Leaving Lines of Gender

LEAVING LINES OF GENDER

A Feminist Genealogy of Language Writing

Ann Vickery

WESLEYAN UNIVERSITY PRESS

Published by University Press of New England

Hanover and London

WESLEYAN UNIVERSITY PRESS

Published by University Press of New England, Hanover, NH 03755

Printed in the United States of America

5 4 3 2 1

CIP data appear at the end of the book

Rae Armantrout's "Special Theory of Relativity," "View," and "Travels," © 1978 by Rae Armantrout, are reprinted with her permission from her book *Extremities* (Great Barrington, MA: The Figures, 1978). "Dusk," "Natural History," and "The Dark," © 1979 by Rae Armantrout, are reprinted with her permission from *The Invention of Hunger* (Berkeley, CA: Tuumba, 1979). "It," © 1997 by Rae Armantrout, first published in *Boxkite* 1 (1997): 135–36, is reprinted by permission of the author. "Necromance," "Context," and "The Garden," © 1991 by Rae Armantrout, from her book *Necromance* (Los Angeles: Sun & Moon Press, 1991), pp. 17, 10, and 11, respectively; and "A Pulse" and "You," © 1995 by Rae Armantrout, from *Made to Seem* (Los Angeles: Sun & Moon Press 1995), pp. 21–22 and 56, are reprinted with the permission of the author and publisher.

Unpublished material by Charles Bernstein, now collected in the Ron Silliman Papers (MSS 75) at the Mandeville Special Collections Library, University of California, San Diego, is used by permission of Charles Bernstein.

Robert Creeley, "Remember . . . ," a section of "Histoire de Florida," by Robert Creeley from *Life & Death*, copyright © 1998 by Robert Creeley. Reprinted by permission of New Directions Publishing Corporation and the author.

Sections from Tina Darrah, "The Best of Intentions," from *Moving Borders: Three Decades of Innovative Writing by Women*, ed. Mary Margaret Sloan (Jersey City, NJ: Talisman House, 1998), and *a(gain)²st the odds* (Elmwood, CT: Potes and Poets Press, 1989); and graphics and quotes from pp. 40, 42, and 48 of *Striking Resemblance: Work 1980–1986* (Providence, RI: Burning Deck, 1989), © Tina Darragh, are included with the author's permission.

A section from Lynne Dreyer's "Tamoka," first published in *Roof* 9 (1979), is reprinted with the author's permission.

Page from Johanna Drucker, *From A to Z* (1976), letterpress, © Johanna Drucker/Chased Press. Courtesy The Poetry/Rare Books Collection of the University Libraries, SUNY at Buffalo. Reprinted with the permission of the author.

Kathleen Fraser's untitled graphic from *HOW(ever)* 3.1 (January 1986) is reprinted with the author's permission. Sections from Fraser's unpublished letters to Carla Harryman, Lyn Hejinian, and Rae Armantrout, collected in the Lyn Hejinian Papers (MSS 74) at the Mandeville Special Collections Library, University of California, San Diego, are reprinted with permission of the author and the Mandeville Special Collections Library.

Continued on page 331

Contents

Illustrations

Acknowledgments

This book would not have been possible without the generosity, encouragement, and great patience of many writers. I remain deeply appreciative of the time spent by Lyn Hejinian, Joan Retallack, and Charles Bernstein in responding to my work at critical junctures. My special thanks also to Rae Armantrout, Carla Harryman, Kathleen Fraser, Mary Margaret Sloan, Bob Perelman, Tina Darragh, Lynne Dreyer, Michael Davidson, Douglas Messerli, Susan Howe, Michael Lally, Barrett Watten, Bruce Andrews, P. Inman, Fanny Howe, Rachel Blau DuPlessis, Diane Ward, and Phyllis Rosenzweig for their various feedback. Their comments and suggestions have been appreciated far more than they can know.

Philip Mead provided the earliest support. I am especially grateful for our ongoing conversations about the project and on poetry in general. I would also like to thank Ken Ruthven for his careful response to an early version of this work. Thanks also to Marjorie Perloff for her illuminating suggestions and Linda Kinnahan and Susan Schultz for stimulating formative discussions. I would also like to thank Emilie Clark, Leslie Scalapino, Maria Damon, Marcella Durand, and Lisa Robertson for material. Further thanks to Anne Brewster, Kirsten Campbell, Steve Evans, Kate Fagan, Alison Georgeson, Barbara Godard, Kris Hemensley, Rosemary Huisman, Romana Huk, Lynn Keller, John Kinsella, Joan Kirkby, Jenna Mead, Lyn McCredden, Jennifer Moxley, Hazel Smith, Juliana Spahr, Stephanie Trigg, Felicity Van Rysbergen, and Michelle Boulous Walker for generating a dynamic intellectual space in which to develop the project, and for their help and/or insights.

This project was significantly shaped by the existence of important archives of contemporary American poetry. I would like to acknowledge the ongoing help and expertise of those at the Archive for New Poetry in the Mandeville Special Collections Library at University of California, San Diego, and the Rare Books Collection at SUNY–Buffalo. Citation of materials from these archives is explained in the abbreviations list that precedes the notes. I am particularly grateful for the continued assistance of Bradley Westbrook at San Diego and Michael Basinski at Buffalo. Thanks also to Kristin Prevallet for suggesting initial, productive directions of inquiry, as well as to Robert Bertholf, Stephen Cope, and Sandra Hochberg.

I would like to acknowledge grants from the University of Melbourne and Macquarie University, which helped to facilitate the travel required to undertake and complete this project.

Many thanks are due to Suzanna Tamminen, who committed herself to this project despite the challenges it faced, its many revisions, and difficulties of distance. All editors should be like her.

Lastly, I wish to acknowledge my family's encouragement over the years. My deepest debt is to Michael, who willingly shared vision with language. This book is dedicated to him.

Some sections of this book were published previously in different form: A version of chapter 12 was published as "The Quiet Rupture: Susan Howe's *The Liberties* and the Feminine Marginalia of Literary History" in *Southerly* 57.1 (autumn 1997): 91–102. A version of chapter 15 was published as "Finding Grace: Modernity and the Ineffable in the Poetry of Rae Armantrout and Fanny Howe" in *Revista Canaria de Estudios Ingleses* (November 1998): 143–64.

Leaving Lines of Gender

SOME INTENTIONS
MINE
The deliberate attempt
from long anticipation
- considering PAUSE -
Not merely PURSUIT of
SEQUENCE
but expansive ACT.
upon EFFECT of action
superceding INSULAR
MARGINALIA
Release from critical
FUNCTION
Felt in
Too
POSSIBILITY.

Summernight:softwarmandbalmy .1 A

Leaping forward to what & why? 2

... seems to be very ants as, 'er has, to & to be ... so's all over all I's wide ope an look in to get what in is ever & ever- 3

O WUZ MUTHA T' UZ AWL BUT O WUZ MON ANGE. WON, WHAT LOOKED UP AND TOOK UP 4

So but did P make it quick or what? While D, mea madre, was the Creature Feature, & A was just gettin to see why- • ...but what did you think of That-supposed-brilliant• 5 C would inquire with conspir atorial lean in the tone A refused tho it caused the breath between them to remain unchanged '6 -it was at any rate least per that P sent A no small interest in the bond they invest as their mutual stock. 7

SUPERFICIALITY
Can I maybe psyche this out a little without getting at all involved? Worth it?

BLASE: hecheckedoutmybustImsureIsawhimlookthatwayrealquick
The first time I saw you I wasn't the least bit impressed. I wasn't even attracted to you. You came in late to a reading and sat down on a bench that was already full. And the way you did it showed how accustomed you were to taking possession, taking control. There was no hesitation, no doubt, in your manner.

Fig. 1. Page from Johanna Drucker's *From A to Z* (1976), letterpress. © Johanna Drucker / Chased Press. Courtesy The Poetry/Rare Books Collection of the University Libraries, SUNY at Buffalo. Reprinted by permission of the author.

Introduction

From *A to Z* (1977) is "an elaborate roman a cléf" satirizing the work and attitudes of poets encountered in the Bay Area in the mid-1970s.[1] (See fig. 1.) Coming from a background of visual or "concrete" writing, Johanna Drucker had initially felt isolated in San Francisco until she met poets like Ron Silliman and Barrett Watten. "[They] affirmed for me what I was already doing with my writing," she later reflected, and they helped to legitimate its value. Becoming "very much involved" with the readings, social life, and poetic conversation in the burgeoning community, Drucker found even more affinity with New York poets and artists (including Bruce Andrews, Charles Bernstein, Abigail Child, and Nick Piombino) when she visited there in 1977.[2] Drucker then went abroad for two years. When she returned to the Bay Area in 1979, controversy surrounding Language writing was already escalating, divisions were being drawn, and she turned instead to graduate school and the art world.

In terms of a documentary, *From A to Z* records the activities of an early Language writing community. Spatially, it maps out the hierarchies and assumptions surrounding poetic practice. While a full poem appears centrally on the page, extratextual events are pushed to the sides. Veiling the descriptions of specific writers by substituting letters of the alphabet for names, Drucker wrote about the anxieties and vanities of the Bay Area scene. Conversations, speculation, and gossip are played out in the margins. Dialogue about careers is entertained but in small "hushed" letters: "did E get the panel appointment?" and "theys both such gentlemen ain't neither of em gonna cop to wanting a CONTRACT?"[3] Her work collapses the distinction between the literary page and social exchange, visually revealing how the two are imbricated in one another.

In "Tamoka," Lynne Dreyer presents poetic practice as blurring into everyday life in the Washington, DC, suburb of Takoma Park. Professional fulfillment competes with looking after a baby, concerns over the body, and always the rush of the day. Even more significantly, Dreyer emphasizes the effects of community:

Chigra. An assembly, fortitude, Chicago, Armands. Folio the books. List poetry. List accomplishments. Mess with words. Love of words. It was the night we all sat down to play double solitaire. No, it was the night they all decided which poets were which movie stars—Ted-Al, Peter-Clift, rich hippies, friendly kisses, more professional pecks on the cheek. A fresh face, a shrimp.

And now busy with the baby, skinny, work study. There was Johnny, such canary friends, window for window. There was one movie that struck as particularly feminine. Books were trapped.

There was not always love. There was sometimes the emptiness of love (a cab from Drug Fair to work to the hitch up to Skyline Drive). Next the intercom morning announcing stops along the way. Pleasant girls reminiscing of long walks, cat walks, imaginable poetry, lost poetry, imagine poetry.

Sometimes it was the absence of love, of particulars, talk producing nosepainting, as Shakespeare explains it, performance over desire. Sometimes it was the imitation of love, and sometimes it was love, with something missing, with kidding aside.[4]

At first instance, Drucker's and Dreyer's texts provide a strong contrast to Bob Perelman's *Marginalization of Poetry: Language Writing and Literary History*—a volume that negotiates a literary history of Language writing while discussing the problems of undertaking just such a task.[5] Both Drucker and Dreyer write from positions of ex-centricity—Drucker experiencing ambivalence and marginality in relation to the San Francisco poets, Dreyer speaking from the third, largely elided community formation in Washington. Alternatively, the blurb on the back of Perelman's book flags it as a "comprehensive account of the language-writing movement" by "[a] leading language writer." Whereas Drucker and Dreyer produced their versions during the early moments of Language writing, Perelman's was written from a fortified retrospective position, long after the structures he discusses have transformed. All these factors influence the way each is read and used as a lens on the past.

Further elements include the form the text takes, both in genre and as a publication. While *From A to Z* was self-published as an artist's book, "Tamoka" appeared as a cross-genre prose-poem in *Roof*, a small press magazine coming out of New York. Both were directed to small local audiences, consisting primarily of other writers. Alternatively, in its Princeton University Press packaging, *The Marginalization of Poetry* has a much wider distribution network and is read primarily by students and academics. While Perelman's account is related through a linear, largely teleological narrative,

Drucker's and Dreyer's works are partial, elliptic, and difficult to read, let alone assimilate into canonical narratives. This is not to suggest that the analytic and the creative are necessarily separate discourses, but that the latter is generally presumed to have little documentary value.

Dreyer is wary of "testimonial dessert[s]."[6] Drucker also analyzes her drive to memorialize: "Am I working through my need to hold onto what becomes established? Do I consider that a part of the work—or just the attachment which generates the conditioning sentimental consideration? On what level the permission? To what end? For the actual purpose of deliberate constructive thought. Mine."[7]

As both a member of Language writing and a more recent member of the academy, Perelman recognizes his dual investment in celebration and critique. In the acknowledgments he suggests that his book reflects an often uneasy balance between the two. By framing his history with two extended poems—or bivouacs, as he calls them—Perelman undercuts not only the authority of his formal style but also the reductive project of literary history itself:

> Language writing beckons
> as modernism beckoned.
>   Critical genealogy is a kind
>
> of art Prose
>   a sort of Poetics,
>   even
>
> a Poem, since the lines it rewrites are new lines
>   read by readers
>   heretofore unaddressed,
>
> unmarked—
>   since their eyes are focused on new media
> (even though formally these were unaccredited.)
>
> No poem is made up entirely of language—since
> the channels it leases are always conduits
>   formerly
>   unarticulated. A
>
> world lost,
>   a world unarticulated,
>   beckons to new genres
> and no poetic value (eternal) is so unnegotiable as the memory
> of value lost[8]

As all three writers show, the writing of community is fraught with difficulties. Cultural memory is always limited by one's own experience and marked through the lived effects of gender, class, race, and age. This book arose partly out of a need to position Perelman's account as one version—and a valuable one at that—among many to open up the field and attend to alternative, sometimes more cryptic and complex narratives. Feminist in orientation, it seeks to recover and celebrate the work of women writers, including not only the poetry they wrote but their involvement in publishing, editing, theorizing, and supporting a broader poetic practice. Following on from this, I hope to position Language writing within a diverse field of innovative poetries and demonstrate how its consolidation as a group practice (within its respective communities as well as institutionally) was both enabling and problematic for the women writers involved.

Language Writing as a Practice of Community

Against a background of American lyricism devoted to the self, Language writing has been particularly active in deconstructing individualist trends in the cultural production of literature, as well as attempting, in various ways, to rethink community. The very term, *Language writing*—or *Language poetry*, as it is also called—has been used to identify a group formation of writers as well as the body of poetic writing that they produced during the seventies and eighties. While many found the tag itself to be limiting, the sharing of a writing practice was generally embraced. In a remark that was typical for many, Joan Retallack states: "My sense of the value of my work must exist in community, must be validated by others whose opinion I respect, must be tied to (perhaps an illusion of) social implication, which I can equate to the implications for the Language and the Literature . . . feeling that I am part of a project which generates new possibilities."[9]

Language writing communities emerged in San Francisco's Bay Area, Washington, DC, and New York City. Although not all knew or necessarily had met one another, a healthy small-press culture generated a sense of intensity. Owing to generational and aesthetic differences, several writers, such as Kathleen Fraser, Clark Coolidge, and Michael Palmer, were involved in other poetry formations and created an independent space for themselves. Yet their interactions or tensions with Language writing would indelibly shape its subsequent projects.

Language writers were concerned not so much with describing the world as with interrogating the possibilities of the social. The public nature of Language writing stands in direct contrast to the privacy of the workshop poem and its therapeutic enabling of the individual. Whereas the workshop poem constructs the poet as self-determining viewer of the world,

Language writing emphasizes the existence of "multiple conflicting per-spectives."[10] Furthermore, it seeks to understand how relations of power that inform the everyday are disseminated and veiled through language. While male Language writers focused predominantly on the dangers of commodity fetishism, an equal number of women writers took gender as an object of critique. Carla Harryman, for instance, agrees with Shulamith Firestone's fundamental premise in *The Dialectic of Sex: The Case for Femi-nist Revolution* that women's oppression is linked to sexual difference. Al-though it matters what form she writes in, what matters more is a commit-ment to challenging how women are currently valued and positioned in society.[11] Much of her poetic game-play and narrative switches displaces conventional sexual roles and their concomitant positions of knowledge and power.

Susan Howe argues that in looking at the terrain of poetry we should ask the following questions: "Who polices questions of grammar, parts of speech, connection, and connotation? Whose order is shut inside the structure of a sentence?"[12] Language writing undermines interpretative codes by self-consciously playing against ingrained habits of reading. The poem reflects upon itself "not only at the level of represented ideas but prosodically, acoustically, syntactically, visibly; which is to say gives these dimensions equal methodological weight as it gives to more traditional no-tions of semantic content."[13]

At a more general level, Language writing also critiques the boundaries of the poem. It challenges formal distinctions between verse and prose, lit-erature and philosophy, aesthetics and politics. In radicalizing the space of its proper object, it overflows into other genres, like talks, essays, politics, and psychology. Alternatively, other genres may spill into poetry. Co-founded by Eileen Corder, Carla Harryman, and Nick Robinson, The Poets Theater (1978–84) involved many Bay Area Language writers. All three, along with Alan Bernheimer, Bob Perelman, and Kit Robinson would write and take part in plays. Leslie Scalapino would also write and direct plays, while Susan Howe's background in the theater is continually brought to bear on her poetry. Another perhaps obvious crossing is between language and music, with Clark Coolidge and Joan Retallack ex-ploring, in quite different ways, the possibilities of sound through complex linguistic, rhythmic, and spatial experimentation.[14]

By opening up the poetic, Language writers foreground the gap between "what one wants to say . . . and what one can say."[15] Accordingly, the poem offers up the possibility of collaboration. Rather than simply consuming the text, the reader participates with the writer in its meaning production. However, there is always a danger that the degree of required attention may alienate a reader. In facing this concern, Retallack wonders if some of the forms we invent to sabotage the cliché . . . may in fact have the very effect on the reader we are trying to avoid: shutting her out to all but her own fantasies, sliding away from an engagement that can be argued with, resisted, or even accepted as genuinely nourishing. Are we creating victims of language when the field of discourse is so idiosyncratic (private), the reader must either wholly capitulate to our designs or retreat?—when we reject common fields of discourse in which, after all, people live and work as too corrupt for our linguistic act are we literally disarming the reader?[16]

Yet it is precisely this risk that distinguishes Language writing as a mode of feminist exploration and critique. Indeed, its poetics stands in direct contrast to much of the feminist poetry produced out of the women's movement. During the seventies, many second-wave feminists sought to bring poetic language closer to common usage in order to "make it more accessible to ordinary women."[17] The poem's content was privileged as a source for message that would help build a feeling of collective experience and empowerment. In its combination of the personal and the communal, such poetry would become a vehicle by which many women from African American, Chicana, and Native American backgrounds, as well as lesbian identifications, could at last feel confident enough to express their feelings of difference. Female experiences of motherhood and sexuality were also articulated and affirmed.

However, the relation of language to dominant systems of knowledge was not fully recognized as a matter of concern. As Cynthia G. Franklin points out, identity politics and poststructuralism were often placed in opposition to one another.[18] Innovative poetry remained isolated and even suspect within many feminist circles, leading Fanny Howe to declare with some frustration:

At a time when women as writers are being given the big break—equal time and interest—there seems to be little focus on the work by women which is aesthetically new. . . . The content of women's work is constantly studied, often by other women, without nearly enough attention paid to the form of that work and why, when the form is new, this newness is intricately tied to the newness of the content.[19]

In order to publish, innovative women writers were forced to start their own presses or journals. Kelsey St. Press became a leading example of this, established by its six editors—Karen Brodine, Patricia Dienstfrey, Kit Duane, Marina La Palma, Laura Moriarty, and Rena Rosenwasser—in order to give the "writing by women we valued a *place*."[20] *HOW(ever)* (founded by Kathleen Fraser and coedited initially by Beverly Dahlen and Frances Jaffer) provided a more frequent and open forum for innovative poetry by women, as well as offering a space for exchange and critique. Around the same time, Lyn Hejinian founded Tuumba Press, featuring writers like Fraser, Susan Howe, and Barbara Baracks in the first series. And on the East Coast, Maureen Owen started *Telephone* magazine after realizing that "a lot of women were around . . . who were writing seriously, [but who] weren't getting published anywhere."[21] Alongside the proliferating print culture, Susan Howe began a radio program, *Poetry*, which brought together her love of innovative poetics and an interest in feminist inquiry. Many of these ventures grounded or ran concurrently with Language writing projects, ensuring a rich cross-fertilization of ideas.

Tied to issues of form, many innovative writers found themselves battling the underlying assumption of consensus in sisterhood. Attracted initially to second-wave feminism in the early seventies, Hannah Weiner found her poetic interests increasingly distanced from the "representative" voice espoused by feminism.[22] Likewise, Harryette Mullen gained inspiration from white academic feminists but simultaneously discovered her own experiences as an African American marginal to their project. She found in Language writing a way in which to negotiate the complexity of subjectivity and identification, using its opacity and play to develop a "mongrelized" poetics that derails gender and racial lines.[23] Mullen engaged with Language writing in the mid-eighties, just as it began attracting institutional attention. At roughly the same time, mainstream feminism started debating identity politics and difference feminism. Gloria Anzaldúa's groundbreaking *Borderlands/La Frontera: The New Mestiza* would not be published until 1987.[24]

Some critics, such as Charles Altieri, have suggested that Language writing is in danger of becoming another sort of modernist formalism, "blind to historical forces and refusing to take responsibility for the political conditions created by those forces."[25] As he discerns, an urgent task is how to address political pressures and hear voices from the margins. While this remains a crucial issue, Language writers have sought to merge an aesthetic practice with a broader cultural awareness. A critique of political structures underscores many of their poetic projects, although these may not take the usual narrative forms. Many women writers have focused on how violent past histories remain a source of loss, shame, and ambivalence—including Leslie Scalapino's immersion in the media coverage of the Gulf War and Susan Howe's, Rosmarie Waldrop's, and Hannah Weiner's complex and quite different investigations into the relationship between colonial and linguistic power in American history. For many years, Joan Retallack has developed a practice of "poethics," designed to plumb history's unintelligible silences.

The emergence of Language writing should also be contextualized against the call for civil rights, the women's movement, the failure of the

European intellectual community in 1968, and reactions to the Vietnam War. Such contexts are not discrete but overlapping, because each challenged the intellectual project by questioning its representative capacity as well as the constituency of communities. Tina Darragh states:

[I]t strikes me that it hasn't been helpful at all to analyze the failure/collapse of the Left in the late '60s/early '70s in political or economic terms—we don't seem to be learning anything about our mistakes, plus we seem like shells in the face of rising militarism, without the desire to unite with others or challenge individually what's going on. The only hope I have . . . is that language "investigations" (if done in an interdisciplinary setting) will renew our sense of ourselves as social beings by illuminating the differences between how private language and public language operate in our lives, how they are two distinct processes that, in their simultaneity, obscure each other and blur the way we address our needs.[26]

Language writing has been in the unusual position of attempting what it knew to be recidivist, that is, naming and performing a shared political practice at the very moment when the modern community is in crisis. As Naomi Schor and others have pointed out, feminism has also been framed as a recidivist project in that it foregrounds a particular form of difference (sexual difference) as a category of analysis.[27] This is not to say that feminism elides other forms of difference but that it views them primarily through their relation to gender. The anxiety of feminism, as with the anxiety of Language writing, is to find a politics that enables subjects of difference to work together.

Like second-wave feminism, Language writing was demonized politically and became the object of both ridicule and suspicion. Both feminism and Language writing were seen to be conspiratorial, an "infectious outside" that threatened the order of the community at large. In San Francisco in particular, Language writing attracted notoriety. Tom Clark's article berating Language writing in a 1985 issue of *Poetry Flash* ran with the headline, "Stalin as Linguist," its very title projecting an image of Communist monster.[28] Charles Bernstein had tried to preempt such thinking in "The Conspiracy of 'Us,'" but its ironic title only provoked ire.[29] Again, when a number of Bay Area writers attempted to argue their relation to one another as an affinity rather than an identity, the force of their argument was defused by having the misrepresentative tag "A Manifesto" subsequently added to their title by the magazine's editors.[30] For both those "inside" Language writing's boundaries and those who saw themselves as either beyond its scope or marginal to its project, there were feelings of anxiety, alienation, and ambivalence. As Ann Lauterbach declares, "Those not so identified are left out, often understandably embittered or con-

fused, as the idea of an individual iconoclastic poet gives way to collabora-
tive and tribal identities."[31]

Recognition of writers through the inflammatory category of "Language
poetry" would make it much easier to ignore them as *marginal*. Throughout
the seventies and early eighties, Language writing remained sidelined by
arts funding systems, the academy, and a broader reading public. Indeed,
the editors of *The Morrow Anthology of Younger American Poets* (1985), an an-
thology typical of the era, described the younger American poet as follows:
"[H]e is rarely a card-carrying group member, political or aesthetic."[32] If
this is the case, Rae Armantrout argues, then the new American poet is
someone with no multicultural, ethnic, class, or gender politics. The image
such an anthology projected was of "an oppressive machismo," the individ-
ual standing alone as poetic frontiersman.[33] Armantrout wrote of another
anthology (*19 New American Poets of The Golden Gate*) published a year ear-
lier by Harcourt Brace: "[I]t features mostly academic poets, listing all their
grants and jobs. It brought home to me how sidelined 'we' really are—how
far from the centers of power, how apt to be forgotten."[34]

Many mainstream feminist poets at the time also suffered from this
form of indirect dismissal. Only when writers like Audre Lorde and Alice
Walker and, later, Judy Grahn, Minnie Bruce Pratt, and Rita Dove began
winning prizes and endorsement from the poetry establishment did this
begin to change.

As Language writing became anthologized during the mid-eighties, its
existence in terms of community was already dissolving. It was becoming
institutionally accepted, gaining the support of influential critics such as
Marjorie Perloff, Jerome McGann, and Andrew Ross. As the use of the
term *Language poetry* or *Language writing* gained currency, it, in turn, inev-
itably began to subsume difference and marginalize other innovative poe-
tries. At the same time, Language writers began to explore other commu-
nity formations. Some writers took up academic positions; others took on
professional roles in publishing, and communications. Many would turn to
family life. In the late eighties and nineties, a proliferation of critical arti-
cles and books appeared that focused specifically on Language writing.
Most characterized Language writing as a literary movement, complete
with leading representatives and manifestoes.

By mapping out Language writing through this familiar narrative, critics
have duplicated mythologies of genius and hierarchized participation in
terms of sexual difference. Even well-known literary histories such as Bob
Perelman's *The Marginalization of Poetry* (1996) and Michael Davidson's ac-
count in *The New Princeton Encyclopedia of Poetry and Poetics* (1993) have
tended to shift women's work to the margins—Perelman devoting half a
chapter to women Language writers and briefly mentioning them in others,

while Davidson names only Hejinian in his summary of its history.[35] Anthologies, too, are marked by amnesia as well as already interpreting what they display. *"Language" Poetries* (1987) showcases only a few "stars" of Language writing, and *In the American Tree: Language, Realism, Poetry* (1986) was constructed through Silliman's highly partial reading of Language writing aesthetics.[36] Finally, Jerome Rothenberg and Pierre Joris's massive *Poems for the Millennium: The University of California Book of Modern and Postmodern Poetry* (1998) sets up a complicated alignment of writers under headings such as "Some 'Language' Poets."[37] In doing so, it fails to include women writers who threaten genre boundaries in their work, such as Bernadette Mayer, Fanny Howe, and Johanna Drucker. In centralizing poetic formations, Washington DC writers are also effectively elided.

In the study of literary movements, the fetishizing of theory has enabled critics to contain innovative poetry and neutralize it along canonical lines. This has certainly been the case with Language writing. Throughout the past two decades, a select number of male Language writers have had their critical work published by eminent university presses. Although their own poetry would sometimes be overshadowed by the authority invested in these volumes, the poetry of their female counterparts remained an object of study through these same theoretical frameworks. Such methodological divisions could only be reductive for Language writers of either gender.

The critical reception of Language writing has therefore tended to represent women as secondary participants or its passive benefactors. From an alternative angle, feminist critics have also overlooked their work. In *The Feminist Poetry Movement*, Kim Whitehead looks more at identity politics than at linguistic subversion in constructing a single feminist poetic tradition.[38] This is reinforced from an unlikely quarter in Rachel Blau DuPlessis's and Ann Snitow's *The Feminist Memoir Project: Voices from Women's Liberation*.[39] Although DuPlessis has long been an enthusiastic practitioner and advocate of innovative women's writing, such voices are absent in this volume's representation of a single movement in sisterhood. Alternatively, Cynthia Franklin fails to mention the blurred genre work of many Language writers in *Writing Women's Communities: The Politics and Poetics of Contemporary Multi-Genre Anthologies*—perhaps assuming a community of sameness rather than of diversity.[40]

To some degree, this double marginalization is now being reversed. While Language writing is still undervalued in its feminist potential, women's contributions to Language writing have been increasingly recognized and celebrated in the past few years. Some have referred to this period as the second front of Language writing, although this risks dissolving the radicalism of the alternative narratives now being produced.[41] Early books of Bernadette Mayer and Lyn Hejinian have been reprinted—Mayer's *Midwinter Day* appearing under the New Directions imprint and Hejinian's *Writing Is an Aid to Memory* appearing as part of the Sun & Moon classics series. Wesleyan University Press increasingly supports innovative women's writing, its list including poets such as Kathleen Fraser, Susan Howe, Joan Retallack, and Leslie Scalapino. The University of California Press is also ensuring a reputation as a publisher of the avant-garde with essay collections by Hejinian and Retallack.[42] Furthermore, the University of Alabama has recently published Fraser's *Translating the Unspeakable: Poetry and Innovative Necessity* and will be publishing a collection of papers on women's small-press publishing (a volume emerging out of the "Page Mothers" conference organized by Rae Armantrout and Fanny Howe in 1999).[43]

Most significant is the recent publication of two anthologies structured around gender. Like the recent Norton anthology on African American literature, *Out of Everywhere: Linguistically Innovative Poetry by Women in North America and the UK* (1996) and *Moving Borders: Three Decades of Innovative Writing by Women* (1998) signal a major redress to literary history.[44] While *Out of Everywhere* draws parallels between British and American innovative women's writing, *Moving Borders* opens the field within North America. At over seven hundred pages, it gives a detailed mapping of innovative women's poetry as well as foregrounding the feminist issues through which such poetry is written.

Mary Margaret Sloan notes that, in editing the anthology,

> it was clear how much a work of writing is not the result of a solitary act but the end effect of a multitude of social activities, the most important of which is reading. We read and are read, and that mutual consideration folds us into a conversation which affects everything about us as writers: our aesthetic choices, certainly, but also where we will publish and what kinds of rewards we receive.[45]

As Sloan suggests, what remains to be done is to contextualize poetry as both text and practice. A genealogy undertakes such a double-barreled process. *Leaving Lines of Gender: A Feminist Genealogy of Language Writing* offers an alternative to reductive originary narratives that read Language writing through a few major sources, such as Ron Silliman's anthology *In the American Tree* and Bruce Andrews and Charles Bernstein's *L=A=N=G=U=A=G=E*. Rather than proposing an organic model of growth or a model of equivalence, a genealogy explores the shifting "mess" that encapsulates actual poetic practice through the traces it leaves. It maps out the interweaving, multiple lines of affiliation as well as the debates arising out of difference, whether these be regional, aesthetic, cultural or ideological.

As the title suggests, this book explores not only the signs of gender in women's poetic practice (including practices of publishing, editing, readings, talks, and collaborations), but also how gender's prescribed tracks have been variously challenged or left behind.

A Feminist Genealogy

Susan Stanford Friedman argues that feminists are becoming more reflexive in producing history, anxious about "the risk of repeating the same patterns of thought and action that excluded, distorted, muted, or erased women from the master narratives of history in the first place." History depends on a fantasy of a reality unaffected by those interpretations, orders, and selections that have shaped it in the present. "As a heuristic activity," writes Friedman, "history writing orders the past in relation to the needs of the present and the future."[46]

Because literary history traditionally treats gender as a normative category, it becomes an invisible effect. Taken for granted, gender is naturalized into the structures of critical narrative. However, as Marjorie Perloff points out, feminist critics should be wary of reading against a dominant discourse and simply giving "pride of place to the hitherto repressed."[47] Such a practice risks being as essentialist as the one it seeks to replace. The aim of a genealogical method is not to discover or consolidate an identity but to inquire into how and why such consolidations are made. As Judith Butler suggests, the best way to understand the construction of gender is not to seek "a normative model against which individual instances can be gauged, but, rather to delimit the field of historical possibilities which constitute this gender, and to examine in detail the *acts* by which these possibilities are appropriated, dramatized, and ritualized."[48]

Like Johanna Drucker's *From A to Z*, a feminist genealogy would draw attention to the vicissitudes of cultural activity by foregrounding the exchanges of this activity rather than the objects that are part of it. It would politicize the structures that frame a text's production, reproduction, and reception. "Even if NOTHING in the writing practice [has] to do with gender," says Drucker, "then almost EVERYTHING ELSE which has to do with the writing—publishing it, seeing it received, being identified with it publicly and professionally, querying its historical position, etc. are ALL involved with gender issues."[49]

Many feminist literary critics have proposed the need for a feminist aesthetic in order to challenge previous representations of sexual difference. Rachel Blau DuPlessis rightly points out in *The Pink Guitar: Writing as Feminist Practice* that instead of only one female aesthetic there should be a constellation of strategies aimed at critiquing hegemonic identities.[50] However, an aesthetic—historically, the ideology of beauty and the sublime—may be viewed as an alternative set of inscriptions, mirror, or artwork for the self. An aesthetic is always overdetermined. What is required is an additional level of critique that engages with historically specific cultural formations and through which an aesthetic circulates and shapes possible roles for women. A feminist genealogy would mediate between a feminist aesthetic (with its necessary invention and artifice) and the operation of subjectivities within the real world. It would emphasize the problems of negotiating both the imaginary and the social by focusing on particulars rather than the absolute.

A genealogy interrogates the cultural space of poetry by approaching it horizontally in time (poetry as practice) rather than vertically (poetry as canonical tradition). This involves reframing many aspects of the poetic practice in order to link text with context. Aspects that must be addressed include the multiple text (its written or performed versions), the text-in-process (drafting, editing, and reprinting), the relationship between readers and the text, the use of particular poetic forms, the structure of small-press culture and its marketplace, and the social politics of poetry (as manifested in how poetic communities relate to one another and to individuals).[51] These may be further contextualized in larger social and cultural structures, including the media and pedagogic institutions. In engaging with such aspects, a feminist genealogy becomes a mode of intervention that may reveal otherwise hidden or elided differences as well as unpredictable relationships.

Kathy Ferguson argues that a genealogy is more of an activity than a theory. It is a practice that seeks to denaturalize the claims of power.[52] As such, a feminist genealogy puts into question the concept of critical distance by demonstrating that every critic is engaged in a double articulation of implication and critique.[53] In being ideologically complicit with the very structures that she seeks to resist, the feminist critic should work in a way that is "specific and contingent upon the cultural field in which [she] operates."[54] A politics of location also escapes the dialectical structure that oppositional critiques often presume. Oppositional discourses that are based on a contrast between margin and center tend to subsume the marginal groups themselves because they are always already grounded on exclusions. Alternatively, a feminist genealogy sees the allocation of boundaries as itself a site of contestation. To focus on a politics of location is one way of ensuring that cultural discourses are investigated from various perspectives and continually redefined.[55] A feminist genealogy, then, should be understood as challenging its own disciplinary context as well as broader processes of knowledge production.

Forms of Witness

A genealogy in my sense of the term is a way of reading texts and their contexts against each other, and in ways that mediate cultural knowledge with textuality. In this framework, poetic discourse is engendered through a range of texts, which, in addition to the poem "itself," includes paratexts such as journals, reviews, interviews, and correspondence. Following Toril Moi, it is possible to argue that once the cultural texts of a practice inform their literary texts, then all sorts of texts (conversations, public talks and readings, gossip, letters, academic institutions, and, of course, poetry) may be considered as elements participating in the same discursive network. "The point is not to treat one text as the implicit meaning of another," Moi states, "but rather to read them all with and against each other in order to bring out their points of tension, contradictions, and similarities."[56] In recognizing that the textual network is over-determined, a genealogical project becomes limitless: it can never result in a final totalization of knowledge. Accordingly, the researcher must arrive at an unstable compromise between a range of factors such as competing voices and discourses.[57]

Given that the proponents of Language writing are still very much informing their own past, the task of genealogy becomes even more complex. The researcher becomes more of a "neographer" than a "paleographer," dealing with a body and its double—the literary corpus and the writer who produced it.[58] In the space of contemporary poetry, the writer "lives on" quite literally, not so much "correcting" as "ghosting" the processes of history making. The structure and breadth of this project has been substantially determined by the input of writers themselves at various stages. This has been a difficult process, for what may have been important for one poet is less so for another. Different versions are remembered, and the significance of an event may change over time. At one level, trying to negotiate these pasts is like sewing together disparate patches of a quilt, but a quilt metaphor is inadequate when it comes to describing the intense affect created by such an undertaking. For many, the genealogy raised great ambivalence. Not only did some feel that present-day relationships were at risk, but there were extremes of joy and regret in looking back. Moreover, what people were willing to share was always partial and often fragmentary—again, an effect of time as much as positionality. Concerned with these and other issues of cultural memory, a group of poets who lived and wrote in the Bay Area during the seventies are now involved in a project in which they share and negotiate reminiscences on a closed Internet site. Such a project is fragile, relying like a genealogy on a certain level of good faith and generosity.

Aside from these connections with the actual writers, the project was greatly enriched by visiting two bodies of public knowledge, one housed at the Archive of New Poetry at San Diego and the other at the Poetry/Rare Books Collection at SUNY–Buffalo. An archive re-presents an idea of community, creating a culture out of an assemblage of texts. For Michael Davidson, archives speak back and forth, thus engendering a kind of dialogue.[59] Dodie Bellamy also reflects that "people you think don't have any connection are suddenly mentioning one another, and it becomes this huge matrix, an organic web."[60] A primary problem is how to approach the social context inevitably constituted by these linkages and alliances.

In the San Diego library, the gaps are as telling as what *is* there. For while the archive holds the papers of Ron Silliman, Susan Howe, Lyn Hejinian, Bernadette Mayer, Sun & Moon Press, and United Artists Press, the correspondence of those who live or once lived and worked in San Diego— Rae Armantrout, Fanny Howe, and Michael Davidson—is notably absent. Instead, Fanny Howe has sold her papers to Stanford. Elsewhere, writers like Clark Coolidge and Michael Palmer have papers archived at Buffalo, and Rosmarie and Keith Waldrop have all material relating to their long-running small press, Burning Deck, at the University of New Hampshire. Others simply dislike the effects of the archival system, with concern being raised over issues of access and control.

As Allen Sekula states, a writer's previously private labor enters the public domain as the property of an institution rather than an individual. As such, archival ownership may not always coincide with the aspirations of the author.[61] To place one's papers in an archive entails also a loss of context, "an *abstraction* from the complexity and richness of use."[62] Archival availability means semantic availability and the possibility that new meanings will compete with and destabilize older ones. Most obviously, "marginal" writing loses its identity as such when its cultural value and importance are confirmed and reinforced by the archive.

Above all, an archive is a business. It predetermines a writer's symbolic capital by placing a value on his or her work on a relative scale with peers. A writer who is not considered popular enough at a particular moment may not be of sufficient interest to an archive. For poets in particular, an offer from an archive to buy one's papers will generally form the largest financial return they can hope to receive from their writing. In plain terms, an archival offer can pay the mortgage on a house, finance the children's education, or simply secure survival after years of pecuniary hardship. It is often larger than any literary grant or personal patronage available. Just as important, it secures one's literary reputation.

An archive functions rather like an editor or publisher in deciding which information is to be available and in what form. Access may be restricted by the archive's own methods of presenting knowledge, by requests for privacy, or by concern over the aging of documents. In collecting the correspondence, ephemera, and work in progress of writers, the Buffalo and San Diego archives enable a very different vision of Language writing from the one offered by literary histories based on "final" texts. In their letters to one another, poets tend to fall into a more intimate mode of address and exchange news that would otherwise remain unprintable or be thought of as trivia. Diaries or journals also engender a more relaxed state.

Archives must be viewed, then, as existing in uneasy relationship to the poetry actually published. Unconcerned with either coherence or discretion, they generally represent the community as much more open-ended— relationships and projects come to be seen as unfinished or dynamic. Archives also create the highly seductive but illusory effect of being closer to "what actually happened." To read letters and drafts, which at the time of writing were never intended to be made public, is to experience a voyeuristic sense of looking over the shoulders of writers at work. Yet Maryanne Dever points out that correspondence is a form of self-representation, whereby different "selves" are performed in response to both the recipient and the circumstances.[63] Letters may be written in shades of sarcasm, jokiness, or self-conscious irony, often discernible only to the target reader. The immediacy of the archive veils not only its institutional impact but also the fictions of authorship.

The placing of one's papers in an archive also can be read as a political act. When writers like Hejinian make their papers available, they do so as part of their ongoing practice to engender an "open community." However, to make public one's private correspondence radically broadens the radius of readership from what was originally intended by the letter writer. Some people believe that letters, usually the most personal form of writing, should remain private. Given that a writer's papers generally consist of correspondence from other people, rather than the writer's own letters, various ethical issues arise. How should a researcher approach such intimate material? What processes should writers have to go through before offering their papers to an archive?[64] How do such issues intersect with or erode the public's "right to know"?

The magnitude of these questions has been witnessed already in the study of Sylvia Plath, where long-running disputes over her unpublished papers have underscored most work to date.[65] Such research raises issues that link the mechanics of literary business with a range of ethical questions concerning the role of writers and writing in contemporary society. Whether a writer is living or dead, issues of editing, censorship, and privacy are of great consequence to subsequent interpretations. Special requests by individual correspondents have resulted in the removal of their letters from the San Diego archive. What, then, are the implications of such processes?

One can understand why those like Charles Bernstein have decided to delay placing their papers in an archive. Access to Bernstein's papers, as well as others like Armantrout, Davidson, and Fraser, would provide alternative frameworks of poetic practice to those that may be garnered from the archives at present. Yet what is sensitive information at one particular historical moment may be less so in another period, and vice versa. Given that Language writing has been increasingly the subject of literary histories (most notably, Perelman's), the eventual impact of such papers may be more limited, now that certain narratives are becoming entrenched.

Marta Werner argues that the work of the archivist is impressionistic, often generating further questions rather than shoring up authority.[66] This is even more true for the genealogist. The use of archival material, along with the use of writers' comments and responses, must therefore be tactical. In both cases the accounts must be seen as coming from "I-witnesses" as much as eyewitnesses, in that events from the real are taken up and translated through an individual's imaginary. The genealogist must then negotiate these partial, contradictory, and shifting constructions of poetic community.

As Foucault claims, a genealogy is "patiently documentary." Instead of focusing on a definitive origin, it constitutes a "knowledge of details, and . . . depends on a vast accumulation of source material." A genealogy records the singularity of events without subordinating them to any finality: "[I]t must seek them in the most unpromising places, in what we tend to feel is without history—in sentiments, love, conscience, instincts; it must be sensitive to their recurrence, not in order to trace the gradual curve of their evolution, but to isolate the different scenes where they engaged in different roles."[67]

The following chapters aim to present some breadth of representation with a detailed examination of specific texts. Through a series of case studies, I examine how poetic practices and authorship were gendered and what sort of textual, rhetorical, and professional strategies women writers employed to disrupt structures of constraint. These case studies focus on particular collaborative texts and individually authored texts. They also attend to specific vehicles of poetic production: small presses (Tuumba), journals (*HOW(ever)*), and radio (Susan Howe's *Poetry* program). Furthermore, they cover practices integral to the formation and consolidation of poetic communities, such as talks, readings, advice, criticism, theorization, and anthologizing. Two chapters also undertake a comparative overview of feminist strategies both within the poetic text and in positioning oneself in the poetic conversation. By selecting such areas, I hope to disrupt the traditional bias of literary histories by showing not only the crucial and multiple roles that women writers have held in Language writing but also how they shaped its direction and force. As with any genealogical project, it soon becomes apparent that other examples would have made equally appropriate subjects of study. It is hoped that this book will link up with other feminist engagements focused on these topics and form part of an ongoing dialogue focused on the work of innovative women writers.

CHAPTER ONE

Cities and Communities: Circling Out of Equivalence

meeting place   (fragments of "meeting" and "place" alternating as object and ground)

"They moved to another locality."
     Seen as   "wood of trees"   given to "stand"
"Not much interest in the contest."

     Seen as "to be between"   given to   "testify"
                                        —Tina Darragh, *Striking Resemblance*

T he city is a crucial factor in the social production of subjectivity. It affects not only a subject's positioning within space but also the way a subject sees others as well as the self. Elizabeth Grosz points out that, "[t]he city orients and organizes family, sexual and social relations insofar as it divides cultural life into public and private domains, geographically dividing and defining the particular social positions and locations occupied by individuals and groups."[1] It is therefore not surprising that Language writing emerged out of quite distinct community formations in San Francisco, New York, and Washington. Given that the city is the most immediately concrete locus for the production and circulation of power, all three poetry communities embraced a *located politics of difference*. This difference has been largely elided in literary histories of Language writing, which continue to stress parallels in poetics as well as a united front. Nevertheless, the Language communities were imagined and practiced at this regional level in highly specific ways.

Joan Retallack notes that, in the early seventies, Washington was more like a *real* city in that everyday life had an element of strangeness.[2] Multiple political movements encouraged an atmosphere of radicalism, as many came to protest at the steps of the country's government. At the same time, a lively arts scene grew at Dupont Circle, which was downtown but off-center from the Federal City and the main business districts. The Community Book Shop on P Street became the site for "Mass Transit" (1971–74), a series of weekly open readings initiated by Michael Lally, who had moved to DC from Iowa in the spring of 1971. Lally was strongly influenced by John Ashbery and other members of the New York school, including Alice Notley and Bernadette Mayer. To complement the readings he began a press, publishing the first books of Bruce Andrews, Lynne Dreyer, Lee Lally, Tim Dlugos, Terence Winch, Ed Cox, and P. Inman. While Lee Lally, Winch, and Cox helped host the reading series, the press soon transformed into a collective venture among local writers and became known as Some of Us Press. Writing from the reading series also was published in a magazine of the same name. The title of both magazine and press reflected the Washington scene as a community of mobile and provisional links.

New York writers were invited to read in the Mass Transit series, and on any one night, audiences could range from twelve to a hundred. Lally tried to pair one well-known poet from out of town with a local poet. Then living in nearby Maryland, Bruce Andrews often discussed his theories of language-centered writing with Lally. Andrews was also in touch with San Francisco poet Ron Silliman, who had been introduced to him in 1971 by Jerome Rothenberg. By 1974, Andrews was corresponding with Canadian poet Steve McCaffery and developing his poetics in conversation with Ray DiPalma, another writer from Iowa. By the mid-seventies, Andrews had moved to New York, excited by the range and intensity of aesthetic debates. With the early Washington community established, Lally, like Andrews, began looking for a broader poetic horizon. In 1974, he made a similar migration to New York, but continued to celebrate Washington writing. Two years later he featured numerous Washington writers in his anthology *None of the Above: New Poets of the USA*.[3] Lally also continued his small-press writing. Later still, he reviewed the poetry of women Language writers like Lynne Dreyer and Diane Ward in various issues of *L=A=N=G=U=A=G=E*.

With Lally's departure, the community nexus shifted to Folio Books. While some writers from the Mass Transit days remained, new figures began taking an active role in this formation. Among the Folio group were poets such as Doug Lang, Diane Ward, Tina Darragh, Lynne Dreyer, P. Inman, Phyllis Rosenzweig, Joan Retallack, Bernard Welt, Connie McKenna, and Julie Brown. Some of these writers would first try out their work at the Mass Transit series, but develop it more fully during this era. Baltimore poets like Anselm Hollo, Kirby Malone, Chris Mason, and Marshall Reese were also regular figures in the scene. A significant force during the Folio years was Doug Lang, who became a kind of "guiding spirit, organizer, and mentor."[4] Lang arranged over eighty-five public readings in a period of four years, continuing Lally's practice of matching a Washington poet with someone outside the District. The writers featured were primarily associated with the New York school, but there were also many Language writers. Diane Ward recalls giving her first poetry reading at Folio paired as a nervous eighteen- or nineteen-year-old with Barbara Guest, who arrived in town with a readymade audience in tow. Lynne Dreyer gave a reading with Barbara Baracks and another with Jim Brodey. Lang is remembered by many to have generated an energetic, collaborative spirit. Inman states that, "the series, without question, created a high degree of excitement about writing & its possibilities & helped push many of us further along our various ways."[5]

When the Folio Bookstore closed in 1978, the poetry community continued but without any centralized location. Tina Darragh remembers a reading of Hannah Weiner's in the late seventies or early eighties in DC, in which she had some of the Baltimore poets positioned in various parts of the audience to read simultaneously while she was center-stage. Abigail Child also gave a talk in the early eighties on narrative deconstruction in film. Also, several performance poetry readings were held at the Corcoran Gallery of Art.

Much of the Mass Transit poetry had been characterized by a politicization of content. Lee Lally, for instance, investigated feminist revisionist mythmaking:

> The horses have ridden off
> with who ever would go.
> The princes should have
> been here by now.
> We are no longer waiting
> We are writing our own stories.[6]

Often the poems in *Mass Transit* and Some of Us Press explicitly resisted existing power structures. Reversing subject positions and describing subcultural lifestyles, they paralleled similar calls within the women's movement and the civil rights movement. Other poems focused heavily on the everyday, including elements of popular culture and slang. "One might say," Retallack states, "that the unifying poetic project in an atmosphere characterized by difference was to create with language, on the page, the kind of figure-ground shift occurring in the socio-political world; to redefine what was at stake, what did or did not lie within the bounds of the poem."[7]

In contrast, some of the poetry read at the Folio series was more recognizably language-centered. Retallack believes that this shift in poetics occurred because the years of Mass Transit and Folio interaction had generated a close-knit or high-context community. Such a community shared a common conceptual framework and could move away from a pre-occupation with "discursive reference toward language and form per se."[8] This is not to say, however, that there were not different influences. As Phyllis Rosenzweig points out, "I don't think there is a common 'our' line-age because I truly think we have all been influenced differently and by dif-ferent writers along the way."[9] While Rosenzweig learned from the exam-ple of poets like Frank O'Hara and John Ashbery, Inman cites Clark Coolidge, Bernadette Mayer, and Aram Saroyan as influences. Lynne Dreyer also saw Mayer as an important influence, as well as Susan Howe. Others, like Joan Retallack, were fascinated by the work of John Cage, Gertrude Stein, and Oulipo.

The transition toward an investigation of form was gradual, with early or proto-Language pieces appearing in *Mass Transit*. One example is Tina Darragh's "Self-Portrait," a photograph of soldiers leading three formally dressed men on horses along a city street. Here, the body politic militates and subsumes the individual subject. In the same issue, she presented a dia-gram of horseshoes with listed descriptions. Through careful excision and rearrangement, Darragh generated unexpected absences (a loss of signifi-cation) as well as tracking sound repetitions. The continual appearance of "Toe" and "Shoe," for instance, transfers attention away from their family resemblance (belonging or appertaining to the foot) to their imperfect se-mantic relation.

The playful experimentation of Darragh's pieces are elaborated and re-fined in *Dog City*. Running for only two issues, *Dog City* was produced by a workshop that occurred at Folio under the aegis of the Poetry Factory, and included writers such as Lynne Dreyer, Doug Lang, Joan Retallack, Phyl-lis Rosenzweig, Bernard Welt, and Diane Ward. The title *Dog City* empha-sizes a poetics of humor, its initials reinforcing a located politics. Indeed, many of the poems featured in *Dog City* focused on the alienating effect and false consciousness of urban experience. An example is this excerpt from Diane Ward's "Home Plate":

> The street sliding away on the sheet metal tops.
> Tiny miniatures of real life. Siren, clouds of smoke:
> inside the dove, sure solutions
> bells when we wake up, bells when we hit the ground
> all bodies filled with input, communicationtrons
> messages from our lips, from our toes messages from the
> space between each hair on our heads.
> Eyes used to be. E[s]pecially internalized. Real life
> becomes so real becomes unreal.
> This conversation has gone back into parentheses. You don't
> have to shout I won't hear you any better.

Falling in love and going back again.
Certain places become special. Not sentimental but unavoid-
able. A writer who uses language. A writer who uses language
and emotion. A writer a language an emotion a philosophy a
wit a system a theory. A writer drinking a writer not
answering the phone on the table with two cups of coffee
a writer taking a shower   Shelley standing clear[10]

The home plate, the point of safety and closure in baseball, is ironicized through Ward's puns on plate—from the metal plates for industrial protection to the domestic plates matching the coffee cups. Here the message becomes lost in the surrounding noise, whether it be the ringing sound of a siren in the distance or of a clock nearby. The limits of language are apparent, as she ends the poem, "No words for what you want to say." Language, emotion, philosophy, and humor are all disconnected. The external becomes internalized, undercutting the Romantic vision of the artist raised above the material world.

Phyllis Rosenzweig turns instead to the divisions and categories that a city constructs:

This is my friend This is my boyfriend
This is my desk where I work
This is my job
This is me
This is the way things go

Merrick Parkway Utopia Parkway
This is the fourth page
This is the fifth page
They offered me a lot of money
so I agreed to do it
Cook an egg Cook another egg
These are the vitamins in your life
You could line people up
Is this pink?
Is this blue?
Is this worth continuing?

. . . .

The teeming metropolis

This is real wool
This is my one true bargain
Everything in your life is fast
but not me
We eat out too much but good food
is good when good food is good
You want to talk about it
and I want to get off the train

> Easy directions Easy to follow
> It is about perception which is
> not memory; to be alone to eat
> a cookie to get dressed up
>
> Assuming for the sake of argument
> Supposing for the sake of argument
> That everything (perception) is based
> on endless temporary experiences
> An absolute fulfillment of human desire
> Stolichnaya. Scientific Valentine.
> Venus in a terrifying light.[11]

Rosenzweig highlights how distinctions are made even when there seems little difference in language use, whether in relationships (the difference between friend and boyfriend), street directions (Merrick Parkway from Utopia Parkway), or work (between desk and job). Clichés of consumption are transformed through a sexual economy—the vitamins of an egg blur into the egg's role in sexual reproduction. Fast food is compared to the fastness of a girl. Rosenzweig leaves us to wonder whether eating a cookie might be somehow linked to getting "dressed up." Through her poem, easy directions become complicated. She seems to suggest that if these everyday distinctions were no longer habitual but viewed as an endless series of temporary decisions, the feminine might appear revamped: "Venus in a terrifying light."

While *Dog City* featured numerous collaborations between Washington writers, others took place outside its pages. Darragh, Dreyer, and Rosenzweig worked together on a detective story. Dreyer recalls that it became a source of immense enjoyment for the three of them. Yet, when finally performed for the workshop group, their idealized and idolized male character was met understandably with less than enthusiasm by many of the men.[12] Such performances, as well as the more public readings, are examples of collaborations that demand a different kind of involvement from their audience. Nick Piombino points out that poems such as Joan Retallack's *Errata 5uite* are best read aloud so that both poet and listener can work together to expand the boundaries of written and spoken language. Retallack, like other Washington women writers, uses "words as they appear to us in the inchoate flux of everyday experience, very much including the experience of silent and spoken reading, as well as associative thinking." This creates "a kind of music that challenges us to listen to the entire complexity of experience in its full density."[13]

The Folio series and *Dog City* would be supplemented by *EEL*. Originally named *Everybody's Ex-Lover*, the first issue appeared in 1973 and was co-edited by Lang, Inman, and Lisa Shea. Inman then became sole editor for the remaining three issues, although Tina Darragh "was very much involved w[ith] the magazine as well."[14] Following Inman's own interests, the magazine shifted from the surreal to more abstract work. It featured many Folio writers, as well as Kathy Acker, Charles Bernstein, Susan Howe, and Hannah Weiner. In the second half of the decade, Douglas Messerli produced *Là Bas* and *Sun & Moon* magazines out of College Park, Maryland.

All four magazines (along with two reading series) strengthened ties between the New York and Washington poets. Like Bruce Andrews and Michael Lally, Diane Ward eventually moved to New York, where she became involved in Roof Books. Washington writers also built upon connections between their work and that of the San Francisco Language writers. This, however, was largely through contributing to West Coast journals and presses like *This*, *Tottel's*, and *Tuumba*, and occurred during the second half of the seventies. Both groups of writers had created high-context communities. However, for the Bay Area writers, the group politics and radicalism of poetics saw them gain increasing notoriety during this period. The oppositional stance that they were often forced to adopt led to a different, more complex function of community from that of the Washington group.

Unlike the crystallization of a community in San Francisco and Washington, Language writing remained initially marginal and dispersed in New York. This was partly because the New York scene was simply so much larger than anywhere else. St. Mark's Poetry Project was in many respects the powerhouse of the poetic community and still the stronghold of a second-generation New York school. Lynne Dreyer points out that while people in Washington felt that Language writing was "really new right here at this time in this space," New Yorkers felt that such innovation "had been there all along and this was just a New Phase."[15] In May 1974, Barbara Baracks told Ron Silliman of the indifference to language-centered writing produced by people such as Andrews, the exception being Clark Coolidge, who was already widely known and had a more varied style.[16] At the end of 1974, Charles Bernstein moved back to New York from Santa Barbara, where he had been working and keeping up a correspondence with Ron Silliman (to whom he had first written in 1973). The following year, Ray DiPalma also moved to New York. "We've got nothing like the sense of community here as you've got," Charles Bernstein nevertheless wrote to Silliman, "at most a few people who read as friends." This lack of community, however, reflects the quality of the city—"Fragmented, decentralized, atomized."[17]

Whereas Dreyer disliked the "high strung" feeling of the New York poetry scene, for others, like Bernstein and Diane Ward, there were advantages.[18] With a concentration of all the arts, Bernstein felt that poets have less a sense of "their own culture import on a glamour or status scale, or, for that matter, public scale." The presence of so many artists means "you can't help but feel as much of a relation to workers in other fields as to people writing poetry, more relation in many cases, & this fact tends to de-centralize the poetry community focus (much less the 'language writing' poetry community focus)."[19] Diane Ward points out that St. Mark's offered the chance to read to a knowledgeable audience and generated publicity for lesser known poets.[20]

Andrews and Bernstein would try to foster a community, first through *Legend*, a five-way collaboration between themselves and Ray DiPalma, Ron Silliman, and Steve McCaffery.[21] Although the project was carried out between the east and west coasts, and across national borders, the distance involved led Andrews and Bernstein to consider the idea of a distribution service. This would strengthen affinities of interest by making available work that was hard to come by or not yet published. Making available back issues of *Big Deal*, *This*, *Tottel's*, and *Toothpick*, the service also offered pho-tocopies of out-of-print chapbooks, such as Andrews's *Edge* and *Vowels*, Lynne Dreyer's *Lamplights Used to Feed the Deer* and *Stampede*, Lyn Hejinian's *A Thought Is the Bride of What Thinking*, and Bernadette Mayer's *Story*. Furthermore, it offered photocopies of manuscripts by writers like Barbara Baracks, Ray DiPalma, Jackson MacLow, Steve McCaffery, Ron Silliman, and Hannah Weiner. The pricing of material covered copying charges as well as a royalty to the author.[22] Unfortunately, the service did not gather much consumer interest, and by early 1980 they began to close it down. Bernstein went on to edit the catalog at Segue with James Sherry and Diane Ward. The major small-press distributor on the East Coast, Segue sought a similar "aesthetic commitment with its choices." It also kept track of "a shifting community of readers" by circulating a mailing list to its affiliated presses.[23]

Besides the distribution service, Andrews and Bernstein envisaged a newsletter that would cut across communal divisions. Finding form as $L=A=N=G=U=A=G=E$—one of the best-known instruments of Language writing—the introductory letter outlined the newsletter's aim to emphasize

that spectrum of work that places its attention in some primary way on language, ways of making meaning, that takes neither form . . . or content . . . , or their rela-tion, for granted. Focusing on this kind of poetic activity, and related aesthetic & political concerns, we hope to open things up more publicly to your correspon-dence, break down unnecessary self-encapsulation of . . . person from person, scene from scene . . .[24]

Circulated to about two hundred writers, it would "include information of magazines & books (price & where to locate) and . . . feature texts (with bibliographic information) on a number of writers." Content was to be "a mix of short essays, texts, letters, statements, reader comments, journal excerpts & reviews (especially of new books etc., by less well-known younger writers—and related non fiction)." Reviews did not have to be expository or evaluative.[25]

Bernstein hoped that $L=A=N=G=U=A=G=E$ would include work that did not usually appear in a "poetry" context, such as art, music composition, performance art, philosophy, or sociology."[26] Accordingly, he envisaged something structured like the poetic scene in New York, contingent and cross-disciplinary in association. However, the writing itself was always to be prioritized, rather than (as in some performance texts or conceptual art) supplementary to the idea. Critical pieces would be chosen for the quality of writing, not merely for their argument.

Despite the general aim to deconstruct community boundaries, Bernstein thought their first issue should establish some roots and sources.[27] New York writers predictably dominated this vision of origins, but perhaps more surprising is the lack of women. Bernstein suggested that in addition to work by the editors, the issue should feature writings by Larry Eigner, Carl Andre, Clark Coolidge, Bernadette Mayer, Jackson Mac Low, Robert Grenier, Steve McCaffery, David Antin, something on Gertrude Stein or Louis Zukofsky, Samuel Beckett, John Enslin, and Ray DiPalma, as well as some intermedia work and found texts. Although Mayer was the only contemporary woman writer listed, Bernstein was hesitant about including her more recent work, which he felt was oriented more toward the New York school. It was envisaged that $L=A=N=G=U=A=G=E$ would distinguish a poetics separate from the New York school (unlike in Washington, where Language writing and the New York school were invariably featured side by side).

Susan Bee designed and produced $L=A=N=G=U=A=G=E$. While Andrews and Bernstein came up with the title of the magazine, Bee designed the logo. Although they had hoped to feature visual art that would articulate concerns similar to the writing (a province to be supervised by Bee), such plans were constrained by the low budget.[28] Until the ninth and tenth joint issue, the magazine was supported solely by subscriptions and donations. Another initial idea was that guest editors be called in to run special feature sections on topics such as sexuality, politics, and collaboration, as well as a forum on language-centered writing and women. Some of these would eventuate, though in varying size. Other early topics of interest, such as schizophrenic writing or the work of Roland Barthes, found fruition in various essays written by individuals. However, Andrews and Bernstein continued to occupy a primary editing role.

Many of the reviews and articles lived up to Bernstein's hopes for opening up the poetic, being written in a fluid and playful style. Yet not all articles in $L=A=N=G=U=A=G=E$ were innovative, many taking a standard argumentative form. Later articles focusing on Marxist-oriented analyses of language, for example, tended to reflect rather than query academic forms. Andrews and Bernstein even reprinted articles or excerpts that they considered particularly influential, such as work by Fredric Jameson, Terry Eagleton, and Stanley Cavell. While more formal pieces focusing on critical theory tended to be written by men, women writers reflected on their own poetics or undertook specific engagements with others. Tina Darragh for instance, wrote on both Susan Howe's poetry and her own use of procedural techniques.

Any characterization of $L=A=N=G=U=A=G=E$ as masculinist in orientation would derive partly from the way in which the magazine's theoretical output was recuperated and deradicalized by the academy. Despite the fact that $L=A=N=G=U=A=G=E$ featured many women writers, their work was often overlooked in critiques of the magazine. Many women remember Andrews and Bernstein as actively encouraging their writing. Lynne Dreyer recalls Andrews's ongoing support for her work, some of which was featured in $L=A=N=G=U=A=G=E$. Bernstein also wrote short articles on Barbara Einzig, Lyn Hejinian, and Hannah Weiner while editing $L=A=N=G=U=A=G=E$.[29] However, while both editors were eager to include women writers in the pages of $L=A=N=G=U=A=G=E$, they were not always successful in soliciting contributions from them. As Bernstein points out in a Keatsian phrase, $L=A=N=G=U=A=G=E$ was "shaped by a lot of what people don't send in . . . [which] amounts to a kind of negative capability."[30]

There are many reasons, of course, why women writers may have felt uncomfortable about sending critical pieces to $L=A=N=G=U=A=G=E$. Aside from the attention given to Marxist critiques, many writers thought of their poetics as already embodied in their poetry. In a letter to Susan Howe, Hejinian writes of her "perpetual confusion about political theory and political acts." If asked the question, "is a poem the result of a political act?" she "would have to say it is. Isn't that the assumption behind the latest issues of L=A=N=etc.?" Too much time was spent analyzing "terms of referentiality and the bourgeoisie."[31] In another letter to Howe, Hejinian writes that she is now thinking about politics, and particularly the Marxist idea of praxis because of "the current . . . L A N G U A G E question re. Capitalism and writing," which she found a rather frustrating question.[32] Howe too found that although she preferred reading the magazine to many others, "[m]uch of the work produced by $L=A=N=G=U=A=G=E$ poets is so damn CERTAIN."[33]

Some of the reviews in $L=A=N=G=U=A=G=E$ also tended to marginalize the work of women by filtering it through the discourse of femininity. An example is Robert Grenier's review of Lyn Hejinian's *Writing Is an Aid to Memory*. To describe stylistic density as "wife-ing quintessence passion" or "[h]ospitality's good behavior" as "womanly devotion's license, romance, logic's guises" is to undercut Hejinian's careful phenomenological meditation on the relation between thinking and writing. Grenier thinks that Hejinian's abstract play with words and her meditation on the philosophy of love is "[f]ine," although by using "too many words," she appears "showy-offy." His final (also playful) quip affirms—in a classic instance of the dancing dog syndrome—the oddity of a woman writer with epistemological concerns: "Darling, god damn, what a thinker, really."[34] While lighthearted, such a summation would never be made of a male writer.

Even though Hejinian and Howe may have seen $L=A=N=G=U=A=G=E$ as limited in addressing feminist concerns, they saw their own involvement as necessary to changing its approach. When Howe experienced an editorial slip-up in the publication of a piece, Hejinian told her to persist in demanding that her work be taken seriously and to "keep telling those guys to do so."[35] Hejinian's sentiments sound curiously like Bernstein's own in "The Conspiracy of 'Us,'" where he quotes the line, "Okay, break it up boys."[36] To Sandra Kumamoto Stanley, this cliché suggests that a "paternalistic ('boys') hierarchy structures [the group's] collective identity." She continues: "Even to challenge, or 'to break,' the group is to assert that the group, as a concept, exists."[37]

Certainly, an effect of $L=A=N=G=U=A=G=E$ (even if unintentionally) was to widen the divisions between poetic communities in New York. This was despite efforts by certain writers like Michael Lally who tried to create an inclusive community. Visiting New York in late 1978, Kit Robinson witnessed a territorial struggle between East Side poets and Language writers, which included some boycotting of readings (although he himself escaped unscathed).[38] Bernstein believed that there was a dangerous but very real "groupism" occurring. He wrote to Silliman on New Year's Eve, 1979, "Circles seem to close tighter & tighter, corral the wagons, in an ever diminishing ability to imagine oneself in some corner other than the one one's been painted into."[39] While he understood the need for people to speak among friends and the anxiety at new formations, the hostility to Language writing was worrying. In "The Conspiracy of 'Us,'" he contends that a group is potentially as atomized in its separation from other groups as a person can be from other persons. "The danger is that we will hide ourselves amidst the shuffle to proclaim who we are."[40]

In the initial planning stages of *L=A=N=G=U=A=G=E*, a three-way editorship between Andrews, Bernstein, and Ron Silliman had been entertained. In the end, *L=A=N=G=U=A=G=E* went ahead without Silliman, becoming wholly a New York–based magazine. For while Bernstein wanted to move toward a more open forum (where an agreement to publish a piece would constitute an "intersection" of poetics),[41] Silliman argued for a more refined editorial policy, with specific objectives. He wanted the magazine to showcase the radicalism and breadth of Language writing to the point that it would be a recognizable force within contemporary American poetry. In San Francisco the community was already a clearly defined presence. It included poets like Rae Armantrout, Lyn Hejinian, Tom Mandel, Bob Perelman, Kit Robinson, and Silliman himself, as well as younger writers like Steve Benson, Alan Bernheimer, Gloria Frym, Carla Harryman, Ted Pearson, and Geoff Young. Some of these writers had been discussing poetry since the beginning of the seventies (Perelman, for instance, had first met Watten in 1971 at the University of Iowa).

The kinds of writing and concerns considered important to the community had been well mapped out in journals such as *Joglars* (edited by Clark Coolidge and Michael Palmer in the sixties), *Tottel's* (edited by Ron Silliman in the early seventies), and *This* (the first three issues were coedited by Robert Grenier and Barrett Watten, the subsequent nine by Watten alone). Running throughout the seventies and into the early eighties, *This* had already linked innovative poetry from the Bay Area with similar poetries produced in Washington and New York. As Watten himself suggests, *This* was "the first continuous, self-conscious, and self-reflexive literary venue of what 'will have been' the Language School once it developed as it did, even if its formal characteristics could be assembled from other sources."[42] Yet it would also feature writers who were generally not considered part of the social or poetic formation of Language writing as it was then defined. The work of writers like Fanny Howe and Leslie Scalapino, for instance, appears in various issues. *This* also featured Canadian writers like Christopher Dewdney and British writers like Allen Fisher. Both *This* and *Tottel's*, along with magazines like Harryman's *Qu* and Perelman's *Hills*, were reinforced by a long-running reading series organized by Perelman and by others at the Grand Piano and Highsmith's.

L=A=N=G=U=A=G=E would have been seen by Silliman as a way to extend such work, creating a space for critical discussion. This was particularly important in the Bay Area, where what was being dubbed "Language poetry" had become the epicenter of a number of political and aesthetic debates. Unlike New York, the arts were strongly differentiated in the Bay

Area during the seventies. Although performance-based poets like Carla Harryman encouraged visual artists to attend readings and talks, poetry was still presumed to be too tied to the page and thus limiting. Harryman recalls a young and prominent artist dismissing Language writing as "just a version of surrealism."[43]

Toward the end of the seventies, there was also dissension within the innovative poetic community by some gay writers. Bruce Boone argued for a community that would work collectively around writing's "interior relation to power."[44] Writing would not be separate from what one does as an intellectual but recognized as much for its instrumental value as for its critique of power. It would be both self-expression and group practice. If viewed in this light, the poetic community could link up with other collective organizations, like the gay movement, feminism, ecology, antinuclear protests, and the prison movement. Narrative opened up such possibilities of liberation.

In a much later article, "Baucis and Philemon (1985)," Robert Glück argues that narration enables both a local, where gestures and ideology are conserved and shared over time, and a sublime, which can destroy or transform the local. Not only are we now aware of our own complicity within the local, but we are aware that different versions of the local are available. "I can take my pick," he states, "but they come with quotation marks and so do their stories."[45] "I write about these forms—that are myself—to acknowledge and then dispense with them, to demonstrate their arbitrariness, how they disintegrate before a secret (the world, the sublime)."[46] Whereas Carla Harryman saw herself as similarly working within narrative to undermine restrictive structures, Boone would draw a line between those who narrate and those who did not—positioning Language writers in general among the latter.[47]

Besides debates within the emergent poetic community, there were territorial antagonisms with more established poets, the most infamous perhaps being an outburst by Robert Duncan at a talk given by Barrett Watten. There also were running battles with more mainstream poets, like Tom Clark, which were played out publicly in the pages of a local newspaper, *Poetry Flash*. By the end of the seventies and throughout the early eighties, the struggle for the Bay Area Language community created "various kinds of frustrations, competitiveness, and feelings of exclusion."[48] To survive and consolidate required an ongoing belief in the value of the poetry being produced. Harryman notes that "[w]riting was an object of belief, and I saw it as a kind of act."[49] Yet another effect was to create a siege mentality in which one could only attack or be attacked. Rae Armantrout believes that "there had to be a wedge driven into the world of poetry, as it existed then, and that it would take a personality like Barrett Watten or Ron Silliman, people that were capable of being aggressive." "I think that what they did," she continues, "was something that probably only they could have done. . . . And so I'm grateful for it."[50]

Unlike San Francisco and New York, Language writing in Washington attracted little controversy. The small poetic community could continue without anxiety. This perhaps had a flow-on effect in making its writers more independent and confident to experiment laterally. Joan Retallack believes that energies could be focused on the work rather than on positioning or promotion.[51] As with the Bay Area circle, the Washington writers formed a strong bond with one another that extended into their daily lives. When Folio Books closed in 1978, they continued to meet at the homes of writers like Doug Lang, Phyllis Rosenzweig, and Diane Ward. These get-togethers occurred sometimes as often as once a week but always at least once a month. They consolidated more public readings and provided a forum in which to discuss work in progress.

In the mid-eighties, Diane Ward rang Tina Darragh from New York asking advice in her reading of Julia Kristeva. Darragh decided to invite a group of Washington writers and artists to discuss *Desire in Language: A Semiotic Approach to Literature and Art*. At that time, she and P. Inman had not been meeting regularly with any group since Mass Transit (they had spent a year away from DC and were as yet only marginally involved in the Folio workshops). Although the ensuing discussion dissolved into an argument between the men, the moment cemented a desire in the women writers to create a space where they could happily remain "inarticulate about things." As Rosenzweig points out, to be "inarticulate" is "a positive condition, indicating that one is thinking over very complex issues and has not yet arrived at a conclusion or explanation for them."[52] For the next eight years or so, Tina Darragh, Lynne Dreyer, Joan Retallack, and Phyllis Rosenzweig met and shared elements from "our lives / our readings / our readings / our latest movie outings / our work." Retallack elaborates:

We talked less about formal aspects of our work more about ourselves as writers, as women who are writers. . . . Exploring personal and social (including gender) implications of the sort of work we do, questioning it, not knowing the answers, identifying concerns which have already begun to appear in the "problematic" of new work; e.g. the question of first person singular subject in our writing.[53]

The four met mostly at Retallack's house but sometimes at Rosenzweig's and less frequently at Dreyer's. They predominantly discussed each other's work in progress, taking the time to analyze it in detail. Upon reflection, Darragh believes

I would not have been able to write the *adv. fans* piece without them. At first, there was a section that was seven pages long, then I narrowed it down to three to read when we got together, and after that I could get it down to a few lines. But I remember thinking that there was no other group that could provide comfortable ears for that sort of thing. I trusted them to be both tough and supportive.[54]

Dreyer, too, recalls the meetings as being the most constructive of times in her writing: "I felt less inhibited about talking," she notes.[55] She also enjoyed having the diversity of theoretical perspectives like Retallack's as a contrast to her own more personal poetics. Phyllis Rosenzweig felt that the meetings encouraged her to begin *Primary Writing*. Each issue was devoted to one long work by a single writer and initially featured writers like Jane DeLynn, Tina Darragh, and Doug Lang. Both the publishing venture and the meetings revealed Rosenzweig's propensity for organization and debate.

The gatherings would culminate in "Intraview," a four-way dialogue or, to be more precise, "polylogue." Although they had written numerous collaborations with one other, they had never written as a foursome or on a project quite so demanding. In 1987, Tom Beckett asked Joan Retallack to contribute to a proposed anthology of interviews. Instead of an individual response, Retallack suggested the four-way "intraview," structured in such way that a series of questions on poetics would be posed and responded to simultaneously. Like the detective story, the "intraview" was undertaken by mail. Rosenzweig notes that while they began writing for pleasure, the process and dialogue became more meaningful as it progressed.[56] They discussed the feeling of alienation within language and within the world, as well as the role of humor and play in poetry. They also shared their poetic influences and the anxiety over whether writing could be considered a political act.

At the same time, Douglas Messerli was also considering a volume of interviews, but more specifically around the question: "How do you see your poetry as being related or as being a product of sexuality or sexual politics?" Believing this to be "an often ignored subject that deserves serious exploration," his proposed list of participants included Bruce Andrews, Steve Benson, Charles Bernstein, Tina Darragh, Jean Day, Lyn Hejinian, Fanny Howe, Susan Howe, David Melnick, and Chris Tysh. He hoped that responses to the first question would generate other questions. Like Retallack, he hoped to re-jig the interview genre to create more of a conversation:

Finally, I plan to reorganize the responses so that related issues, comments, etc. can play off one another, to re-edit the responses, so to speak, to create a more connected document. In all cases, participants will have the opportunity to see the final draft and to make changes in their individual comments and to offer suggestions for the entire "symposium."[57]

Retallack's "intraview" was probably close to what Messerli had in mind. Significantly, neither the "intraview" nor the volume on sexuality and poetry was ever published. Having already considered the question of masculinity and writing in *Legend*, Andrews and Bernstein undertook responses to Messerli's initial question. In "Poetry and (Male?) Sex," Bernstein argued that language was no more "phallic" than it was "clitoral," and "while standard grammar may reflect the (patriarchal) social order, alternative (nonphallic) grammars are simultaneously being realized and repressed."[58] He proposed a move away from essentialist framings of gender, adding that "the struggle for men is to unlearn masculinity, without substituting any positive value to this gender differential."[59] Andrews, on the other hand, continued the rather phallic economy generated by *Legend*. In "Be Careful Now You Know Sugar Melts in Water (On Sexuality)," the female "you" is a tabula rasa, occupying a position of virtual alterity.[60] Such a representation lies at odds with other, perhaps later examples of his writing like "Lip Service," which lyrically contests stereotypic gender categories.

Given Messerli's association with Washington writers, it is perhaps not surprising that there should be a synchronicity between his proposed volume on sexual/textual politics and the appearance of "Intraview," with its focus on gender and writing. It is also not surprising that Andrews's and Bernstein's responses found publication in contrast to "Intraview." Retallack notes that the Washington community's marginality and relative independence from New York and San Francisco has left many of its writers "pretty low on the horizon."[61] While a political center of power, Washington has often been lost between the equal signs of Language writing maps. It is only through alternative topographies—engendered through feminist charting—that it gains symbolic capital.

CHAPTER TWO

Poetic Fields and the "Painted Birds" of Language Writing

Feminism has broadly been defined as those practices that articulate women's experience as something culturally differentiated from the experience of men. As such, feminism foregrounds the possibility of a communal bond around the sign of a sexual difference that is sometimes marked corporeally. It is also implicitly a critical discourse about relations of power in social formations and the possibility of change. Systems of representation in Western culture have traditionally recognized one constitutive speaking subject, which is unitary, European, and masculine. While those systems offered men an identity of social agency and possession, they restricted women to lives of constraint, idealization, and silence. The onset of democracy and the ideological presumption that every subject has a right to speak led many women writers to demand access to hitherto closed public discourses. As a privileged site of individual expression, poetry was a desired medium of self-determination. However, until the revival of the women's movement in the late sixties, poetry was not popularized as a political discourse.

Much second-wave feminism was grounded on a desire not only to express individual "truths" but to link them into a collective awareness.[1] Self-expression and visibility were key aspects of this project. The act of writing became a political and communal strategy, empowering individual writers toward a newfound authority as well as helping other women to realize their inner selves. This idea of an underlying authenticity may be seen in the titles of contemporary poetry anthologies, such as Florence Howe's and Ellen Bass's *No More Masks!: An Anthology of Poetry by Women* (1973).[2] As Erica Hunt points out, this meant that any writing that was difficult to assimilate into a centralized or coherent narrative became problematic:

One troubling aspect of privileging language as the primary site to torque new meaning and possibility is that it is severed from the political question of *for whom* new meaning is produced. The ideal reader is an endangered species, the commit-ted reader has an ideological agenda, both open and closed, flawed and acute, that we do not address directly. (Italics added)[3]

Language writing did not address a reader who might be looking for a predetermined or instant form of affirmation. Rae Armantrout suggests that ambivalence toward Language writing was also related to the belief that women's lives could be described only through transparent and imme-diate forms of representation.[4] In many cases, the desire for agency and control overrode the attractions of innovative writing. "For a writer," as Kathleen Fraser states, "whose awareness has been turned by a growing need to claim her own history and voice/s, such as Feminism provides, Language writing's concerns are often experienced (if not intended) as di-rectives she cannot afford."[5]

Feminism, then, was predominantly articulated through a single ideol-ogy of opposition, that is, of gender *as* difference. With writers like Adrienne Rich spearheading the women's movement, there was further impetus for poetry in particular to be read as confirming a separate vision. Rich herself claimed: "[T]he poetry of women's liberation . . . was women's antiestablishment poetry, challenging not just conventional puritanical mores, but the hip 'counterculture' and the male poetry culture itself."[6] In contrast, many formally innovative poets felt distanced from this process of political instrumentality, as well as alienated through their activities within nonseparatist poetic communities.[7] Often they were situated on the mar-gins of a recognized feminist practice, as approved by the women's move-ment, and of a mainstream field of poetry that was defined by systems of funding and teaching appointments.[8]

The early framework of "gender as difference" also replicates many of the structural problems that were symptomatic of a phallocentric logic. As female academics tended to focus on texts that reflected their own predom-inantly white and middle-class experience, institutional feminism fostered a self-generative field of interpretation. Preference was given, as Rae Arman-trout notes, to poetry centered on a single image or trope and narrated by a voice of both sincerity and authority.[9] In its challenging of the prevailing symbolic order, the poetic "I" became emblematic of female experience, speaking for and resembling women beyond the text. Gayatri Spivak argues that, in the desire for synthesis, feminism unwittingly ventriloquized the voices of Third World women in its approach.[10] Yet because cultural iden-tities involve racial or ethnic difference, nationality, familial responsibility, and sexual orientation, all produce a different relation to the feminine and may vary in their political sensitivity during an individual's life.[11] Further-more, such differences are contingent on recognition. Their "significance" is continually asserted and assessed by the unstable and overdetermined "meanings" with which they are privately and socially invested.

The arguments circulating within feminism in the early seventies were echoed from a quite different viewpoint within Language writing. In an article for *Socialist Review,* Ron Silliman contends that the socially marginal are involved in a different sort of challenge from that of the avant-garde. As a traditionally white and male-centered formation, the avant-garde could be seen to occupy a double relation to the cultural dominant by being both part of a hegemony and oppositional to it. In this respect, experimental writing is a less effective means of critiquing gendered and racially disparate practices.[12] Leslie Scalapino responded that, until the constitution and perception of the conventional changed, political discourse aimed at challenging cultural hegemony would largely be ineffective:

In order to get at what you're seeing as oppressive, the writing must be aware of the way in which one (and the writing) is formed and reformed by exteriority, and the solidification of a pattern coming to "one" from the exterior world. The writer may express the difference between what is interior (different from what's "socially" articulated) and what is being shaped, which is itself a reintegration vis-à-vis the "whole," placing the person (again) in a conventional relation to that supposed whole.[13]

Cora Kaplan makes a similar argument when she notes that the decision by women writers to "storm" the canon merely recognized and reinforced the importance of high culture while undercutting a more radical critique of the values embedded in language itself.[14]

In the anxiety surrounding second-wave feminism, individual politics were deemed "declared" through social as well as textual practices. This framework meant that the way in which one was positioned by others in the field of cultural production was considered offset by the way in which one "chose" to be positioned. Rather than "engaging" with a poetic community, writers were interpreted as "belonging" to a social formation. In such a logic of allegiance, one could choose to be part of a separate feminist community or of a mixed group like the Language writers. A third alternative was to position oneself independently of any recognizable group. Such logic necessarily reduced and oversimplified an ongoing and complex poetic interchange into cultural stasis.

Although more women have been visibly associated with Language writing than with other poetic formations, its group nature was seen as deleterious to the critical reception of their work. "[E]ven here when the history of this sub sub group gets written even *here* women get shut up or out," Susan Howe states.[15] "When articles are written about Language poetry," she adds, "it's usually the men who do the writing and fighting."[16] Marianne DeKoven also views Language writing as continuing an avant-garde agenda that maintains many of those modernist characteristics that either exclude women or elide their achievements. Following Scalapino's response to Silliman, DeKoven concedes that, like the avant-garde, many feminist projects question representation. However, while the stylistic characteristics of the avant-garde (postmodern, antirealist, metafictional, surfictional, and innovation) are often indistinguishable from techniques of the feminine, she maintains that both the contemporary and historical avant-gardes have deliberately prevented women from playing a significant or even active role there.[17] The presence of female figures in the avant-garde is merely the effect of tokenism.

In such an argument, what marginalizes the women involved is the cultural formation of the practice. In an article entitled "Gertrude's Granddaughters (1986)," DeKoven focuses more on their critical reception. In both cases she imagines a gloomy future for women poets who choose to associate with Language writing:

As long as the experimental writer whose "signature" is female aligns herself with the language poets, for example, . . . she has a place on the literary map. The price she pays, a price familiar to all of us, is twofold: the question of gender will be erased, declared a non-issue, and at the same time it is less likely than if her signature were male that she will become one of the stars, even in that tiny firmament.[18]

Certainly, recent histories and overviews seem to bear this out. The *New Princeton Encyclopedia of Poetry and Poetics* (1993) mentions only one woman poet in its section on Language writing. While Robert Grenier, Ron Silliman, Charles Bernstein, and Bruce Andrews each receive a separate chapter in Bob Perelman's *The Marginalization of Poetry*, Hejinian's work is chiefly read in relation to Silliman's New Sentence; and the work of Beverly Dahlen, Susan Howe, Rae Armantrout, and Carla Harryman is compressed into half a chapter (although he does give a convincing and careful reading within the chapter on gender politics and American literary history). George Hartley's *Textual Politics of the Language Poet* does briefly mention the work of women writers, but focuses more on a Marxist analysis of Language writing. And while Susan Howe is one of the three writers that Linda Reinfeld attends to at length in *Language Poetry: Writing as Rescue*, there is little contextualization of Howe's work in light of other feminist innovation.

DeKoven's argument about self-marginalization blames the women writers themselves instead of analyzing the structures through which poetic practice is perceived and interpreted. In this respect, DeKoven views women who choose to associate with avant-garde group formations as "Othered" by patriarchal contamination from them. Such a logic is similar to that of Mary Daly, who proposed in *Gyn/Ecology* to banish such "Painted Birds" from her "true elect" of feminists, because they are either aberrant or have "sold out" on their feminist politics.[19] The alternative that DeKoven envisages is a specifically female canon, a separate literary tradition of women writers. She elaborates: "Even when feminists claim for women or for the feminine a privileged, transgressive marginality in relation to hegemonic culture, it seems necessary also to claim sole occupancy of that margin, exclusive rights to the territory of the Other: women must *be* difference."[20] Such a rhetoric of essentialism, as Meaghan Morris discerns, is itself a form of colonization. As a tactic, it implies a "pure" line of feminist practice competing necessarily against contaminated lines. Furthermore, it suppresses the possibility of feminist critique between politically diverse subjects.[21]

In *Poetics of the Feminine: Authority and Literary Tradition in William Carlos Williams, Mina Loy, Denise Levertov, and Kathleen Fraser* (1994), Linda Kinnahan accepts DeKoven's proposition and maps out an alternative tradition of feminist-informed poetry. Focusing on a group of experimental writers surrounding *HOW(ever)*, she suggests that in the late seventies and eighties a number of women writers sought their maternal forebears in writers who similarly explored linguistic innovations earlier this century. Kathleen Fraser, Beverly Dahlen, Frances Jaffer, Susan Howe, and Rachel Blau DuPlessis began reconstructing "a forgotten line," a "modernist counterstrain" that included writers like Emily Dickinson, Gertrude Stein, Mina Loy, Djuna Barnes, H.D., Virginia Woolf, Marianne Moore, Laura Riding, and Lorine Niedecker.[22] According to Kinnahan, "[t]he work of current women writers interested in language innovation suggests . . . that experimentalism in America is gendered in its various responses to such issues as lyric, voice, and audience." She adds that the "condemnation of the lyric voice by Language poets almost automatically marginalizes [a woman writer's] experiments with the lyric."[23] In making such a statement, Kinnahan overlooks Language writers like Armantrout, whose poetry—like Loy's and Niedecker's—is sharply lyrical. Furthermore, Kinnahan's female tradition elides other histories of poetic dialogue, such as Loy's exchanges with Marinetti or Niedecker's close association with Louis Zukofsky. While these discussions may have been sexually and textually ambivalent, they nevertheless motivated further explorations into the multiplicity of language. Indeed, all the writers Kinnahan lists as a "modernist counterstrain" were involved in productive debates about current poetics with male counterparts.

In "Sexifesto," Anne Waldman also outlines an alternative tradition of women writers but incorporates writers from a diverse range of poetic communities. She envisages a "class where women writers were to be summoned as muses and pilots, as old tests and trails or trials . . . of past time. Eternally present in the imagination." Waldman describes a liberated space, an experimental topos of the feminine, doubling up on the dominant vision. This "other old place" is where the Muse, Laura Riding, Stein, or the "sibylline H.D." creates the atmosphere. Waldman argues that "diPrima, Kyger, Notley, Mayer, Acker, Lauterbach, Howe, Scalapino, Hejinian will now cast you [the reader] in a more contemporary net. But the experiments you might muster will change the way you see 'her' thinking-grammar forever."[24]

The construction of such countercanons is not new. Ellen Friedman and Miriam Fuchs's influential *Breaking the Sequence: Women's Experimental Fiction* (1989) may be seen as a significant intervention in avant-garde traditions; like Kinnahan's and Waldman's more recent efforts, it also seeks to construct a feminine canon.[25] In putting together a selected list of women experimentalists, Friedman and Fuchs fail to comment on what limitations such a list might have or what its purpose might be. While their list includes many of the writers discussed in the essays collected in their book, they do not discuss how the articles themselves were selected nor what is absent from such collections. Their list is divided into first generation, second generation, third generation, and literature in translation. Far from "breaking the sequence," Friedman and Fuchs consolidate it by reinforcing a "corrected" tradition of writing. Although the list mentions Kathleen Fraser, Fanny Howe, Laura Chester, and Bernadette Mayer, it fails to include many of their contemporaries. As in Kinnahan's list making, many women writers fall through the gaps.

Rather than deconstruct the process of canonization, the arguments of critics like Kinnahan or Friedman and Fuchs run along the same logic that first prescribed a gendering of influence. Instead of investigating how or why the canon is engendered in specific ways, they merely attempt to reverse negative attitudes to the feminine. A different set of exclusions and silences is thus produced.[26] In this respect, a separatist female canon creates another type of categorization that excludes the valuable connections made between writers working within a variety of formations and affiliations. Christine Brooke-Rose notes that the focus on feminist recovery also tends to elide those structures that contemporary writers are struggling against: "that sisterhood is, with some notable exceptions, generally so busy on feminist "themes" and on discovery or reinterpreting women authors of the past . . . that it has not time to notice or to make an effort to understand, let alone to back, an unfamiliar (experimental) woman writer who does not necessarily write on such themes."[27]

In terms of her border position within political and poetic communities, the innovative woman writer would seem to be "out of everywhere." Rosmarie Waldrop suggests that such alterity or nomadism is the position of poetry in general—and potentially emancipatory.[28] In contrast, Brooke-Rose argues that it leaves women writers in a disabling situation: caught in a canonical conundrum, doomed if they seek some sort of feminine margin and doomed if they align themselves with any larger poetic community. Of the latter, she remarks: "On the one hand, they will not get the encouragement, or the serious criticism that a male experimental writer will get, which can help them develop. On the other hand, an indifferent experimental male writer will get more attention, qua experimenter, than any woman experimental writer—good, bad, or indifferent."[29]

Of course, there have been individuals and projects that have made a difference in how women Language writers have been positioned in relation to both their male counterparts and to other women poets. Manuel Brito sought initially to focus entirely on male poets for his series of interviews with Language writers until Rae Armantrout advised him to widen his scope.[30] Armantrout offered similar advice to Alan Golding after reading the predominantly male-oriented chapter on Language writing that formed the draft for his book on poetic canons.[31] Joan Retallack, too, wrote a detailed article on contemporary experimental poets so that they would be properly represented in *Feminist Measures: Soundings in Poetry and Theory* (1994), one of the first collections focusing on critical theory and women's poetry.[32] More recently, Mary Margaret Sloan's ground-breaking women's anthology, *Moving Borders: Three Decades of Innovative Writing by Women* (1998), offers an important corrective to past histories by working through and alongside poetic communities not formed primarily around gender.

As Sloan's collection suggests, the question of marginality is perhaps in need of further review, as gender is only one of a number of cultural positionings that map and inform the poetic field. Harryette Mullen argues that even when a space for innovative women writers is temporarily located and named, the work of Black writers or other minority writers continues to be elided or ghettoized.[33] This is made particularly apparent in volumes like *The Oxford Companion to Women's Writing in the United States* (1995). Along with Mei Mei Berssenbrugge, Myung Mi Kim, Theresa Hak Kyung Cha, Trinh Minh-ha, and Erica Hunt, Mullen occupies a subcategory, displaced from the more general category of innovative writers as well as the category of Black poets. An even more startling example is the anthology, *Out of Everywhere: Linguistically Innovative Poetry by Women in North America and the UK* (1996), which promises to showcase "the extraordinary range and diversity" of linguistically innovative poetry by women in North America and the United Kingdom.[34] Despite such a promise, writers of color remain absent from its mapping of North American poetry. A somewhat fitting irony is Carla Harryman's contribution, "After Theresa Hak

Kyung Cha's *Dictée*," which pays tribute to Cha's own testimony of cultural erasure. Apart from this trace, what is "out of" formally innovative poetries is Black or ethnic writing. Once again, this confirms Mullen's suspicion that the two are viewed as mutually exclusive categories.

Alternatively, Black or ethnic writing seems to have been taken up in mainstream anthologies more for its value in portraying a range of "emblematic" experiences of race and gender than for its degree of innovation. An example is *The Norton Anthology of American Literature* (1998).[35] Of the ten represented poets born after 1935, there are two Anglo-Americans, two African Americans, two Asian Americans, two Latin Americans, and two Native Americans—and from each of these cultural groupings, one male writer and one female writer. The danger here lies in ethnic writers being read purely in terms of authenticity rather than for the way in which they may challenge, critique, or diversify particular stereotypes and cultural boundaries.

Sloan successfully negotiates such issues in *Moving Borders*. The margin itself disappears as the work of writers like Harryette Mullen, Erica Hunt, Myung Mi Kim, and Mei-mei Berssenbrugge is represented alongside that of other innovative poets. Like the transatlantic scope of *Out of Everywhere*, *Moving Borders* is one of the few anthologies that cross national borders— overlapping thematic concerns and responses to feminism are found between Canadian and American writers, even as they are shaped by cultural differences.

Case Debates on Language Writing and Feminism

In the mid-eighties, women poets like Rachel Blau DuPlessis and Kathleen Fraser were asked by journals to "arbitrate" poetic debates between the proponents and critics of Language writing. A peculiar choice as fence-sitter, the feminist was seen to work both in and alongside a tradition of marginality.[36] Ultimately, such arbitration foregrounded issues of gender over race as DuPlessis and Fraser focused on the possibility of merging feminist practice with the community practice of Language writing.

DuPlessis was brought into an ongoing debate between Eliot Weinberger and Michael Davidson in the pages of *Sulfur*. In positioning herself as a third term, DuPlessis hoped to collapse the "rules" of their adversarial exchange. She posits that the primary difference between Davidson and Weinberger is one of degree. Viewing both as obsessed with influences and traditions, DuPlessis writes, "I've always been startled, fascinated, put off? By how neatly male writers construct originating genealogies as part of their critical analyses. How that tactic fixes and defines 'ink' lines, lines of descent."[37] Yet, DuPlessis's gendering of this practice falters in light of her own remapping in *The Pink Guitar*, as well as in other works by women, such as Waldman's "Sexifesto," Susan Howe's *My Emily Dickinson*, and Alice Notley's *Doctor Williams' Heiresses*.

DuPlessis also wants to reject poetry as a communal act or to recognize that her own writing may be a consciously dialogic practice. Identifying herself as part of Woolf's Society of Outsiders, she states: "As a devotee of working cohorts rather than declared and centered groups, I regard the activity with curiosity and amazement tempered with suspicion at the self-limiting aspects of any concerted enterprise."[38] Such a tradition of nontradition, however, is paradoxical, since elsewhere she cleaves to a collective identity of gender. After discussing with DuPlessis the effect of gender in poetic formations, Armantrout told Hejinian that

[Rachel] seemed to want to make generalizations about women writers. For instance, she said it was "no accident" that she and I don't write a lot suggesting that this was a special problem for women writers. I thought of a number of quite prolific women. We seemed polarized as feminist (her) and other (me), though I have always thought of myself as supporting feminism. I said that there seemed to be more women writers than ever before accepted in the various "movements." She said that her studies have shown that there were always a lot of women involved especially in early stages of movements, but that most tend to disappear due partly to lack of critical attention leaving usually one woman per "group". . . . I don't know enough about literary history to evaluate her argument—but it was interesting and disturbing. At any rate, she seemed warm and bright and I liked her.[39]

To some degree, the *New Princeton Encyclopedia of Poetry and Poetics* proves DuPlessis's theory, since Hejinian features as the sole woman in its section on Language writing. Again, this may have more to do with the critical transformation of poetic practice into recognized canonical patterns than with the actual formation of communities.

In other forums, such as the collaborative "For the Etruscans" or her talk for "The Tradition of Marginality" symposium (published as "Otherhow"), DuPlessis suggests that drawing on an avant-garde practice is often fruitful. The woman poet, she suggests, can have a tactical relation with various communities, based on nation, sex, subculture, race, or aesthetic. By maintaining a "both/and vision," she can embrace a movement of "not choosing" and thus avoid a final or fetishized position.[40] In "Otherhow," DuPlessis further argues that she finds the avant-garde's "idea of power and language . . . interesting: [particularly] the resolute lack of synthesis, the non-organic poetics, the secular lens." She is cautious, however, on the following points: "Where is/are its women?: where in the poems, serving what function? where in its social matrices, with what functions? where in its ideologies? How does it create itself by positioning its women and its women writers?"[41] In asking such questions, she forces a further response by Language writers to interrogate their own practice.

Like DuPlessis, Kathleen Fraser raises a number of questions about the effects of a community ethic. In 1985 she wrote an article entitled "Partial Local Coherence" for *Ironwood*, as a framing response to a special feature on Language writing. As she notes, its editor, Michael Cuddihy, wanted a different angle from that provided by someone not "in the family" but who followed Language writing with interest. Fraser sent a draft of her article to Steve Benson, who then showed it to Carla Harryman. Through Harryman and Benson, Lyn Hejinian also read a draft copy. Before publication, both Robert Glück and Frances Jaffer gave advice about the article. Rather than ask questions from a distance, as DuPlessis did, Fraser actively sought out opinions.

In her draft version, Fraser suggests that women poets are working under the wing of male Language writers. This marginal position potentially constrains creative and theoretical flight. Fraser further argues that the group formation of Language writing has interrupted and changed the poetic practice of women who were already writing strongly by themselves. By way of illustration, she suggests that Silliman has systematically helped create an audience and frame for Hejinian's work: "She'd been writing beautifully, for years, before she was claimed as a Language writer, but her emergence as a figure in American poetry has been due in very real ways to Silliman's naming and championing her work."[42] Fraser also argues that Silliman has done the same for David Bromige and Rae Armantrout. Finally she raises the issue of referentiality when suggesting that a political writing practice must be tied to the experiential. Fraser concludes: "While the structural preoccupations of language-centered theory and practices are both stimulating, and, at times, concretely useful in this enterprise, their [a]esthetic distaste for self-referentiality and/or evident personal investment in one's subject immediately introduces a series of prohibiting factors."[43]

Although the aim of the article was otherwise, writers such as Carla Harryman felt that Fraser was specifically attacking her own and other women's poetry on account of its alliance to Language writing. Part of Harryman's sensitivity came from the fact that she had always treated gender as a real concern in her writing, particularly in its relation to power and the subsequent marginalization of women. She wrote back a point-by-point response, sending a copy to Hejinian as well. In particular, she took offense at the suggestion that Language writing promotes a "patriarchal" poetics, arguing that she did not see herself as "huddling under the protective 'wing' of the male Language writers." While some of her work, as well as Hejinian's and Armantrout's, had taken place "in the structure of the wing," "we have made charming and perhaps enduring contributions to the tail, the beak, the eyes, the storage bin for the eggs, the singing voice and the brain—what there is of it."[44] While Silliman has encouraged Armantrout, Harryman argues that Armantrout has likewise helped Silliman. Where Fraser sees a hierarchical relationship, Harryman finds evidence of equality and variance.

While they view Language writing differently, Harryman suggests that she and Fraser share many of the same influences. *All* writers, she continues, are influenced by various contemporaries and elders. Harryman also points out that Hejinian had been a small-press publisher well before the emergence of the term "Language writing." Furthermore, Hejinian parallels Silliman in championing the work of others and in being "an outspoken writer who shares her views on writing in a number of public formats."[45] As for Fraser's grouping of writers into one community around the term "Language poetry," Harryman remarks that it had "been coming into being for many more years than four. I have had close association with some of these writers for nine and ten years. And some of us have known others of us for twice that long." As such, distinctions between "inner and outer circles are blurred. . . . There is no church or lodge."[46] Such a presumption inscribes an elitist poetics onto Language writing. Rather, poets crave community as a consequence of working in isolation.

Writing back, Fraser conceded that by "not giving credit to the true powers of women individuals in the [Language writing] movement," she had merely "reinforc[ed] the dominance of men, which I was complaining about." Admitting she had been "wrong," she promised to "try to do further fixing, if Michael will let me."[47] Before it was published, Fraser revised her article, cutting out all references to "patriarchy" as well as the phrase about the "wing."

At a more personal level, Fraser sympathizes with Harryman's anger at being categorized as a Language writer. Identifying herself as a committed feminist, Fraser notes by way of analogy that she too does "not like being lumped together with a great deal of boring, didactic, and politically diffuse stuff that has appeared linked to that general term or ideology." Fraser adds that she recognizes the desire for community, because it is "essential for survival." She confesses that she was too easily led by George Lakoff's

approach to Language writing, acknowledging that by treating it as a phe-
nomenon she "short-changed the individuality of the writers associated
with the term." Yet she continues to disagree with the idea that Language
writing might be a scattered or dispersed community:

Clearly, there is a group of friends of varying intensities and tolerances that com-
prise an inner group who are in constant dialogue, socially or by letter exchange,
etc. I *do not* say this with any intent . . . to be divisive. I am simply trying to describe
a movement something like protoplasm, I guess, which *does* have a kind of perme-
able boundary and a nucleus.[48]

Fraser also stands by her argument about channels of readership.
Readers, she states, have to be alerted, led, and cultivated, adding that this
became particularly obvious in Hejinian's publication of Fraser's *Magritte
Series* through Tuumba Press.[49] The creation of a readership has generally
been gendered masculine: "Men have a tradition of doing that well and
being supported in this kind of assertion. Women, on their own, without
any help from male editors or mentors, have been viewed quite differ-
ently, if they sought out a serious audience."[50] While male Language writ-
ers are serious in attacking hierarchical value structures, there remain im-
plicit hierarchies of aesthetic choice, dismissals, and gestures of
arrogance. Fraser views the politics of poetic communities as having been
historically mediated by a specifically masculine entrepreneurial process
and rhetoric.

She also sees her own poetic position as shifting and contingent. Using
Benson's concept of "testimony" as "a growth or manifest construct of an
individual and a cultural complex at a particular juncture in their history,"
Fraser finishes her article with a list of writers influencing her current
poetics. In publishing the article and its concluding testimony, she was
hoping to show that Language writing was "providing all kinds of stimula-
tion and intellectual excitement which I took seriously and was affected by,
but that it finally wasn't the whole show for me."[51]

Glad of the dialogue between herself and Harryman, Fraser says that
she had "often thought that talks among you, Lyn, Frances, Bev and I
could be extremely interesting and useful." For years, Frances, Bev, and she
had been "threshing through the effects of [Language writing] on us, both
socially and in the writing . . . where we can share the values and stimulates,
where we feel threatened, annoyed, shut-out, etc." However, she con-
cludes, one important question still remains: "Can one attempt to locate
one's own differences, aesthetically, politically, without committing insult
and injury? Can one try to describe structures of patriarchal style and be-
havior, without further constituting them, as you suggest I do?"[52] As Fraser

herself discovered, for a woman poet the question of position-taking is heavily loaded. It is further complicated by the degree to which a position is claimed by a writer or designated by critics or other writers in the poetic field. It was largely on this issue that many women associated with Language writing remained defensive about the question of gender. Only as the field began to change did many feel more comfortable about discussing their role in communal formations.

CHAPTER THREE

In the Middle of Writing: Feminism's Ruptured Vocabulary

An ongoing problem in focusing on a specific poetic community is highlighting the points of departure between writers. Walter Kalaidjian, for instance, aligns Hejinian's epistemic investigations of the subject to what he views as a distinctively feminist constituency within Language writing, which included Beverly Dahlen, Rachel Blau DuPlessis, Kathleen Fraser, Fanny Howe, Susan Howe, Frances Jaffer, Leslie Scalapino, and Rosmarie Waldrop.[1] Unfortunately, Kalaidjian does not critique distinctions within this feminist body, preferring instead to reduce any "regional" difference to a landscape of similitude. We need a map of Language writing as a field of rich and diverse feminisms.[2] Such an exercise would investigate a range of practices, many of which cross over, interrogate, and refigure what Linda Kinnahan has called a "poetics of the feminine." In detailing the various border strategies that inform such writing, this chapter also becomes a response to many well-articulated feminist concerns about the uniformity of political direction presumed in Language writing.

With the emergence of poststructuralism, linguistic critiques of subjectivity put into question many assumptions about gender, particularly its presumed transparency. The view that women's experience was constituted in language (rather than merely "reflected" by it) was specifically espoused by French feminist theory in the late seventies. In 1980 two of the most influential texts on French feminism were published in the United States. Providing an alternative to primary texts of American feminism such as Kate Millett's *Sexual Politics* (1970), *The Future of Difference*, and *New French Feminisms* tied the issue of sexual difference to discursive formations of the subject.[3] In relating cultural values to their discursive inscription, such theories implicitly questioned the nexus between language, knowledge, and power.

Following Jacques Lacan, French feminism suggested that the social order is regulated through the symbolic, which is itself structured around the centrality of the phallus. This system of signification marks the masculine with value and prioritizes it as a dominant discursive term; the feminine occupies the space of the Other, or that which is blank or abject. Metaphysically, the feminine is associated with the body in being beyond speech, while the philosophical self engenders itself as masculine. Constructed through such symbolic relations, the subject is always already inscribed with corporeal and epistemic hierarchies.

With the symbolic thus viewed as relentlessly masculine, many women writers felt that they were in a bind, either cast out of representation or at least denied any possible agency. As Frances Jaffer put it, "Stein says we no longer have the words people used to have so we have to make them new in some way but women haven't had them at all and how can you deconstruct a language you never constructed or it was never constructed by others like you, or with you in mind?"[4]

Writing after a long hiatus, Jaffer noted that feminism gave her the permission she needed in order to write about things that others found uninteresting or unacceptable.[5] Hélène Cixous's theory was attractive to women like her because it prized an identity of difference *as women*. In "The Laugh of the Medusa," Cixous inverts the metaphysical value system by viewing the semiotic or presymbolic as positive. The semiotic is not only the space of the feminine but is also associated with women's language and the female body, on account of its fluidity and loss of boundaries. Such a theory promotes feminist discourse as outsiders' discourse.

The idea of an alternative space of femininity was attractive to many women writers. In her early work, Joan Retallack combined Julia Kristeva's distinction between masculine and feminine writing with Carol Gilligan's feminist theory of masculine and feminine thought. Whereas male modes of thought were linear and hierarchical, female thinking tended to work in web patterns. For Retallack, the textual space of the feminine signaled contingency, play, and indeterminacy, as well as unintelligibility. This coincides with "the typical female structure, always somewhat provisional, occasional, things depending on constantly shifting contexts" where some universal principle or structure "breaks down."[6]

For Jaffer and other editors of *HOW(ever)*, French feminism confirmed the validity of an alternative tradition of women's writing. Kathleen Fraser recorded her experience of reading French feminism in "this.notes.new year":

I wanted, suddenly, to speak French because of certain French women thinking about layers, thinking *in* layers, but as yet not translated. They had moved ahead but not in a line. It occurred to me that growing up inside of, yet opposing, a tradition peculiarly French and masculine appeared to give them a certain authority because the tradition itself assumed a dialectical plane and invited the next position, while echoing "I baptize thee in the name of the father and the son."[7]

The poem marked a new narrative form for Fraser. Like much of Language writing, it focused on the unit of the sentence. Another poem, entitled "Medusa's hair was snakes. Was thought, split inward," directly recalls Cixous's central image of excessive femininity. Because such femininity is expressed beyond language, it may figure as "[f]lashes of light or semaphore waves, the sound/of rules, a regularity from which the clouds drift/ into their wet embankments."[8] Fraser also turns to the work of Julia Kristeva in outlining a poetics modeled on the maternal body. The poetics of the "gestate" is an "unfolding process" that presents "all the uneven and emotional curves" of female experience. Such a form encourages interruption and digression, "welcoming those unexpected and mysterious and necessary leaps in human consciousness."[9] In an interview, she recalls being fascinated by the idea of "female time."[10] French feminism, then, offered a range of exciting theoretical models that could challenge traditional poetic form.

In contrast, Dahlen worked through French theorists like Lacan and Kristeva, not only to negotiate the relation between gender and language but also to critique the models themselves. By alluding to or quoting directly from the texts, Dahlen used a mode of citation to read them back as self-commentary. As Perelman comments of Dahlen's epic work in progress, *A Reading*, "The more the writing tries to objectify its content, or perhaps to call a content into existence, the less real any content becomes."[11]

Dahlen herself writes of the relation between fantasy and the real in *A Reading* as such: "*Phallus the first division, woman atomized . . .* what is real in this fantasy of the real is the phallus. everybody believes it. I believe it. you can't touch it with a ten foot pole because it isn't there. that's how it comes to be real. it isn't there. and I'm not here. nobody's here and that's reality."[12]

As that which is desired, Woman (the projection of desire) becomes interchangeable with the phallus. In the process, the actual figure that is marked as "Woman" is removed from a speaking position. Dahlen therefore suggests that the possibility of the woman possessing a subjective agency is scandalous:

(All this language is floating. The men make statements. They use the forms of the verb 'to be' with confidence. What I write is provisional. It depends. It is subject to constant modification. It depends. . . .

(They are so sure this equals that. Reading their sums.)

on the other hand. all dark. blank. the blank wall waiting. in it. waiting for something, The Other.[13]

In this passage, Dahlen contrasts the undecidability of language with the definitive roles of gender cast by the symbolic. The men, under the sign of the Father, can "be" a subject with confidence, while the woman writer's occupation of the role is provisional or tactical: "It depends." Under the logic of the symbolic, a logic where "this equals that," the masculine is a stable force that reads, while a feminine identity exists as that which is "dark," "blank," or "The Other" that is read by the male gaze.

While Dahlen re-presents this inevitable logic of gender, she foregrounds the limitations it imposes on sexual difference: "what this yes means. the binary. symmetry. open-ended. the limits of yes. the limits of no . . . I think like a ouija board. lay your palm on the table. the answer must be yes or no. there are no other choices.[14]

Like Dahlen, Hejinian was receptive to certain concepts offered through French feminism while rejecting other aspects, particularly what she saw as an overly essential argument. Writing to Armantrout in 1982, she stated: "One of the themes that runs through what little stuff I've read so far is that 'feminine' language seeks to do away with hierarchy, or to attack the power base, which is the dominant or normative vocabulary and style." Viewing as highly questionable the designation of the semiotic as "female" and the symbolic as "male," Hejinian observed that descriptions of *parler femme* were similar to those describing postmodernism, including "disjunct grammar, disjunct narrative devices, paradox, rejection of closure, etc."[15]

Hejinian would also write to Susan Howe about reading an interesting group of "French women critics . . . in cahoots with or rebellion against (or both) Derrida and Lacan and Barthes." Throughout the late seventies to late eighties, Hejinian and Howe engaged in an ongoing dialogue on feminism and its relation to their writing and to their everyday life. Their correspondence reflects "working through" the revolutionary possibilities of language as raised by French feminists such as Julia Kristeva and Luce Irigaray. Considering some of their thinking "good, and some incredibly hokey," Hejinian expressed a wish that Howe lived closer so that they could read the translations together and share opinions. She adds: "I'm not interested in denigrating nor enthroning the point of view—merely in fathoming it and pulling out what is of use (if anything)."[16]

Later, Hejinian wrote to Howe about working on a paper on narrative closure for the "Women and Modernism" issue of *Poetics Journal*. She noted her discovery of *New French Feminisms*, "which deals with the open text, or unbounded text, or multifaceted text, as 'feminine.'" In this respect, her "literary interest in this issue of closure, and [her] personal and political concern that the poetry community . . . be made to embrace a wider notion of valid and relevant issues and styles" seemed to be "coinciding." [17] Michael Davidson argues that the eventual essay, "The Rejection of Closure," works from the possibility of a "woman's language" as outlined by Cixous.[18] Yet as her letters reveal, Hejinian, although certainly attracted to particular concepts such as the open text, had a relation to French feminism as ambivalent as it was enthusiastic. At one stage to be called "Closure and Confusion," this early title for Hejinian's essay is suggestive of her struggle to think through a productive relation between French feminism and poetic method.

Whereas Howe found the idea of a feminine alterity attractive, Hejinian sought to move away from the gender categories of "masculine" and "feminine" as given oppositional differences. She was joined by writers like Johanna Drucker in viewing French feminism's sexualized imagery as utopic and reductive. As Drucker states, "To hide ourselves inside of language, to claim the body against the law as if it were our own, to use the tropes of sensation, fluidity, reception—these are positions I do not find viable in the face of the realities of women's real lives."[19] Like many others, Hejinian and Drucker read Cixous's and Irigaray's metaphors in their most literal sense, overlooking the deconstructive politics that also informs the writing. In working both metaphorically *and metonymically*, theorists like Irigaray simultaneously reproduce the system of sexual difference while foregrounding an overdetermination of the system. In thinking otherwise but from within, Irigaray reveals the excessive sites of Western philosophies of the subject; in doing so, she undoes the dualistic logic of gender.

In her 1984 article "Women and Language," Johanna Drucker proposed a third term between the feminine of alterity and being co-opted into the masculine. This, she elaborates, is a movement beyond the opposition between masculine and feminine, an improvisation with language that moves sexual difference beyond two poles or categories.[20] This improvisation first requires a recognition of the symptoms of phallocentrism and its existing order of identity and then the choosing of a position in relation to it. Such an approach is tactical rather than strategic. It is also contingent, taking account of one's historic specificity.

Although Drucker's view of language and subjectivity is argued through the psychoanalytic framework of French feminism, it has more in common with the work of feminists following on from Louis Althusser or Michel Foucault. Theorists like Denise Riley and Judith Butler have variously critiqued how the subject is a site for the inscription of various social discourses, including that of sexual difference. Denise Riley, for instance, views *women* as a historically dynamic category that interpellates individuals within socially specific roles.[21] Judith Butler also suggests that the unity of the category, *women*, like the notion of experience, is not an essential attribute of that category but the effect of regulatory laws that attempt to "institute and maintain relations of coherence and continuity among sex, gender, sexual practice and desire." As such, the category must "be understood as the regulatory fiction it is—rather than the common point of our liberation."[22] This is not to suggest that there are no women, but that the unmet needs and suffering spring from the ways in which women are positioned in the social *as women*.[23] Socially, *women* has figured as a hegemonic norm; to try to move beyond the assigned roles would be to position oneself nonhegemonically.

Denise Riley suggests that being a woman is a state of fluctuation, that "there are always different densities of sexed being in operation" depending on the historical moment.[24] The classification of *men* and *women* is entangled with other culturally specific formations such as the polis and the body.[25] Riley argues that an understanding of the indeterminacy of the category *women* enables feminists to develop new and effective strategies that both refuse and pragmatically reuse it. Butler, too, states: "The deconstruction of identity is not the deconstruction of politics; rather, it establishes as political the very terms through which identity is articulated."[26]

Hejinian discussed feminism with Riley and with Margaret Whitford, a prominent critic of Luce Irigaray's work. Many women Language writers, including Hejinian and Howe, considered sexual difference not only in relation to textual practice but also in terms of the social construction of authorship. Lynne Dreyer speaks of feeling angry at needing praise or recognition, "like the good girls we all were raised to be," when she wants to stand alone, confident in the knowledge of having written something worthwhile.[27] Drucker, too, writes of the difficulty in breaking out "of the good behavior to which I thought myself addicted."[28] She found that she had internalized the prohibitions imposed by male writers as her own taboos against certain modes of writing, particularly narrative. Alternatively, Hejinian felt frustrated at what she saw as a gendering of intellectual practice by feminist writers, which celebrated women having a nonlinear style of mind. She notes that she tried to hide her intellectualism in adolescence, seeing it as unlovable and unfeminine: "Finally I freed myself from those fears (more or less) and allowed myself to develop as an intellectual woman (to the best of my abilities) and now it is the women who are telling me I am unacceptable as that—that I have been co-opted by men. I find this enraging, and disheartening."[29]

As Bruce Robbins posits, "The subject of intellectuals is about as gender-neutral as pro-football."[30] The profile of the intellectual is traditionally the image of an individual who, while relatively autonomous, is able to perform a function as representative or speaker for a collective. Robbins suggests, "If women have not been [historically] invited into the conversation about intellectuals, they have also had good cause to feel that the conversation has nothing to offer them. A discussion centered on the ideal of universality without ties, on intellectuals unattached and disembodied . . . could easily appear to occupy a realm of male fantasy."[31] He argues that the refiguring of intellectuals through a recognition of ties, bodies, and situations is "a necessary step toward the demasculinizing of the discourse."[32]

Hejinian discussed with Howe the role of the female intellectual in relation to her own development as a writer. Being the oldest child and the "smart" one gave her privileged access to the adult world. She desired that privilege immensely, feeling a sense of anxiety at "an inability to be good at things that counted" as feminine: "flirtation, clothes, hairdos, etc." Instead, she developed qualities that were not "particularly associated with girls." As she states, "What the men were talking about was more interesting to me." She began to feel territorial about such talk, partly due to a need to be both included and appreciated.[33]

Hejinian's childhood anecdotes show the desire for recognition of her "masculine" qualities, that is, her intellectualism. She wanted to enter the same field of cultural evaluation that men inhabited. Accordingly, she hid her gender in early publishing ventures. Writing under the name C. H. Hejinian, Hejinian notes that she received some fan mail afterward addressed to Mr. Hejinian. "[W]hen I responded and said I was a woman the mail ceased—so my instinct for attempting to 'pass' wasn't entirely misplaced or unnecessary at the time."[34] At the same time that this was occurring in her professional life, Hejinian began entering into the traditional private roles of wife, mother, and homemaker.

By leading a life between poetic community and family commitments, Hejinian shifted back and forth in her intellectual performance, blurring the masculine and the feminine in her various roles. As Joan Riviere argues in "Womanliness as Masquerade," "Womanliness . . . could be assumed and worn as a mask, both to hide the possession of masculinity [intellectualism] and to avert the reprisals expected if she was found to possess it."[35] This trope of femininity as mask or masquerade is one that Hejinian constantly circles around in her writing, not only in *A Mask of Motion*, but in the repeating figure of the double, as well as the genderless person of the Tuumba icon (fig. 2). Wearing a mask over its face and presenting a sartorial superego, the Tuumba figure deflects any defining gaze of identity.

Riviere argues that many intellectual women ward off the anxiety over displaying knowledge by a reversion to womanliness. Hejinian's dual anxiety over being both intellectual *and* feminine is revealed in a

TUUMBA

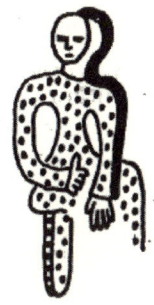

I have re-invented many things.

Other men, for example.

— Paul Valery

Fig. 2. Frontispiece of Lyn Hejinian's *A Thought Is the Bride of What Thinking*. (Willits, CA: Tuumba Press, 1976)

letter about feminism in general to Armantrout. "I don't know what to think about my feminism," Hejinian confesses, "or rather, I have various positions in it, depending on the context . . . there was the period of feeling that, in fact, men and women were the same . . . and now there is a period of feeling as if women were different from men." As to whether women have a different kind of imagination, Hejinian begins to "sincerely hope so—not because I dislike what men do, not at all, but because it is thrilling to discover further grounds for individuality on the one hand and commonality on the other."[36]

Similar to Hejinian's Tuumba icon, Fanny Howe's figure of Erato reveals a complete collapse of sexual difference. In *For Erato: The Meaning of Life*, Howe writes, "I was told, by a stranger, that Erato, is *so thin, there's no gender there*, just a plate of light rays criss-crossing the sky. And it's this very form of androgyny which attracts me" (italics added). Howe notes that in Aristophanes' definition of the term, the sexes were viewed as three in number: "there was man, woman, and the union of the two, having a name corresponding to this double nature which once had a real existence, but is now lost." The possibility of error in identity, the space of Erato, is seen as utopic. Howe's definitions of this third identity are playful and contrary:

1. untempted by sex
2. solitary
3. busy every minute
4. occupied half the time with philosophy; the other half with trivia
5. a service to others
6. self-absorbed
7. so still, no one can see you
8. so fast, everyone wants you
9. petrified
10. above suspicion[37]

Like Hejinian and Fanny Howe, many women associated with Language writing found the cultural positioning of the feminine limiting. Its continual imposition often led to a different set of aesthetic expectations for women's writing compared to writing by men. Armantrout, for instance, recounts to Hejinian that Rosmarie Waldrop "decided not to include my collaboration with Ron in my book because my writing was 'so delicate' it would be overwhelmed by something (partly) by Ron." She notes that this "made me feel like I was ready for handicapped parking."[38]

Like Armantrout, Tina Darragh felt that the rhetoric of femininity was disadvantageous, especially when mobilized within the Language writing community. She suggests that postmodern techniques are still negatively interpreted when used by a woman poet. In an interview with Joan Retallack, she states:

I think I'm still sort of angry about it . . . but . . . in terms of writing there's still very much a product orientation in this "language" community. You know, "are you just playing with this or are you serious about what you're doing?"—as though playfulness and seriousness don't go hand and hand.[39]

Retallack responds that the division is itself gendered, in that "when a woman is playful it is more suspicious than when a man is being playful. Her seriousness in the 'professional' world is always in question."[40]

Diane Ward also points to this phenomenon, arguing that it "may be more common . . . [for] women to fret over not asserting the ego enough, of losing a certain 'credibility of content' by not relaying a thought in a linear (quick and clear) way." However, she feels a frustration "in the (often) automatic connection between women and a preoccupation with emotions (especially in poetry)." She maintains that it is "limiting and destructive as is any narrow categorization." While Ward finds herself unable to abandon this aspect (emotion, empathy, compassion), she has come to see it as a result of the form she chooses and as a way to draw parallels between otherwise unconnected thoughts or events or dreams. By contrasting two disparate objects or events, she can create a third feeling (state) or perception: "It's with this 'creating' that I hope to transcend that feminine tag of pointless and self-referential emotionalism."[41]

Rae Armantrout suggests that, as a response to these social labels and expectations, women writers have developed sophisticated strategies to textually challenge the feminine and to search for freedom. Her own writing employs subtle layers of irony that, in Donna Haraway's definition, "is about contradictions that do not resolve into larger wholes, even dialectically."[42] An example may be seen in the first part of "Necromance":

> Poppy under a young
> pepper tree, she thinks.
> The Siren always sings
> like this. Morbid
> glamor of the singular.
> Emphasizing correct names
> as if making amends.
>
> Ideal
> republic of the separate
> dust motes
> afloat in abeyance.
> Here the sullen
> come to see their grudge
> as pose, modeling.
>
> The flame trees tip themselves
> with flame.
> But in that land
> men prized
> virginity. She washed
> dishes in a black liquid
> with islands of froth—
> and sang.[43]

The poem investigates the relationship between the individual and collective voice. In the first half, the association of female sexuality with the flower is joined to the more specific symbolism of the poppy as a sign of remembrance for those soldiers who have fallen in battle. "The Siren always sings / like this" not only recalls its warning sound during wartime but the articulation of desire itself. Both the Siren and the poppy represent the negative pull of social prescriptions, signalling death through man's loss of control.[44] Recalling Plato's republic, which banished the poets and elided the role of women, the second stanza forms a critique of the "morbid glamor of the singular," including the "correct names" of gender. An alternative, Armantrout proposes, is for the person to be viewed as "dust motes." As with Hejinian's *The Cell*, these elements of matter that form life "float in abeyance" to the regulatory laws of femininity.[45]

According to Plato, the feminine is dangerous because it is a "pose," a representation. Like poetry, the feminine is a medium of artifice and seduction. While the "young" pepper tree matures, it ignites into flame, recalling the vivid colors of the poppy in bloom. Here, the "flame trees tip themselves with flame," suggesting an autoerotic capacity in excess of the cultural logic. The republic, however, still recuperates the cultural value of femininity (as virgin and pure) through the sign of Woman.

In her own rite of passage, the female character learns the art of necromancy. Necromancy is both the art of magic and communication with the dead. Although "she" performs the feminine role of domesticity, some agency is claimed. Thus, dishes are washed in black liquid, and "she" finds her own voice and sings. Armantrout therefore maps out an ambivalent female position, as "she" is seen to exist between the dead of the presymbolic (with song being viewed as communication beyond the symbolic) and the symbolic (as "she" implicitly still sings from within the kitchen). While "she" can only repeat the cultural feminine, there is the possibility of performative subversion via mimesis. Yet this possibility remains, as Armantrout ends the poem, "The mermaid's privacy."[46] Such privacy is an area of mystery, "[h]ard to say where / [it] occurs" but always "just a bit further" from definition.[47]

As Armantrout writes in another poem, "Ventriloquy / is the mother tongue." The song in that poem repeats the refrain, "I'm not a baby. / Wa, wa, wa." The assertion of womanhood, "I'm not a baby," is contradicted by the "Wa, wa, wa" that follows it.[48] The baby doll of femininity is performatively reinforced but, as Armantrout later points out, possibly "feigned." Donna Haraway declares that "[i]rony is about humor and serious play," destabilizing relations of power through a tactical use of rhetoric.[49] Kathy Ferguson also argues that "[i]rony is a particularly appropriate strategy for feminism in that it calls upon two virtues historically associated with women . . . the recognition of limits and the struggle to continue."[50]

In an interview with Manuel Brito, Armantrout outlines her practice in relation to a female writing or separate language. While she is attracted to the idea of a writing that eschews logic or that offers a "limitless sensuosity," Armantrout distrusts definitions such as "masculine" or "feminine." Although, she admits, "I feel most female when I am resisting or subverting systems." As systematic thinking is not "easily jettisoned," it tends to have a comedic function in her work. Her writing becomes "compelled by starts and stops, silences, and (the trappings of) logic."[51]

Hejinian points out that both Armantrout and Carla Harryman use the oxymoron as a textual strategy of subversion. Pairing words with opposite connotations can produce "an immensely powerful figure." "I've been trying to learn to use it too," Hejinian writes to Armantrout; "one can get both sides of the question so to speak, to play against each other in the absolute minimum of words. Endless reflection is possible afterwards."[52] An example from Harryman's work may be found in *The Middle:*

As she goes about her day to day, she doesn't care about the end. She lives with what's around her, and not with some big fate to be held up, compared to her modus operandi. Cinderella loved luxury, as would any dreamy floor scrubber. Exotics love evil, without families, on the fringe, with minds, and adventurers. Nature is luxury. Meaning is evil.[53]

Similar to Armantrout's dishwasher, the "day to day" figure of a "dreamy floor scrubber" is figured as both exotic and of the everyday. Harryman also sets up a contrast between nature and luxury and between meaning and evil. Both pairs jolt the reader, who must reevaluate what is thought of as "natural" and what is thought of as "meaning." Domestic drudgery alongside escapist dreams of luxury are suggested to be consequences of the same system.

Harryman herself argues that narratives such as femininity continue but that a narrative holds "within its boundaries both its advantages and defects." In preferring to "distribute narrative rather than deny it," its blindspots might further be considered.[54] Joan Retallack suggests that "the idea of play is important as a middle term between believing and doubting, ideology and dead-end skepticism."[55]

Yet, while she sees irony as essential in starting a movement away from an undesirable but deeply entrenched state of affairs, a second movement is required to then depart from irony. As Retallack argues, "The ironic mode is so heavily parasitic on the object of its critique that it is, if anything, a sign of the robust life of its host." While irony "places us crucially on the threshold of movement beyond the position it critiques," writing should always be imagining alternatives.[56]

To some degree, Harryman's and Retallack's sense of play echoes the theoretical framework of Gillian Rose's "broken middle." Rose states: "Whereas postmodernity remains dualistic and pits its others against domination, the broken middle is triune. It will investigate the breaks between universal, particular, and singular, in individuals and in institutions."[57] To hold forth a feminism of the middle does not offer any individual or collective security. It is not actually a position (because it does "not posit anything, and refuses any beginning or end"), but it might be considered a point of departure.[58] As a performative concept, it is specific to surrounding circumstances. The poetry of women Language writers often undertakes this lateral shift, working within and around constricting appellations of subjectivity. Accordingly, it can never be fixed by some overarching explanation but contests as it describes linguistic and social boundaries.

CHAPTER FOUR

Supporting a Scene: Tuumba Press

Like so many other Language writers, Lyn Hejinian actively promoted the practice of community through collaborations, reading groups, and more informal discussions. Running for eight years (1976–1984), Tuumba Press was a way in which she could more explicitly support the emergent Language writing community. Publishing is best seen as a form of resonance, which, according to Karen Burke LeFevre, occurs "when an individual act—a 'vibration'—is intensified and prolonged by sympathetic vibrations,"[1] The term *tuumba* is itself associated with the making of vibrations, as in Africa it signifies the "mother" drum of a drum family. Hejinian says she came up with the word from a nonsense phrase chanted by her husband, the musician Larry Ochs, while beating out polyrhythms.[2] In this respect, "tuumba" is associated with music but not with harmony.

Hejinian told Andrew Schelling that she saw publishing as an extension not only of her responsibility as a poet but also of her own writing and thinking about writing: "I had the sense that my poetics included other writing than my own, by definition." Her decision to begin publishing a series was determined partly by living in "an extremely isolated situation in northern California; it was rather as if I had decided to be a newspaper reporter in order to hear the news."[3] Cultural or geographic isolation seems a motivation for many to start a press or magazine, publishing providing a way of creating a community of one's own. Alice Notley and Tom Beckett started *Chicago* and *The Difficulties*, respectively, for just these reasons.[4]

Tuumba Press built on the dynamic collective activity already occurring in the San Francisco poetic community, that had been fostered in journals like *This*, *Hills*, *Tottel's*, and *Miam*. According to Jerome McGann, "[the] process of printing and distribution is essential to the record that fiction makes of itself" because "[i]t locates the imagination socially and historically."[5] While a journal has a certain flexibility in the range of writing it can showcase, a book press enables longer works to find a forum, as well as to be read in alternative contexts. Robert Grenier and Barrett Watten, the editors of *This*, were well aware of this distinction and had already begun to publish books, most notably Clark Coolidge's *The Maintains*.[6] Tuumba therefore emerged out of a healthy scene. During the seventies and eighties, there were a number of small presses focusing on innovative poetry, including This, Burning Deck, Roof, The Figures, Angel Hair, Sun & Moon, Some of Us, Gaz, and Telephone. Allen Fisher argues that the overall activity of a small press may be political, for it works against established norms of consumer practice in creating "communities" of artists interested in having some autonomy of production.[7] Mary Biggs also believes that independent and noncommercial presses are the primary source of exposure for poets and provide a vital role in fostering a poetic community.

Women were particularly prominent in editing and publishing innovative small-press books and journals. Apart from Lyn Hejinian, other women editors included Barbara Baracks (*Big Deal*), Bernadette Mayer (*o to 9*, *Unnatural Acts*, United Artists), Rosmarie Waldrop (Burning Deck), Carla Harryman (*Qu*), Madeleine Burnside (*Gnome Baker*), Laura Chester (The Figures), Phyllis Rosenzweig and Diane Ward (*Primary Writing*), Anne Waldman (Angel Hair), Maureen Owen (*Telephone* magazine and press), and Kathleen Fraser, Beverly Dahlen, Frances Jaffer, Susan Gevirtz, Carolyn Burke, and Rachel Blau DuPlessis (*HOW(ever)*).[8] Other roles also were occupied by women: Susan Bee designed and produced every issue of L=A=N=-G=U=A=G=E, as well as designing most of the Roof books in the eighties; Diane Ward also designed Roof books and did editorial work for Segue; Lee Sherry designed the artwork for *Roof* magazine; and Jean Day worked at Small Press Distribution. Susan Albertine points out that women have always been active in publishing. Yet in the rush to position women writers within refigured canons, literary historians have often elided women's *other* contributions to textual production, ensuring that "women's writing—especially published, literary writing—stands at the top of a hierarchy."[9]

One reason that small-press publications proliferated was that funding from sources like the NEA (National Endowment for the Arts) was more readily available than it is today. Furthermore, there had been a rapid change in print technology with what some have called the mimeo revolution. Not only could writing be reproduced fairly easily, but the "scrap and replace" mentality meant that printing presses could be bought fairly inexpensively. Many writers could now feasibly become involved in the publishing side of literary production.

Given the rocky conditions of production, small presses often operated on an irregular basis. This was certainly so for magazines like *Big Deal*, as its schedule was dependent not only on solicited material arriving when promised but also on the hectic lifestyle of its editor, Barbara Baracks. The frequent and punctual appearance of Tuumba books was fairly unusual. Yet the press had a place in everyday domestic life, with Hejinian's two teenage children helping occasionally to get an issue out on time.[10] As Nigel Wheale points out, small presses tend to be run by one or two individuals, usually in their spare time and at their own expense.[11] The life of a small press is normally quite short because the activity occurs at the margins of viability and at the expense of the editor's other occupations, particularly his or her own writing. Most little magazines last only from two to five years, or until the editor or editors are exhausted by the process. Instead of maximizing their readership by promoting more accessible or assimilable material, small presses by definition promote the marginal and the partisan. As such, in capital terms, they are more likely to run on what Charles Bernstein has called a "negative" economy of loss rather than accumulation.[12] On the other hand, Jennifer Moxley speaks of an alternative symbolic economy underlying the small-press world, in which the returns are often in the form of books and magazines rather than cash. In such exchanges, continuing support for one another's work is crucial.[13]

Certainly, Tuumba Press often struggled to stay afloat. "I do really want you to see [*Poetics Journal*]," Hejinian wrote to Susan Howe, "but have been stingy with free copies as Tuumba already loses money, as does *This* Press (Barry's) and we absolutely have to make PJ pay for itself."[14] The economy of loss in small-press culture has generally been reinforced by a failure to establish regional and national networks. Personal correspondence enabled many Language writers to overcome this problem. One attempt to establish a more formal network was the Women's Distribution Group in New York, which included editors from small-press journals such as Barbara Baracks (*Big Deal*), Maureen Owen (*Telephone*), Fran Winart (*Violet Press*), and Roberta Gould (*Poetry Review*).[15] The idea was to run it as a collective and put in place a larger infrastructure of distribution than a small press could traditionally manage to do. This networking enabled the group to compete with larger presses and go beyond regional or specialist readerships. Members could exchange books and reach more bookstores through joint efforts. Mary Biggs further notes that, during the seventies, money from the NEA began to pour into the CCLM (Coordinating Council of Literary Magazines) for distribution to literary periodicals. The motivation for funding and continuing magazines was significantly altered by this change in institutional support.[16] Collectives such as the Women's Distribution Group were encouraged. The economic climate in the seventies was, in many ways, more conducive to small-press production than it is at present.

Hejinian started from scratch in acquiring professional skills as a publisher. According to an early interview she gave in the *Poetry Project*

Newsletter, she slowly gained confidence from using the commercial printer near her home in northern California. "It was unheard of for a woman to do any printing," she states; "the printer would only hire me as a janitor." She recalls that when she first tried to adjust something on a press, "one of the press crew slapped my hand and said, 'Don't *you* touch that, girlie.'"[17] However, eventually, she was allowed to come in at nights and was taught how to use a letterpress by the shop's manager.

Making use of a more informal network of women editors such as Barbara Baracks and Rosmarie Waldrop, she began a modest venture to publish chapbooks and postcards. Although Susan Coultrap-McQuin's *Doing Literary Business* focuses on writing in the nineteenth century, her description of how women learn to intertwine private with professional matters still holds true for the late twentieth century.[18] Certainly, in Hejinian's case, the running of Tuumba press was often linked inextricably to her emerging or ongoing relationships with other writers. It was largely through Tuumba that Hejinian came into contact with a number of writers, including Susan Howe and Kathleen Fraser.

The first title in the Tuumba series was Hejinian's own *A Thought Is the Bride of What Thinking* (1976). This was followed by Susan Howe's *The Western Borders* and later still by Kathleen Fraser's *Magritte Series* (1977), which was featured as the sixth title in the series. Fraser's first publishing experience had been disappointing. Publishing her book as a foreseeable loss, Harper & Row failed to advertise it and pulped it within a year. In contrast, the Tuumba publications helped Howe and Fraser gain an appreciative audience, and this partly explains why Howe and Fraser have been associated with Language writing or brought within its rubric. Both subsequently sought to distance themselves from such categorization.

Tuumba Press published bimonthly. As Jed Rasula notes, its frequency of publication meant that some titles were works in progress, and others were more finished and sophisticated. He argues that the absence throughout this century of a committed chapbook series like that of Tuumba Press has obscured the fact that chapbooks are the prime space for the fifteen- to twenty-page poem, which is usually too long for most magazines to consider, even though it is the most popular length in American poetry.[19] Tuumba chapbooks varied in size, but with their binding and high-quality paper they were usually larger or more substantial than octavos or pamphlets. Occasionally, Tuumba would move beyond the limits of the book form, as when publishing the 265 poems of Robert Grenier's *Cambridge M'ass* (1979) in the form of a large poster.

Tuumba certainly had its teething problems. The second issue, Howe's *The Western Borders*, was printed with a page missing. Apologizing to Howe,

Hejinian wrote that she felt "badly about the missing page" that Howe must have "worked over . . . for so long, and with so much attention." But the subscribers' copies had already been mailed out. As a last option, she suggested, "Maybe I should make another massive hustle for distribution, sell out this printing, and redo it." "The only consolation," she added, "is that people who have seen THE WESTERN BORDERS have all been admiring—of your writing and of the chapbook."[20] Hejinian vowed to "do my best to try to make IRELAND complete." Meanwhile, she was "going tomorrow to try to find a course in printing—if I had my own press it would be an easier thing, even to tear apart the chapbooks and redo that part."[21]

Subscriptions made Hejinian nervous. "I never know when to write and remind people," she told Howe, "lest it appear to be pressuring them, and so, etc. bumble."[22] Later she wrote about "testing the support system for Tuumba now when I have to find new subscribers (or renew old ones) and have no grants to support the press without subscribers—so find myself indeed thinking hard over who gets free copies, what that means." She had had "a great talk" about such matters with Rae Armantrout—who "sensed a kind of snob system, who gets publication without having to pay for them vs. the payers"—and also with Ron Silliman, who (like Howe) "always pays, as support—putting his money where his mouth is."[23]

Hejinian also writes about how the rigor of being an editor partly involves going through work that does not meet one's personal standards and therefore having to battle feelings of negativity:

[U]nsolicited manuscripts . . . sometimes make . . . me think all writing is terrible; surely there are too many writers out there with their words. The clichés echo in my brain, and the lumpy rhythms, and I can't work at all. I don't get many manuscripts, however. I'm sure some good ones will come along now and then—some already have.[24]

In the subscription flyer sent out after completing the first series, Hejinian outlined an inclusive rather than exclusive editorial policy for Tuumba Press. She described a broad and generically open forum for poetry, poetics, and art, similar to Andrews's and Bernstein's agenda for *L=A=N=-G=U=A=G=E:* "Each chapbook is devoted to the work of one writer or the written work of one artist; this includes fiction, poetry, essays, interviews, statements, and manifesto[e]s. Occasional issues include broadsides, postcards, and other written graphics by assorted writers and artists."[25]

Various issues could be termed position statements, including *A Thought Is a Bride of What Thinking*, which Hejinian saw as "close to a manifesto in tone." But the only essay as such was Alice Notley's *Dr. Williams' Heiresses*, which was given originally as a talk at 80 Langton Street, San Francisco.[26]

There were no interviews, nor any performance art or intermedia after the first series.

Although Tuumba focused increasingly on poetry, its production would reflect its original leaning toward the aesthetic possibilities of the material book or page. Tuumba books have always been noted for their impressive presentation, which involve a combination of carefully chosen fonts, sizing, covers, illustrations, and ink colors. Tuumba postcards were also meticulously designed. The postcard series was fairly popular at the time as a form of self-promotion. Other forms were book markers and calling cards. Featuring the work of a number of Tuumba writers, Hejinian negotiated each postcard design with its author. She found the material for her postcards at Willits Printing, salvaging scraps when she was working there. The postcards are now extremely hard to trace, primarily because of their categorization as ephemera. Literally sideslips of the printing trade, they were also viewed as such by institutions: not even major research libraries, like the Rare Books/Poetry Collection at Buffalo, were interested in acquiring such items when they first appeared.[27] The few that survive were kept not for their own sake but for the correspondence scribbled on their unprinted side. Perhaps more than any other type of publication, then, the postcard tested traditional categories of literary value.

Rae Armantrout's Tuumba postcard (fig. 3) features the poem "Special Theory of Relativity," which is particularly apt in reminding the receiver of the transience of such ephemera. The textual form of the postcard is homologous with the face of the woman featured on it, in that both are classified as mere cultural ornamentation. However, in an alternative reading, the woman who gazes out of the picture at us challenges not only the gendering of subject-object relations in the image itself but also the systematic erasure of women from history. The poem's title also suggests a perspective beyond the logic of history. It is perhaps not surprising that Susan Howe chose the same poem when seeking something representative of Armantrout's work. Its few lines embody much of Armantrout's feminist poetics in exploring "mysteries without boundaries."[28]

While most cards simply printed a few lines or a short poem by the author, others were more sophisticated in design. Hejinian wrote to Susan Howe that she was searching for old engravings of a thorn, thistle, or animal for Howe's card. Howe referred to all three in a passage in the *Secret History of the Dividing Line* (1978):

Thorn, thistle, apron leaf

through each scene
man covers his body

calling "I have heard"

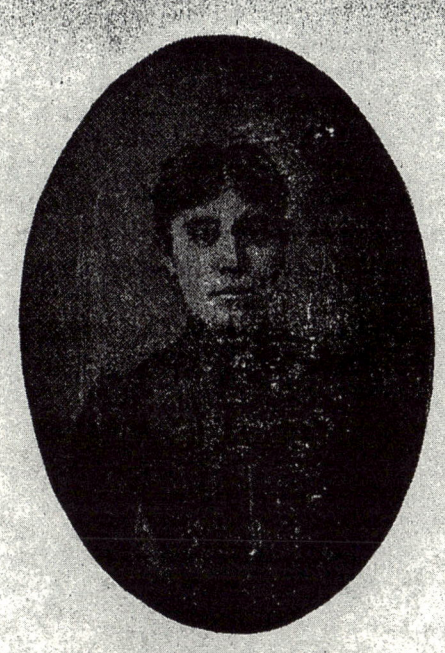

**SPECIAL THEORY
OF RELATIVITY**

You know those ladies
in old photographs? Well,
say one stares into your room
as if into the void
beyond her death in 1913

Fig. 3. Rae Armantrout's Tuumba Press postcard. (Mandeville Special Collections Library, University of California, San Diego)

> to a cadaverous throng
> of revelers
>
> who pose and gesture
> acting out roles.
>
> It is a dream
> Enchantment
>
> the animals speak
>
> impaled again
> in a netting of fences.[29]

This passage foregrounds both her ambivalence toward the gendering of cultural identity and the role playing that she later emphasized in *The Liberties*. Howe thought "the set of postcards . . . lovely,"[30] and Kathleen Fraser also thanked Hejinian for her Tuumba postcard: "I really don't think you should have to spend your time painting leaves for me . . . but I do love them!!! They add so much to the poem . . . and such a nice thing to send out for spring."[31]

Hejinian's attention to the design of postcards illustrates the care she took in general with the design of Tuumba books, especially in attempting to achieve a symmetry or commentary between the artwork and the written text. For instance, on the cover of Fanny Howe's *For Erato: The Meaning of Life*, Hejinian used a black ink drawing (by her sister-in-law, Diane Andrews Hall) of a rose in full blossom (fig. 4). The text itself circles around the metaphor of roses and the growing of a rose garden as "the meaning of life." The following passage has especial affinities with the cover drawing:

A thick-set rose dangled at a ninety-degree angle off a shrub overlooking a thin branch of water. It was one of those so red, it's nearly black, and fiercely scented. Like a certain brand of Czech wine, popular that summer, the rose was too thick for its own good, and before the petals had a chance to express their individuality, the whole clump fell on the checkered cloth. Every rose that falls is not free from the attention it desires, like ears, to escape.[32]

Another example is the cover design for Michael Palmer's *Alogon*. Hejinian's image of an archaic horse was drawn from a prehistoric French painting. Palmer notes that the term *alogon* is from the Greek and has "all kinds of resonant meanings." Apart from signifying the irrational, it also refers to something that stands apart from the Logos, from logical speech, and is therefore outside the Word. But it also "means horse, because horses were 'crazy' as was pointed out to me by the poet and Greek

FOR ERATO:

The Meaning of Life

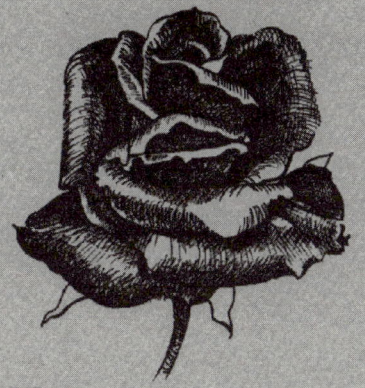

Fanny Howe

Fig. 4. Front cover of *For Erato: The Meaning of Life*, by Fanny Howe. (Berkeley, CA: Tuumba, 1994)

scholar Duncan McNaughton when I was working on the poem."[33] Hejin-
ian worked so closely with Palmer that she could personalize the cover de-
sign almost as the signature for his own sense of the term.[34]

In a letter to Howe in 1977, Hejinian wrote that although "the post-
cards make a nice little assortment," she would "do postcards very seldom
from now on" because she found books "much more interesting as a pro-
ject—or as an object."[35] Her book designs—like Waldrop's or even Jo-
hanna Drucker's more limited editions—recall the print renaissance of
early modernism. "The page becomes an object of attention," Claire
Hoertz Badaracco suggests, "a place to demonstrate language rather than
merely print letters,"[36] although it would be more accurate to say that the
book itself reinforces the materiality of language. Indeed, Drucker felt that
she "'[held] language in my hands'—lines of letterpress type shaped in a
composing stick whose weight and presence were as much physical as lin-
guistic."[37] "Printing a book is always satisfying at the tactile and material
level," she states. "You flip through the pages. You feel the heft and bulk or
slipperiness and opacity."[38] Tuumba became a means, then, through which
Hejinian could develop her interest in the graphic and physical side of tex-
tual production. It would even be picked up as a model for Torque Press, a
British small press, whose editors were impressed with its front covers.[39]

In the early Tuumbas, Hejinian published writers who were neither
identifiable with any group nor primarily poets but who worked in prose
and performance. Jed Rasula finds the first dozen or so chapbooks from
Tuumba "disparate" and "unfocused."[40] But they are significant for the sort
of community that Hejinian was building for herself in the isolation of
Willits. With writers like Howe and Fraser, Hejinian was exploring an
overlap in poetics. Another early contributor, T. R. Uthco, was associated
with Hejinian's brother, Doug Hall.

Another early contributor, Barbara Baracks, gave invaluable advice
about how to set up and market a small press. Editorial judgment and a
quality printing job, she believed, were the key elements of a successful se-
ries. In the formative stages of Tuumba, she suggested that Hejinian find a
professional to supervise the final stages of production and to focus her at-
tention primarily on editorial matters.[41] Baracks herself had financed *Big
Deal* by working the entire process single-handedly and warned that sub-
scriptions, library orders, and single-copy orders take time to build up.
Furthermore, there was publicity to consider.[42] She would later remind
Hejinian to send promotional copies to reviewers, obtain bookstore lists,
and personally encourage bookstores to stock Tuumba books. Once Hejin-
ian had begun printing, Baracks advised her to strengthen Tuumba's finan-
cial base with a giant benefit reading. She also offered to send her the *Big
Deal* subscriber list, as well as information on how to approach libraries.

Finally, she would suggest that Hejinian apply to the NEA for funding as a book series.[43]

After completing the first series of Tuumba, Hejinian considered purchasing her own printing press. Baracks pointed out that while letterpress requires buying type and lengthy periods spent typesetting, an electric press might be more dangerous if one was tired or distracted by children.[44] Like many poets running small presses, Hejinian preferred a more hands-on approach. Following others, like Maureen Owen, she chose letterpress over more recent methods of printing. Hejinian wrote to Susan Howe about her "wonderful" day spent in the Bay Area looking at used printing presses:

I went first to a dingy warehouse full of printing press parts, and discovered cases and cases of old type, including floral decorations and assorted similar old fashioned printing devices. . . .

After the first printing warehouse, I went to another company that sells new equipment—waxed linoleum floors, shiny presses, slick catalogues. I bought some colored ink and some type and was invited out to lunch by one of the men who work there—I accepted and we ate sandwiches while he gave me lots of information about paper, ink, other printing companies. . . .

After lunch, I went to a third place—the high point of the day. It is a place that specializes in letterpress, has endless sorts of types and fancy borders, etc. I met an old man there who showed me how to do hand sewn binding. He showed me some books he had printed—one an inch high filled with tiny colored engravings. Then he introduced me to a woman who collects handprinted poetry books—beautiful, beautiful things by people known and unknown. It was a museum of printing. . . .

I still worry, though, that I spend too much time at all this.[45]

Clearly, Hejinian was much taken by a craft-based method of book production. Following writers like Emily Dickinson, William Blake, William Morris, and Rosmarie Waldrop, Hejinian turned toward a romantic tradition of printing that focused on the personalized handmade form.[46] She finally found a press, "an 8 by 12 Chandler and Price—quite an old press—it is styled rather like the old treadle Singer sewing machines—cast iron and hard wood."[47] She set up the press in the utility room, where space had been designed for the washing machine. Tuumba no. 12 was the first chapbook Hejinian published completely by herself.

As editor of Tuumba, Hejinian also advised and promoted a number of writers as they went on to other projects. Holly A. Laird argues that such involvement is both a primary "responsibility" and potential "risk" for feminist editors: "[W]e surely are as responsible to the authors we publish . . . as to the readers we seek, yet in the delicate balance of our multiple responsibilities, mentorship risks upsetting a . . . schedule or deflecting energy away from maintaining readership."[48] However, as many editors realize (Hejinian among them), the relationship between editor and writer is not so much one of mentorship as of affirmation and counsel.

An example of the value of Hejinian's editorial involvement may be seen in her relationship with Fanny Howe. Like many women writers, Howe was constantly anxious about the reception of her writing. Viewing Hejinian as a potentially sympathetic editor, she asked whether a small selection of her work could appear in the Tuumba series. "I sort of dislike even asking," she writes. "But a failure, on my part, to send things out, to imagine even, anyone there, has begun to worry me, as if I were a hen with chickens under my wings, first for protection, then for suffocation. I have, in any case, quite a lot of material littering my room, and I'd like to try some of it out on you."[49] Although Hejinian explained that her energy for Tuumba was waning, she agreed to fit Howe's writing into her schedule. Hejinian viewed each Tuumba publication as a collective project between herself and the writer. When *For Erato: The Meaning of Life* was eventually published, she wrote to Howe: "I hope you like the book—my part of it, that is. Your part is wonderful. Though I suppose it is redundant for me to say so, since the gesture of publishing it is supposed to show all-out approval—at least, I mean it to."[50]

Rasula maps a turning point in the history of Tuumba with the publication of Hejinian's own *Gesualdo*. At that moment, he notes, she "took hold of a burgeoning local scene and rode it out to the end of the series four years later." Silliman's appearance in the Tuumba series with *Sitting Up, Standing, Taking Steps* indicated even more clearly the series' newfound focus: "[a] swift succession of titles by Andrews, Bernstein, Perelman and Watten indicated to anyone in the know that Tuumba was throwing in its lot with a particular nexus of publications and their contributors."[51] The effect, Rasula observes, was to make Tuumba appear as a kind of "'house organ' for 'language poets' in general." The disadvantage of this group identification was that Tuumba risked being oversimplified as a publishing project.[52]

Certainly, the association of Tuumba with Language writing elides Hejinian's expertise as an editor. Added to this is the difficulty literary critics continue to have with the material basis of poetic production. Given the centrality of Tuumba Press in consolidating the appreciation of Language writing, it is surprising how little has been written on it apart from Rasula's survey. Rasula himself argues that Hejinian's skill as an editor may be seen in her selection of publications, since many Tuumba titles are "their author's best and/or most approachable works."[53] Hejinian was demonstrably careful with her selections and sometimes a hard principal in the editorial process, as when "making Bob Perelman work on his book for

Tuumba."[54] The book in question was Perelman's *To the Reader*, which marked a distinctive change in Perelman's writing, according to Charles Bernstein: "There . . . was a very dramatic move . . . this playing with call and response, which really worked. I mean, you open that book up and it's talking to you, even talking back, and the work has been that way since then."[55] Hejinian would turn down Alan Davies's manuscript, feeling perhaps that the work was not yet ready for publication or that the chapbook form was not an appropriate medium. It was not that she disliked his work, for she cited it appreciatively in her talks.

According to Rasula, the press adhered "too strict[ly] . . . to its documentary aspects, the sense of chronicle, so that the charges of being merely a house organ for language poetry have some truth."[56] His long list of "absences" include writers such as Don Byrd, Charles Stein, Ted Pearson, Jackson Mac Low, Rosmarie Waldrop, Diane Ward, John Taggart, Gerald Burns, Gustaf Sobin, Robert Duncan, Duncan McNaughton, Ronald Johnson, Leslie Scalapino, Tom Raworth, Barbara Einzig, Michael Davidson, and Christopher Dewdney. What he overlooks, however, is Hejinian's view of the Tuumba series as an extension of her own poetics, which differed considerably from the poetics of several writers Rasula mentions, such as Taggart and Duncan. There may well have been other difficulties, both geographical and temporal, in publishing some of the others, like the Canadian poet Christopher Dewdney.

For Erato was among the last of the fifty chapbooks in the Tuumba series. Hejinian had long contemplated finishing at this number. "I do think I might continue to publish," she wrote to Erica Hunt in February 1983, "but if so I'll switch to larger, offset, perfect-bound books—i.e. work my way free of the actual production process. It has become too time-consuming—which is to say, I want to spend my time doing some other things now."[57] She intended "to stop for a year or two and then turn Tuumba into an occasional offset enterprise."[58] Habitual attention to clarity and precision in the Tuumba Press books had turned her into "an almost compulsive self-editor."[59]

During the eighties, the dynamics of running a small press were rapidly changing. The economic climate made life increasingly difficult for those wishing to publish poetry. In 1989 the editor of *Poetry Flash*, Joyce Jenkins, called for evidence of funding discrimination against experimental writing. Douglas Messerli responded by noting that although Sun & Moon always included books of poetry in their grant proposals, were they to apply *only* to publish poetry, they would quickly find themselves in the same straits as many excellent presses and magazines, including The Figures, Burning Deck, Roof, Gaz, and *Poetics Journal*. Messerli pointed out that even established presses such as these have "found it increasingly difficult in the past few years to receive NEA funding." Furthermore, as the size of the grant is based on overall budgets, they "have received such extraordinarily small amounts that one cannot really describe it as 'funding' in any true sense."[60]

Despite this, the end of the twentieth century has witnessed a sudden resurgence in small-press production. The Buffalo small press, Leave Books, published several impressive series of chapbooks comparable in size to those of Tuumba, and its low-budget form enabled it to present a wide range of lesser known writers alongside more established ones. Journals and series like *Chain* (Jena Osman and Juliana Spahr), *Shark* (Emilie Clark and Lytle Shaw), *The Impercipient Lecture Series* (Steve Evans and Jennifer Moxley), *Tinfish* (Susan Schultz), and *Tripwire* (Yedda Morrison and David Buuck) continue to publish innovative writing and poetics. While many editors find it an ongoing struggle to fund such small-press production, there is a healthy determination to find alternative ways to keep such enterprises going.

One factor explaining the growth in small-press production is the relative ease and inexpensiveness of computer technology. Charles Bernstein suggests that a side effect of the computer revolution is that visual aesthetics are becoming less important.[61] Given that design is partly what made presses like Tuumba and Burning Deck distinctive landmarks in the poetic community, this shift appears particularly unfortunate. Yet Bernstein is perhaps overly pessimistic, as presses such as Tender Buttons have since emerged to complement the work of Hejinian and Waldrop. Begun in 1989, Tender Buttons is (apart from Kelsey St. Press) the only specialist publisher of experimental poetry by women in the United States. It takes its name from Gertrude Stein's famous text, from which so many Language writers derive their poetic tradition. Its editor, Lee Ann Brown, brings to it the personal touches that Hejinian gave to Tuumba Press, as is clear from her contribution to *Chain*'s "Gender and Editing" issue, in which she describes how she put together the front cover of her first publication, Bernadette Mayer's *Sonnets*: "For the cover I made a stat of a drawing by [Mayer's] daughter, Marie and asked Thomson Shore to print it in blue with a black background. We matched the blue to Bernadette's favorite in her Ukrainian scarf—that blue in late evening when the sky is about to turn to black.[62] This combination of attention to detail with a community ethic parallels Hejinian's work with Tuumba.[63] Hejinian, too, has returned to publishing, with Atelos Press (which she runs with Travis Ortiz); others, like Maureen Owen are restarting their original presses. Such a resurgence of activity bodes well for the small-press culture, promising women writers even greater control over poetic production in the decades to come.

CHAPTER FIVE

Making Waves: Radio and Susan Howe's *Poetry* Program

R adio offers an additional vehicle to the small press in supporting innovative poetry and giving it exposure. As Harriet Monroe proclaimed as far back as 1930, "[P]oetry is a vocal art; the radio will bring back its audience."[1] Yet critical histories continue to focus on the print culture of poetry, partly to preserve a tradition of poetic genius and partly because of sound's elusive and unstable nature. Exceptions to this trend are Adalaide Morris's *Sound States: Acoustical Technologies and Modern and Postmodern Writing* (1997) and Charles Bernstein's *Close Listening: Poetry and the Performed Word* (1998), both of which explore the shared nature of listening as well as the role of sound in innovative poetic practice.[2] Morris's collection in particular traces the effect of wireless in the work of avant-garde artists and writers such as futurists, Dadaists, and more recent writers using found or invented language.

New technologies in the early twentieth century offered quite radical power. Some, like Rudolph Arnheim, saw the wireless as engendering alternative forms of community, defined by use and interest rather than proximity or economic relation.[3] It was a democratizing device. Others were less optimistic, pointing to radio's manipulation of not only voice but also the sensibility of its audience. Joseph Harrington argues convincingly that the mass orientation of poetry broadcasts was viewed by many as a significant threat to the separation of high art from "low" culture.[4] They also disrupted the gendered aesthetics on which this hierarchy was based. For while the wireless catered to a largely female market and held a classless democratic appeal, poetry was still regarded as the vehicle of an elitist and predominantly masculine Modernism. Radio's very popularity saw it condemned for reducing art to an industry and, more particularly, for transforming poetry into an everyday feminized commodity.[5] Deeply entwined in the perceived commercializing effect of radio was the danger it posed to the romanticized role of the poet as a solitary and inevitably male genius.

The difficulty and abstraction associated with modernist writing reinforced the reading act as an isolated rather than a social formation. While key modernist figures like Virginia Woolf, Rebecca West, and Vita Sackville-West talked "live on the air," literary historians have ignored their involvement with this medium in order to perpetuate a narrow construction of textual engagement. Both West and Sackville-West broached social and political topics such as marriage and militarism. Woolf, however, used the radio to stage discussions of the modern reader, the market for books, and craftmanship.[6] Poetry readings by H.D. further supplemented the early field of poetry and broadcasting.

Since then, numerous women poets have been attracted to this particular medium. In the sixties, Anne Waldman hosted a poetry series at WRVR in New York that included panel debates on topics like "the little magazines." Waldman notes that radio gave an extra dimension to her engagement with poetry, enabling her to meet with writers whose work she admired and to engage in dialogue with them.[7] During the late seventies, Howe produced a program at WBAI Pacifica Radio, simply titled *Poetry*. It too combined readings and interviews. On the West Coast, Lyn Hejinian (along with Kit Robinson) began a weekly program, *In the American Tree: New Writing by Poets*, on the Berkeley community radio station. It was later run by Erica Hunt. And in Washington during the eighties, Joan Retallack was a regular commentator for the radio program *All Things Considered*. In tandem with this work, she wrote "word plays," plays for voices intended for a utopian radio series.

While print culture focuses attention on poetry as writing, radio shifts linguistic value back to speech or sound. Producing and receiving sounds under the conditions of radio involves a negotiation between proximity and distance, presence and absence. In print cultures, a text is contained and stabilized by its physical form as a document. Sound, on the other hand, is spatially infinite. As Susan Stewart writes, "We see properly only what is before us, but sound can envelop us; we might, as we move or change, having varying experiences of sound's intensity, but it will not readily 'fit' an epistemology of spatiality, horizon, or location."[8] In radio, no two readings are the same. Rather, recordings of a single composition will foreground its textual variance, and alternative meanings may be revealed through a simple change in stress or intonation.

The listener, too, is involved in a complex process of reception. Philosophers like Kant and Hegel sought to separate the poetic imagination from the sensual surroundings invoked in performance, arguing that poetry was essentially an abstract or cognitive form. Yet the sounding of a poem transforms the poem into an event, and it is through this event that the poem communicates. What it communicates through this "sounding out" may be an experience beyond language but apprehensible all the same. The elliptical moments produced in a reading enable the listener to incorporate certain elements of her or his internal experience into the poem. In *On Language*, Roman Jakobson states, "We have . . . failed to appreciate properly the subjectivism of the hearer who fills in the elliptic gaps creatively."[9] A poem's aurality provokes a heightened consciousness of reception.

Both in sound production and reception, then, radio enacts a very different sort of generative economy from that of print. It is not surprising that writers like Susan Howe, whose work plays radically on the aural complexities and resonance in the production of meaning, should turn to radio. Her visual strategies—the unorthodox spacing, word grouping, and crossover of lines—help increase the voicing possibilities in her text. Radio was a way for her to explore the staging of poetry, particularly how the dramatics of voice might be orchestrated.

Running for five years from New York, Howe's *Poetry* program featured readings by and interviews with contemporary writers. Among these were readings by Barbara Guest, Ron Padgett, Robert Creeley, John Ashbery, May Sarton, and Helen Adam. Howe also maintained an archive at WBAI of taped readings by Jack Spicer, George Oppen, Charles Reznikoff, and Charles Olson. These recorded an innovative tradition of American poetry, framed specifically by Howe's concerns with an "outsider" literary history. In her program, Howe also defined "poetry" more broadly as a cultural production that goes through various stages of writing, editing, publishing, and distribution. As such, she ran a number of interviews with publishers like James Laughlin (New Directions), magazine editors such as Bruce Andrews and Charles Bernstein (*L=A=N=G=U=A=G=E*), and distributors like the New York–based Women's Distribution Group.

Within the genealogy of *Poetry* that Howe was constructing, women writers were strongly represented. Many were contemporaries of Howe, including Armantrout, Dahlen, Fraser, Harryman, Hejinian, Mayer, and Owen. Just as Tuumba enabled Hejinian to contact other writers from her farm in Willits, so too the radio program gave Howe a social context for her work. "[B]efore my radio thing," she told Hejinian, "when I was utterly alone here except for my family . . . and felt a total failure and was struggling away with *Hinge Picture* and *Chanting* and *Boston Harbor* and *Sandycove*—I was doing my best work. But no-one was reading it."[10] Other activities, such as editing the *Poetry Project Newsletter*, were less attractive. Radio gave Howe more scope to seek out and present work that interested her, as well as more control. In 1977 she described to Hejinian the pleasure of radio's "hands-on approach": "I like producing programs. The way you like printing books. I love that process of editing and producing a finished product."[11]

Hejinian was an appropriate person to write about the possibilities that radio offered for poetry. For a period both Hejinian and Howe were involved in radio, and they shared their various experiences as well as their hopes for and frustrations with the medium.[12] When Hejinian wrote to Howe with the news that she was leaving *In the American Tree*, Howe responded: "I understand about not wanting to continue live radio work. It does become a case of personalities and the poet etc. The personality exchange between host and guest. Also one program a week takes quite a bit of planning and thought even if done live."[13]

As with Howe's *Poetry*, Hejinian and Robinson's program has not been mentioned in literary histories of Language writing. One reason that radio programs are generally excluded or marginalized is that they shift away from the traditional roles of reader and writer to more fundamental categories of audience and producer. Although Grenier's "I Hate Speech" was ironic in its first announcement, the way in which it was taken up as emblematic of Language writing's focus on the *scriptible* made radio's emphasis on voice correspondingly problematic. Voice seemed to reaffirm the authenticity and primacy of the author as producer of meaning. While Howe herself sometimes found it difficult to challenge the cult of personality that radio encouraged, the fact that *Poetry* was mostly preedited enabled her to decenter and distance its effects.

Like one of her favorite writers, Virginia Woolf, Howe's actual experience of live radio was frustrating. Woolf wrote, "There's a certain thrill about writing to read aloud—I expect a vicious one. It's the talk element that upsets it." To Vita Sackville-West, Woolf joked, "Just off to broadcast; not a bit nervous, more likely to be deadly bored. I know what will happen—I shall yawn and say, [11 words omitted]. This will be broadcast and ruin the chastity of 12 million homes."[14] Howe, too, wondered at the value of the talk show when fielding phone calls about Allen Ginsberg's workshop at that Naropa Institute. As it became increasingly clear that women were not considered part of Ginsberg's version of American poetry, she kept asking herself "what the Hell I am doing—I should be working." Furthermore, would Emily Brontë, Christina Rosetti, or H.D. "have wasted their time listening to this junk"?[15]

Howe's roles as radio interviewer and producer were instrumental, even crucial, in fostering her skills as a critic and increased her confidence in the value of her own ideas. "It is amazing what a slow process it was for me to gather the courage to conduct my own interviews rather than finding someone else to do it and just producing," she told Hejinian. "The idea that I might be knowledgeable enough to question someone intelligently or sensitively had never occurred to me." Radio further enabled her to interact with a public without feeling that her own writing self was somehow up for judgment as well. Howe also enjoyed "the archival aspect" of the programs she did, as well as editing "the sound of the poet reading his or her own work."[16]

Just how far those editorial skills that Howe gained from WBAI *Poetry* translate into her subsequent literary engagements is open to conjecture. The role of editor, however, is strongly apparent in her work, from *The Liberties* and *My Emily Dickinson* to *Melville's Marginalia* and *Eikon Basilike*. "Howe adopts the mask of an editor, reviser, or 'redacter,'" Susan Schultz observes in her review-essay "Exaggerated History." "That is, she takes as given that our histories and literature have already been written, and makes it her task to alter rather than reinvent the record."[17]

The *Poetry* program gave Howe the chance of meeting in person a range of writers, including Lyn Hejinian and Kathleen Fraser. Wanting to organize a reading for WBAI while Fraser was in New York, Howe asked Hejinian to help her locate Fraser (Fraser appeared on both Hejinian's and Howe's radio shows).[18] In November 1977, a couple of months later, Howe wrote: "Thanks for sending *Gesualdo*. I will follow your instructions and let you know in advance the exact date of broadcast. . . . Within two weeks to have met you and Kathleen Fraser! A heady experience. One that makes this radio work very much worthwhile."[19]

Two days before Christmas, Howe told Hejinian she had just finished editing the broadcast of *Gesualdo:*

[T]he last part of the half hour is *Gesualdo*. I play a Gesualdo piece before the poem and read a summary of his life. This I think makes the [piece] far more accessible . . . for the listener who cannot read it on the page. One can then listen to you use the life and music and float with the words. It is really an ambitious piece, I left a lot more in than you had marked along with everything you had marked.[20]

This reveals Howe's own input into Hejinian's work, particularly in planning how best to present it to an audience unfamiliar with Gesualdo's history. Her selection of Gesualdo's music as an entry point for Hejinian's poem was not unusual, as Howe contextualized many of the readings and interviews for her listeners by opening with a carefully chosen track of music. These exemplify what Erving Goffman calls a frame space for the eventual speaker.[21] Howe did the same for Bernadette Mayer, selecting music to complement Mayer's "Eve of Easter," which focuses on Milton:

I found great music for your program. I was thinking . . . it should be something Messiah like. I went to the record section to search for Handel and found he had written gorgeous music to Milton's *L'Allegro* and *Il Penseroso*! . . . It seemed like a message from Milton himself, there in the musty BAI record library.[22]

Radio work also firmed up Howe's thoughts on feminism and writing:

If I have learned anything from all this tape work—it is that women are pretty generally ignored in serious discussions about the history of American Poetry. Dickinson, Stein, and H.D. and sometimes Marianne Moore are often mentioned in passing, but never as being seminal to some kind of growth process. There is always Ezra, WCW, Olson, Eliot, Stevens, and now Ashbery. They did have similar great threads running through etc. but I feel something building among women aside from feminist self-pity. I see in the work of you [Lyn Hejinian], Kathleen, Barbara Guest, me, Maureen, Ann Lauterbach at times, and Helen Adam too—something related. Some attempt at a personal mythology that is interesting and strong. Of course we still lack the confidence to start with, that those men had. But maybe its building.[23]

In addition to a program on Dorothy Wordsworth, Howe did one on Virginia Woolf in whose work she "got completely immersed": "It was a tremendous learning experience for me," she wrote to Hejinian. Howe contrasts it with recording an interview with Adrienne Rich, done in order to try to understand her feminism and "intellectual passion" better. Although Rich had "written very truthfully in *Of Woman Born* about the conflicts of being a mother and a writer," Howe discovered that interviewing her was "[n]ot the rich experience the Virginia Woolf program was, but interesting nevertheless."[24] In June 1980, she admitted to Bernadette Mayer that she found a good deal in Rich's prose and that Rich had "forced me to do a lot of serious thinking about all the feminist ideas."[25] Having done "some interesting reading about H.D. in the Yale Library," she also decided "to produce a program about her and am trying to think of what way to do it."[26]

Another feature program was an interview Howe conducted with Bruce Andrews and Charles Bernstein as editors of *L=A=N=G=U=A=G=E*. Over "a long lunch" she "found them so lively, so full of opinions and ideas" and had a "wonderful" time. Writing to Hejinian, she imagined that "[y]ou must get the same sort of boost from Silliman, Perelman, Eigner, Rae (there I go, woman's first name). Why do I do that? BRAINWASHED. It's nice to have a dialogue with people. I am very cut off usually."[27] Howe felt it was important "for women to be included in their [Andrews and Bernstein's] particular dialogue, because their tendency is to leave them out."[28]

Significantly, the archival tape of the interview is different from the transcript that was eventually published in *L=A=N=G=U=A=G=E*.[29] In the version published as a supplement to "The Politics of Poetry" feature, questions of gender are completely edited out.[30] On the tape available at the New Poetry archive, Bernstein and Howe briefly discuss gender as an issue in language as well as in constructing a literary tradition. It is unclear as to quite how much editing was done and by whom, given that the interview seems to have gone through two stages of editing—first by Howe herself (the unedited tape to an edited tape) and then by Bruce Andrews and Charles Bernstein (presumably from the edited tape to a transcript). The issue of gender is perhaps elided to draw more firmly together the issues of capitalism, ideology and public space that were also being discussed.

At first, Howe tries to position the magazine within a broader tradition of experimentation. She notes that in the sixties, journals like *Artforum* and *October* featured similar dialogues among artists and that *Artforum* took chances in the innovative work it focused on. *Artforum* also featured some early critical writing by Kathy Acker, Barbara Baracks, and Johanna Drucker. For Andrews and Bernstein, however, *Artforum* and *October* were limited by demarcating between criticism and other sorts of writing. Andrews argues that "what $L=A=N=G=U=A=G=E$ seeks to do is to get that discourse out into a more public realm where participation can be less restricted."

In contrast, they want to build a sense of community and to make information more accessible without being mediated by a critical establishment, which Bernstein sees as involved in repressing knowledge. He notes that work written in the early part of the twentieth century has been circumscribed by very conservative approaches, giving as examples the American reception of Pound and Williams in the fifties and sixties. Society, then, was primed for a certain sort of consumption of art. "Poetry had to get an immediate hit," he states. Alternatively, by exploding genres and moving beyond a recognizable verse tradition, $L=A=N=G=U=A=G=E$ sought to negate such reductive approaches. Bernstein points out that modernist women writers like Laura Riding, Virginia Woolf, and H.D. similarly undermined culturally dominant values by showing language to be in a state of flux rather than neutral or fixed. At this point, Andrews attempts to introduce a more Marxist orientation by saying that critique should focus on the structure of power—not on instrumentalities but on things in themselves.

Later in the tape, Howe suggests that the political genealogies of $L=A=N=G=U=A=G=E$ tend to exclude her, focusing as they do on theories that take little account of women's experience. She argues that language as a system is also constructed along gender lines that are specifically masculine. This made it more difficult to write or to be acknowledged seriously as a woman writer. "Stein found being a woman a problem," she observes. "She wanted to be seen as 'one of the boys' most definitely." Alternatively, Laura Riding's ideas were appropriated by men.

Bernstein responds that feminism has changed his consciousness signif-icantly and (citing Shulamith Firestone and Kate Millett) argues that his own writing has been affected by feminist investigations of language and perception. He also concedes that Marxism has presented a strongly mas-culinist model of social realism. Andrews then introduces the idea of de-sire, suggesting that change could be achieved by exploring the psycholog-ical. Unfortunately, at this point, the interview changes direction and once again dissolves into a dialogue between Andrews and Bernstein. In the published version, feminism is removed so that the discussion can focus fully on Marxist frameworks for relating language and society.

Over time, Howe would have different feelings about the interview. In a letter to Ron Silliman in 1985, she rejects Silliman's idea that it could be seen as "critical writing of mine," because "[it] is me asking one meager sentence and then Bruce and Charles going on like gang busters for ever." Although she felt "deflated" by the interview and its subsequent multiple editing, she was proud to have given them "an hour and a half air time." She continues: "Since then I have grown very fond of them both and less in awe which is good for everyone."[31]

Another extensive interview on magazine production was focused on the feminist journal *Signs*.[32] Both its founding editor, Catharine Stimpson, and her coeditor, Elsa Dixler, agreed to be interviewed at Howe's request. At the time, *Signs* was only in its fourth year of publishing, and given its ap-parent lack of engagement with poetry, Howe's interview with its editors seems an unusual addition to her radio corpus. In one respect it may be viewed as an early gesture on Howe's part to open up a space in which poetry and theory could interact. In particular, French feminist theory—as presented to Americans—parallels Language writing's own investigations into the relations between language and knowledge. As Claire Moses points out, *Signs* figures prominently in the anglophone construction of "French" feminism in the United States. *Signs* not only published the first English-language translations of Julia Kristeva and Hélène Cixous in 1975 and 1976 but also featured (in articles by Elaine Marks and Carolyn Burke in 1978) the first critiques of the women's movement in France. As Moses adds, because *Signs* was the only academic journal to reach a wide cross-section of American women in its interdisciplinary scope, it became an in-fluential distributor of French feminist theory.[33]

Howe says that she came across *Signs* quite by accident in a bookstore and was fascinated by it. The interview is highly provocative, because it not only considers the relation between innovative women writers and aca-demic writing but also provides information about the early position of feminist criticism in the academy. Each relationship reveals a degree of anxiety. On the one hand, Howe is clearly concerned about her own access to such material, as well as somewhat in awe of the intellectual capacities of contributors to the new feminist knowledge. On the other hand, the editors of *Signs* reveal a comparable anxiety about their current status in the academic marketplace.

One of forty or so journals published by the University of Chicago Press at the time of the interview (1979), *Signs* had the highest sales in bookstores. Stimpson places *Signs* within an intellectual movement that includes academic feminist journals such as *Women's Studies, Feminist Studies,* and *Sex Roles* but notes that *Signs* represents more disciplines than the others. Because it represents a subject that many academics despise, in its first year it overcompensated by including more footnotes per article than any other journal.

For Howe, the most innovative aspect of *Signs* is the letter section, which she finds "really very exciting." As a space for feminist discussion, it could be seen as a forum for crystallizing a feminist academic community. Howe appreciates the passion of the debates that occupy *Signs*, as women respond to one another and to articles published in previous issues. Stimpson notes that by responding in these ways, women feel that they are actually shaping the matrix of feminist thought. She sees the development of academic feminism as homologous to a certain extent with the women's political movement. But *Signs* was just beginning to encounter a backlash at the time of Howe's interview, when sexual conservatism was becoming more visible. Stimpson and Dixler had already received instructional letters or articles that reproduced patriarchal didacticism, citing as example, one simply titled "Sweet Things." Significantly, the style of such letters— powered more by anger than argument—parallels many of those produced out of the backlash experienced by Language writing.

Howe asks about the excerpt from Kristeva's *On the Women of China,* which was published in the inaugural issue of *Signs*. Attracted to Kristeva's framework of historical change as a slow structural process, she contrasts it to what she saw as an oversimplified or overgeneralized approach in American feminism. She notes that European women such as Kristeva, Simone de Beauvoir, and Hannah Arendt achieved so much as intellectuals; their success is to be found in the fact that their books are now standard texts used by both men and women. Having invested her own poetics in a highly American tradition of innovation and thought, Howe queries the apparent Eurocentrism of academic feminism. "Even the writers—Lessing and Murdoch," Howe says, seem to be part of that phenomenon.

Stimpson's answer is that American academics are more apt to give European women permission to be different, for two simple reasons: "One, they don't perceive them so much as competition. And two, they seem like exotic strangers. They seem less like potential wives." Stimpson concedes the existence of a double standard in the reception of European and American feminism but notes that some American women have radically altered their field, such as Susan Sontag and Margaret Mead.

Another concern of Howe's is the issue of access, especially responsibility for broadening the audience for the kind of work done in *Signs*. Stimpson agrees but suggests that the present emphasis has to be on institutionalizing feminist knowledge. She argues that the new scholarship on women is highly political in negotiating the movement of feminism toward institutionalization. As yet, this process is still highly selective, excluding what constitutes knowledge for Third World women.

Stressing her point again, Howe gives Stimpson a concrete example: "Why haven't I seen Kristeva's translation? Why isn't it available?" Stimpson replies that, as a small-press publication, access to it is still limited. Nevertheless, its very publication signals an intellectual revolution: "Ten years ago, it wouldn't have been published at all. *Signs*, as an academic journal, legitimated the work being done by women. Yet, it accepts only 2% of the articles submitted."

Howe also questions the framework that makes symposiums and debates on feminism unavailable to women outside the academy. Many of the women who listen to her poetry program want to read more than *Ms.* magazine, but other feminist material simply cannot be found. Stimpson locates the problem in the nature of academic life in the United States. Because America produces very few independent intellectuals capable of speaking influentially to their peers and the world at large, "we have made a fetish of intellectual specialization." For Stimpson it is a matter not only of opening up professional meetings but also of publicizing them widely. The answer lay in mass education—perhaps cable television could rectify this lack. Howe, however, is skeptical of this solution, believing that the capitalist structures that underlie the media would block or resist such a move.

Her response would be in some respects prophetic, as Howe subsequently had to fight to keep her own program on the air. Despite her devotion to the program, as well as an increasingly strong base of listener support, she received little financial help. In January 1979 the National Endowment for the Arts stopped funding poetry projects in the media. In August of that year, Howe told Hejinian that she had "no money from grants for my program this year, and as of now no job. Four years of work seems to have gone for nothing."[34] By mid-September, the prospect was a bit rosier. Howe received a grant for a series of twelve readings, but the money was to go specifically to poets, even though it would involve her in "hours and hours of work. . . . And not work done at home." Lack of funding compelled her to discontinue the program: "It does make me bitter. As I took so long to build it and worked so hard."[35]

Howe planned running a radio program called "The World Viewed" with Bernstein, but it did not eventuate because they had no success in their grant applications to the National Endowment for the Humanities.[36] Pragmatically, Howe admitted defeat and moved on to other ventures. "Suddenly there comes a point where what had been a labor of love becomes loves labor lost—or just labor," she told Hejinian in late 1982. "Then it really *is* time to stop and go on to another thing."[37] Bernstein, however, became involved in another radio show focusing on poetry, namely, the LINEbreak series initiated by Martin Spinelli. Spinelli asked Bernstein to host and coproduce the national program, which like Howe's *Poetry*, featured both readings and interviews. The first two shows (which were part of the many pilots made to consider the format of the series) were with Susan Howe. While it remains an important program in its own right, the editing does not have Howe's distinctive emphasis, an emphasis that was not only feminist in orientation but that idiosyncratically explored the palimpsests of poetic production.

CHAPTER SIX

Kathleen Fraser's Feminist Alternative: *HOW(ever)*

Founded by Kathleen Fraser, *HOW(ever)* sought to create an ongoing exchange between women writers and feminist critics interested in innovative writing. Fraser had moved from New York to San Francisco in 1972 to direct the Poetry Center and to teach at San Francisco State University.[1] She was curious and stimulated by the emergent Language writing, and participated in its early social scene. Yet she strongly resisted the demarcations increasingly made between poetic forms and hoped for a community that would confirm her own feminist explorations. While other women writers negotiated the given print culture, Fraser looked toward a figure-ground shift. *HOW(ever)* presented not only an alternative forum for innovative women poets but also a way for women readers to gain access to such writing.

The impetus for *HOW(ever)* arose through a regular writing group, a subcommunity including Fraser, Frances Jaffer, and Beverly Dahlen, who had met through various connections to San Francisco State University. As Fraser notes, "We shared our uncomfortable feelings of marginality vis-à-vis the women's writing community and our attraction to the various writings coming out of the modernist project."[2] They discussed the influence of gender on perception and the growing evidence of various gender-oriented preoccupations in one another's writings. Fraser thought that "without each other's support at that time, none of us would have written as much or as well."[3] Yet their meetings also reinforced a feeling of isolation from both the avant-garde and feminist orthodoxies of the time.

Fraser found in their writing an "unresolved drift towards privacy."[4] The writing group eventually dissolved, but the three remained friends. Dahlen and Fraser participated in Bay Area literary activities organized by Language writers like Bob Perelman (with Dahlen's talk, "*A Reading*: a Reading" eventually appearing in *Writing/Talks*). Jaffer turned to more specifically feminist activities, such as reviewing Ellen Moers's *Literary*

Women for *Chrysalis: A Magazine of Women's Culture*.[5] In 1979 she attended a workshop (as part of a conference in "The Scholar and the Feminist" series) run by Rachel Blau DuPlessis on the possibility of constructing a female aesthetic. The proceedings from the conference were later published as *The Future of Difference* (1980), a groundbreaking volume of early interdisciplinary feminism.[6]

DuPlessis was the only coordinator to contact all the members of her workshop to ask for their critical responses. She incorporated this feedback into an essay collage entitled "For the Etruscans" and featured substantially material from Jaffer's then unpublished manuscript, *Procedures for Having Lunch*. Other members of the workshop included Carol Ascher, Sara Lennox, JoAnn McNamara, Lou Roberts, Mira Schor, and Louise Yelin.[7] Another workshop coordinator was Carolyn Burke, who was then introducing French feminism into the United States and working on a book about Mina Loy. The inclusive form of DuPlessis's essay signaled a willingness to disrupt the traditional hierarchies of academic discourse. The workshop also was significant in confirming academic interest in contemporary innovative writing by women. When DuPlessis sent Jaffer and Fraser copies of "For the Etruscans," they were "hooked."[8] Sharing a similar passion for feminism and writing (such as the poetry of George Oppen) strengthened the friendship. DuPlessis's own interest in the work of the writing group continued in her publishing of Dahlen's and Fraser's work in *Feminist Studies*.

The methodology and issues raised in DuPlessis's workshop were reflected in Kathleen Fraser's course, "Feminist Poetics," which began in the fall of 1982 at San Francisco State University. Fraser notes that this course solidified many of the issues she had been grappling with over the years and strengthened her desire to explore questions outside the hierarchical framework of teaching. As happened with Susan Howe, *Signs* also provided a turning point in Fraser's thought. "I felt I'd found 'my people,'" she recalls in a recent interview.[9] She was excited about the nonlinear feminist textuality outlined by Burke and Irigaray, particularly in its parallels to her own style. She invited Burke to lunch and to speak to her "Feminist Poetics" class. *Signs* further provided an example of how effectively a journal could change the intellectual climate.

Another formative moment was a conversation with Bob Glück, who advised her to "decide who your audience is and then address it."[10] Glück's words mobilized Fraser to rethink her growing solipsism. Charles Bernstein also encouraged her to create community options for herself.[11] Fraser began cementing her ideas about a magazine forum in which poets and critics could enter into a dialogue over poetics. Writing to Annette Kolodny as both friend and critic, Fraser asked her if such a project would be taken seriously by academic feminists, and whether it would be helpful to include the working notes of poets. Kolodny's response, being immediate and positive, was the final encouragement that Fraser needed.

HOW(ever) began in 1983, more as a broadsheet than a journal, with sixteen to eighteen pages (8½ by 11 inches) stapled together in an inexpensive format. It was modeled on Carla Harryman's journal *Qu*, of which each issue could be read in one sitting. After considering titles such as "Parts of Speech," "Feminine Endings," "Indefinite Article," "Alice Blue Gown," "Red Tulips," and "Para/phrase," Fraser, Dahlen, and Jaffer finally decided on *HOW(ever)*. These provisional titles point to a range of possible influences from Gertrude Stein to French feminist theory. The eventual title alludes to Marianne Moore's lines about poetry: "I, too, dislike it./However, there is a place for it." As Frances Jaffer suggests, the very title of the journal suggests a second take after all the givens, or the "exception."[12] There are no equal signs here; language is seen to inscribe processes of power rather than a democracy of phonemes.

Significantly, the shorthand occasionally used for the journal's title was *H(er)*, which foregrounds not only the journal's feminine focus but also its ties to a modernist avant-garde of women's writing. The possessive pronoun signals a territorialization, the mapping out of an alternative space to other poetic formations. *H(er)* also echoes H.D.'s abbreviated title for *HERmione*. It would be particularly appropriate for Dahlen, whose admiration of H.D.'s writing (including *Helen in Egypt*) moved her to write *The Egyptian Poems*. Like Language writing, *HOW(ever)* emphasized process and method in foregrounding the word *how*. As Fraser pointed out much later, "Perhaps the most pivotal factor in *HOW(ever)*'s creation was the urgency to provide alternatives to the romantic *I* of fixed unilateral authority."[13]

The opening editorial statements suggest that *HOW(ever)* began with a complex editorial policy, only part of which was to reclaim forgotten or marginalized modernist women writers and artists. According to Fraser, "*HOW(ever)* proposes to make a bridge between scholars thinking about women's language issues, vis-à-vis the making of poetry, and the women making those poems."[14] She thus aimed *HOW(ever)* at two potential audiences: one academic; the other, comprising women writers not affiliated with institutions. As Fraser notes, the first issue of *HOW(ever)* was published when "women's writing" was beginning to be recognized in the academy. Issues that continued to be the focus of scholars or editors at this time included the following:

- the creation of place: (magazine/book/essay/caucus) where women's editorial choices could be asserted & exercised
- the foregrounding of lesbian subjectivity/its literature

- the celebration & legitimization of female body/"female language" as basic grounds for investigation
- "common language" (as in Adrienne Rich's *Dream of a Common Language* or Judy Grahn's *The Work of a Common Woman*), asserted as the superior agency of literary exchange . . . often seen as the only valid way to empower a female community
- a growing sensitivity to class/race issues in women's lives.[15]

In particular, Fraser was interested in theoretical issues that arose when women's innovative writing was combined with political practice. However, she resisted the idea of a "common language" because it was another way of prescribing the field of "women's poetry." Building on the idea of difference within community, Fraser hoped to move away from both master narratives and prosodic patterns in order to show that "our hearts did not belong to Daddy" or, for that matter, to a substituted "mommy" figure still common in feminist strategies of reversal.[16] She argued that an all-woman editorial collective was a necessary part of the *HOW(ever)* project: "It is probably realistic to speculate that even as many male writers were extremely supportive of our undertaking, had any one of them been an active voice in our collective editorial labors, a discretely different sum 'product' would have emerged."[17] Fraser felt that men would bring along their own histories, as well as a specifically male style of logic and argument. By working independently, the *HOW(ever)* editorial group was free to figure out issues one by one.

In this respect, Fraser seems aware of the likely epistemic and behavioral inflections of gender. Frances Jaffer, in her opening editorial statement, also outlined a praxis that focused on "what can be written in other than traditional syntactical or prosodical structures [that] may give an important voice to authentic female experience."[18] As the writing, working notes, and letters featured in *HOW(ever)* reveal, the "truths" of female experience were interpreted broadly, covering a diverse range of subject positions. What became apparent was that no one tendency in form or style captured experience more accurately than any other.

Looking back at *HOW(ever)*, Fraser reflects that it was a model "not just for a different kind of writing but for the assertion of editorial choices by women."[19] There was no hard-and-fast editorial policy: "We had to trust our individual responses, our discretionary sense of authenticity and difficult pleasure, to acknowledge variable tastes and persuasions as the work began arriving." Primarily, they were looking for "that which had not yet been uttered because forms were still being imagined to contain those unsayables." She notes that although conflicts often occurred in the editorial process, the use of a collective form helped clarify the reasons for their choices. It was important to argue for the "necessity and value of a certain work, to ask for reconsideration when there was a strong difference, [and] to think even more closely about why or how a particular piece was causing excitement in one of us and not in another," for to do so was to open up and interrogate powerful and persistent ideas of cultural value.[20]

This editorial conversation was supported by the inclusion of a "Working Note" for each poet, the only requirement that *HOW(ever)* imposed on its contributors. The "Working Note" was to give some idea of the processes that had gone into the production and of any formal problems proposed or encountered. This was to reinforce the idea that no text is produced in a vacuum but always within a social and aesthetic field. The end of each issue also included a section called "alerts," set aside for informal commentary and information on new or neglected books by innovative women poets. Its informality encouraged a flexible form of criticism, although it still maintained a far more traditional form than the reviews published by *L=A=N=G=U=A=G=E*.[21] There was also a "postcards" section, which included letters that commented on past reviews or offered information on forthcoming work. Finally, the editors' notes provided updates on forthcoming books, conferences, and readings.

While focusing primarily on the literary, *HOW(ever)* also drew attention to relevant topics in film theory and art. The second issue initiated a visual aesthetic in order to promote similar conversations along a parallel track. Subsequent issues presented artworks that generally foregrounded the structural, such as "alphabets, words, [and] de-composition." This initiative was Fraser's, whose interest in art was both intense and longstanding. Fraser thought that to juxtapose visual work alongside written texts would enact a convergence that would provoke further processes of thought or points of attention. She hoped to give space to "writing as different in its goals and its 'product' as a painting by Nancy Spero or Elizabeth Murray was from a picture by [Willem] DeKooning or David Salle."[22] Such expansions complemented the business of exploding genre and showed innovative poetry on a broader and more interdisciplinary scale than traditional literary histories.

HOW(ever) further set out to show that American and Canadian women writers participate in a common tradition. Frequent postings in the "alerts" and "postcards" section of new Canadian books or forthcoming events in Canada are evidence of this. To a lesser extent, British news was forwarded by writers like Wendy Mulford. By listing Simone de Beauvoir and Luce Irigaray alongside Shulamith Firestone and Nancy Chodorow in the very first issue, Fraser also brought together what were seen as quite separate—even conflicting—directions in feminism, namely, French feminism and

Anglo-American feminism. In doing so, she foregrounded differences within feminism, as well as framing the multiplicity of feminisms that *HOW(ever)* hoped to feature.

One of Fraser's declared aims in *HOW(ever)* was to present a set of writings from both "established feminist scholars and working poets" that would move critical discourse beyond those "readings" that sought to impose interpretations on texts from without. As such, she hoped that her journal would enable the two disciplines to cross-fertilize in an encouragingly unofficial space. While poets were already implicated in this endeavor by being required to supply a working note, Fraser notes that the editors were largely unsuccessful in soliciting any material from critics that did not simply develop an argument with the usual footnotes. She and the other editors put considerable effort into encouraging submissions:

I sent out a large number of personal letters of friendly invitation to feminist scholars and essayists whose work I discovered in my reading. We handed out flyers at regional and national MLA sessions and at conferences on H.D. and E[mily] D[ickinson] and V[irginia] W[oolf], inviting contributions . . . but with mostly silence in return.[23]

Although Fraser suggests that academic feminists were not yet ready to move out of a male-dominant academic practice, *HOW(ever)* was also competing for attention against emergent scholarly journals such as *Signs, Feminist Studies, Frontiers,* and *Heresies,* most of which were refereed and therefore preferable outlets for the work of career academics.

Fraser says she had "envisaged . . . a place for informal, incomplete response to current and historical works, with particular emphasis on recovery of texts, letters, critical reputations of lost or dimming modernist women writers." The issue of preservation and cultural memory was of fundamental importance. The parentheses around the "ever" in the journal's title could be seen as a symbolic closing off of any future for women's work. "[W]e hardly ever heard about their poems where I was sitting listening," she writes. "You mean in school? I mean where poems were being preserved and thought about seriously and carried forward as news."[24] Borrowing from Pound's "literature is news that STAYS news," Fraser is concerned here not only with the cultural recovery of past women writers but also with those canonical processes by which the work of present women writers will be made over into a past. She astutely realizes that such survival will depend, for the most part, on the community of feminist academics. While staging itself as opening up a dialogue between writers and critics, *HOW(ever)* is also, importantly, an early intervention into the institutionalization of poetry. As Fraser notes in an editorial preface, "*HOW(ever)* hopes to create a place in which poets can talk to scholars through poems and working notes on those poems, as well as through commentary on neglected women poets who were/are making textures and structures of poetry in the tentative region of the untried."[25]

Her project focused on the academy in several ways. Significantly, the editorial group formation was quite traditional in structure, with a chief editor (Kathleen Fraser), associate editors (Frances Jaffer and Beverly Dahlen), and contributing editors (Rachel Blau DuPlessis and Carolyn Burke). The inclusion of the last two guaranteed an academic perspective. DuPlessis actively promoted innovative writing in scholarly journals and at conferences while publishing her poetry in small presses. Given her interest in *écriture féminine* and the French women's movement, Burke could elaborate on the aesthetic and political connections between French feminism and experimental women's writing. Both editors would therefore be invaluable in shaping an intertext between the academic and the poetic. Another function of *HOW(ever)*'s editorial structure was to indicate the degree of individual involvement in its publication. The withdrawal of Beverly Dahlen enabled Susan Gevirtz to take on the workload of an associate editor. As *HOW(ever)* evolved, its editorial constitution gradually changed. Toward the end, Myung Mi Kim and Meredith Stricker produced three issues as guest editors.

Perhaps the major site of contestation in *HOW(ever)* was the debate over poetic form. This was particularly evident after the publication in a guest-edited issue of an article by Annie Finch titled "The Sonnet Transfigured" in October 1990. Three original members of the editorial collective—Dahlen, Fraser, and DuPlessis—were moved to respond to Finch's call for a reclamation of the sonnet form. All three disagreed with Finch's contention that "poetry is to stop fear" and that "the structure of the sonnet" as "a way of organizing, channeling and making familiar" is particularly well suited for doing this.[26]

DuPlessis argued that the desire to situate oneself in relation to power—to take hold of or "ride" power, as Finch suggests—does not make it necessary to opt for the sonnet form. And for DuPlessis, the use of fixed forms as "stylistics counters" to anxiety or fear was implausible. In such circumstances, it is best to ask what "romantic" might mean in the context of the sonnet. Its recuperation, she suggested, "is only possible within a full analysis of lyric ideology, beauty, and pleasure." As a genre, the sonnet is "already historically filled with voiceless, beautiful female figures in object position." Since these are rendered as muses, the sonnet is more of a "sonnet," (or medium of a male subject) than a "sound-net" which emphasizes different voices.[27]

While DuPlessis recognized that for some women writers the muse is arguably a male force, she argued that for many others it is female—"maternal, mirroring, lesbian." DuPlessis seems to add difference per se as a recognizably female force, for she continued to list the female muse "as a child; a family configuration; a community; an old, wise, mischief elf; a dark-colored person; a light-colored person; a force transcendent; a force chthonic." DuPlessis then encompassed all other difference in a binary model of sex/gender, stating that "[t]he muse for women is labile & bisexed, bigendered."[28] This is problematic because it not only elides sexualities within an either/or model but also attempts to fit different sorts of influence into a prioritized sexual paradigm.

Fraser responded by expressing her concern at Finch's either/or attitude toward the use of traditional forms. For Finch, the surviving poet might choose to align herself, as struggling writer, either with the sonnet of the humble and lowercase *i* or with the sonnet of the powerful and even frightening uppercase *I*. Fraser suggested that to surrender to traditional binary descriptions merely reinforces such "false" structures and that Finch's bind "is indeed double since it seems to dismiss or discount a third existing position provided for us by dozens of formally transgressive works written by women poets," namely, the exploration of "alternative poetic models and strategies." As Fraser pointed out, much "breakthrough works of poetry by women and men have engaged the traditional sonnet, etc., by brilliantly reversing, unhinging and transfiguring it."[29] Her examples included the sonnets of Laura Riding, Bernadette Mayer's *Sonnets*, and Alice Notley's *When I Was Alive*.

Fraser found Finch's position further problematic in privileging the sonnet tradition as some law or authority that must be addressed, "as if it were a Jungian shadow to be conquered." Her point is that "[w]hen one linguistically links the act of making a poem to that hierarchic purpose of winning and/or maintaining control over chaos with familiar 'technology' and methods of 'writing efficiency,' one risks courting the clichéd counterpart of this male tradition: 'female inadequacy.'" Furthermore, arguments about the sonnet tradition illustrate a larger debate over margins and center: "Isn't it that very attempt to align oneself with an acknowledged center, to win approved product status from the representatives of *any* established center, that throws the marginalized poet into a condition of fragility and mute chase?"[30]

Significantly, in the same issue as the responses by Dahlen, Fraser, and DuPlessis (summer 1991), Norma Cole emphasized the importance of determining who speaks when considering poetic form. As Cole points out, readers "are accustomed to having male writing in female characters' mouths."[31] She points to the recent practice of gender reversal, as when Carla Harryman puts words into the mouths of androgynous or genderless figures or when Leslie Scalapino puts words into the mouths of male characters. Arguing for the highly subversive effects of such practices, Cole's observation rests uneasily alongside Jaffer's call for the representation of women's lives. Indeed, such strategies are perhaps more contentious as a feminist practice than a return to the sonnet form.

While the term *HOW(ever)* is often used to denote a specific group of feminist poets (such as Fraser, Dahlen, Jaffer, Gevirtz, and DuPlessis), the journal itself managed to include a wide variety of feminist practices. Black writers and poets from ethnic minorities, such as Sheila K. Smith, Mei-mei Berssenbrugge, and Myung Mi Kim, were presented alongside British writers like Wendy Mulford and Pamela Stewart. For the first time, working projects by both Canadian writers of the feminine (écriture au féminin) and Language writers could be presented in the same forum. The range of contemporary poetry featured in *HOW(ever)* undid the presumption that there was merely one tradition or politics of practice. The journal also included writing and information about modernist women who were otherwise considered noncanonical, such as Mina Loy, as well as writers associated with later poetic communities such as Lorine Niedecker and Barbara Guest.

During its lifetime, *HOW(ever)* was positioned confusingly as either a rival venture to or a subset of Language writing. In his debate with Michael Davidson in *Sulfur* (1988), Eliot Weinberger took the opportunity to stage a critical appraisal of *HOW(ever)*. He argued that, unlike Language writing, *HOW(ever)* was "the most exciting group activity occurring in American poetry today."[32] Adrienne Rich, by contrast, collapsed the project of *HOW(ever)* with that of Language writing, when she referred to Susan Howe, Rachel Blau DuPlessis, Kathleen Fraser, and Frances Jaffer as "the Feminist Language poets."[33]

Each of these framings of *HOW(ever)* and Language writing is misleading. *HOW(ever)* is best viewed as operating alongside the community practices of Language writing, such that some women poets chose to participate in both. At the same time that Fraser was forming *HOW(ever)*, Lyn Hejinian and Barrett Watten were entertaining ideas for a similar project to be featured as a special issue of *Poetics Journal*. This was the "Women and Modernism" issue, which they began planning almost from the inception of the journal. Originally, they had set a 15 March deadline for what was expected to be the spring/summer 1983 issue. If that schedule had been kept, it would have coincided roughly with the first issue of *HOW(ever)*, which appeared in May 1983.[34] Early that year, Hejinian outlined the "Women and Modernism" issue in detail to prospective contributors such as Susan Bee, noting that she and Watten wanted to present two types of essays: "[O]ne dealing with questions in terms of earlier women writers and artists (Stein, Laura Riding, H.D., etc.) and the other discussions by and about current writers and artists and their own personal thoughts. Which is to say, I am interested in both the historical and the personal approach."[35] Such a framework distinctly parallels Fraser's own editorial statement. Together, the "Women and Modernism" issue and the ongoing project of *HOW(ever)* confirm and contextualize one another, as well as providing a clear example of the illusory nature of strict community boundaries. Indeed, three of *HOW(ever)*'s editors, Beverly Dahlen, Carolyn Burke, and Kathleen Fraser, contributed essays to the "Women and Modernism" issue.

Apart from those writers mentioned by Adrienne Rich, others associated even more closely with Language writing, such as Rae Armantrout, Carla Harryman, Hannah Weiner, and Leslie Scalapino, also contributed to *HOW(ever)*. Generally, this posed no problems. But conflict did arise once, over the issue of critical writing. For although the feature of Rae Armantrout's work in progress had gone smoothly, her later review of Lyn Hejinian's *The Guard* underwent a tougher editing process, which saw her manuscript returned with various suggestions by members of the collective (Fraser, here, wished to show that the comments were not necessarily her own, particularly as Armantrout had been a past student).[36] Although Armantrout considered withdrawing her piece, she and Fraser negotiated a reedited version of her article.

The changes between the draft sent to Hejinian and the published version of Armantrout's review are revealing because they show a tendency toward a more traditional academic criticism rather than the informality that *HOW(ever)* professed. In the published version, Armantrout is more explanatory and less at ease with her statements. She is more specific about *The Guard*'s publishing history, notes two of "several magazines" by name, and mentions Hejinian's more popular *My Life*. The editors' questioning of the term *resonance* led Armantrout to define it: "Resonance is inherently pleasurable, as this work shows us, and requires no *raison d'être*." The draft phrase about "the density/solidity of matter" was also revised into "the solidity/reality of matter" in the published version.[37] This change actually shifts the meaning away from the texture of the language, to which Armantrout originally seemed to be referring, to the constitution of the real.

In her response, Fraser apologized by saying that "[n]one of us knowingly had anything 'different' in mind than what you did." But the original review presumed a background in Language poetics, which the editors thought would be unfamiliar to most of *HOW(ever)*'s audience. In accordance with its editorial policy, the collective tried "to imagine a reader who hasn't read a certain book or even literature resembling that book's aesthetic attitudes towards the language usage it is practicing."[38] The policy was underwritten by academic circumspection. For although

critics "are wanting to extend their interests," they still "feel varying de-
grees of wariness and fear and inadequacy when it comes to thinking
about or reading with any satisfaction, the poetries coming out of the
modernist and avant-garde traditions." At the same time, the *HOW(ever)*
editors were trying to be less informal than a scholarly journal.[39] Despite
the initial difficulties with Armantrout's review, Rachel Blau DuPlessis
would reinforce the *HOW(ever)* editors' esteem of Armantrout and
Hejinian's writing by publishing a sample the following year in *Feminist
Studies*.[40] By positioning innovative women's poetry within such an aca-
demic space, DuPlessis was actively combatting the unfamiliarity de-
scribed by Fraser.

Criticism of *HOW(ever)* tended to focus less on its choice of writing
than on its politics, particularly its exclusive interest in women's writing
and the prioritizing of gender issues. Some felt that *HOW(ever)* was in ef-
fect essentializing or decontextualizing the writing. According to Jane
Miller, for instance, "[t]here is always a new sentence, a new voice, a new
timing that needs to be found, and it may come out of a female experience
but must be transformed into something else, larger, to move from construct
into art and from report into rite." Although Miller agrees that it is impor-
tant "to have one's own sexual imaginings" or environment "mirrored in
art," she believes that "[g]reat poetry is always . . . about more than one
thing." Besides, "there's a time and perhaps the time is now, when femi-
nism blocks transcendence (not to another world, but in this one) and is
another crutch."[41] Although Miller's desire for a sublime is problematic,
her point about exploring multiple avenues is astute. While contributors to
HOW(ever) hailed from various cultural, racial, and national backgrounds,
issues of race and class were generally not developed in relation to either
gender or an experimental poetics.

Susan Gevirtz notes that many reactions to *HOW(ever)* were grounded
in old debates about the "woman question." She cites a review of
HOW(ever) by Robert Peters that illustrates the persistence of Victorian
anxieties about women writing. Noting that Gertrude Stein and H.D.
"seem the primary goddesses behind this sort of writing," Peters stated
that he had yet to meet anyone who could remain excited "after twenty
pages or so." Arguing that "[a] poem is not a set of easy metaphysical spec-
ulations on the nature of grammar, guilt or the primal flood," he con-
cluded, "Let's not keep the trope flying, let's strangle the little creature in
his crib before he soils his pants and screws up our life."[42] The metaphor of
infantilization parallels the one used by Wayne Koestenbaum in theorizing
the results of collaboration between male writers.[43] While the "child" of
such masculine literary processes is culturally acceptable, textual births by
women writers are deemed unnatural creations.

Peters's comments are part of a general backlash against the proliferation of feminist magazines. In the face of this narrow-minded and negative reception, both the format and practice of *HOW(ever)* have become a model for many other magazines. Apart from journals like *Big Allis, Black Bread, Chain, Motel,* and *6ix,* which are edited by women and present a forum for contemporary women's writing, the Canadian broadside *(f.)Lip* most closely reflected *HOW(ever)*'s editorial practice.[44] As Fraser points out, *HOW(ever)* was deliberately modest in size and therefore something that could be read between work commitments and familial obligations. One of *(f.)Lip*'s editors, Angela Hryniuk, states that their journal took a similar form for the same reasons; indeed, it got its title partly for being something that women could "flip" through. Aimed at formally innovative writers and women in the academy, it also hoped to attract a broader community of women readers. This ambition was not altogether successful. As Hryniuk notes, "A lot of people who weren't already reading similar writing or weren't in the academic community didn't know what to do with us." Consequently, "[w]e had to deal with feminist anger that we weren't like everyone else."[45]

In 1992, after seven volumes, *HOW(ever)* came to an end. "As you might imagine," Fraser told Daphne Marlatt,

The decision has been extremely difficult to make, provoked by major and unexpected depletions of time and energy for editing competing with the more private pull of one's own writing. Also, funding for our "modest proposal" has been nearly impossible, between an intentional page limitation and our peculiar hybrid of innovative poetry with feminist critical writing.

As with *(f.)Lip,* the radicalism of its form accelerated its demise in a period of increasing conservatism. Fraser, however, held hopes for the future and ended her letter to Marlatt on a positive note: "We've got a good start on building a much-needed community; the talent and invention of women poets is clearly burgeoning; and the once non-existent dialog[ue] among scholar/critics and innovative writers has warmed up. Surely there is more to come."[46]

Fraser's optimism was well justified. Seven years later saw the first issue of a daughter magazine, *HOW2*. The journal emerged out of Fraser's realization that "more registers and more vernaculars" were still required for women's voices following the Assembling Alternatives conference in New Hampshire (1996).[47] Her reflections finally took shape through an ongoing e-mail discussion between herself and Kathleen Crown. Through Crown's initial groundwork and the support of many others, Rutgers University agreed to develop and maintain a web archive of the original *HOW(ever)*

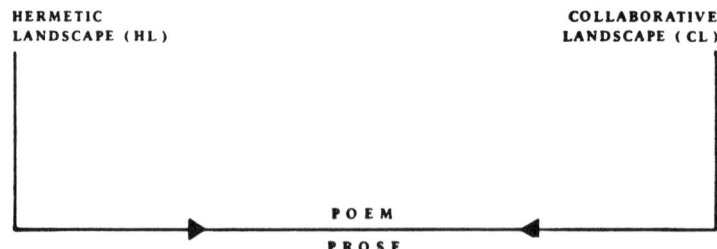

Fig. 5. Kathleen Fraser, Untitled graphic, *HOW(ever)* 3.1 (January 1986).

volumes. Cynthia Hogue then helped to persuade Bucknell University to house *HOW2*. The willingness of two prestigious universities to accommodate *HOW2* is a strong sign of how the relationship between the academy and innovative women's writing has changed since the first issue of *HOW(ever)*.

Like *HOW(ever)*, *HOW2* is in a form that challenges the current print culture. As an electronic journal, it invites multiple, nonlinear reading strategies. There is also greater accessibility, as readers from around the Western world can return again and again to old and current issues (the web site has links to both a *HOW(ever)* archive and the *HOW2* archive). Because of this broader audience, *HOW2* has an advisory editorial board with members from Australia, Canada, New Zealand, Germany, and the United Kingdom. This, in turn, promises a greater range of innovative poetries and concerns being debated on the *HOW2* site. So far, there have been forums on the issue of class, and why nontraditional women's writing may still need a separate critical and creative space.

At the same time, *HOW2* maintains many familiar sections from *HOW(ever)*, including alerts, the postcards, and the readings. These sections are still recognized as fulfilling a valuable function in sharing information between readers and providing a commentary of poetic texts and events (perhaps even more vital in a globalized context). While many of the original readers and contributors to *HOW(ever)* are now becoming involved with *HOW2*, younger writers and critics also inform the journal's concerns. As its title suggests, the journal is—like the DIY feminism of the nineties—still challenging gender structures, not least being its use of what is still often viewed as a masculine technology (the Internet), to its own advantage.

CHAPTER SEVEN

Models, Manifestoes, and Morphogenesis: The Role of Theory

Glas: "One has to understand that
he is not *himself* before being

Medusa to himself . . . To be oneself
is to-be-Medusa'd . . . Dead sure of self . . .

Self's dead sure biting (death)." Whatever
this might mean, and it's possibly

aggrandizing post-feminist, man swallowing woman, nevertheless
in its complication of identity it

seems a step towards a more
communal and critical reading and writing

and thus useful.
　　　　　　　　　—Bob Perelman, "The Marginalization of Poetry"

I n his collapsing of poetic language and critique, Perelman foregrounds the monstrous role of the feminine in the theoretical tradition. From Aristotle onward, woman has been the first Other of the genres of "man" "en route to becoming a monster."[1] The law of genre is simultaneously gendered, as Derrida points out: "[Once] genre announces itself, one must respect a norm, one must not cross a line of demarcation, one must not risk impurity, anomaly, or monstrosity."[2] For woman to be theorist was to negate the maternal feminine, as well as to cross unnaturally between object and subject. For a male poet to engage in theory is to likewise occupy this Medusa-like position. Yet in doing so, Perelman leaves the female critic—where? What sort of role did theory play in the practice and reception of Language writing? Was it associated with particular positions of authority within poetic communities, and what was its impact on the formation of individual literary reputations?

Traditionally, women's discourse has been seen to equal description, whereas the work of theory is authored by men. A significant aspect in the masculinization of Language writing's literary history is the construction of theory as a base for authority through which the writer may then speak for others. As Ann Lauterbach reflects, while male Language writers are remembered as "theoretical architects," the women are seen either as exemplary practitioners or "sort of live-in girlfriends."[3] Mary Margaret Sloan believes that limitation of time may have been a contributing factor "to why women innovative writers have not produced as much theoretical writing as their male colleagues." Sloan argues that, for many, it is hard enough to find time to write the poetry, let alone write *about* the poetry. Aside from participating in the community infrastructure of readings, corresponding, editing, and publishing, many have family and work responsibilities. "And since theoretical writing often frames the issues which define canonical choice," she points out, "this economic/time limitation that some women face may still be a determinant in their permanent presence in—or absence from—the canon."[4] Only recently has the theoretical work of women writers exacted academic recognition comparable to that of male writers during the eighties and early nineties. Aside from the willingness of University of California Press, University of Alabama Press, and Wesleyan University Press to publish the critical work of poets like Lyn Hejinian, Joan Retallack, Kathleen Fraser, Susan Howe, and Leslie Scalapino, Susan Howe was part of the Modern Language Association's presidential forum in 1997. Yet, as Sloan cautions, women may have appeared in the canon, "but it's not clear yet to what extent we're staying."[5]

The struggle over the nature and value of theory is another example of the complex process of gendering within Language writing, not only in terms of a group definition but also between a collective and the individual. Traditionally, poetry has been "the bride of what thinking," that is, the figure of the lover or the feminine absolute in the intellectual community.[6] Absorptive and all-consuming, it *invites* criticism but is never fully knowable. It embellishes and escapes the paths of reason. Theory, on the other hand, is a "pure and simple metalanguage."[7] The tradition of modernity that many Language writers felt they were coming out of was one, however, in which the theoretical was in close conceptual tension to the poetry. Writers like Laura Riding critiqued poetry's "truth" to the degree of outright disavowal, while both Louis Zukofsky and Gertrude Stein produced poetics that would challenge its foundations.

The collapsing of the poetic and the theoretical is showcased in two early collections of writing: *The L=A=N=G=U=A=G=E Book* (1984), which reproduced pieces from various issues of *L=A=N=G=U=A=G=E*, and *Code of Signals*, edited by Michael Palmer (1983). While these volumes celebrated the genre crossings that occurred in the seventies and early eighties, a shift began occurring in the eighties toward more conservative forms of theoretical writing. The shift itself may be seen in the difference between *L=A=N=G=U=A=G=E* and *Poetics Journal* (which started in the early eighties and was edited by Lyn Hejinian and Barrett Watten). In publishing articles in a recognizably academic form, *Poetics Journal* may be read as an attempt to bridge the gap between the poetic sphere and the university. The mid-eighties also saw a proliferation of collected criticism, including Charles Bernstein's *Content's Dream: Essays 1975–1984* (1986), Ron Silliman's *The New Sentence* (1987), Barrett Watten's *Total Syntax* (1985), Steve McCaffery's *North of Intention: Critical Writings 1973–1986* (1986), and Alan Davies's *Signage* (1987).[8] While some of the essays offered in these books were playfully experimental, many were framed through an academic argument, complete with footnotes and references to past avant-garde traditions. In taking up a more authoritative mode of discourse, they could not help but reproduce its implicit structures of power. It has largely been these collections that have been taken as the doxa or underlying logic informing the politics of Language writing.

Reproduced in literary histories of the poetic community, they have often been viewed as more representative than the less assimilable poetic criticism. Bob Perelman, for instance, argues in *The Marginalization of Poetry* that, "[a]long with Andrews, McCaffery, Silliman, and Watten, [Bernstein] has been one of the leading theorists of the group."[9] Joan Retallack went so far as to suggest that, in its early days, the "official permission slip" for identification under the sign of "Language poetry" was a contribution to the debates surrounding language, thought, and reality begun by philosophical progenitors such as Marx, Wittgenstein, and Derrida.[10] In being seen to *not* write theory, women writers were perceived as leaving the significant work of defining Language writing to the men and, as such, taking a secondary role.

Writing to Erica Hunt, Hejinian noted that *Poetics Journal* gave her the opportunity to do some "scholarship." More specifically, it offered an indirect means by which she could overcome a "sense of ineptness in writing criticism and theory."[11] In their correspondence, Hejinian and Susan Howe discussed the pressures and difficulties surrounding the critical act. Although Hejinian considered writing an article about Howe's work, she was fearful of stating the obvious and thought that her own perceptions would be of slight interest. In laboring through numerous drafts of *My Emily Dickinson*, Howe shared similar anxieties. However, both recognized the value of producing feminist criticism, particularly as a means to redress the often narrow theoretical approaches to poetry. While Hejinian had avoided feeling inadequate by simply not writing criticism, she increasingly saw it as "part of the general literary responsibility."[12]

Kathleen Fraser also saw the writing of theory as *crucial* to canonical survival. In a letter to Carla Harryman in 1982, she argued that the "high-powered" role and resultant "pressure" of theoretical writing "has come largely out of male experience."[13] Fraser contrasted this sort of theory with the writing that was "coming from a group of women in their 30s and 40s who are trained academic theoreticians but deeply feminist (& usually Marxist) in their politics." She adds, "We share, in our deepest fiber, recognition of what it has been to fight for a legitimate existence as thinking, writing women in this culture."[14]

For Fraser, the writing of theory was inextricably linked to the relationship between visibility and power—the greater the visibility, the more enhanced the political power. In the margins of the same letter, she noted:

On the other hand, you and Lyn never wrote much theory and unfortunately it is those who write the theory that command . . . more of the attention. It's not that . . . the poem and prose works by any of you are of lesser value or importance. But when you . . . see who finally . . . puts their imprint upon a movement or its reception, it is most often the writers of theory. And that's why women have to be willing to do it more—you and Lyn doing your [publishing] is one good assertion of choices.[15]

To some extent, Fraser is absolutely right. An example is perhaps illuminating. In *The American Poetry Wax Museum: Reality Effects, 1940–1990* (1996), Jed Rasula's representation of Language writing is dominated by male poets. Arguing that a schism generally existed between the poetry and the poetics, he lists a page of theoretical works without mentioning a single woman. Furthermore, these critical works are seen to be *prescriptive* of the poetry produced.[16] It is only through a critique of Eliot Weinberger's anthology, *American Poetry Since 1950: Innovators and Outsiders*, that he raises the question of gender imbalance. Rasula points out that although many innovative women writers fitted Weinberger's editing prerequisites, they were simply elided in the actual selection process.

In a corrective gesture to Weinberger, Rasula lists the women writers, piling them together into a single footnote with seemingly little awareness of self-recrimination.[17] Leslie Scalapino is the one woman whom he does mention in light of theory. She is viewed as one of the exceptions to the "separate theory" rule in Language writing, in that she actively collapses theory and practice in the one text. Yet, once again, Rasula relegates her book, *How Phenomena Appear to Unfold*, to a title listing within a footnote, preferring instead to focus on Barrett Watten's *Conduit* and Alan Davies's *Candor* in the main body of his argument.[18] In such an instance, women writers are performatively marginalized, literally sentenced to the margins in the body of criticism.

One reason for the increasing acceptance of Language writing within the academy is undoubtedly its relation to theory and the inflation of theory's value in general. Language writing has addressed its form through a mode of self-reflexive criticism. Like theory, it requires the reader to fill in textual specifics and to give embodiment to abstract meaning. An example of how Language writing has grown in stature through its engagement with theory is the double issue on poetry of *Diacritics*, a high-profile scholarly journal "concerned primarily with the problems of criticism." The first volume of *Diacritics* to feature poetry in many years, the 1996 issue featured a host of writers and critics predominantly associated with Language writing. To many, such a critical event signals Language writing's coming of age in the academy. For the past decade, Language writing has also been a frequent topic of scholarly journals, conferences, and course syllabi.[19] This is not to suggest that pedagogic attention to a few high-profile poets such as Jorie Graham or James Merrill is waning but that Language writing is slowly gaining space as a subgenre somewhere between poetry and theory.

With the academy showing a growing tendency toward economic rationalism and its attendant emphasis on constant publishing and renewal, there has been a heightening of the debate and stakes involved in writing that is perceived as theoretical. According to John Guillory, the theory-canon has been fortified by the emergence of charismatic "master thinkers."[20] To be able to recall and apply the work of such theorists guarantees symbolic capital. In "The Race for Theory," Barbara Christian critiqued this fetishization, suggesting that it distances the critical work being done by those more marginal to the institution, such as women and ethnic minorities.[21] In its awareness of theory, Language writing offers a "hard" alternative within the relatively "soft" area of poetry.

William Lavender has recently argued that the theory generated by Language writers was central to their projects because they were marketed to the same audience and circulated in the same way as the poetry.[22] This audience, he suggests, became increasingly academic in orientation.[23] The appetite for theory that the academy engenders is sharply satirized in Harryman's "There Is Nothing Better Than a Theory." First given as a dramatic reading by the Poets' Theater in April 1984, it may be seen partly as a deferred response to Fraser's letter (although not specifically intended as such) but more generally a critique of what could be called a theory explosion.[24]

A book of manners for imitators
Might sell like hotcakes
To twins
If we could only write our theory down
Oh, theory
Yes
There is nothing better
Than a theory
But confess
What?
You know . . .
We will eat anything
Anything?
The book, the idea
Or the product . . .

Airing in the sun
For the sake of a technique
We couldn't master
For we were enjoying ourselves
While the technique was enjoying us
But could not master our enjoyment . . .[25]

Here, Harryman suggests that theory is generated for easy and quick consumption, a fast-food resolution for the desires of an audience hungry for control and expediency. What is left out are elements of pleasure, humor, and play, which defy pedagogic containment. For Harryman, the immediacy and uniqueness of performance resists the continuity demanded of much theoretical interpretation.

In "The Gender of Theory," Catherine Lutz maintains, "Theory has acquired a gender insofar as it is more frequently associated with male writing, with women's writing more often seen as description, data, case, personal, or, as in the case of feminism, 'merely' setting the record straight."[26] In making such an assertion, Lutz may at first seem to join the ranks of feminists like Elaine Showalter, whose suspicion of what she terms "male theory" is outlined in "Feminist Criticism in the Wilderness."[27] While Showalter investigates the Other of theory, Lutz is more concerned with *how* the theoretical value of a text is determined. She believes that part of the problem is with the very definition of theory. "Something called 'theory,'" Lutz states, "is intentionally or unintentionally signaled to and consciously or unconsciously picked up by readers *as* theory."[28] This "something" is not in itself inherently gendered. Yet it is clear that there is a pattern by which writing by women is generally perceived as less theoretical and thus of lesser value as intellectual knowledge.

One of the more obvious ways in which texts are recognized as theoretical is through self-categorization, such as Pierre Bourdieu's *Outline of a*

Theory of Practice. This theoretical marker may also be imposed on the work by others. An example of this was the publication of an article collectively written by Steve Benson, Carla Harryman, Lyn Hejinian, Bob Perelman, Ron Silliman, and Barrett Watten, which appeared in *Social Text* with the phrase "A Manifesto" attached to the title.[29] The six writers were hoping to show the very impossibility of theorizing their practice in such a manner in arguing the case for a "contaminated" poetics, a poetics where poetry was indistinguishable from theory. By adding the phrase "A Manifesto," the editors of *Social Text* drastically misread the actual argument of the paper, translating it instead into an agenda made familiar by past literary movements. This desire to read works for an overriding or explanatory theory may be seen as a kind of critical "frame lock."

Lutz suggests a second signal is one that "allows readers to imagine that the writing describes a wide variety of instances rather than a single case." In this respect, the critical work of many male Language writers has represented itself as inclusive or indicative of a broader phenomenon. Ron Silliman, for instance, defined New Sentence writing as a West Coast form, adding:

While, in general, the new sentence has not been nearly as visible on the East Coast as it has in the west, something much like or tending towards it can be found in the writings of several poets, including Peter Seaton, Bruce Andrews, Diane Ward, Bernadette Mayer (especially in her early books), James Sherry, Lynne Dreyer, Alan Davies, Charles Bernstein and Clark Coolidge.[30]

Silliman therefore purports to map a contemporary tendency that not only covers numerous writers but more than one poetic community.

Responding to a draft version, Bernstein took issue with Silliman's contention that the New Sentence was the first significant challenge to literary convention by Language writing.[31] He also criticized the New Sentence's implicit construction of a united definable practice:

[T]he way it comes off it tends to profile regional divisiveness & to suggest some universalizable Idea underlying this work rather than a series of overlapping practices with no common center but with things in common to one another and the other to a third & so on Venn Diagram style—what Wittgenstein calls family resemblances.[32]

Lutz argues that theory is "seen as consisting of more rather than less abstract statements, widely relevant or universalistic or 'deeper' statements of more ultimate or timeless value than others."[33] Drawn from the world, theory is not touched by the world. It is given social license akin to the power of poetic license. This quality enhances the authority of the writer, so that the perception of authority is enhanced in proportion to the distance with which the speaker appears in relation to his or her subject matter. As Bob Perelman points out, Silliman's proposal of the New Sentence was framed as a canonical injunction, with its emphasis on the "new" suggesting an alternative form to traditional structures of narrative.[34]

Similarly, in *Total Syntax*, Barrett Watten mobilized the term *total* to align his work alongside the order of "high theory" or "grand theory." Watten noted that the small communities of Language writing were alone in redressing the role of the contemporary intellectual. In filling this gap, the question of theory became "immediately relevant in that it leads to the absence of social equivalents for the 'collective state of mind' that is literature at present."[35] Watten then declared even more broadly that the result of Language writing's resistance to current critical practices "is a new order of thought."[36] In making such a claim, he unintentionally echoes Silliman's New Sentence.

In contrast, the titles of McCaffery's *North of Intention* and Bernstein's *Content's Dream* suggest a desire to remain off-center as well as to maintain a lack of definition. Yet even the sweeping generality of these titles may be contrasted to the specificity of Susan Howe's *My Emily Dickinson*, which not only reads the American poetic tradition through a single writer but emphasizes the positionality and affective investments of the author.[37] Such an example strengthens Joan Retallack's argument that in much innovative writing by women, "there is the warmth of the personal in language; but the privilege, placement, status, and access of the egocentric authoritative voice is entirely absent."[38]

Following Trinh Minh-ha's observations in *Woman, Native, Other: Writing Postcoloniality and Feminism*, the use of academic jargon will provide further signals of the work as theory.[39] Again, the use of critical terminology is heavily evident throughout the critical work of many male Language writers. Of course, there are exceptions such as Charles Bernstein. Using everyday phrases like "Here's the thing," Bernstein presents his ideas more as conversation starters than as masterful narratives. He often digresses from, interrupts, or reflects on his own statements. In "Optimism and Critical Excess," for instance, he reaches a point of comedic self-deflation: "Yet this approach enabled me, empowered me I think is the term often used now . . . I mean what would it be like to empower white, male heterosexuals? It's a curiously warped notion."[40]

Bernstein argues that "[p]oetics is all about changing the current poetic course. Putting on a dress, not strapping yourself into a uniform."[41] Rosmarie Waldrop also states, "I don't want to write 'about' any issues, not even feminist ones. I prefer exploring the forest to hewing the road, even if the road is in a good direction."[42] In using a philosophical form such as the Wittgensteinian proposition, she sought in *The Reproduction of Profiles* "to subvert its closure and logic from the inside, by constantly sliding between frames of reference." She continues, "I especially brought the female body in and set into play the old gender archetypes of logic and mind being 'male,' whereas 'female' designates the illogical: emotion, body, matter."[43] She hoped that the constant sliding would challenge these categories.

The difficulty of theory is, to some degree, ideological. Following Bourdieu, theory may be seen as a demarcating factor in sorting readers into those who have been encouraged in the culture of knowledge from which it arose and those who have not. It becomes a differential of power relations and is generally gendered and racially disparate.[44] As a value, difficulty itself remains gendered. Susan Howe, for instance, wrote to Hejinian: "I have come to dread that word 'difficult.' Its [*sic*] all right for Language Poets such as Watten, Silliman, Bernstein, and all to be 'difficult' but with me it means dismissal as I have found so far."[45] Again, difficulty is associated with the original or new for male writers, but with women writers it is seen as being obtuse or confusing. In another example, Leslie Scalapino discovered that a letter she wrote was refused publication by *Socialist Review* on the grounds that the use of language was "too poetic and did not qualify as political discourse." Scalapino felt that the incident brought home the fact that she "must speak a language recognized as discourse before it can be regarded as public and as germane."[46]

Catherine Lutz notes that, positively framed, "theory's abstractness requires or creates a more active reader. Like poetry, it allows for imagination." Yet "[s]tated more negatively, theoretical writing is like a capitalist enterprise: it exploits or appropriates the labor of readers. . . . A reader may often imagine that the writer has written or said or implied all of the ideas that her or his reading has actually provided."[47] Bernstein also confirms this anecdotally: "Recently, a scholarly poet friend was telling me that he thought he would have to undertake two years of background reading in philosophy and literary theory and linguistics to find out what $L=A=N=G=U=A=G=E$ was all about." He argues that, had his friend done so, "he would have read far more comprehensively in [the] area than most of the poets published in $L=A=N=G=U=A=G=E$."[48] Like the worker who does not recognize the source of the commodity's value, the reader fetishizes the theoretical product.

Certain styles of citation will also signal a work as theory. "Theorists cite other theorists," Lutz discerns, "and appear to tend to cite more deeply into the academic past and to cite even more males than does the average piece of academic writing."[49] Certainly, Silliman's essay "The New Sentence" claimed more than its fair share of theoretical alliances. The context he constructed for the proposed New Sentence included, among others, Ivic's *Trends in Linguistics*, Saussure's *Course in General Linguistics*, Hjelmslev's *Prolegomena to a Theory of Language*, Chomsky's *Aspects of the Theory of Syntax*, Volosinov's *Marxism and the Philosophy of Language*, Wellek and Warren's *Theory of Literature*, Todorov's *The Poetics of Prose*, and Macherey's *Theory of Literary Production*. Watten also relied heavily on the citation of a critical tradition that included Russian Formalism, Surrealism, and Charles Olson.

Citation, then, has to do with paternal anxiety and with control. It is a means to guide the reader away from errancy and back into the fold. Clark Coolidge noted that "[s]ome [Language poets] write a great deal of method essays, theory, which isn't native to my procedure. I'm thinking here of Barry Watten and Ron Silliman in particular. I find their emphasis on the word fascinating, though I sometimes feel that they want to describe a poetry almost before it exists."[50] Anxious at being manipulated by signs, Watten and Silliman were determined to reinforce their role as the operators of signs. Watten's anxiety over control was symptomatically revealed in allegorical narratives of linguistic, Oedipal contestation. Language became a tool through which past paternalisms may be defeated: "As in losing one's virginity, once one sees the world from the standpoint of language there's no going back. Realism becomes the father waiting up late to no avail—'It's already happened, Dad.'"[51]

While discursive anxiety may be just as visible in the work of women writers, the response is more likely to be grounded in a politics of location. Certainly writers like Susan Howe were as much concerned with canonical position taking as either Silliman or Watten, yet her work was generally at the level of the particular rather than the universal. Andrew Levy has pointed out that the series of talks on politics and poetry that Bernstein curated in 1988 reveal a gendered difference in the relation between politics and form. He suggests that only Hunt, Howe, and, to some extent, Rosmarie Waldrop (having missed Nicole Brossard's talk) "clearly challenge the inability to think a materialist politics without the rather hackneyed notion of the liberatory 'free play of the signifier' and the always consequent claim that the revolution at the level of the signifier is on hand." Levy argues that the women writers contextualized their innovations through a specificity that challenged prior modes of thought and their relation to material structures. He further suggests that writing like Leslie Scalapino's continues to be treated with critical intolerance because it eludes capturing ideas and instead presents writing as other to the "tactics of power."[52]

Although the theoretical efforts of women poets have been elided in the majority of literary histories, women are viewed by some as having produced the most adventurous critical work associated with Language writing. In a 1996 interview, Robert Creeley notes that, despite the inability of writers to respond to the "awful . . . consternations of the literal world," a "cluster of women" are engaging in "intellectual explorations [that] are vivid and terrific." Of these, he mentions Susan Howe, Rosmarie Waldrop, and Leslie Scalapino. What Creeley finds most exciting is the poetic work, which is, in itself, self-reflective or theoretical. Many women poets associated with Language writing have rejected the theoretical model of a text that is transcendent to other texts. Furthermore, they continue to explore forms that have transgressed genre boundaries, often working somewhere between the theoretical and the poetic or the critical and the personal.[53] However, this is not to say that their writing does not register a range of formality or that such explorations are limited to the work of women.[54]

While Bernstein, McCaffery, and Perelman have all written recognizable theory in the form of poetry ("Artifice of Absorption," "Lyric's Larynx," and "The Marginalization of Poetry," respectively), works such as *My Emily Dickinson*, Carla Harryman's *There Never Was a Rose without a Thorn*, Joan Retallack's *The Poethical Wager*, and Leslie Scalapino's *How Phenomena Appear to Unfold*, have challenged poetically the boundaries of the essay. In her preface to *There Never Was a Rose without a Thorn*, Harryman describes her cross-genre poetics:

These hybrid writings, staged as they are between fiction and theory, the domestic and history, abstractions and androgyny, the rational and the nonrational, the creator and her artifact, organize themselves against normative ideas while using whatever tools of novelistic, philosophic, autobiographical, or poetic discourses present themselves to advance these tellings. . . . The writing is also a response to literature and things of the world: it does not separate one from the other. . . . Complex ideas and simple rhetorics mingle, yielding impure theories, precarious stories, and fabulist games.[55]

Harryman's work, along with Howe's, Retallack's, and Scalapino's, may be viewed through what Bernstein terms an "*applied* poetic." Yet, shifting to a focus that looks at the form rather than an application of a rule, such work is more effectively spoken of in terms of "*differentiated* essays or statements." The function of such pieces is generally feminist in that they conceptualize theory out of the lens of gender, often celebrating sexual difference. Rather than being removed from a discursive real, the theory emerges out of and in response to a historic materiality. As there are multiple versions of feminism, so there may be multiple functions. Differentiated writing does not so much seek to posit a new form as to transform or reenergize an old one. They are morphogenetic, or "shape-generating." As Abigail Child suggests, morphogenesis is a process or "active theory."[56]

According to Teresa de Lauretis, "Strategies of writing and reading are forms of cultural resistance. Not only can they work to turn dominant discourses inside out (and show that it can be done) . . . they also challenge theory in its own terms, the terms of a semiotic space constructed in language, its power based on social validation and well-established modes of enunciation and address."

As Rachel Blau DuPlessis points out in her important work on the essay ("f-Words: An Essay on the Essay"), innovative women's writing is less likely to be recognized as *theory* because the theory runs through and informs at the level of form.[57] None of the typical signs are present. As such, this theoretical double-take is often misread or viewed as revealing a lack of skill or mastery. Also, its use of iteration is interpreted as blank or poor imitation. Carla Harryman, for instance, opened *Vice* with a quotation from Derrida:

> Genres are not to be mixed.
> I will not mix genres.
> I repeat: genres are not to be mixed.
> I will not mix them.[58]

David Lehmann's review of Harryman's work isolates this passage from any context, viewing it as a form of straight dictation. In doing so, he misses the irony with which Harryman actually uses the quotation, especially when the term *genre* is played out in other citations with its etymological slippage, *gender*. Harryman becomes an easy target, not only the representative scapegoat of Language writing but "a critical cartoon"—as feminist work tends sometimes to be considered.[59] Lehmann argues: "[T]hese poets have a distinct predilection for fancy theorizing: so-and-so is said to have 'subverted patriarchal assumptions' or maybe 'deconstructed the Romantic image' in a poem consisting exclusively of the word *tampon* repeated twelve times in a vertical column."[60] Lehmann's joke relies on the absurdity of such an exercise in sexual politics. As an alternative, he cites Bob Perelman's "Movie." Overlooking Perelman's carefully integrated critique of Reagan's militarism, media, and masculine presence, Lehmann judges Perelman "a master of comic invention."[61] Poetry, he seems to suggest, should keep to its proper place of amusement and fancy and away from mixing the poetic with the political or the theoretical.

In 1990 the Canadian journal *Raddle Moon* published a series of conversations between women writers in a forum entitled "Women/Writing/Theory." Johanna Drucker initiated this more formal space for debate. By doing so, she hoped to "promote exchange, foster discovery, find a network of women involved in pursuit of their own metalanguage."[62] In other words, she wanted to encourage a community of women that would investigate the theory question in a collaborative and coherent frame of production. Drucker sketched out a number of questions that mapped the territory of interest:

How would you theorize . . . your work? How does your writing already articulate a theoretical position? What attitude do you have toward theoretical and critical writing? Do you find conventions of critical/theoretical writing inherently masculinist, or masculinist by association? What is the relation you posit between your gender and your writing practice? What is the relation between your gender and your attitude toward, or use of, or resistance to theory and/or theorizing?[63]

As Susan Clark recalls, the dialogue not only generated an overwhelming "bulk of exchange" but in its multiple forms of correspondence produced a "recordless" paratext. The limit of the written was thus foregrounded and put at issue against "talk" and other mediums. Clark suggests that the published effects of the first misrepresents this "invaluable, intertextual, supratextual 'mess.'"[64] One issue later, the "mess" became more apparent as disagreement and individual anxieties emerged and work was withheld. These effects were symptomatic of the ambivalence about not only the relation between knowledge and gender but also about the idea of a feminist theoretical community.

Drucker believed that those who perceived theory as outside or other to their own writing articulate a sense of powerlessness as well as defensiveness in terms of their own authority. Those who were more involved in theoretical work—being affiliated to an academic institution, for instance—tend to "*assume* an authority in their writing, even in its thematics, which is markedly different."[65] She further pointed out that, although academic feminists have an investment in the discourse of theory, its jargon continues to alienate them. Viewed as an instrument through which an interpretative community could reproduce and maintain its authority, the role of critical vocabulary remains problematic. Drucker adds: "How to learn to speak theory in the vernacular? This, indeed, may be the real challenge, and the only means to dissolve the (to my mind) destructive and useless opposition to theory from within a community which I think has only to gain by feeling that the authority of the writer's voice is her own."[66]

The debate over critical vocabulary and its difficulty had previously been raised in forums such as the Canadian feminist journal *Tessera*, in which an editor stated: "Academic discourse is discouraged."[67] Janice Williamson notes that "accessibility" is as ideologically loaded a term as "difficulty" and requires address. She responded to a similar editorial statement in the feminist broadsheet *(f.)Lip* by asking: "Will you edit out words [in my paper] like 'overdetermination' which are not 'acessible' to my interested mother who would perhaps be moved to look it up in a reference book? Isn't that part of what feminist 'innovative' writing should do? Propel readers to exceed themselves."[68] As Williamson makes clear, the problem is not with the critical vocabulary itself but with how it is taken up and used in particular situations.

Drucker herself suggested that it is limiting to demarcate women's theoretical writing through a particular stylistics that demands writing always be "diffuse," "plural," and "polysemous."[69] Such divisions between male and female theory merely perpetuate the current tradition of the feminine as irrational and illogical, and the masculine as rational and definitive. Chris Tysh also believed that this form of essentialism fantasizes a dangerous version of pluralism: "[It] designs a panel, say, a hunting scene where the master on horseback gallops in a correctly gendered fashion while we, fluid bodies, are crossed, bridged or evaporated according to the weather, tearing hounds on the moor."[70] Rather than an instrument of imposition, theory becomes a means by which such gender constraints may be questioned. Theory by women, Drucker argued, should not be "deferential, lady-like, and polite" but a mode of assertion.[71]

Moreover, it enabled her to interrogate the otherwise invisible relations of power that writing can reproduce:

What has become absolutely clear over time is that the possession of a metalanguage of theory is an essential aspect of claiming a place from which to write. Theory, for me, is the perspectivizing tool, that which permits the two-dimensional plane of the page to be located in the multiple dimensions of the world, of the discourses of power and politics. If I cannot articulate my own position, it will be spoken for me, and I will be, as women have been, an object, not a subject, of language.[72]

Framed as an objective overview, Drucker's response to the forum was itself a model of the scholarly essay. While many of the other participants quoted one another, whether formally or informally, Drucker's arguments were decontextualized. In terms of strategy, it was a far stretch from her own innovative writing.[73] Jean Day viewed Drucker's statement as "troubling" in the way that it reflected and maintained the privileged position of academic discourse in shaping theory. Day herself wanted to expand the intellectual field: "There are no right ideas, only situations. The writing that means most to me is situational, speculative, wants to know what it doesn't know already."[74] She suggests that distinctions between academic and lay discourse, between privilege and lack, between articulation and obscurity, are redrawn with every new situation.

Continuing over two issues of *Raddle Moon*, Abigail Child's "Active

Theory" provided a vivid contrast to Drucker's statement and response as well as to the essays in Silliman's *The New Sentence* and Watten's *Total Syntax*. In it she moved beyond the traditional essay form by mixing anecdotes, the poetic, and the academic. Child argues that, having taught in universities for the past twelve years, she did not feel the need to reproduce theory according to academic definitions.[75] She had previously used the manifesto form in a piece she wrote for *L=A=N=G=U=A=G=E* on the revolutionary potential of film and language as mediums for critique. In that article, Child contrasted the practice of filmmaking to Language writing, defining the latter as "A COMMUNITY OF SLOGANEERS."[76] In "Active Theory," she ironically and self-consciously takes up this very position as "sloganeer."

Janet Lyon proposes that the manifesto is characterized by an assumption of audience, an audience constituted as "we."[77] The manifesto, then, has a communal morphology. Child herself acknowledges a collective context for her thinking. In the first version of "Active Theory" she named and thanked three other women for a dialogue that occurred outside the particular forum. "Women are always talking theory," Child writes, "only they don't name it as such."[78] With her retrospective meditation and poetic interjections, the dialogue performed Child's "active theory," but its speakers constitute only part of the "we" included in its manifesto—the other part being the prospective reader.

"Active Theory" was the only forum response of *Raddle Moon* to consider the possibility of theorizing beyond language. In addition to Child's interest in film, two of the other women worked as a painter and a sculptor. Unlike a typical manifesto, this dialogue fractures the "we," as the women's conversation reveals disagreements and tangents of concern. Child's work, then, could be said to engender what Rachel Blau DuPlessis calls an "(ambiguously) non-hegemonic" "we."[79] Janet Lyon posits that a multiple "we" is advantageous in foregrounding the speaker as a self-made fiction "superimposed ironically over or against the prior fiction of a textual subject." Rather than circulate one dominant fiction of identity—be it feminism, femininity, or community—an ambiguously nonhegemonic "we" can circulate versions or alternatives. Second, as Lyon remarks, "this unspecified 'we' suggests and affords participation, on the part of its interpellated subject(s) in a provisional community whose power is located in the potentially infinite 'non-I' of the 'we.'"[80] Child's "active theory" becomes

a body of errors

Not words as codes, but words as agents.

Models. Capable of eluding their own vigilance.

AN ANTI-MATTER THEORY
an anti system theory
a system plus error
a theory of what has been erased

use impatience[81]

In her refiguring of the manifesto form, Child suggests that the boundaries between theory and practice, the abstract and the emotional, are highly nebulous. As Lyon contends, "[F]or the manifesto-writer who must create feminist speaking-positions, the production of a manifesto is no mere 'sketch' job: it is a palimpsest's task, a decoding and recoding of inherited discourse, a creation of ironic and transitory political subjecthood."[82] Child's form resembles this tactical morphology, shaping and reshaping to problematize the programmatic. It enacts a politics of struggle outside the binary of theory versus poetry and, in the process, raises such chaotic realities as race, sex, and class.

"Active Theory" may also link up with other manifestoes, such as Tina Darragh's "The Best of Intentions":

Manifesto:	given	public domain
Contents:	intentions	a stretching agent
	opinions	think + to put
	objectives	toward + throw/or/ against + throw/or/ inversely + throw
	motives	serving to move[83]

As with the essay, this revamped form of the manifesto enables a space for alternative articulations. It only remains for such forms to be critically recognized as theoretical interventions so that their radical potential to be realized. Given the current climate, this already seems to be occurring—at least with the essay. It remains to be seen how such recognition will challenge the theoretically narrow versions of Language writing previously produced, as well as what is produced by its writers in the future. Barrett Watten's more recent work, *Bad History* (1998), certainly interrogates the embodied act of criticism as much as it explores a broader cultural politics.[84] While many women writers are now producing collections of essays, it is to be hoped that such work—by its very nature—resists the call for an expedient illumination of their author's poetry, encouraging instead new ways in which poetry will be identified, read, and valued.

CHAPTER EIGHT

"I Hate Speech": Gendering Poetic Talk

It is not surprising that

It is not surprising, that.

where in the placement of
saffron this is simple "you"
are listening "I" am alert
enough "she" is learning how to
talk "we" are reconstituted.
—Rachel Blau DuPlessis,
"Draft #1: It"

Talk is perhaps the most primary form of community, being at once commerce, intercourse, society, and intimacy. Poetry readings have provided an integral part of the contemporary feminist movement, bringing together women and energizing others.[1] For Language writing, readings and talks fostered local group formations as well as larger constellations. As Charles Bernstein suggests, they provided a forum for poets "not only to read their new work but also to meet with each other and exchange ideas."[2] They also established an important space in which young and unpublished writers could gain access to a public.

New York readings in the late fifties and throughout the sixties saw groups of poets reading in each other's houses and in bookstores, galleries, and cafes.[3] However, in being accommodated at such venues, they tended to operate sporadically. These provisional occurrences, along with the occasional academic gathering, scarcely gave enough space and time to foster and enable a community practice. Anne Waldman felt that poetry required a larger arena.[4] Through a collective effort by herself and—over the years—a great many others, St. Mark's Poetry Project became a regular space for readings and talks. The Poetry Project was directed by several influential female figures, such as Waldman, Maureen Owen, and Bernadette Mayer. This would be reassuring for some women writers who felt that their own work was being taken seriously for the first time. Later, Charles

Bernstein and Ted Greenwald began the Ear Inn reading series (1978), and in the early eighties, Abigail Child curated Image Talks, a cross-disciplinary series of talks about film, poetry, and performance.

In Washington there was the Mass Transit reading series in the early seventies, followed by the Folio reading series. Begun by Barrett Watten in 1976 and later managed by writers like Rae Armantrout, Steve Benson, and Carla Harryman, the Grand Piano series offered a similar venue for writers in the Bay Area. In 1977, Bob Perelman also began a series of talks in his Folsom Street loft, which would continue for the next five years. Both of these series offered an alternative to the Poetry Center, which featured readings and talks by innovative writers like Rachel Blau DuPlessis, Kit Robinson, and Jerome Rothenberg but also by more mainstream poets like Sharon Olds, C. K. Williams, Jorie Graham, and Charles Wright.

The division between poetic experimentation and more traditional styles was reinforced by poets like Robert Hass, who joked to a large crowd at the Center that his bucolic poem, "Blackberries," ended with three lines of "language poetry": "'blackberries,'/'blackberries'/'blackberries.'" Recording the event but escaping unrecognized, Carla Harryman remembers the large and appreciative audience applauding wildly, cheering and whistling.[5] It brought home to her how powerfully the political force of a text could change through its rendition and how a reading charges the text with further investments in self and community.

As Erving Goffman suggests, public talks are simultaneously an occasion for performance, exegesis, and a social event.[6] The content of the speaker's text is only one dimension among others, including the cultural position of the speaker, the mode of delivery, and the constitution of the audience. "Who is speaking to whom," as Linda Alcoff discerns, "turns out to be as important for meaning and truth as what is said; in fact, what is said turns out to change according to who is speaking and who is listening." Alcoff uses the term "rituals of speaking" to identify "discursive practices of speaking or writing that involve not only the text or utterance but their position within a social space that includes the persons involved in, acting upon, and/or affected by the words."[7] As a Poetry Center employee merely taping the proceedings, Harryman was not part of the presumed audience. If she had been Barrett Watten or Ron Silliman or Kit Robinson, she may have been recognized.[8] Such recognition would very likely have changed the dynamics of Hass's joke.

Attached to San Francisco State University, the Poetry Center obviously engendered a different audience and rituals of reading to the communally run spaces of the Grand Piano and Folsom Street. Less institutional, these latter reading series could afford to feature less well-known writers and to test the boundaries of the reading itself. At the Grand Piano, for instance, a performance of Zukofsky's "A 24" involved numerous local writers: Barrett Watten was Poetry; Kit Robinson was Thought; Steve Benson and Carla Harryman were Drama; Lyn Hejinian was Story, while Bob Perelman played the piano. The series would eventually end as audiences grew to an uncontrollable number. At the final performance of Frank O'Hara's "Try! Try!" (with parts played by Benson, Harryman, and Nick Robinson), people filled the coffee shop and overflowed onto the street. This performance was the precursor of Poet's Theater, which began soon after at a space called Project Artaud.

Perelman, too, would start the Folsom Street talks with the desire to encourage a lively interchange of poetics. Breaking away from the structure of journals, which defines the role of reader and writer in terms of private and public, anyone could participate. He points out that "in all cases the talk was not for talk's sake, but for the sake of writing."[9] Richard Rorty uses a similar model of "conversation" or talk as a model of cultural practice and social change."[10]

Many of these talks were fruitful in interrogating the communal nature of poetic knowledge. In "Walking Back through *The Maintains*," Carla Harryman explored the relationship between the work of others and her own drive to write. Invoking Kierkegaard's analogy between walking and thought, she staged the conceptual limits of *The Maintains*, then still a relatively new text by Clark Coolidge that Harryman believed would radically transform the field of poetry. The performance distanced itself from what she saw as the normative but retrogressive reading of poetry, where the reading follows an interpretation built around continuity and codification. In its place, she offered a creative reading that encouraged a different way of thinking about the poetic act. In Brechtian fashion, Harryman focused attention back on convention—or what has become invisible—by giving individuals domestic tasks to perform throughout the event. While she read from Coolidge's text as an androgynous and still figure (the author as central but unknowable), the surrounding activity satirized her own authority as the "influenced' writer. Influence, she suggests, is traditionally assumed to be unoriginal, passive, and ultimately feminized. In her reading of Coolidge's poem, Harryman induces the audience to consider alternative characterizations for someone who writes out of other's texts.

Harryman's performance foregrounds the inequality of positions that can structure poetic exchange. Even in a space that is other to more established or mainstream readings, not all are in a position to participate as equals in conversation. According to Nancy Harstock, those who are more marginal than others will fail to be overheard if more pragmatic issues of access and standing are not addressed.[11] As "Walking Back through *The Maintains*" illustrates, the Folsom Street talks were often as much group performance pieces as presentations by an individual to a group.[12] While Perelman envisaged an ideal of exchange, the dynamics of power sometimes circumscribed the act of speaking in practice. The constitution of the audience often shaped a talk as much as the identity of the speaker and his or her delivered text. Some talks were interrupted by interjections from the audience; other talks actually referred to members of the audience by name.

Both would prove alienating for those in the audience who remained silent or unidentified.[13] In particular, Perelman recalls David Antin's talk in 1978 in which Antin broke from his usual monologue to address specific individuals from the audience, all male. As one of the first of those invited from out of town, Antin clearly "had the most literary capital" as speaker. "Issues of power and literary genealogy were clearly relevant," Perelman says of the event.[14] Antin had previously given one of his earliest talk poems at the Poetry Center, but Perelman argues that the different venue—80 Langton Street—influenced Antin to change the nature of his talk. It became, in fact, a conversation about the talk form itself and the usefulness or impropriety of audience participation. Antin cited specific individuals as examples, comparing the sentence "I wonder if Ron Silliman will be here tonight?" with "I wonder if there will be a Ron Silliman tonight?" and asking if George Lakoff's new book was about metaphor.[15]

Those who are used to being dominant in group activities are generally more comfortable participating in such open formats. Certainly, Silliman, Lakoff, Tom Mandel, and Bob Perelman all responded to his encouragement, and asked questions or illustrated points "with extended comments."[16] Significantly, they were also seated in the front row. In the discussion following Antin's talk, one man stated how uncomfortable he had been made to feel, particularly as he could not even see any of the people who were in face-to-face conversation with Antin. Finally, Eleanor Antin interrupted her husband and spoke to the audience about the machismo dominating the night: "We're all prisoners of five guys. Is that what these things are? Everybody comes to hear these five guys?"[17]

Perelman believes that the controversy generated by the evening was less about the difference between Antin's oral-based art and Language writing than about gender. Alcoff suggests that "in many situations when a woman speaks the presumption is against her; when a man speaks he is usually taken seriously."[18] The gender of the speaker will influence how an argument or idea is received and certainly the power of its force. In terms of cultural expectations, a female speaker is more vulnerable to criticism in a public forum. Here, however, Eleanor Antin's authority was bolstered through her positioning as Antin's wife.

Most women feel uncomfortable using traditionally "male" registers of public speech, which are often authoritarian in tone and even polemical.[19]

Partly, this is because women have not been able to speak in the first-person, universal voice but also because they are socially conditioned to "wait their turn" in the conversation. Alternatively, men in both single-sex and mixed-sex situations tend to "construe conversation as a competition where the aim is to be the speaker . . . their conversational strategies involve trying to seize a turn whenever possible, and trying to hold onto it."[20] Discourse analysts Candace West and Don Zimmerman repeatedly found that males interrupted more than females and that females were more likely to have verbal deference.[21]

Hejinian would dwell on the dilemma she felt over participating in talks. On the one hand, she saw response as part of the commitment to the poetic community. Writing to Susan Howe, she noted the conflict "between wanting to 'speak my mind' about issues vs. a hesitancy to inflict my attitudes on others." "Is the latter a liberal cop-out?" she wondered, "I find this particularly perplexing in terms of feminist issues—when a woman speaks up, she takes certain risks, socially. So it is doubled as a political issue. Politics vs. politeness."[22] In her landmark study of men and women's communication patterns (*Language and Woman's Place*), Robin Lakoff argues that women's use of language is markedly constrained by expectations of politeness. She further suggests that women are placed in a double bind in relation to such a role.[23]

In spring 1980, Perelman published a volume of the Folsom Street talks in his magazine *Hills*.[24] Perelman states that in putting together the issue he was concerned more with the strength of each presentation in itself than how it would appear as a whole. He believed Hejinian's 1977 talk, "Chronic Ideas," lacked the strength of argument found in her later well-known talk, "The Rejection of Closure."[25] Other talks, like Harryman's, which relied heavily on performance, could not be included. Harryman notes that she did not want to document the event, even on videotape, as it would undermine the power of her text. In performing its own object-status, Harryman's text becomes what she calls "recalcitrant." Because it is unable to be imitated, it cannot be exploited or transgressed.[26]

In a letter to Hejinian, Susan Howe criticized the overwhelmingly gendered map of Language writing that Perelman unwittingly produced: "If you examine that issue . . . [y]ou will see that . . . Fanny is the only woman." She adds:

Hers is like the rest of us—nervous, tenuous, suggestive. No discussion from the men, no feedback. Now examine the other pieces in the book. Men, talking about and to men. Only the occasional tentative question, usually very brief—from a woman usually identified by first and last name—along with all the other unfamiliar men who make tentative additions to the ongoing . . . dialogue.[27]

A month later, Hejinian responded, denying Howe's charge in full: The lack of women in the talks was "as much our fault as the men's." Although Perelman "has tried hard to get any and all of us to give talks," many chose not to speak. Hejinian herself had given two, but "I didn't want them published, as neither stands for all of what I think about the subjects and I didn't really want to rewrite them." "Melissa Riley gave a very good talk, but it wasn't literary," Hejinian continued, "That left Fanny. And I should tell you that when Fanny gave that talk she refused to give it herself . . . claiming that she 'was a terrible reader.' "[28] The problem was "not that the men are ignoring us here—but that women are extremely hesitant to expose their opinions; and that is a problem with roots in the past far more than it is rooted in present conditions."[29]

Somewhat shocked at Hejinian's harshness, Howe replied: "Do you really feel it is the fault of the various women who like Fanny sit down and have [others] read their words . . . or like you—for whatever reason decide your own should not be published, or like me, hide behind fragments of ideas rather than stating them[?]"[30] Although she envied Hejinian's inclusion within a stimulating group of writers, Howe experienced a sense of anger at the inadequate representation of women.

To some degree, this difference of view would be a testing point of their correspondence. Hejinian wrote back quickly to confirm the importance of their exchange: "I want . . . to keep up the dialogue with you—not just about the feminist and/or female issues—at least keep the distance between letters small enough that there [is] a dialogue." In the same letter she admitted to changing her mind over the gender rhetoric of the *Hills* issue. "Well—you do convince me in part, if not that the HILLS issue is unfair, at least to keep watch over that issue here. That is, you have made me vigilant. Perhaps I have become lax, being comfortable."[31] As if in response to the *Hills* issue, Hejinian soon thereafter published a talk by Alice Notley in Tuumba Press, notably the only talk or lecture to be featured in the series.[32]

In early 1983 the issue of gender and talk arose again, this time in the context of a residency by Charles Bernstein at 80 Langton Street. Susan Bee noticed that there was a general gendered division in who was doing the talking at such events. Hejinian wrote to Rae Armantrout, recalling that the discussion following an early Bernstein talk was mostly restricted to the usual people, "and I suddenly felt extremely alienated and unhappy, and went home. I stayed home the next day."[33] As Perelman points out, Bernstein's residency highlighted conflicting definitions of Language writing that were then emerging. These were not only about a difference in poetics (Watten's constructivism versus Bernstein's open textuality) but about the role of theory and the relationship between professionalism and politics. For writers like Bernstein and Watten, the talk provided a chance to debate seriously the consequences of this division. Yet, as Perelman notes, "A number of writers who attended the talks spoke (afterward, off the record) of being 'terrified' to speak."[34]

The final day of the residency did not feature a talk as such but a "play-let" called "Entitlement" in which Bernstein took the part of John Milton, Hejinian acted as Popova, and Jean Day was Jenny Lind. Although Hejinian found it "quite a lot of fun," she thought that "only the men were doing the talking, and not even all the men." She noted that Susan Bee raised the issue afterward "and got us all talking and thinking about it."[35] In a letter to Howe, Hejinian elaborated:

Susan and Johanna Drucker and I have had some great conversations in which Johanna and I were able to articulate our feelings and ideas about the power structure and power imbalance in the West Coast literary community—a woman's issue but also a larger issue, since so many of the "peripheral males," as Susan calls them, seem to be [similarly] inhibited in public discussions.[36]

Writing to Erica Hunt, Hejinian restated that it was not entirely a "woman's problem" although it was "in fact, the women who are talking about it." She further admitted that it was an ongoing problem, recalling that it "reminds me exactly of the moment I came on the scene here [mid-1977], when there was a meeting to discuss why don't the women talk at the talks."[37]

Hejinian relayed developments to Susan Howe, adding that she felt "like a detective . . . as all the pieces begin to fall into place." Yet, as with her earlier response, Hejinian still believed that the blame lay with the individual women at such events rather than any larger structural problem:

I am quite excited, really, as I feel that the non-talkers will talk when they realize that their (our) failure to speak out or speak up in public events is a) limiting the creative potential of the community as a whole (i.e. only one kind of issue is being addressed and only one style of analysis or theoretical proposition is being advanced) and b) that people want to hear them (us).[38]

Hejinian further noted that many whom she talked to about the issue seemed to have turned their "frustration and anger against themselves," adding that she had also done so to the point of becoming "paralyzed with self-doubt."[39]

Johanna Drucker subsequently organized a public panel entitled "Who is Speaking: The Power of Discourse." A group of women writers, including Drucker, Hejinian, Melissa Riley, and Jean Day, met to map out the issues to be addressed. Hejinian lists them as follows:

Who/what is the authority that "permits" one to speak? What authority does one gain by speaking a) in the immediate act of speaking? b) as one who often speaks? Why is or isn't it important to speak in public—is it necessary to speak or can one "participate" without speaking? What is the relationship of speaking in public to publishing one's writing (or showing one's work)—are these similar public acts? Is art formed by its social context—or is it formed and then it becomes part of the dialogue? What does it mean when one feels one "doesn't have anything to say"? Who/what determines valid and relevant styles and topics of discourse? What is the relationship of public speaking to the creative imagination?[40]

As the discussion continued, Hejinian began to change her mind about the implications of the gender imbalance in talks. She wrote to Bee and Bernstein that "[t]he more we talk about the specifics of that, the more clearly I've been able to see how widespread—or how many . . . elements . . . contribute to the problem." Hejinian understood that certain members of the audience might be made to feel that they were outsiders if they were not part of any of the groups socializing. Part of the problem, she suggests, is that "the transition from private event . . . to public event has never been made conscious and complete."[41] Another problem might be the fact that the events started so late. Although Hejinian realized that this might be a problem for people with a limited amount of time, she did not specify the actual group for whom such timing is most obviously problematic, namely, those who have to look after children. In not recognizing the often gendered nature of child care, Hejinian manages to maintain a gender-neutral framework for the issue.

Hejinian told Susan Bee that the public panel was set for March 28: "There has been no publicity etc. for it yet, but I have heard already that several groups of Women Artists plan to attend as well as other women's groups, etc. . . . The four panelists (Johanna and me being two of them) will have the responsibility of keeping the evening in focus."[42] Hejinian's letter indicates that the issue had broader cultural interest, particularly a feminist one, than otherwise demonstrated. The New Poetry archives are silent over the content of the actual presentations, but the event itself seems to have attracted quite a bit of energy. Hejinian described the atmosphere to Howe:

When I was on the panel . . . listening to people in the audience express their feelings before, during, and after speaking in public—the heart beating faster, the flush, the inability to attend to anything else that was going on until one got the chance to say what one had to say, the slumping back in one's chair when one had asked one's question or said one's thought, the let down, near remorse. Sounds like Eros to me. Happily I didn't think of this until after, and so spared myself the effort of formulating the idea on that occasion, which was already fairly emotional and highly charged.[43]

The evening discussion became a catalyst for Hejinian's extended thought on language and desire, which would eventually be published as "Language and 'Paradise.'"[44] "For the panel, of course, what is relevant is the psychology of speaking," she reflected. But that "is actually only peripherally about the psychology of language." She told Bee that the panel has provoked both enthusiastic and self-parodic responses, the latter coming from Tom Mandel who declared jokingly that he had prepared "a paper on how much he likes to hear himself talk." She also confessed that the event had made her analyze her own process of socialization into a feminine model: "I actually find that the issue itself brings up a lot of painful areas for me vis-à-vis the psychology of the self-in-public, etc., that go way back to my childhood, fears of being unpopular if I was smart, etc."[45]

One possible effect of the public interrogation of gender and discourse was that a more encouraging forum would be created for women writers. As Carla Harryman points out, even though she was frustrated by the way men could lock horns in public events, it was preferable to the more traditional talks by conservative or mainstream writers.[46] Feelings of marginality began to be addressed, and were discussed repeatedly. On hearing that Bernadette Mayer had been invited to take up a residency at 80 Langton Street, Fanny Howe told her that she would not be disappointed. At a stage in her work when she was exploring "new beginnings as yet undefined," she had found that "the people who came to hear me were really attentive, not unkind, and . . . [gave] me lots of nourishing questions."[47] For Howe, it was invigorating to have one's work placed at the center of community attention.

Another effect was that some women writers began exploring alternative speaking forums. Writing to Armantrout at the end of 1983, Hejinian states that she is participating in a "women writers" group that meets once a month and talks about writing. Other writers in the group included Gloria Frym, Laura Chester, Lindy Hough, and Summer Brenner. The group photocopied works in progress, passed them around, and talked about them. Hejinian noted that she often found "more interest in talking about women than writing." Although she sometimes felt alienated aesthetically, the group provided support in other ways: "We drink coffee and chitchat in a warming way, and I learn about how other people read work—which is extraordinarily unlike how I read work."[48] She also found the group useful in motivating her to explain and sometimes defend her poetics.

Hejinian thought that the group worked from a broader base in their discussions than seemed to be the case in the talk series: "when we get off the subject of specific work and talk about exploitative fiction, say, or ethics or whatever it is especially interesting."[49] Similarly, while Tina Darragh, Lynne

Dreyer, Joan Retallack, and Phyllis Rosenzweig continued to participate in a broader poetic community, they found it valuable to meet and discuss one another's work as well as their role as women writers. Rae Armantrout also participated in a women's writing group for a while. Of course, the editors of *HOW(ever)* had already discovered the benefits of this talk structure.

Several studies of talk in all-female groups suggest that women's discourse often operates on a collaborative or mutual basis, with lived experience and relationships as the primary source of conversation. There is a connection between private and public activity that transforms the act of writing/reading as part of, rather than separate from, other aspects of everyday life. As Anne Ruggles Gere has shown in her work on nineteenth-century women's clubs, writing groups of women provide an alternative to concepts of authorship and authority that mark the dominant culture. This alternative is generally communal rather than agonistic.[50]

Given the controversy surrounding the *Hills* "Talks" issue and Bernstein's residency, the eventual publication of the talks series by a university press redressed the issue of gender. Five of the sixteen contributors in the volume, fittingly called *Writing/Talks*, were women. The gender division in the style of talks is telling and is apparent even in the choice of titles in the *Hills* "Talks" issue as well as in the *Writing/Talks* book. Fanny Howe's talk, "Artobiography," examines the fictiveness involved in writing or reconstructing her own life. Beverly Dahlen gave a talk, or rather, more accurately, a reading of her own work in progress that was itself titled "A Reading." These topics may be seen as personal, with Howe and Dahlen speaking only for themselves or for their particular writing practice. Rae Armantrout's "Poetic Silence" stands in contrast to Bill Berkson's "Talk" and Kit Robinson's "Song."[51] In addition, Carla Harryman and Lyn Hejinian elaborate on the "middle" and "open form," both of which are strategically undefined.

Talks that were published in the *Hills* issue but not in the *Writing/Talks* book included Berkson's "Talk," Michael Davidson's "The Prose of Fact," David Bromige's "Intention and Poetry," and Benson's "Views of Communist China."[52] Such titles suggest authority or at least some broader power in the imparting of knowledge. However, Perelman also may have thought that some, like Benson's talk, would be even more difficult to translate into book form (Benson's talk was actually a performance piece in which, having moved his own effects into Perelman's loft, he then proceeded to juxtapose the reminiscences of a man living under a communist regime with his own life and work). In light of the public response to the talks, Perelman thoughtfully positioned Robert Glück's article, "Who Speaks for Us: Being an Expert," at the beginning of the volume. As a result, many of the key issues of the Bay Area debates were addressed as a way of contextualizing the subsequent talks. "[M]ost experimental writing has an adversary relation to professionalism," Glück argues, "a resistance to fetishizing the 'expert' or whatever is authoritarian." However, he adds a significant qualifier, noting that "when the avant-garde talks about itself, it becomes extremely professional."[53] He thus points out that public speaking is usually an act of self-legitimation.

In a lengthy review of *Writing/Talks* in *Poetry Flash*, George Lakoff calls attention to the careful positioning of the articles: "Hejinian's 'The Rejection of Closure' ends the book, providing just the right kind of closure, while rejecting closure in both form and content. Carla Harryman's 'The Middle' is just where it ought to be—in the middle. Rae Armantrout's 'Poetic Silence' is followed by Kit Robinson's 'Song.'"[54]

Conveniently, Lakoff overlooks the fact that Armantrout's "Poetic Silence" comes after Bernstein's talk, "Characterization" (which was one of his residency talks that initiated the subsequent debate about gender). Even in *Writing/Talks*, Bernstein's piece stands out for the frequent interjections right from the beginning of the talk. Only two of the interjections are by women. In the talk, Bernstein used a notice placed in the *New York Times* by one of the biggest advertising agencies in the United States. Paying homage to the recently deceased Bill Bernbach, the piece reads: "He said, 'The real giants have always been poets. *Men* who *jumped* from facts into the realm of imagination and ideas.' Quoting from this, Bernstein focuses on the emphasis given to the words *men* and *jumped*." Unfortunately, he does not follow up the relation of gender to poetic "greatness," although he considers the impact of reputation. "[Once] characterized as excelling in your field," he states, "they want to jump you into another field."[55]

Bernstein's talk thus raises issues of naming, of how one is spoken of and of who speaks. What he is exploring are possible responses: "how you can deal with these things in poetry itself [by creating] a music of contrasting characterizations, so that you can have not only this monoplanar or dyadic movement to characterization, framing the frame, but that you can have lots of different angles in composition so that the whole sounding of the various characterizations gets heard and made palpable."[56] Bernstein raises possible strategies of critique: straight expository writing, the "composition as explanation" mode with which Stein engaged, and silence. He admits that entering into the discourse of power can be painful. Yet to remain silent is to cede such a discourse to those who are willing to use it. It is not only "politically foolish" but of itself an anti-intellectual gesture.[57] In the ensuing discussion, Michael Palmer disagrees, stating that a contextual use of silence "can be an enormously powerful political act." As he goes on to say, "It can be an absolutely articulate rejection of the procedures themselves."[58]

In this respect, one could say that Rae Armantrout's essay "Poetic Silence" is strategic (just as it was a strategic editorial move by Perelman to place it straight after "Characterization"). Armantrout's impulse to silence provides a strong contrast to Bernstein's impulse toward expository discourse. In mapping out different types of silence, Armantrout covers silences that: admit mistakes, concede a personal limit or finitude, indicate the presence of the ineffable, are imposed by the presence of the Other, wait for an unknown response, or occur "when someone you have been considering from a distance turns and stops you with their look."[59]

Armantrout adds that there are many negative interpretations of deliberate silence. However, the point of her talk is to argue for the value of the lyric format in its greater potential for evoking silence. She lists various ways in which silence may be accommodated:

1. She may end a line or a poem abruptly, unexpectedly, somehow short of resolution.
2. She may create extremely tenuous connections between parts of a poem.
3. She may deliberately create the effect of inconsequence.
4. She may make use of self-contradiction or retraction.
5. She may use obvious ellipsis.
6. She may use anything that places the existent in perceptible relation to the nonexistent, the absent or outside.[60]

Armantrout states: "I often feel overwhelmed by the likelihood of error, my apprehension of the inexactitude of thought, and the impulse comes to cross out and start again from scratch, whatever that is."[61] A talk given by Beverly Dahlen (as part of a panel discussion, "The Tradition of Marginality") also focused on the issue of silence. Dahlen suggests that silence has become a figure, almost allegorical, in contemporary writing. She notes that it is not a unified figure, that her own silences are not the same as the silences of Susan Howe or of Rae Armantrout, of Tillie Olsen or of John Cage.[62]

Talking at Cross (Cultural) Purposes: The New Poetics Colloquium and the Debate on Feminine Rhetoric

Held on 21–25 August 1985 in Vancouver, the New Poetics Colloquium was a cross-cultural discussion between American and Canadian poets. Organized by the Kootenay School of Writing, participants included Charles Bernstein, Susan Howe, Nicole Brossard, Gail Scott, Daphne Marlatt, Sharon Thesen, Bob Perelman, Carla Harryman, Barbara Einzig, Michael

Palmer, Lyn Hejinian, Diane Ward, George Bowering, Steve McCaffery, and Barrett Watten. The colloquium marked the literary entrée of a new generation of language-centered writers in Canada, such as Jeff Derksen (one of the coordinators of the colloquium), Lisa Robertson, Christine Stewart, Catriona Strang, and Nancy Shaw. Diane Ward recalls that she "got to know a little bit about how a true collective (Kootenay School) could function."[63] For writers like Ward, the colloquium also provided an opportunity to see the role of poetry in other Western cultures.

Significantly, the colloquium was held a mere two years after the Women and Words Conference, also held in Vancouver. This previous conference was a feminist landmark in marking the emergence of a woman-oriented multicultural community of Canadian writers.[64] As Di Brandt recalls, "feminism was no longer an idea but a group of women talking working together. It was like a dream, the beginning of feeling, connected to other writers, women, becoming part of a women's community."[65] The conference also saw the first editorial meeting for *Tessera*, which remains the only journal of feminist criticism in Canada. Writers like Daphne Marlatt, Gail Scott, and Nicole Brossard, who participated in the New Poetics Colloquium, were intimately involved in the activities of that previous conference, particularly in the crossover in poetics between English Canada and Quebec.

Furthermore, Janice Williamson notes that prior to the New Poetics Colloquium, the first West Word Summer School Retreat was held in Vancouver.[66] A number of women writers remained in Vancouver for the colloquium. While the colloquium promised "A Celebration of New Writing," the retreat was a radical feminist project, the first of its kind, in which for two weeks women would live and work within a community of women readers and writers. Gail Scott ran the prose workshop, and Daphne Marlatt led the poetry. These workshops were divided between critiques of each other's writing and a discussion of various innovative texts. As with the colloquium, the retreat organizers were interested in opening up a cross-cultural dialogue between the United States and Canada. Accordingly, the writers introduced by Marlatt in the poetry workshop featured a range of American and Canadian poets, including, among the former, Barbara Einzig, Kathleen Fraser, Lyn Hejinian, and Susan Howe. Meanwhile, Scott included writers from Kathy Acker to Nicole Brossard in hers. French feminist theory was also discussed in both classes.

Williamson notes that as the workshops proceeded, the gendered nature of genre distinctions became evident. "It became clear at West Word," she argues, "that a woman's writing practice is very different" from the project of "masculinist postmodernists" who may also be concerned with deconstruction and investigating the open form. She adds that this became even more evident at the New Poetics Colloquium, where the politics of the various writing practices greatly diverged.[67]

The New Poetics Colloquium continued many of the issues raised in the 1983 conference, that is, issues concerning language, subjectivity, and desire. However, it drew heavy criticism for the way in which language was used, with deconstruction in particular being seen by writers like Paulette Jiles as enabling a depoliticization in its theorization of writing.[68] As Williamson suggests, Jiles's summation of the colloquium itself bordered on the antifeminist as it dismissed many of the experimental feminist writings as well.

Smaro Kamboureli believes that what was at stake in the colloquium and more generally in Canadian innovative writing was the rift between the academic and the writerly, which were viewed respectively as masculine and feminine.[69] Certainly, the structure of the conference and the papers as they were presented tended to reinforce such a distinction. As the conference was organized, two talks ran consecutively, one pair presenting in the morning and another in the afternoon. For some reason, this pairing followed the same pattern throughout the conference: first a male speaker, then a female speaker. Structurally, it was already setting up the primacy of male critique.

The American Language writers approached the colloquium with enthusiasm and with little sense of the heightened, radically feminist atmosphere that they were entering. Diane Ward found it "a lot of fun" and was pleasantly surprised at the positive reception to her recent work.[70] For the Bay Area writers the colloquium encouraged a group reflection on the various characterizations of Language writing and the range of poetics it now seemed to accommodate. Ward, for example, notes that the emphasis on play in a recent essay by Joan Retallack ("The Metaphysick of Play: L=A=N=G=U=A=G=E U.S.A.") caused some debate.[71] Writing to Susan Howe, Hejinian reflected that

[the colloquium] didn't seem like an "everyday occurrence" . . . despite the many years of Talks (informal and formal, institutional and noninstitutional). In fact . . . the colloquium didn't have any feeling of bringing to a conclusion a history of Talks—rather it seemed entirely new. New formats, new formulations, new ideas, new approaches. I think everybody was . . . making a great effort for the occasion.

There were two somewhat extra-literary currents that I have come away thinking about. . . . First, the "social rhetoric" that the occasion elicited . . . [and second] [t]he ways in which social rhetoric can be catastrophic, or can, on the other hand, invite attention to the work—these seem distressingly important to me.[72]

She noted that many of the Canadian audience seemed to be paying more attention to the social rhetoric than to the poetics. However, such rhetoric was necessarily linked to the way in which the writers tended to frame their poetics. Williamson recalls her own reaction to the colloquium: "This was literary history in the making . . . and like other feminists in the listening audience, I could feel my public discursive space shrinking towards either hysteria or silence."[73] For Williamson it was precisely the confidence of the male presenters in presenting their poetics as either factual or straightforward that was problematic. While many of the male writers seemed to be *speaking at* an audience, the women writers continued to practice a dialogic method in making space for other positions. Many of the women writers presented their knowledge as localized (such as Diane Ward's "Being Another * Locating in the World"), whereas the men tended to present theoretical overviews (an exception to this was Bob Perelman's specific analysis of his own poems from *The First World*).[74]

However, a comparison of Ron Silliman's talk and Susan Howe's helps illustrate the otherwise general difference of approach. Silliman's paper, "'Postmodernism': Sign for a Struggle, the Struggle for the Sign," was a wide-ranging but fairly abstract critique of postmodernism as a social structure. By contrast, Howe's statement, "There Are Not Leaves Enough to Crown to Cover to Crown to Cover," confirmed her poetics as highly invested in particular strands of a personal history.[75] Her paper "The Captivity and Restoration of Mrs. Mary Rowlandson" also raised questions about colonizing the female voice in public history.[76] Whereas Silliman used a linear, academic mode of argumentation, Howe's personal criticism emphasized openness and lack of continuity.

For Hejinian, the two modes of address were complementary rather than oppositional. She wrote to Susan Howe:

But I hear your Talk . . . not as from a different world than Ron's but as a complement to Ron's—both parts of the poetic universe. I heard all the Talks . . . as building—no, something more organic is required here—as flowering from some magnificent tree, some grotesque tree, with little red fruits and enormous yellow-pink fruits, and softer-skinne[d] elongated fruits and hard-shelled nut-contained fruits, etc.[77]

Hejinian's metaphor of food in describing the colloquium parallels similar imagery used by Janice Williamson in her poetic response to the colloquium. Writing a text entitled "Ratatouille," Williamson states, "It was intended to challenge the authority of the masculine voice canonized in academic institutions and to refute its universalist claims about 'what matters'" in cultural production.[78] By focusing on the domestic and the private, Williamson hoped to shift the discursive center away from the abstract. Here is a short extract:

> *Ratatouille*
>
> INGREDIENTS (*ingredi*—to enter):
> bruce andrews/charles bernstein/nicole
> brossard/barbara einzig/michael gay/carla
> harryman/lyn hejinian/susan howe/daphne
> marlatt/steve mccaffery/michael palmer/bob
> perelman/ron silliman/diane ward/barrett
> watten/others/talk. . . .

Gather together the poets in their all weather coats absorb themselves in work-in-progress/totalizing textuality.signs of pleasure etc. the women talk among themselves between questions refuse to speak the same language of difference talk among themselves

over and over again they wouldn't couldn't stop talking over   he said again "I am no feminist essentialist"   we believed him when he said "you're not going to read our books"   she said "but what about our books"   he said again (exasperated) what he said before. . . .

he remarked on the difference between american and canadian writers "the american men and women are so together: the canadians so divided" as though this was a difference[79]

Hejinian also was "disturbed" by "the Woman issue" in the context of the colloquium but more with how a nonlinear style of argument was continually cast as feminine. "The more I think about it," she wrote to Howe, "the more troubled I feel about it." Hejinian thought that there had been an inadequate discussion of many of the ideas in the talks "because so much energy was coming from people challenging the male authority of the presentation." However, she adds, "I have had a very nice and long letter from Janice Williamson, who seems to have thought back over the events herself and come up with some serious questions."[80]

While the rhetoric seemed divided, the content of the writing was sometimes in direct contradiction as well. Daphne Marlatt subsequently noted her difficulty with Bruce Andrews's use of language. She states: "He was supposedly writing against the kind of corrupted language that obtains in advertising. But he was using all . . . that commercialized sexual imagery [in his reading]."[81] Silliman's reading of *Paradise*, with its disregard for the power dynamics of lines such as "The tip of his penis against the back of her throat," also offended some writers like Williamson.[82] For a number of Canadian women, such imagery—interacting with and no doubt influencing the social rhetoric at the colloquium—did much to damage the early

reception of Language writing in Canada. It would be the newer genera-
tion of poets, clustered around the Kootenay School, that would continue
to invite Language writers to Canada and engage in a cross-cultural dia-
logue with them. Jeff Derksen argues that this connection still draws criti-
cism from more established Canadian writers and networks, as poetic out-
put is offset by suggestions of American colonialism.[83] Perhaps because of
their ongoing negotiations with issues of margin and center, it would be
the Kootenay poets who developed a community of difference (or what
Derksen calls "articulated linkages"), as well as generating one of the most
innovative and strongly feminist of poetic communities existing in Canada
today.

CHAPTER NINE

Cabinets, Closets, and Consumption: Analyzing the Anthology

KOALA—To survive you have to be willing to do anything. Anthologies! That's where the money really is, or might be. At least so I imagine from my fuzzy animal distance. Reprint the material! Dominate the gene pool! Rise like Godzilla and make them read you for fucking ever!

PANDA—If you use language like that, you'll have a hard time even making it into the La Brea tar pits.

—Bob Perelman, "The Manchurian Candidate: A Remake"

O geography My Great Flat Home

—Maureen Owen, *Amelia Earheart*

Perelman's lively exchange between koala and panda may be read as a parable contrasting two approaches by the marginal toward taking up the position of the culturally dominant. The Australian perspective is not only survivalist and potentially criminal (reflecting the convict mentality), but also implicitly immature (reflecting the naiveté of a young nation). In contrast, the Chinese perspective is stereotypically reflective and passive, philosophically reminding the koala of the importance of manners and ritual. Their countries' most popular icons, the koala and the panda, do hold an illusionary family resemblance (given that the koala has mistakenly been considered a bear), but their scripted dialogue reveals significant cultural differences. As John Yau suggests, such representations display "an acceptable confluence of mythology, geography, history, and the exoticizing view of the *Other*."[1] Taken from a larger work that critiques Cold War politics and the media's use of such stereotypes, Perelman allegorically stages America's own anxiety.

Anthologies have traditionally divided the geography of a poetry world into quasi-nations with impermeable borders, thus provoking political anxiety among poets. In addition, they have tended to reproduce anxiety in seeking legitimate heirs for the past and reducing diversity to type. In Oedipal fashion, poems are often presented as isolated rather than collaborative, the authors enjoined by a summary of accomplishment. In contrast to the heroicization of poets, the poems occupy a feminized role. Such a view is supported by Jed Rasula's metaphor of the way poems are featured in anthologies: "Poems, like women on view in a Miss Universe pageant, look more like one another than anybody around them."[2] In describing textual objects as such, Rasula fails to note the role of the woman writer in such a scene. Between the male gaze and the author-subject, she is doubly cast.

The fact that one of the anthologies of contemporary innovative poetry by women writers is called *Out of Everywhere: Linguistically Innovative Poetry by Women in North America and the UK* seems to confirm that an anth[rop]ology of poetry is still largely rendered through a logic of male observation.[3] Its editor, Maggie O'Sullivan, drew the title from a public discussion in which Rosmarie Waldrop was asked if she, as an innovative woman writer, experienced difficulty in being excluded both from mainstream women's anthologies and also, the questioner implied, from radical male-edited anthologies. "You are out of everywhere," lamented the audience member. Waldrop responded somewhat ambiguously, "I take that as a compliment. I've more or less claimed this is the position of poetry."[4] O'Sullivan exploits the suggestiveness of this exchange in her title by pointing both to the past experience of innovative women writers (excluded from everywhere) and to a possible new horizon (women writers coming from all over the place and appearing "everywhere"). Indeed, both *Out of Everywhere* and another recent anthology of women's poetry, *Moving Borders: Three Decades of Innovative Writing by Women*, create a new vision of poetic space by chronicling women's innovations in their "Great Flat Home" of the published page.[5]

Anthologies have traditionally played a major role in canon making, in recording and shaping the poetic territory for future readers. While Amy Lowell involved herself in this process, modernist women poets were generally much more active as editors of journals and presses. Second-wave feminism in the early seventies brought about the first collections of women's poetry. Anthologies like *No More Masks! An Anthology of Poems by Women* (1973) and *Rising Tides: Twentieth Century Women Poets* (1973) attempted to create a tradition of American women's poetry and included numerous modernist writers.[6] A third anthology, *The World Split Open: Women Poets 1552–1956* (1974) was even more ambitions in scope, beginning with sixteenth-century writers and ranging to the mid-twentieth century.[7] Understandably, these first collections did not include any women associated with the still emerging communities of Language writing.

By the mid- to late eighties, anthologies were beginning to focus solely on contemporary women's writing. However, women's poetic production

continued to be defined in strongly essentialist terms. Published by a pre-
stigious press (Faber and Faber), *Deep Down: The New Sensual Writing by
Women* (1988) featured a combination of innovative women writers like
Kathy Acker, Nicole Brossard, Lydia Davis, Rachel Blau DuPlessis, Kath-
leen Fraser, Bernadette Mayer, Erin Mouré, Leslie Scalapino, and Ntozake
Shange alongside more mainstream poets such as Judy Grahn, Audre
Lorde, and Sharon Olds. In her introduction, its editor, Laura Chester
wrote: "I feel that poetry and prose written by women in the past decade
has become more truly female, and by that I mean more vitalized, self-
affirming, and whole. Not only has the writing of women become a greater
part of the literary dynamic as new forms have pushed new limits, but the
writing has blossomed inward, into the realm of the feminine."[8]

Chester, here, is far more confident than she was in her introduction to
Rising Tides, which she coedited with Sharon Barba. In the earlier anthol-
ogy, Chester and Barba had justified their project, writing defensively of
the need to present women's lives—particularly their domestic lives—
through poetry. As Mary Margaret Sloan points out, the appeal for permis-
sion must be read in light of prevailing social ideologies at the time.[9] How-
ever, after fifteen years, Chester's second anthology still seeks to legitimate
women's experience through allocating it a separate, identifiable sphere.

Much of the poetry featured in the volume uses quite traditional form
such as Sharon Olds's "First Boyfriend":

> We would park on any quiet street,
> gliding over to the curb as if by accident,
> the houses dark, the families sealed into them,
> we'd park away from the street-light, just the
> faint waves of its amber grit
> reached your car, you'd switch off the motor and
> turn and reach for me, and I would
> slide into your arms as if I had been born for it.[10]

Although Leslie Scalapino's poetry radically challenges perception and
the representation of time through her use of repetition and minimalism, it
seems to have been selected more for its daring erotic content:

> the
> women—not in
> the immediate
> setting
> —putting the
> lily pads or
> bud of it
> in
> themselves

a man entering
after
having
come on her—that
and
the memory of putting
in
the lily pad or the
bud of it first,
made come[11]

Another anthology, *Early Ripening: American Women's Poetry Now* (1987) featured a strong selection of poets from diverse cultural and ethnic backgrounds, as well as poems by well-known lesbian writers. Its editor, Marge Piercy, argued that even with such a broad range of experience, gendered patterns could be discerned in poetic practice: "Contemporary women's poetry tends to be, far more seamlessly than contemporary men's poetry, of the body, the brain, the emotions fused."[12] While Piercy hoped to show the "densely populated and beautifully planted" landscape of women poets in her anthology, she believed that it was time for an anthology of poetry to show the "exciting work that women are producing" as occurring in the same field as [writing by] men.[13]

In the same year, Joel Lewis wrote that "[t]he works of Bernadette Mayer, Joanne Kyger, Alice Notley, and Maureen Owen (to name a few of the many women writers whose work is published through small-press publishers) are invisible to the substantial readership for woman-centered texts."[14] Certainly, women poets associated with the second generation of the New York school or with Language writing do not appear in Piercy's anthology.

In fact, innovative poetry more generally was difficult to register outside small-press journals and publications. An exception to this was Michael Lally's *None of the Above: New Poets of the U.S.A.* (1976), which featured all four women writers mentioned by Lewis.[15] It also featured an eclectic range of New York and Language poets, including among the latter Bruce Andrews, Lynne Dreyer, Ron Silliman, P. Inman, and Ray DiPalma. In his introduction, Lally notes that he sought to represent "important developments in the poetry of the past five years that have never before been presented in one collection." While it had a fairly successful distribution, its small-press status meant that it was largely overlooked by critics (although Marjorie Perloff gave it a mixed review) and a broad poetry-reading audience.[16]

It was not until 1986—the year before Lewis remarked on the difficulty of expanding the audience for innovative women writers—that an anthology attempted to present in a systematic manner work specifically associated with Language writing formations. It took Ron Silliman well over five years to finally see *In the American Tree: Language, Realism, Poetry* (1986) in its published form.[17] During this time, Helen Vendler's *The Harvard Book of Contemporary American Poetry* (1985), A. Poulin Jr.'s *Contemporary American Poetry* (4th ed., 1985), and Dave Smith and David Bottom's *The Morrow Anthology of Younger American Poets* (1985) created a view of contemporary American poetry as a homogeneous entity[18] Besides narrow thematic outlets such as those created in Chester's anthology, the innovative poem remained closeted in small-press journals and publications. Most of these remained unknown outside the literary circles in which they were produced and distributed.

Silliman's anthology, along with Douglas Messerli's *"Language" Poetries* (which appeared a year later), signaled "a radically new emergence, even eruption, on the scene of contemporary writing in the United States."[19] Although they were not marketed for an academic audience, both anthologies quickly became handy pedagogic tools. In offering an introduction to the poetry, they were more accessible than many of the samplers that had been published in journals like *Alcheringa, Paris Review,* and *Ironwood.* Furthermore, they had a much longer shelf life. Hank Lazer characterized them as "the two most important anthologies of contemporary American poetry since Donald Allen's *The New American Poetry* in 1960.[20] Certainly, mainstream presses could no longer ignore the presence of Language writing. By the nineties, Language writers had significant representation in the Norton anthology, *Postmodern American Poetry* (1994), and the University of California's double volume anthology, *Poems for the Millennium* (1995; 1998).[21] Given that *In the American Tree* and *"Language" Poetries* had such an overwhelming impact on the poetic field, it is worth asking how they represented innovative women writers and whether such representation had any effects (advantageous or otherwise) on the future reputations of individual women poets.

In the American Tree and *"Language" Poetries*

With *In the American Tree,* Silliman hoped to map the innovative work produced over the past decade by the poetry communities commonly thought of as Language writing (although he repudiated the reductiveness and uniformity that such labeling implied). As the work of writers like Jerome Rothenberg, Barbara Guest, and Robert Kelly threatened to be forgotten in canonical accounts of the sixties, Silliman was particularly aware of the consequences of not producing anthologies. In a symposium on poetry and community, he stated: "Both ironic and aggressive, interventions such as ours seem to be entirely necessary in a world in which the right to define is a critical aspect of hegemony."[22] To some degree, whose right to define became the basis for a serious territorial dispute.

The full title of the anthology—*In the American Tree: Language, Realism, Poetry*—reflects this concern, for it recalls an avant-garde tradition that includes both *The New American Poetry* and, in a different sense, William Carlos Williams's *In the American Grain*.[23] As Perelman suggests in *The Marginalization of Poetry*, Silliman reproduces Allen's generic division between poetry and poetics in dividing the volume into two sections: "First Front" (poetry) and "Second Front" (poetics).[24] The *New American* zoning of poetic communities is also paralleled by the collection being structured into two geographic regions: East and West.

Douglas Messerli also was concerned with the fate of innovative poetry, believing that instead of struggling to distinguish boundaries or circles within itself, attention should be given to the gap that lay between established writing schools, like the Iowa School and Bread Loaf, and the experimentalism of Language writing and the New York school. Messerli's volume did not intend to be representative like Silliman's. Indeed, New Directions originally asked Messerli to select only four poets. Messerli hoped "to represent a few of the many poets currently writing a poetry focused on or highly attentive to language—to the play of language, to its structures, and to its current social and political [context], and its potential uses to (re)create the world around us." For this reason, he chose individuals "who might not normally be thought of as being in "the heart of 'Language' concerns" and to "exclude others who may be more central to whatever 'group' aesthetics there are."[25] Gradually, Messerli negotiated a larger collection with New Directions, primarily because a number of writers felt that it should be more wide-ranging. In calling his anthology *"Language" Poetries*, Messerli foregrounds the problematic "group" nature of Language writing, suggesting that it should be seen as a multitude rather than as a unified movement. He states in his introduction, "Particularly in San Francisco, and to a somewhat lesser degree in New York and Washington DC, the 'Language' poets—despite obvious differences in aesthetics—came together out of what Lyn Hejinian has called 'motivated coincidence.'"[26]

Silliman had begun planning his anthology as early as 1980. Editorial selection was shaped by the previous publishing activity of writers, with Silliman considering those who had contributed to a core set of publications such as *Tottel's*, *This*, *L=A=N=G=U=A=G=E*, *Miam*, *Roof*, and *The Difficulties*. This adherence to a central set automatically limited the aesthetic and political range of writers to be included in the anthology. Washington-based magazines and presses like *Dog City*, *Là Bas*, and Some of Us Press were not considered to be part of this "core." Nor were a number of small presses run and edited by women, such as *Big Deal, Telephone, HOW(ever)*, and Kelsey Street Press. This meant that women writers like Beverly Dahlen, Rachel Blau DuPlessis, Kathleen Fraser, Joan Retallack, and Rosmarie Waldrop were overlooked, as well as writers otherwise active in the poetry community like Messerli and Lally.

Silliman also chose not to publish those whose primary medium was other than poetry. This further excluded a number of innovative women writers engaged in interdisciplinary work or prose-poetry, such as Kathy Acker, Abigail Child, Lydia Davis, and Johanna Drucker. Silliman argued that writers like Beverly Dahlen and Leslie Scalapino were excluded because they were not a presence in the print culture that specifically featured Language writing. More recently, he has suggested that he saw them as occupying something of an adversarial role. Scalapino believes that this was because they were not writing the syntax by which Silliman characterized Language writing.[27] At the time of the anthology's compilation, Joan Retallack was told that the decision to exclude her work was due to aesthetic difference.[28] Messerli points out that other women writers, like Fraser and Waldrop, did not figure in either anthology because they too were generally thought to stand apart from "language" concerns of the period.[29]

Linda Reinfeld notes of Silliman's anthology, "Woman, too, makes herself heard nearby, but her voice, though never least, remains irreducibly marginal."[30] Yet, in its gender distribution, *In the American Tree* reflects the gradual social change wrought by feminism, with twelve of its forty contributors being women. This was compared to the four who were represented in the Allen anthology. Furthermore, it opens the poetics section with a poem by Carla Harryman that questions the reliance of writing on either prescriptive abstraction or photographic representation. Silliman also reproduces Rae Armantrout's "Why Don't Women Do Language-Oriented Writing?" in which Armantrout specifically addresses the wealth and diversity of innovative poetry by women.

Of all the women contributors, Susan Howe occupied the most difficult position within *In the American Tree*. Both Charles Bernstein and Lyn Hejinian had advised that she be included if the anthology aimed to present work important to the context of innovative poetry or sought to give "something like a report on the climate."[31] Silliman eventually decided to use her review of P. Inman's *Platin*, not only to illuminate Inman's work but also because it solved the need of addressing forms of criticism like the book review (which was a central part of so many small-press journals). However, he also featured a section from Howe's *Pythagorean Silence* that gave an effective sense of her concerns with history, absence, and feminist revision:

Two sisters at work under an oak
spinning and weaving   Idea

and Echo wavering so
I wish I could see them (mist)

into clear reason (air)
Music murmurs double discord[32]

Howe herself felt that she was "only a lyrical twig" on Silliman's *American Tree*.[33] She would have preferred some dialogue over the work that was to be included. But neither she nor Silliman attempted such a discussion until Howe wrote to Silliman in support of Messerli's forthcoming *"Language" Poetries*. Silliman later told Howe that she had proved a controversial choice and that he had received criticism for her inclusion as well as for not including enough of her work. In its final form, *In the American Tree* served Howe well by featuring a review of her poetry by Tina Darragh as well as her own poetry and poetics sections. This triple representation could only have helped her growing reputation.

Silliman and Messerli seem to have had differences about the aesthetics of some women writers as well as about the importance of poetic lyricism, which Messerli favored. It is somewhat surprising then, that all the women poets who appeared in *"Language" Poetries* were represented in *In the American Tree*. Lyn Hejinian's *My Life* and *Writing Is an Aid for Memory* can be found in both volumes, and even the chosen sections from Susan Howe's *Pythagorean Silence* overlap. However, different selections were made from the writing of Tina Darragh, Carla Harryman, and Diane Ward. *"Language" Poetries* not only chose work from a broader cross-section of publications but it often gave more of a sense of each individual's literary scope. Whereas Darragh, Harryman, and Ward have only one piece featured in the poetry section of *In the American Tree*, there are three or more pieces by each in *"Language" Poetries*.

"Language" Poetries would therefore mirror roughly and even reinforce the same grouping made by *In the American Tree*. Writers who do not appear in either volume—such as Kathleen Fraser, Joan Retallack, Leslie Scalapino, Rosmarie Waldrop—were effectively rendered marginal in terms of their reception to Language writing projects. All four would later appear in *Out of Everywhere*, fulfilling its title far more than did other contributors like Susan Howe, Carla Harryman, Diane Ward, Lyn Hejinian, and Tina Darragh. They would also appear in Dennis Barone and Peter Ganick's *The Art of Practice: 45 Contemporary Poets* (1994), which showcases those excluded by Silliman and Messerli as well as featuring the work of younger poets.[34]

Among women associated with the Language writing communities, there was both hesitation and support for anthologization. Messerli himself notes that anthologies "have often been something poets have worked against rather than supported."[35] Alternatively, "a good anthology can shed light on the relationships between poets."[36] Carla Harryman was concerned with the potential effect of depoliticizing the poetry. "[T]here is a trend in said literary world," she wrote, "to commodi[fy] literary products to such a degree that what is significantly radical in the works is undermined, at least to some extent."[37] While aware of such risks, Lyn Hejinian felt that an anthology might clarify "other people's sense of what we care about, are interested in the broadest sense."[38] An anthology would act as a timely intervention into the categorical dismissal that the term "Language poetry" often engendered. As with several other writers, Hejinian acted in a mediatory role between Silliman and Messerli, hoping that both anthologies might be produced in relative harmony. Given that *"Language" Poetries* would be published by a well-known small press (New Directions) and was far smaller in scope (it featured half as many contributors), Silliman felt that it might threaten the eventual impact of *In the American Tree*. However, the sheer size and number of contributors to Silliman's volume meant that it was more likely to be taken up as the definitive anthology.

His disagreement with Messerli's projected anthology was viewed by many as being emblematic of divisions occurring more generally in Language writing. Susan Howe saw the conflict as emerging out of differences between East Coast and West Coast Language writing—both aesthetically and politically.[39] Tina Darragh viewed Silliman's frustration as being caused not so much by the Messerli anthology itself but by the failure of the logic of community:

It may seem sort of far-fetched to you, but the break-up of Some of Us Press had a similar devastating effect on me because it meant that we had failed to create an ongoing means of production & collective lifestyle to match what we thought of as a common collective basis for our work. It's not a full analogy, but I think that a good deal of your anger regarding the N[ew] D[irections] anthology is frustration over the fact that the *Legend* crew couldn't back up the collaborative impulse in that work with a means of production that could handle *In the American Tree*, as it exemplifies a full flowering of that collaborative effort.[40]

The epigraph to *In the American Tree* certainly foregrounds the collaborative nature of Language writing (the poem was written by Kit Robinson in a collaborative project with Steve Benson and Bob Perelman). Silliman features more poems from the same collaboration by Robinson, as well as some by Perelman. There were also two collectively authored pieces: "Experiments" by Bernadette Mayer and her workshops at St. Mark's, and "For *Change*" by Silliman, Barrett Watten, Steve Benson, Lyn Hejinian, Charles Bernstein, and Bob Perelman. In its turn, *"Language" Poetries* does not feature any collaborations. Against an ongoing deconstruction of authorship in Language writing, it largely reproduces the authority of the individual in poetic production.

Despite Silliman's concerns, the fact that *two* anthologies devoted to Language writing appeared in the mid-eighties only highlighted its significance within the poetic field. And perhaps the very difference in size and structure (one featuring poetics, the other not) meant that instead of the public choosing one over the other, both volumes would be read. This was helped by Messerli's distribution of *In the American Tree* through Sun & Moon Press. Throughout the eighties, Messerli would also publish numerous collections by innovative women writers through Sun & Moon Press. In 1994 he produced another and more substantive anthology. At well over a thousand pages, *From the Other Side of the Century: A New American Poetry 1960–1990* was far more inclusive than *"Language" Poetries*, presenting not only poets like Scalapino, Retallack, and Waldrop but also Nicole Brossard, Abigail Child, Alice Notley, Fiona Templeton, and Marjorie Welish.[41] It also included numerous male writers left out of the two previous anthologies.

Out of Everywhere and *Moving Borders*

Besides *In the American Tree* and *"Language" Poetries*, only a few women associated with Language writing were featured in anthologies in the eighties. Even then, their work was generally filtered through specific themes or other poetic formations. One exception to this trend was a special issue of *Mirage* (1989) that focused on innovative women's poetry.[42] Edited by Dodie Bellamy, it included more established writers like Rae Armantrout, Kathleen Fraser, Fanny Howe, and Rosmarie Waldrop, as well as newer writers like Harryette Mullen and Susan Gevirtz. Significantly, each writer gave a short statement of her poetics. Although some of these statements focused on gender and language, other aspects were noted, such as the various processes of writing (what might be considered as experimentation), structuralism, fetishism, and the relation between race and linguistics.

Yet an actual anthology of innovative writing by women would not be published until 1996. At roughly 250 pages and with thirty contributors (twenty of them North American), *Out of Everywhere: Linguistically Innovative Poetry by Women in North America and the UK* stands as the first rousing announcement of the strength and diversity of women's innovative writing on both sides of the Atlantic. Originating in the United Kingdom, the collection made a radical entrance there. The situation was strikingly similar to that in the United States (whereas *écriture au féminin*/writing in the feminine could be said to have created other patterns in Canadian poetry). Like American anthologies of women's writing, British anthologies of contemporary women's poetry continued to focus on traditional forms. The editor of *Sixty Women Poets* (1993), for instance, chose only poems that "successfully order thought, emotion and imagination into a form that communicates itself effectively and unequivocally to the reader."[43] Alternatively, women were also scarcely represented in anthologies of innovative British poetry. Veronica Forrest-Thomson was the sole woman included in Andrew Crozier and Tim Longville's *A Various Art* (1987).[44] Only five of the thirty-five contributors to the more recent *Conductors of Chaos* (1996) were women (although it does open with an adventurous selection of Caroline Bergvall's more performance-based work).[45]

In contrast to these collections, *The New British Poetry* (1998) features a large and diverse range of contemporary women poets.[46] Yet it was peculiarly divided into four categories: Black British poetry, feminist poetry, experimental poetry, and poetry by younger writers. Such divisions meant that Black women writers were distinguished from being either feminist or innovative. There is also an implied break between the poetry and projects of Wendy Mulford, Denise Riley, and Gael Turnbull and those of Maggie O'Sullivan and Geraldine Monk. The unfortunate effect of this structure was to produce a fragmented and artificial picture of contemporary British poetry, as well as to close down the potential links that could be made between the techniques and concerns of various writers.

A particularly valuable feature of *Out of Everywhere*, then, is its distinctive display of the diverse range of poetic practices among experimental women writers and, most notably, its emphasis on the politics of the page. Compared to the largely left-margined or centered poem placement of both *In the American Tree* and *"Language" Poetries*, a scan of its pages reveals a range of startlingly radical approaches to territory of the page. Beginning with the scattered multidirectional lines of Susan Howe's poetry, the anthology maps work that visually challenges reading habits, including the bisected, historically bifocal pages of Retallack, Darragh's play with the dictionary's own geography of meaning, the documentary cut-ups of Diane Ward, the blank spaces of Carla Harryman and Rosmarie Waldrop, and the ticker-tape progression of Hannah Weiner's words. Although the book's length is limiting in scope, it gives a reasonable taste of each writer's work by allowing between five and eleven pages per poet. Furthermore, it introduced unfamiliar poetry to readers on both sides of the Atlantic and gave an idea of parallels between two poetic cultures previously seen as fairly separate.

Two years later, a more substantial anthology of American women's innovative writing was published. Whereas *Out of Everywhere* sets the stage for a transatlantic exchange between women's experimental poetries, Mary Margaret Sloan's *Moving Borders: Three Decades of Innovative Writing by Women* (1998) meticulously traces the growing public presence of innovative women writers from the sixties to the nineties in North America. Sloan notes that she hoped to construct a space within which poems and statements of its writers speak back and forth to one another.

The title, *Moving Borders*, announces Sloan's intentions to redress the poetic map of North America and, at the same time, to take up Sillliman's injunction that "intervention such as ours seems to be entirely necessary in a world in which the right to define is a critical aspect of hegemony."[47] Using a grammatically ambiguous word (*moving*), the title enacts the values of provisionality but also signals the importance of positionality for women writers within poetic practices. It suggests that the space of poetry is always already changing (the very parameters are being rethought) because of experimental women's writing and, furthermore, that such writing is being repositioned institutionally through Sloan's anthology.

The volume undermines the borders set by most previous anthologies—both woman-centered and innovative. While the contributors to the anthology do not define their work wholly or partly through the identity of gender, the anthology enables readers to see how gender boundaries have been interrogated and contested through a multitude of strategies. Like Silliman, Sloan recognized the importance of little magazines in the development of innovative poetry. However, she was also interested in calling attention to the emergence of women's writing into a public sphere by using each contributor's first publication date as the chronological organizing principle of the book. This gesture foregrounds Sloan's belief that writing and publishing are not equivalent acts and that writing's survival and institutional recognition is directly linked to its positioning in a public world.

Ed Foster, the publisher at Talisman Press, initially proposed the idea of undertaking such an anthology to Kathleen Fraser, given her experience in founding and editing *HOW(ever)*. Perhaps because of her extended effort on *HOW(ever)*, Fraser declined and instead suggested Mary Margaret Sloan, whose work Foster also knew and respected. Foster gave free rein to Sloan, even agreeing to double (or very nearly) the number of pages from the original goal of four hundred. Sloan found him a generous and enthusiastic publisher, maintaining support throughout the four years it took her to compile the volume. She agreed to take on the project because the topic was special to her, even unique, "since I had a personal stake in the history."[48]

From the start, Sloan claimed an interested position. "Impartiality is a fiction," she discerns in her introduction, "one is partial to as one has taken part in, how one has been a part of."[49] Nevertheless, Sloan distinguishes between a partial approach and a partisan one, arguing that the latter more fervently supports a party or cause and is likely to be more defensive. Sloan's own poetics were first formed by wide reading in American and European literature and philosophy. In the early seventies she immersed herself in feminist theory and a broad range of contemporary women's writing. Brief membership in the Feminist Writer's Guild in 1976 ended when she felt its agenda was too narrowly focused on the subject matter of women's poetry (how it related to women's experience) at the expense of issues of form. In the late seventies she studied creative writing with Kathleen Fraser at San Francisco State University and went on in the mid-eighties to further study of poetics at the New College of California, with Robert Duncan, Michael Palmer, and Lyn Hejinian. During this period she became more actively engaged in the Bay Area experimental writing community, forming friendships within the group of women surrounding *HOW(ever)*, most notably with Fraser and Susan Gevirtz. She also met and established friendships with poets associated with Language writing; Tom Mandel has been particularly important to her. Sloan sees feminism as a "momentous force" in the era of her own writing and as inextricably linked with other interests (such as the history and impact of the scientific method and the political and aesthetic dimensions of spatial orders) in her thinking.[50]

In considering questions of structure and representation, Sloan decided not to mark out regional divisions, thus generating a more fluid concept of poetic community. Moving away from anthologies that herald a "next generation," *Moving Borders* followed Messerli's *From the Other Side of the Century: A New American Poetry, 1960–1990* in its cross-generational scope. Starting with Lorine Niedecker and finishing with Melanie Nielsen, *Moving Borders* reveals particular issues to be of continuing concern but approaches them through historically specific engagements. In covering only three decades, Sloan is able to emphasize a rhizomatic association between the contributors, rather than a clearly definable or linear tradition.

Like Maggie O'Sullivan, Sloan found it difficult to find many of the small-press books and magazines. Eventually she discovered that much of the material had been archived at Stanford University. Sloan also visited other libraries and scoured used-book stores. Once she had undertaken an extensive survey, Sloan then read through the complete output of each potential contributor at least once before assembling a list of writers, then again when making a selection of actual pieces. In her reading process she wondered: "What is going on here; how is this innovative, or if it doesn't seem so now, how was it radical or startling or useful when it first appeared; is it still; where had it led; how did it influence others in fruitful directions?" She found that many of the writers she continued to consider had formed "conversational networks" and had generally received few major prizes or "other kinds of recognition beyond that of their peers."[51]

Initially, Sloan sent a hand-picked selection to each writer for a response. A few accepted them outright; others requested changes. Even then, Sloan discussed the selections with the writer: "I didn't override anyone's preferences," she recalls, "but sometimes I argued hard for my point of view."[52] Her choices would be vital to the feminist tenor of the book.

Sloan hoped to avoid encoding a hierarchy that eventuates in some anthologies wherein the contributors' work is featured in widely discrepant lengths. However, the career spans and circumstances of the contributors to *Moving Borders* varied, and their output ranged from one book to thirty. Selection length, therefore, ranged from five pages to eighteen. Unlike most other editors, Sloan made a point of including writers who blend poetry with other genres and mediums. Examples of these others areas are: film (Theresa Hak Kyung Cha and Abigail Child); performance art (Fiona Templeton and Hannah Weiner); music (Julie Patton); art (Johanna Drucker); and drama (Carla Harryman, Leslie Scalapino, Camille Roy, and Nicole Brossard).

At first glance, Sloan appears to have maintained a split between poetry and poetics, as Silliman did. Her purpose in doing so was "to represent the crucial political role that writing about writing plays in canon formation."[53] Sloan hoped to foreground the functional and political uses of writing. At the same time, she highlights the way in which innovative women's writing can accommodate both modes in a single form. The poetry section therefore contains a selection by Leslie Scalapino on "the analytical mind," representing her position that thinking does not lend itself to categories. On the other hand, the poetics section includes manifestoes and polemics in poetic form (Tina Darragh, Alice Notley). Selections from Maureen Owen's *Zombie Notes* and Bernadette Mayer's *Midwinter Day* can further be found in both the poetry and the poetics sections.

Sloan felt that the poetics section was particularly important in a historical anthology because it could show how innovative women writers "have supported each other and discussed work among themselves . . . and pushed each other in certain directions."[54] Accordingly, she arranged each piece so that "some aspect of each selection, whether central or minor, suggests a feature of the one that succeeds it." "As in actual conversation," Sloan states, "some of the connections carry on a central issue from the preceding statement, while other links are associative and occasionally whimsical."[55] At over 150 pages, the size of the section underlines Sloan's sense that women's participation in public discourse is valuable, serious, and still underrepresented.

Over half the work in the section had never been published before. Sloan solicited specific pieces from Carla Harryman and Fanny Howe on motherhood and writing, as well as from Tina Darragh, Cole Swenson, and Susan Gevirtz, among others. Whereas Ron Silliman had turned down an early section of Joan Retallack's *Errata 5uite* for *In the American Tree*, Sloan emphasized the importance of error tracking in history. The extensive range of topics includes applications of feminist theory to women's writing (Susan Howe, Rachel Blau DuPlessis, and Norma Cole), elaborations by women of male-derived poetic practice (Fraser on Charles Olson and contemporary women poets), the relation of writing to film (Gevirtz, Scalapino), contemporary writing by men (Rae Armantrout on Bob Perelman), philosophy (Retallack and Laura Moriarty), and the interrogation and use of scientific method (Swenson on Howe and Albiach, Darragh on Donna Haraway).

Looking back over the process of producing the anthology, Sloan notes that she would not do anything differently, "except to try to keep all decisions provisional until the very end so that I could assemble the manuscript in its entirety as a collage." She found that the anthology closely resembled her own way of writing poems in becoming "essentially an architectural construction."[56] While *Moving Borders* could be said to fall into what Marjorie Perloff calls the "blockbuster" trend of anthologies, its expansion is synchronic as well as diachronic.[57] Accordingly, it keeps a focus on the importance of poetic communities while suggesting multiple vectors continually in practice.

Not only have *Out of Everywhere* and *Moving Borders* cultivated a wider interest in innovative women's writing, but their success confirms that there is a growing market for work of this kind. The proliferation of poetry and essay collections by individual writers featured within these two anthologies suggests that they have had a real and significant impact upon the field of contemporary poetry. While *Out of Everywhere* and *Moving Borders* were published by small presses, there remains a danger with anthologies that the very culture in which the writing was originally produced may be marginalized or erased. As Lynn Keller and Cristanne Miller point out, it is worth remembering that Susan Howe's work was first published by small presses run by women: Maureen Owen (Telephone), Lyn Hejinian (Tuumba), Lita Hornick (Kulchur Foundation), and Brita Bergland (Awede).[58] This history is elided when her poetry is reproduced in the anthology form. An anthology may revise canonical borders and draw attention to otherwise unknown work, but it is limited by its very form in the challenges it can pose to the way we read innovative writing as well as the way we think about poetic practice. Yet given these constraints, *Out of Everywhere* and *Moving Borders* have been incredibly important in shifting away from narrowing terms such as Language writing and revealing such poetry to have much in common with a broad range of innovative women's poetry.

CHAPTER TEN

Desire Not a Saint: The Pathography of Bernadette Mayer

> Don't take what I say too seriously
> Or too lightly,
> I'm sorry
>   Nevermind
> I was just playing around, I'm trying to find
> What I guess I'd rather not know consciously
>   I'd like to know
> What kind of person I must be to be a poet
>   —Bernadette Mayer, *Midwinter Day*

An anonymous band of feminist activists working out of New York, the Guerrilla Girls made a poster which listed ten advantages of being a woman artist. One of them included the relief of never having to worry about being labeled a genius.[1] While Bernadette Mayer is one of the leading experimental poets on the East Coast, her position within the literary history of Language writing has been, at best, ambivalent. She is overlooked by Perelman's and Davidson's overviews and, until recently, received little critical attention.[2] Her lack of academic recognition forms a contrast to the five male poets who collaborated on *Legend*. In describing the 1980 volume, Reinfeld reaches a state of explicit reverence: "[T]he study of *Legend* is analogous to the spiritual exercise of Christians who move toward perfection by reading saints' lives, aspiring to that state in which all men come together with God."[3]

However, hagiography is more fitting for Mayer than for most of her contemporaries. Writing that began considering the formal concerns of Language writing featured in *0–9*, a journal that she coedited with Vito Acconci in the late sixties. Her unusual workshops (1971–1975) generated a good deal of excitement and were enthusiastically attended by a number of Language writers, including Bruce Andrews, Charles Bernstein, Barbara

Baracks, Lynne Dreyer, Peter Seaton, and Nick Piombino. Her "Experiments" was the only piece repeated in Ron Silliman's anthology, *In the American Tree: Language, Realism, Poetry*, and Andrews's and Bernstein's *The L=A=N=G=U=A=G=E Book*.

Yet a return to traditional forms saw Mayer fall from grace. Peter Baker suggests that some poets viewed collections like *Poetry* (1976) and *The Golden Book of Words* (1978) as a betrayal of her earlier teachings. While Mayer managed presses and magazines—United Artists and *Unnatural Acts*—and went on to direct St. Mark's Poetry Project for four years (1980–1984), the joyous celebration of her heterosexuality made her a difficult subject for feminist critics wanting to expound on the constraints of sexual ideology. Despite disavowals in both these quarters, Mayer nevertheless maintained a faithful following among New York writers. Such belief found confirmation in the nineties when *A Bernadette Mayer Reader* (1992) was published by New Directions, a high profile poetry press. As with all saint stories, Mayer also experienced this trial and transformation corporeally. Suffering the equivalent of a stroke in 1994, she defeated death and became, inadvertently, a literal "living legend."

Hagiographies typically transport individuals to the level of myth, but Mayer continues to locate herself within the everyday. Her narrative is more a narrative of dys-sanctity or pathography. Whereas hagiography informs institutional status, pathography articulates that which is excessive to the canon. As Mayer herself has argued, "Saint bernadette was made a saint by devil's advocate."[4]

The cycle that Mayer's reputation takes is particularly fascinating for tracing the gendered nature of authorship and the expectations that are brought to bear on a female signature. Often blurring together issues of vocation and sexuality, Mayer meticulously investigates the identity that lies overdetermined not only in a woman's life of writing but also in her life-writing. She was among the first to explore seriously the nature of consciousness and linguistic modes of thought, taking up Gertrude Stein as a model long before many Language writers did. "Some part of me wants to write a book of descriptions," Mayer told Hejinian. "I had one idea to describe in any old style at all one person or thing every day till I had exhausted all the descriptive possibilities of focusing on one thing, an idea much like [T]ender [B]uttons perhaps."[5] She saw such "annotating & computing & even describing" in her writing as "a kind of history, or writing of history." Writing history "as a woman" was "still a sparse field."[6]

Mayer began what she called an "emotional science project," collecting data that eventually resulted in *Memory*.[7] Memory, of course, has a complex relation to history. In "Between Memory and History: *Les Lieux de Mémoire*," Pierre Nora distinguishes between "real memory," which he sees as retaining the secrets of a community, and history, which organizes the past into tradition. As oral culture, memory has traditionally formed a feminine counterpart to the masculine inscription of Western history. The gap between history and memory, Nora argues, has stretched in modern times so that memory is being slowly eradicated by history.[8]

In seeking to foreground traces of memory, Mayer went about transcribing "every event, every motion, every transition of . . . her own mind."[9] Starting with photographs, Mayer shot a roll of film every day over July 1971; the month had been chosen at random. Rather than trying to make the photographs beautiful, she aimed to take photographs of "what you're really seeing, not trying to isolate objects and put them in the center of the frame." This, she hoped, would "reflect what actual vision is, and not romanticize it."[10] In the end she had 1,200 color snapshots. During the month, Mayer also kept notes that were then turned into tapes. When played back, they totaled seven hours of narration. Experience was translated through the lens as well as through speech. This double exposure enables both a critique of vision as a truth discourse (the documentary powers of the photograph) and of the dominance of language in the telling of history.

Mayer first showed *Memory* as a gallery installation. She recalls that, "[t]he pictures were mounted side by side in row after row along a long wall, each line to be read from left to right, 36 feet by 4 feet." They were placed in chronological order, so that they could be "read" like a book. A reel-to-reel tape took the pictures "as points of focus, one by one, & as taking-off points for digression, filling in the space between."[11] As a public site, the gallery emphasized memory as existing through a shared social space. Voice and image were pieced together by each audience member in varying degrees. *Memory* was therefore presented not only as a staging of the past but as a collective reenactment.

The installation received a positive review in the *Village Voice* and attention from the art world. Praeger, a large publishing house, expressed interest in turning *Memory* into a book. However, Mayer soon discovered that the textual transaction was conditional on a sexual one and was forced to look elsewhere.[12] The small press North Atlantic eventually took on the project but kept only a few photographs for the cover design. While the book fails to capture the multidimensional breadth of Mayer's original project, it does keep something of the experimental underpinnings. The introduction, written by Freudian psychoanalyst David Rubinfine, confirms Gertrude Stein's approach to writing as a science. Rubinfine argues that *Memory* is a "new kind of autobiography," one that re-creates "archaic modes of presentation of inner and outer sensory data."[13] In registering shifts of consciousness, it is close to how children remember events and

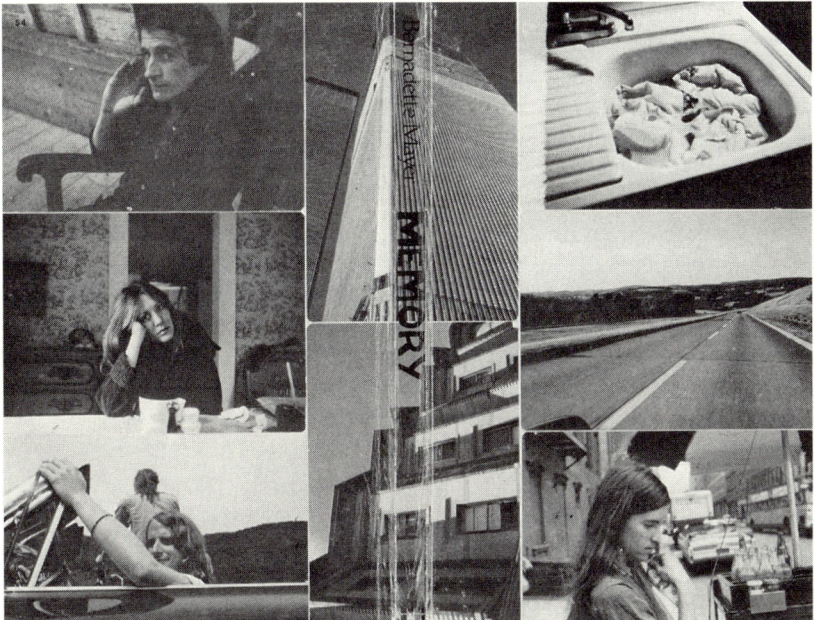

Fig. 6. Front and back cover of Bernadette Mayer's *Memory* (Plainfield, VT: North Atlantic, 1975). Reprinted by permission of the author.

incidents. Dream is also recovered as an additional plane of reality. In externalizing the emotional, Mayer follows a largely modernist tradition of psychological exploration embodied in figures such as Proust and Joyce.

The written text of *Memory* recalls Stein's own development of a continuous present in putting together *The Making of Americans: Being a History of a Family's Progress* (1925). Stein wrote with evident frustration, "I can never really be knowing all the ways there are of feeling living."[14] In *The Gradual Making of* The Making of Americans, she discusses the problems of accurately capturing the history of an individual:

When I was up against the difficulty of putting down the complete conception that I had of an individual, the complete rhythm of a personality that I had gradually acquired by listening seeing feeling and experience, I was faced by the trouble that I had acquired all this knowledge gradually but when I had it I had it completely at one time."[15]

As Stein began to realize, she had been mistaken in projecting *The Making of Americans* as an all-encompassing retrospective narrative. She reflects that

I began to get enormously interested in hearing how everybody said the same thing over and over again with infinite variations but over and over again until finally if you listened with great intensity you could hear it rise and fall and tell all that there was inside them, not so much by the actual words they said or the thoughts they had but the movement of their thoughts endlessly the same and endlessly different.[16]

Subjectivity could thus be found in the *movement* or *process* of thought. In a lecture given at the Naropa Institute in Boulder, Colorado, Mayer states that she composed the text of *Memory* around the pictures and notes she already had, in order to contest Stein's claim that "you can't write remembering."[17] When the writing of *Memory* nearly drove her crazy, she was forced to admit defeat: "Dear g.s., when I think of you I think I am you but not so harsh you were right o.k. to be harsh."[18]

At first glance, *Memory* seems to have a traditional autobiographical structure, with its daily journal–like sections patterned in chronological order. Yet events from the present increasingly resemble the past and blur together in synchronous affect. A friend's illness recalls her own mother's death and her subsequent feelings of rootlessness. Addressing her sister, Mayer writes:

secrets are ours I'm talking to you, rosemarie, keep the order keep the peace. . . . Watch my black eyes: the large skies of queens with the large clouds of wyoming neat vistas, rows, fields no life anywhere, do I want to be cut off from all people or from all of my family, when I saw GP I thought of my mother mouth open gaping into the atmosphere of a room hospital room no power neither protesting I don't want to die in a hospital: hear the thrusts deaths & sighs or was each a soul scream head-rending at its heart & horrible[19]

"I'm a history her coil mark time," she writes elsewhere.[20] Mayer switches between collapsing the traditional distance between narrating self and narrated self in autobiography and playfully foregrounding it: "The I-character is usually a she."[21]

In a continuous present, "all experience is of equal value, that which was future . . . is in no way different from that which was past."[22] This equivalence may be found in the numerous lists and the endless repetition of phrases. She also echoes other writers, such as in the line that so obviously recalls Hannah Weiner, "I love you you are deer we dont hear images from you anymore."[23] This undermines the traditional privileging of authorial voice. The food of a dial-a-steak service is described in as much detail as an emotionally explosive fight. Clichés such as "Bright lights big city," billboard signs, and the words of popular songs ("I wanna take you higher") also resound throughout the text, sometimes in fragmented or interrupted form.[24] Everything is included, even the physical process of producing a text:

what can a diary be not a reconstruction, something put in, use the time, pass it, stain it, pass it, it's stained, it's magnified, it sticks, it sticks in my mind & my hand always hurts always hurts still does when I write in this book: book, took three rolls to be developed into seen.[25]

By placing otherwise disjunctive elements side by side, she creates meaning through association. An example is the opening line, "& the main thing is we begin with a white sink a whole new language is a temptation."[26] The white sink next to the new language suggests the whiteness and blankness of the page before her. This process of making connections, often illogical ones, is similar to dreamwork. In the last section, entitled "Dreamings," Mayer suggests that "dream makes memory present, hidden memory the secret dream."[27] Dream becomes a memory kept in process. As closure is impossible, the last page of *Memory* can only be a "false ending."[28]

Clark Coolidge felt that *Memory* was not "talked about that much by the poets," and even Mayer notes that many friends admitted they could not finish it.[29] Yet Simon Schuchat suggested that its challenge to the conventions of writing were the most radical since William Burroughs's cut-up novels.[30] Peter Baker also argues that *Memory* "helped establish Mayer as one of the leading experimental writers of her time."[31] Mayer, however, had already gained attention. She experienced what many saw as premature recognition in 1970 when featured in a prominent New York anthology edited by Ron Padgett and David Shapiro.[32] Mayer was the only female contributor among twenty-six male poets, while leading women writers like Barbara Guest were excluded. This put Mayer in a difficult position. As Marcella Durand points out, "Being the 'only woman' chosen by male editors, brought the wrong sort of responsibility, separated women out from the community, made them carry the burden for other women."[33]

Coolidge notes that, even in the early part of the seventies, people were more intimidated by Mayer's work than by his own. "I figured at the time it had something to do with the fact that she was female in a male dominant poetry climate," he states, "and she was feisty and wouldn't take shit from any of these guys, wanting the same opening for her work." Coolidge notes that throughout the seventies they encouraged each other, "[a]lways to go further, no matter what reaction, or lack of, by anyone, known or unknown."[34] The writing that both were doing had very little to do with "poetry" as it was then understood. Extending *Memory's* study of states of consciousness, Mayer undertook an even longer work, the "Studying Hunger" journals. At several hundred pages of single-spaced text, it remained problematic for publishers. Mayer managed to publish only a few lectures she drew from the journals in 1975. Ten years later, Sun & Moon turned down the complete manuscript on the grounds that it was a long work and that there was not a large enough audience for journals at that particular moment.[35]

Barrett Watten and Robert Grenier's inaugural issue of *This* is often taken as a point of origin for a predominantly West Coast framing of Language writing. However, in the same year as its publication (1971), Mayer began teaching her influential workshop, "Experimental Writing," at St. Mark's Poetry Project in New York. The workshop provided much of the impetus behind the emergent Language writing on the East Coast. Her teaching included the work of Stein and Wittgenstein, which would stimulate, even ground, the poetics of many Language writers. Blurring the philosophical and poetic was still a highly contentious act at the time, and Mayer notes that she had to deal with varying degrees of dissension. She introduced her students to Dadaism, psychoanalytic theory, and semiotics and also sponsored an interdisciplinary lecture series for her classes.

Lynne Dreyer moved to New York to go to St. Mark's but more specifically to study in Mayer's workshop. Her writing had already been compared to Mayer's, and Dreyer was impressed by *Moving, Memory,* and *Poetry*. The smallness of the workshop was reassuring, and the experience had a strong impact on her writing. "[E]verything became much faster, darker, and extremely internal," she recalls.[36] Mayer states that when she began the workshop, "I noticed a lot of people, women, would want to study with a woman teacher . . . [b]asically because they have something different to say, different attitudes, understand different things from men."[37]

The scarcity of female role models often places additional pressure on women in pedagogic positions to give emotional as well as vocational support. Diana Hume George argues that "women are in effect asked to extend the work of mothering from the domestic to the professional sphere."[38] Mayer gave care and advice, but she attempted to move beyond the hierarchies that maternal relationships produce, often in tandem with more traditional paternal relationships. In her 1971 workshop she began the experimental magazine *Unnatural Acts*, which was devoted wholly to collaborative writing. Still only twenty-six herself, she was initially terrified of teaching and "did a tremendous amount of over-preparing."[39] However, by the final year, there was a revolving leadership "so that every week somebody in the workshop would do something else."[40] Through such teaching mechanisms, she challenged her own authority as a repository of poetic knowledge. She also encouraged students to argue back.

In her notes for the workshop, Mayer argues that writing should be seen as a "long-term process & lead-in to more experiments & investigations in whatever tradition to achieve things you think could not be achieved in writing, to liberate words." She adds that the aim of experimental writing is "to find out what more is communicable, or, what is communicable now."[41] She also wanted to explore a language that seemed to separate, but just barely, the distinction between observation and analysis. In other words, she wanted to explore the extent that language's materiality shaped meaning. In attempting to describe something as fully as possible,

language seemed to be demanding its form . . . colors plotted the outline-sound of a language, an unmarked language, not controlling it. Forget any substance of naming, forget substantives & their color & get it gradually paler, seeing sound vibrations in sleep-closed eyes. A lamp hanging is a sound. It lowers & disappears.[42]

The sound, of course, arises from the rhythm invoked by the repeated soft *s* in "seeing sound vibrations in sleep-closed eyes." "The Poem may have to mean nothing for a while or reflect in its meaning just the image of meaning," Mayer states in "The Obfuscated Poem," "The best obfuscation bewilders old meanings while reflecting or creating a structure of a beauty that we know." Experimentation could thus transform language and offer a "chance for liberation."[43]

Mayer was soon recognized as one of the few women who were able to intervene in the various canonical groupings of male writers. By 1980 her profile was such that Susan Howe would tell Hejinian to "go back and rummage through recent LANGUAGE issue[s]—and HILLS and see how often she is mentioned and how seldom you or I or any other woman is."[44] In the seventies, Mayer and Stein seemed to Howe to be the only women writers promoted by Language writing, and even then Stein was problematic. Terming her "Mr. Stein," Howe saw Stein as occupying a masculine role in her relation to the Left Bank community.[45] Mayer, on the other hand, had succeeded as a woman against the traditional gendering of authorship.

Mayer's workshop notes, known simply as "Experiments," mutated over the years as different members of workshop groups added and transformed the list. Jerome McGann argues that "Experiments" outlines "a number of the most important characteristics of $L=A=N=G=U=A=G=E$ writing."[46] His essay "Contemporary Poetry, Alternate Routes" was one of the earliest academic interventions into Language writing and informed many later debates. Unfortunately, his discussion of Mayer's work fails to recognize the often humorous edge to its aphoristic statements, interpreting "Experiments" more as an instructional "mini-manual" or "do-it-yourself" text of Language writing. Moreover, the importance of "Experiments" in relation to Language writing is offset by his constant use of the descriptive term "*L=A=N=G=U=A=G=E* writing." This has the effect of making the magazine edited by Bruce Andrews and Charles Bernstein the key signifier in his historicization of Language writing. In a strange twist, Bernstein himself recently updated and expanded Mayer's "Experiments," foregrounding their playful nature.[47] Unfortunately, the effect of aligning "Experiments" with Bernstein's own signature, particularly in the forum of a scholarly journal such as *Boundary 2*, is likely to (however unintended) displace Mayer's original signature and frame the piece in terms of Bernstein's.

In the mid- to late seventies, Mayer came to believe that one can go too far with experimentation. Citing Joyce's *Finnegans Wake* as an example, she felt that there was a danger in moving too far from what was communicable: "It's simply if you go too far in one direction, you can never get back & you're out there in complete isolation, like this anthropologist who spent the last 20 years of his life on the sweet potato controversy (which way it floated)."[48] Mayer began turning toward a more traditional form, strengthening ties with the second-generation New York school. This can be seen in "The Complete Introductory Lectures on Poetry," which is dedicated to Ted Berrigan:

> It was when the words on the covers of books,
> titles as true as false leaves led me to believe
> in inviting the ultimate speculation of love—
> that I could learn *all* of the subject—
> that I first began to entertain what is sublime
>
> Like a moth I thought by reading *Jokes and
> Their Relation to the Unconscious* or *Beyond
> the Pleasure Principle* or *Eat the Weeds* or
> *The Origins of the Species* or even a book on
> *Coup d'Etats* or *The Problem of Anxiety* I
> could accomplish all the knowledge the titles implied.

In contrast to language or the theories surrounding it, Mayer suggests that there is more science in the notes on the back of a discarded envelope, or in shadows on the wall in the night when the babies awaken. She concludes:

> It is to think this or that might include all
> or enough to entertain all those who already know
> that in this century of private apartments
> though knowledge might be coveted hardly anything
> is shared except penurious poetry, she or he
> who still tends to titles as if all of us
> are reading a new book called *THE NEW LIFE.*[49]

Given that Dante's *Vita Nuova* speaks of "The New Life" as that which occurs after an ecstatic experience, Mayer speaks with the faith of the converted. She was interested not so much in the possibilities of language as such but in its relation to a more pressing subject, the concerns of everyday life. Her writing shows more interest in the narrative layering of perception and is at times reminiscent of the immediacy of the Beats. In a radio interview with Susan Howe, Mayer cited as her role model Alice Notley.[50] Both wrote in a seemingly transparent style in order to focus on "unspeakable" areas of experience—sexuality, motherhood, and desire. While Mayer and Notley focused attention on the importance of family, it was presumed, mistakenly, that they were leaving their partners, Lewis Warsh and Ted Berrigan, to get on with the more serious business of writing.

For poets like Fanny Howe, the blurring of roles between domestic and professional was refreshing. She argued that Mayer's work is a "radical human gesture" in its level of emotion and regard for everyday life." "[S]he does, in fact, seem to be writing at the same time as she is living," Howe wrote, "The effect of this illusion on the reader is welcome; you are invited, without fear, to participate in experience and interpretation."[51] In contrast, Lyn Hejinian had some trouble with the way in which she saw Mayer trying to make domestic life into a "romance."[52] However, she told Rae Armantrout that she "would like to be friends with Bernadette—I admire her writing very much and there are few enough of us women."[53]

Others thought Mayer's focus on the domestic gave her poetry a lack of political orientation. In *Total Syntax*, Barrett Watten takes Mayer as an example of an avant-garde that has "too much possibility/not enough necessity":

While the advantage of Mayer's techniques is their adherence to the quotidian, there is no further integration. The "permanent avant-garde" vaporizes, leading to more conventional roles. As actually happened—in the course of Mayer's later editing of United Artists, the stylistic opening-up returns all these techniques to "the self."[54]

In her study of Simone de Beauvoir, Toril Moi points out that prolific female figures are quickly tagged with an inflammatory reputation. In approaching such a figure is to "find oneself in a web of hotly disputed opinions and entrenched public myths."[55] Under such conditions, "Bernadette Mayer" is not simply the name of a person who wrote poems, edited magazines, managed presses, and directed the St. Mark's Poetry Project but a site of ideological and aesthetic conflict. Mayer's shifting poetics made her a contentious figure, and as with Beauvoir, so did her personal relationships. It is worthwhile considering Mayer's reputation in relation to that of another influential yet contrary figure in Language writing, John Ashbery. Ashbery also turned from the radical experimentalism of earlier work such as *The Tennis Court Oath* to more traditional forms. While Ashbery was seen to "compromise" in his later poetics, he nevertheless remains central to projects aimed at building a tradition for Language writing.[56]

The Desires of Mothers to Please Others in Letters reveals that, far from abandoning the principles informing *Memory*, Mayer was extending them to explore a poetics of connection. Like *Memory*, *The Desires of Mothers* is a long prose work. Much of it is also written as a stream of consciousness and requires similarly heightened attention. Even concerns of the relationship of memory to language and knowledge are continued:

Funny how you mention having fun or something, we are having a hard time re-membering and now the images and the powers of talismans might be sought and rendered bereft or even just forgotten for their powers, we are so unsure, we are back in the shops of forbidding the exclamation like the exclamation of leering or of the structure I was begging you to allow me to show off with, instead of having to talk about snakes and mirrors and all that stuff, Maldoror, Lautréamont, Rimbaud, more chances and temptations, hashish rumors and art objects, there's too much stuff and only an enormously fat or very skinny person can even begin to try to fathom it in literature and without and what it is and what her powers among it might turn out to be, a young one, an old one, a sacrosanct one, originally lost but lost with such fortitude.[57]

In *Memory*, Mayer frequently uses an epistolary form of address. Such directed thought is found more explicitly in *The Desires of Mothers*, which takes the form of a series of letters, written (but never sent) during the period of 1979–1980. There are also temporal constraints on the project, although instead of one month, Mayer allowed herself nine—covering the pregnancy of her third child, Max. In using a unit of what Kristeva calls "women's time," Mayer investigates authorship as a gendered process.

In compiling the volume she wrote both to and of earlier women writers like Gertrude Stein, Virginia Woolf, and Lady Mary Wortley Montagu, as well as contemporaries like Alice Notley, Hannah Weiner, and Fanny Howe. In a note to Notley, she reflects, "I began to write letters I would never send so I could at the same time have a person to write to and not have to worry about what I said."[58] Hejinian shared similar musings with Fanny Howe: "I've been thinking about you, and thinking this letter to-ward you, a lot recently. That partially comes of writing fewer and fewer letters and therefore harboring conversations in my imagination."[59] The composition of letters, as Lola Lemire Tostevin suggests, provides "an op-portunity for women to digress from daily routines, help . . . them to conjure another person with whom to share both the turbulent and the quiet within."[60] It helps them to tap feelings and ideas that otherwise would have gone unformed.

Letters form a genre that not only demarcates the feminine and the private but which foregrounds relationship. Carroll Smith-Rosenberg critiques a women's culture of love and ritual in nineteenth-century America by examining the letters written by women to one another.[61] This culture took place outside but necessarily alongside the public economy, constituting an alternative but interrelated social structure. Mayer's letters, with their feminist desires and failed address may be seen as doubly illicit, as both public and cultural objects. More than anything else, they are best viewed as confessions, revealing a compulsion to speak of everyday anxieties, reflections, and admissions as writer and as mother. Only recently have they been viewed as a viable publishing venture. As with the trouble she had in publishing her journals, Mayer's letters failed to please others, perhaps primarily because they do not attempt to please. Instead, Mayer explores the possibility that mothers have *other* desires, including the desire to write, to claim agency as subject.

Mayer writes of her need for dialogue as a means of mirroring back identity:

[W]hen I was first trying to learn about the world, I remember it clearly, I realized easily that I couldn't apprehend it at all . . . and I decided the only thing to do to be able to speak at all was to find another person I loved and respected, find out what his or her opinions . . . about the thing I was wondering about were, and say they were my own.[62]

Through repetition, Mayer could sound out the boundaries of cultural knowledge and thus begin to experiment through mimicry. In an unsent letter to Notley, she declares:

So thus I could find out in the talking from the words what thoughts were because I couldn't find out from my silence as it seemed. . . . So I got the habit that way to experiment. To, like the other Alice, see what I could say. Which is also why I never could believe you or anyone could take my writing seriously because I knew I was just trying out for a world, even of words, everyone but me was the master-mistress of, at least apparently.[63]

Mayer's writing invokes an echo chamber, a sympathetic context of past and present writers, through which she attempts to validate her practice. Yet this context is itself uncertain. "Don't get me wrong," she states at one stage, "I don't fault them, Kerouac or Hemingway. Who are the great

American women novelists, I don't even have a saint here, there's no field, Willa Cather."[64] Yet Mayer does map a field, one that includes Hawthorne, Whitman, Williams, Kerouac, Woolf, and Stein. These are the writers who experimented with the sentence. Looking back to women writers such as Gertrude Stein and Virginia Woolf, Mayer reflects on how their own cultural and historically specific position enabled their innovations with language. In this retrospective project, Mayer joins contemporaries like Susan Howe, who felt more in common with dead writers like Emily Dickinson, Emily Brontë, and again, Woolf.

Both Howe and Mayer looked to Woolf as a role model, but one whose success as a woman writer is countered by her failure to be part of society. Susan Howe writes with empathy of Woolf's anxiety over (and despite of) her success:

BUT I thought as I lay tossing and turning unable to sleep last night—this same successful woman, widely published, surrounded by successful men—and a loving husband. Walked into a river one March day. All the layers in work that the critics never never never reach—like the fathomless bottom of the sea—are in that fact.[65]

In contrast to Howe's Romanticism, Mayer writes with humor of the dangers of intellectualism for women: "I only worry all the time, I worry about my cervix, I worry about my uterus, my ovaries, my pleasant vagina and that reading too many books by women about things will turn me into an even more unbearable crank than the cranky poets who write hate letters." "I had a dream last night," she adds, "that two men I know in New York City wanted to . . . strike matches on me, this from reading A ROOM OF ONE'S OWN which is an odd book to read when you're broke and worried about your female sexual organs."[66]

Whereas Howe interprets Woolf's literary success as resulting from being surrounded by a supportive community of men, Mayer viewed Woolf's economic ease as a more significant factor. However, like Woolf, Mayer was particularly concerned about the material constraints imposed on women's cultural agency. She reflects: "The news about women is dismal, their voting in Japan, the new prostitutes in China, the female doctors who can't find the time to have children because their husbands won't help them, all the disapproval of having both babies and abortions, the expensive sterilizations, all deduced and argued by the vainest males of choice."[67] Elsewhere, she relates how she used to fear the possibility of being institutionalized with other women. Between the lines there is a recognition that they are always already institutionalized through the regulatory divisions of work and gender. "[T]he presence of men," she realizes, "seemed to enliven or enlift the irreducible sentence from its gloom. Now I don't feel that way."[68]

As a woman and a writer, Mayer experienced a split identity in being known both through her work and her family. These are roles that Mayer had to take up and perform involuntarily: "Since I am a woman I got accustomed to the other part of life too as if there were two parts, I don't forget I am a poet but I forget to be being one except for the writing or I even pretend love is the same and all the rest."[69] She notes that earlier writers, like Williams and Hawthorne, had devoted wives. Even Stein had Alice Toklas. Whitman, however, allows her to "think of him as a woman like me."[70]

These familial and professional identities are continually reinforced in everyday life as being mutually exclusive. In one letter, she tells how she got into trouble for attempting to place an ad in the "faculty bulletin" to start a play group: "It seems like you're not supposed to act like a person or a mother when you're a teacher."[71] In another, she considers the effect of motherhood on her reputation as a writer:

Remember that woman I told you about who came to take a picture of Lewis and he said I was a poet too, and she looked at me and Sophia and Marie carefully crawling on me and she said, oh really and when do you get to write? There's no use ever actually saying you're a poet, it's a disservice to yourself except for the wonder you can sustain among the moths, but you'd better say it anyway.[72]

In using the imagery of moths, Mayer recalls Woolf's metaphor to describe creative impulse.[73] Like Woolf, she views women as still culturally alienated from the labor of writing. Mayer repeated the image in describing her desire, even necessity, to write: "Families are so seriously whole, worked at not like poems, not gotten from the air, still the spirit in the moth attracted not to the light but to my hands . . . , if I don't see it, scares me."[74]

While Mayer wrote of the demands of the family, her identity as a mother also motivated meditations on identity. In *Studying Hunger* she describes her relationship with her daughter Marie: "That's what started me off again & that's what opened the question of who is the you. You private person. And now, while you keep in mind my intentions at the beginning & what I've said to try to explain how they got transformed & where they came from, I'll go on."[75] The difference between the speaking "I" and the "you" is rendered ambiguous.

Mayer desired a utopic space where sexual difference does not constrain what one can be or what heroic acts one can do. "Kerouac loved Proust," she wrote, "and did you ever hear the story of his reading Henry IV out loud with somebody and then the other person realized he was doing it from memory, remember when I did that once on Demerol with NAKED LUNCH."[76] Such a space would be genderless and outside historical time:

"Then the water seems to talk and I am Joan of Arc or Jean Arthur hearing voices, I am neither a woman nor a man but an ethereal person leading two horses in another world; where my sex is . . . something I can't recognize."[77]

Yet this vision of androgyny is tempered, as "the dream of perfection like romances or families, fails you."[78] The failure of heroic logic, particularly for women writers, is made apparent by the economically grim realities of family and working life. As Mayer states, "Whenever we buy some food it disappears right away, unlike Jack Kerouac's food."[79] Living in New Hampshire further marginalizes her: "I am invisible, we have no mirror, the students sneer at everything, there's no place to publish poems, no one to read them, they're all too long."[80] Of domesticity, she writes: "I wonder why when everyone is doing the opposite of the very things that women have always detested and abhorred, and run away from, especially women poets, I have to be stubbornly doing them."[81] This split identity is something she embraces, even though she cannot resolve her frustrations. The desires of mothers to please, she seems to suggest, will always be in conflict with the desire to write.

The Desires of Mothers to Please Others in Letters was published in 1994, well over a decade after it was written. Following similar works, like *Midwinter Day*, it reveals the interlinking of private to public history and a feminist poetics that openly proclaims its contaminations and contingencies. In the same year, Mayer suffered the equivalent of a stroke, which left her unable to work for a lengthy period of time. As a way to provide Mayer with some financial support during her rehabilitation, the Bernadette Mayer Fund was established. In addition, twenty-five friends and colleagues contributed poems and prose to a limited edition boxed set of broadsides called *Writing for Bernadette*.[82] This collection was limited to twenty-six copies. Automatically marketed as "rare," the volume inadvertently replicates the inaccessibility of much of Mayer's past writing. At the same time, it attests to the strong level of community support for Mayer.

While publications like *The Desire to Please* or *The Bernadette Mayer Reader* intervene canonically to retrieve Mayer's textual body from the realm of cultural forgetting, others, such as *Writing for Bernadette*, more directly aid the author herself. Indeed, such volumes serve to remind us of the strange but inextricable connections between a writer's work and her life. The excerpt from Robert Creeley's "Histoire de Florida" states by way of dark parable:

> Remember German artist
> (surely "conceptual" or
> "happenings") ate himself,
> cut bits from his body
> on stage while audience

watched, it went well
for awhile. But then
he did something wrong
and bled to death.
The art is long
to learn, life short.[83]

Writing for Bernadette served as a tribute not only to Mayer but also to
the poetic community she helped to shape. Often chosen to emphasize an
aspect or aspects of Mayer's poetic practice, each piece stands as an un-
canny response to the title of *The Desires of Mothers to Please Others in Let-
ters*. As Hejinian wrote on the back cover, "the desire to please is always a
prolongation of the power to please." The poems on the broadsides, with
their subtle reveling in the signature of Mayer's poetics, attest to this pleas-
ure. Individually marked from A to Z, they may be seen as the letters writ-
ten back in the same vein as Mayer's own letters a decade earlier.

Michael Palmer's contribution recalls Mayer's *Midwinter Day*, her he-
roic and other-world imagery, experiments in dream-writing, and love of
Stein in "Anode (27 XII 94)":

> The words she spoke in sleep
> That the city would disappear
> In winter a walk through the Summer Gardens
>
> We all recognize ourselves in *Stanzas*
> Peter, as in a lake of ice
> blue as a lake of ice . . .

Fanny Howe's "The Practice" may also be read as a testament to
Mayer's advice and her exploration of the continuous present:

> *Go on out but come back in*
> You told me to live by, so I went . . .
>
> I did this several times, out and in,
> it was of course a meditation . . .
>
> Past? Present? Future? No such things.

Clark Coolidge's "What Is Thought But Won't Hold Still" speaks of es-
caping from "chambers/of intellectual mood" toward "the nothing that
you see." Hejinian also focuses on Mayer's autobiographical self, the writ-
ing of a perceptive self that investigates how it knows through language
and time:

> The imagination is useless unless the mind is free of prejudice
> So as to follow its objects
> Turning day to night,

Appearance to lightsource, fountains to rice,
And what is knowledge in this condition?
Flight?
I think, the Nightingale Girl said to the Singing Man,
That time requires anecdotes to contradict it.
No answer.
Time longs undividedly for something.
We'll wait
For an uninterrupted look at the border,
The interpretation,
the pass,
Not only through adventures but through to tomorrow . . .

Hejinian's faith in a critical "tomorrow" is perhaps already being assured. In 1992, *The Poetry Project Newsletter* ran a special issue on Mayer.[84] Aside from her work appearing in numerous magazines and anthologies, the past decade has seen the publication of *The Formal Field of Kissing*, *Proper Names and Other Stories*, and *Another Smashed Pinecone*, as well as a reprint of *Midwinter Day*. As Peter Baker suggests, "It may be that when the publishing process begins to match up to Mayer's actual production a clearer picture will emerge of her more recent work."[85] It is to be hoped that the growing audience for Mayer's work will continue to read it in terms of the radical challenges it offers to past institutional narratives—the hagiographies that praise poetic order and virtuous female constraint. For to borrow a line from Gertrude Stein's own dys-sanctity, "To know to know to love her so/Four saints prepare for saints."[86]

CHAPTER ELEVEN

Taking a Poethical Perspective: Joan Retallack's *Afterrimages*

If knowledge has nothing to do with certainty, if certainty is instead a property of belief in the viability of the social game, then knowledge is always a tentative matter of bearings—taking in linguistic, spatial, temporal cues just well and long enough to contemplate, capitulate, or, move on.

—Genre Tallique, *Glances: An Unwritten Book*

W hile writers like Bernadette Mayer show poetry and life to be mutually informing (often in strange and unexpected ways), Joan Retallack explores this relationship more fully in a practice she calls "poethics." Poethics describes the use of a positively constructive imagination in relation to the complex conditions of society and the world. Yet it is also analytic, requiring one to ask whether a form is enabling or damaging in the context of its use and value at a particular moment in history.[1] To view its joining of aesthetics and ethics as some variation on the Wildean credo to live according to the rules of art would be misleading. Rather, poethics critiques the reductive logic of Western history and charges us with the task of considering what would make a viable future-redeeming past.[2] This requires rethinking the past through its relationship to the present. Furthermore, poethics confirms the role of writing in encouraging thought to move in new, unfamiliar directions.

As a philosophy graduate at the University of Chicago, Retallack studied under the aegis of G. E. M. Anscombe, known not only for her own influential book, *Intention*, but also for her definitive translation of Wittgenstein's *Philosophical Investigations*. Like J. L. Austin, Elizabeth Anscombe advocated a pragmatic approach to language, one that removes humor and poetry from the philosophical engagement. Retallack was deeply attracted to the certainty that Anscombe's theories held, as well as the almost crystalline structure that theories of the sublime offered to art. Yet at the same time, she was discovering an enjoyment in performance, particularly the act of writing poetry and its attendant free-fall through language and genre. This yearning to have *both* (order and chaos, theory and praxis, desire and enjoyment) rather than *either/or* becomes apparent in all of Retallack's future ventures.

Moving to Washington, DC in the sixties, Retallack became active not only in the local arts scene but in the civil rights and antiwar movements. In 1968 she was hired by R. G. H. Siu (author of *The Tao of Science*), whom Lyndon Johnson had appointed to run a newly formed interdisciplinary institute at the Department of Justice.[3] The institute had a broad mission to develop a social value framework for government policies. Retallack recalls that she hoped, in the long run, to contribute to a rethinking of the language of government in the United States.[4] She also planned to start conversations between the Justice Department and citizens from disparate economic classes and communities, and to promote community arts projects as a proactive alternative to incarceration. More immediately, Retallack set about interviewing a variety of people already involved with issues of social justice, including John Cage and Buckminster Fuller. Both Retallack and her interviewees were optimistic, believing that here was a chance for the arts to directly influence governmental policies. However, not long after the interviews were transcribed, Nixon came into power. Retallack's work was confiscated and "classified," and her contract was not renewed. Far from destroying her belief in the social power of art, this experience confirmed in Retallack the need to find escape paths from the overbearing imprint of hegemonic authority.

Retallack suggests that poethical work begins when "you no longer wish to shape materials (words, visual elements, sounds) into legitimate progeny of your own poetics." It requires the ego to be relinquished as the point of control informing the work. She adds that poethics can occur only "when you realize that your present project is insufficient, that it has not moved towards the unintelligibilities of the present." In rejecting expected patterns, poethical writing effectively undertakes the work of genealogy. It changes "your sense of the relation of your language to the world beyond the page—to everyday life and death. And this will in turn affect the world of the page—the formal intersections of space-time with linguistic forms of life, recovery and loss, silence and art."[5]

Because it works outside legitimate, even recognizable models, poethical writing often goes through a period of invisibility and misunderstanding. Similar to Pascal's philosophical wager on the existence of God ("Oui, mais il faut parier. Cela n'est pas volontaire, vous êtes embarqué" [Yes, but you must wager. This is not voluntary, you are embarked]), Retallack argues that every writer is also always already engaged in a poethical wager. That is, the writer must gamble on the "very realistic, if improbable chance" that his or her contribution will have some sort of significant effect. While the effects of any one person's work are unpredictable, one can but try to produce a generative outcome. This is achieved partly by basing one's actions on a conscious framework of values.[6] Once writing is seen to have a future charge, it is then possible to consider how to "add positive, even constructive, initial conditions" to the work of generations to come.[7]

Such a poetics of possibility is not foreign to Language writing, yet Retallack's work stands apart from many of its projects. Her major serial poem, *WESTERN CIV*, for example, uses new dimensions, extended time frames, and all kinds of media. As an ongoing composition, part of it (*WESTORN CIV CONT'D, AN OPEN BOOK*) involved a three-dimensional installation requiring the reader to walk from one site to the next.[8] Another section demands a quite different kind of embodied reading practice, "*WESTERN CIV CONT'D:* A Brief Experiment in Linguistics" (1998), actually directing the act of reading through a sequence of physiological positions.[9] What this does is to dislodge poetry from its resting place as something abstract, repeatable, or containable. Instead, the reader must enter the space of the poem and perform it self-consciously according to some sort of procedure or score. Gender always figures (or transfigures) within Retallack's work as an imperative of ethical analysis.

As Hank Lazer points out, Retallack's compositions sometimes seem like a form of "radicalized anthologizing," an overwhelmingly dense stockpile of literary, musical, philosophical, scientific, legal, and linguistic leavings dating from the near to ancient past.[10] But given her poethical premise, Retallack is doing far more than simple bricolage. Instead, she carefully assembles a confluence of coordinates that will generate a paradigmatic shift in the very way we think about our own positioning within time and space.

"All images are after. That is the terror they hold for us," reads the epigraph by Genre Tallique to one of Retallack's more recent volumes, *Afterrimages* (1995).[11] Jacques Derrida suggests that although the past is absolute and unable to be reduced to any form of presence, we find ourselves attempting to bring the dead back, trying to recall through image. Yet this image is only an image of ourselves, for the dead can never answer to it or share in it.[12] A tradition of centering knowledge around the self can be traced back to the Greeks, with Homer generally pinpointed as an origin of Western civilization. In the *Iliad*, for instance, at the height of the battle of Troy, Achilles cries out to his victims, "Look at me! Do you not see how beautiful, noble and great I am?"[13] Here, the hero and history, too, become ineluctably linked to the modality of the visual. In Greek the word for "to know" (*eidenai*) is semantically and morphologically cognate with the word for "to see" (*idein*).[14] The analytic gaze was part of the anatomy of a

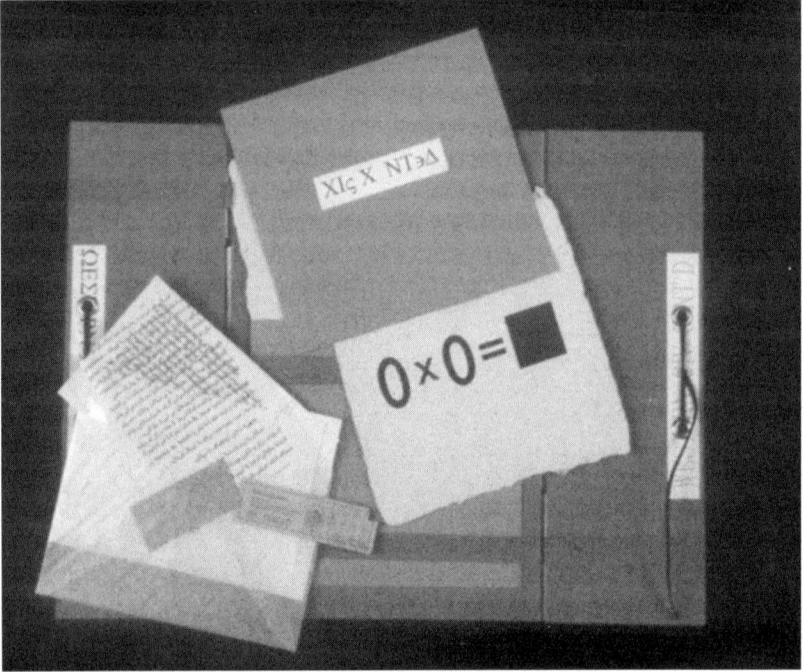

Fig. 7. *WESTORN CIV CONT'D: AN OPEN BOOK*, Joan Retallack, 1996. Cardboard, metal grommets, cord, acetate, handmade paper, silk-screened and moveable images, text cards, tickets.

subject's claim to know. Although Plato shifted from the dominance of the corporeal image to the abstract image in his analysis of the Republic, the link between epistemology and vision was firmly established.

In *Afterrimages*, Retallack critiques the terms of our encounter with past elements of Western culture and their aftereffects. What she attempts to do is not to dislodge the mirror effect of history but to show how our desires for the past influence our understanding of it. An afterimage occurs when we focus our sight steadily on one area and then shift it to another, resulting initially in a pattern of the first over the second. In terms of history it could be said that in switching attention from the present to the past, we also produce an afterimage—by seeing it through the familiar. Images of the past, according to Retallack's analogy, will be completed by each individual viewer and are therefore varied in their local effects and contrasts. The eye chart of inverted words at the beginning of *Afterrimages* playfully reinforces this by transforming the volume's title into "Afterthoughts," "After/Ors," and "Aftermath."

Although afterimages have traditionally been discounted as aberrations, Retallack suggests that they are valuable because they demand a more complex understanding of knowledge's relation to vision—that vision itself is never clear and unclouded. We need to look again at how and why we construct the past through particular frameworks and constellations, and to examine how this might affect our current sense of the world. Retallack's theory of afterimage is similar to Walter Benjamin's dialectic of history. While firmly rooted in the "time of the now," it is a reality that looks back to moments in the past that speak to the present and to the future.[15] Traditionally, the Cartesian subject has engendered the self through a separation—even denial—of the Other, the external world, and even its own senses. By looking again, we can see fractures in the coherent objects we have built of the past. We might then see the past as not only reflecting our own (self-supporting) fantasies but as containing the fragments or shards of an Other. The self would subsequently be estranged in the resulting revelation of being constituted against a background of misrecognition and disorder.

Retallack is interested in this edge between present and past, self and Other. The very title of her poem, *Afterrimages*, contains the term *rim* as a hidden supplement, an excessive syntax that threatens the stability of meaning. Retallack's poetry reads the rim of Western knowledge, revealing it is as an imaginary construct that represses what would otherwise be recognized as cracks in the picture. As Retallack suggests, this unintelligible space is feminine, phallic, and phobic.[16] "The feminine . . . as we understand it in the intercourse of culture," she argues, "may be nothing more or less than the fluid drive zone of unintelligibility."[17] This psychoanalytic gendering of knowledge (which follows the Aristotelian paradigm) is a primary distinction between Retallack and other Language writers.[18] For Retallack, the feminine is the Other of knowledge—or rather, it is "know ledge," the edge of the knowing "I." She argues that history's condition imposes a particular kind of structure on one's Time and Space that may leave one blind.

In "Afterrimages" (the serial poem opening and lending its title to the volume), the pages are divided in the middle by a steady or dotted line. The poem in the bottom half of the page has been created by the chance procedure of scattering thirteen paper clips of various sizes on the poem in the upper half, and recording what remains within the eyes of the paper clips. Retallack chose thirteen, not only because it was the date on which she was born but because the number (while "lucky for some") has portentous or "dicey" associations in Western culture. Through this process, the original poem may appear to hold previously unseen resonances. As might be expected, the resulting second poem or "aftermath" is much sparser. Some of the spaces beneath the line are completely blank or silent. Occasionally, the remaining groups of letters may lead to the creation of further poems. For example, from four residual clusters of one poem—"snagge," "od," "in pastel," and "twa"—Retallack begins a new poem with the line: "1. No God can be snagged in a pastel twang."[19]

Retallack argues: "The results of 'chance operations' . . . are just that, nothing more, nothing less than a turning of attention to the silences that lie beyond the habits, desires, fears of our intentionally directed eyes and ears. What results from the use of chance procedures may shock or delight." She adds: "The selective foregrounding of chance makes it possible to bring to light and sound things that are otherwise potently absent or ominous."[20] Western modernity has tended to reject the presence of chance in the world because it takes control away from the knowing subject. Retallack believes that a procedural use of chance is a strategy for making visible through the local material detail of the poem what is otherwise a global condition.

Afterrimages' poems resists any sort of consistent, lyric voice by being themselves made up of fragments. While each poem is open to an infinite range of readings, Retallack continually challenges the reader to question the linguistic and epistemic categories that they might bring to the poems. There is a metatextual focus on the process of reading itself—specifically on the patterned, often hierarchical assumptions that are automatically made in producing meaning in the poem. The opening poem of the first series is a good example:

> pull of gravity
> balance between
> spherical form
> covering of short hairs or fur
> something on or near the surface
> i.e. specificcrystallineformoftaxonomiccategories
> ....
> *So reulith hire hir hertes gost withinne,*
> *That though she bende, yeet she stant on roote*

> rs o
> ne th su
> orm onomi ate
> .. ..
> *e hir hert*[21]

The beginning of the poem literally balances between the "pull of gravity" and "spherical form," while schematically graphing the eye's binocular line of vision. Reminding us of the unseen curve of the globe itself, the poem suggests alternative dimensions to what Retallack calls elsewhere,

"Flatland."[22] This is the plane of history in which reality appears mapped with the "geometric ironies of misogyny and denial." A surface is also a single plane but tends to be more complex than first thought. There is no surface without depth, except in fractal terms. The skin, for instance, might have a "covering of short hairs or fur." Retallack also quotes Chaucer, "though she bende, yeet she stant on roote." Although the woman seems to bend with the emotions, her heart, in fact, may prove her steadfast. This is reinforced through the chance operation that Retallack performs, for one of the surviving parts of the poem is "hir hert." Yet this time "hir hert" is uprooted and remains in a fragment, anatomically an island.

The fragments of the second poem in the series recall Sappho's joyous, sensuous writing of the bedroom. Again, there is a contrast between female surface and depth, "deep in her body" and the "yellow smile."[23] As Page DuBois points out in *Sappho Is Burning*, Sappho herself is an anomaly—a thing apart—in the stories we tell ourselves of the Greeks.[24] As a woman who spoke her desire, she challenges modern constructions of the desiring subject. Like Retallack, DuBois wonders what would occur if we think outside the set patterns of history. "What would it mean temporally," she asks, "to scramble the linear sequence of time, to set Sappho the archaic aristocrat in the middle of the classical age, either Socrates' or Plato's time, to place this noblewoman in the scene, the symposium, of the democratic city?"[25] How would this affect the sense of ourselves today?

The "morning" of Retallack's first line returns us to the beginning of Western civilization, a primary scene of modern translation. While Homer spoke as a conduit of divine inspiration, Sappho was among the earliest to use the first person singular.[26] An epistemic *clinamen* or swerve occurs as Sappho's poetry gives us, for the first time, individual subjectivity—an "I" with the "heart" referred to by Chaucer. This heart is a private space of the individual's desires. Precisely because these desires are interior, they remain unintelligible or "beyond translation." Retallack makes this blindspot of translation apparent in her line, "Saph [. . . . .]gment."[27] The heart of the line is missing. Instead, the poem leaves us to ask: whose words are being spoken when we read translations of Sappho's verses? Any "acknowledgment" is cut off or circumscribed.

Following this is a sequence of signs denoting poetic rhythm. As C. R. Haines points out, we are multiply disadvantaged in understanding Sappho's rhythms and music, not only by our general ignorance of Greek music but because of the mutilated condition of many of Sappho's lyrics.[28] In Retallack's text, both the line of measure and the fragmented quote beneath it end with a question mark. The brackets around the quote by Sappho, along with its small, almost unreadable font, reinforce the gap between ourselves and her poetic song. Interpretation and measure can only be conjecture. What Retallack offers us in the poem is "know ledge." In "Blue Notes on the Know Ledge," she suggests that only this form of knowledge, with its recognition of insufficiency, can bring about "the possibility of reciprocal alterity." Even though we have only fragments, language offers us "the largesse and futurity of an engagement." Language becomes a navigational tool through which we can actively and consciously orient ourselves outward, looking "toward and with."[29]

The poem underneath the dividing line or break may, in fact, provide clues on how to continue reading. The letter clusters, "ne," "e," and "ns" are all abbreviations for directions: northeast, east, and north-south. "[L]at" lends itself both to "latitude" and "lateral." Furthermore, "[O]d" could describe the odd and fragmented corpus of Sappho's writing, while "gh" could refer to its ghostly presence throughout Retallack's text. Indeed, Sappho's pervading specter "calls attention to the varieties of pasts we have still insufficiently come to know."[30]

The third poem in the series continues to undermine the chronological trajectory of history by combining a number of different temporal periods, including the pre-Socratic moment, St. Augustine, and the twentieth-century era of radio. The opening phrase "vol low on radio" brings to mind the opening epigraph of *Afterrimages*, in which Victor Weisskopff, a Manhattan Project physicist, notes that the countdown to the first atomic bomb was accompanied by a Tchaikovsky waltz because it was being broadcast on the same frequency by a nearby radio station. Through this chance incident the actual explosion is remembered (or triggered in the memory of many) by the waltz. In this unintended context a piece of Western high culture engenders a new constellation of meaning. Similarly, a mundane everyday phrase like "nice being out here in the sun" becomes, in this context, not only absurd but comically black.

Retallack argues that after learning about the explosion she began seeing images in which all of civilization was blown up, falling back to earth in scattered fragments. *Afterrimages* enacts a similar crisis but on far less a dramatic scale. Out of the remaining pieces (still imbued with cultural memory), the reader is left to compose a new mosaic of meaning.

The bold circular dot in the first line, with its surrounding blankness, may be read as symbolizing a target point in cartography. "[N]o smoke but smell of alarm" brings to mind the cliché, "no smoke without fire." While an atomic bomb requires some sort of heat or energy for fusion to occur, there is no actual smoke (although an obvious aftereffect is a mushroom cloud). Another fire without smoke is intellectual passion, a "pre-Socratic fire in the mind."[31] Retallack points out that the pre-Socratic acknowledgment of the physical world involved an ethos of knowing as transitive and paradoxical.[32]

The ecstatic experience was a revelatory, fervent moment confirming the self's own alterity. It embraced the gap between perception and understanding. A "sage of the ectopic eye" might well describe one whose sight or spirituality is unbounded by the self or, conversely, someone who finds wisdom in the surface of the eyeball itself.[33]

Beneath the line, chance provides an unerring reinforcement of the poem's concerns of interiority and exteriority. Leaving the bracket open, the reader "sees" an "i in e" and "in e in." The "i" may be read as both "I," "eye," and "e," the latter being the scientific symbol for energy. Rather than the mimetic tradition of looking out over the world, a redirection inward might be considered. This inward gaze would include the presentation of dreams and impressions, or what is known in philosophy as *phantasia*. *Phantasia* joins the language of viewing and desiring so that sight becomes part of an erotic economy.

Just as the unintelligibility of desire is rendered an afterimage of knowledge, so is the agency of women as bearers of knowledge. The citing of Geoffrey Chaucer's *Canterbury Tales* throughout *Afterrimages* generally relates to some aspect of women's character. As Anne Laskaya discerns, these representations are filtered through several layers of male perception, including the pilgrim-narrator, the persona "Geoffrey," and Chaucer himself.[34] Yet the text precludes unqualified authority to any one human voice. In an interview, Retallack points out that *The Canterbury Tales* accommodates multiple voices and tones, "enacting the fact that language belongs to the community of all language-users present and past." Its style is "rich enough to move out of originary self into struggle and play" so that it cannot be wholly homogenized by either self or state.[35]

Retallack quotes from the strongest female voice of the *Tales*, Dame Alysoun, or the Wife of Bath. In the prologue, Dame Alysoun speaks "of wo that is in marriage." She further states that "[m]en may devyne and glosen up and doun / But wel I woot expres withoute lye."[36] Men love to interpret, distort, and imagine the truth, she says, but I would express myself without lies. Masquerading under this female voice, Chaucer indirectly criticizes St. Paul, St. Jerome, Ovid, Jean de Meun, Walter Map, and others for their negative characterization of women. As Alice Jardine notes in *Gynesis: Configurations of Woman and Modernity*, the Middle Ages was a period when the word *woman* was at a height of discursive circulation and, as such, a matter of contention.[37] In the Wife of Bath's story, Chaucer challenges the cultural assumptions about femininity otherwise raised in the pilgrims' narratives.

By giving us fragments of such representations, Retallack reveals stresses that might lead to alternative constructions of gender. For example, she quotes from an episode in the "Man of Law's Tale," where Custance is attacked by a sailor intent on rape. Dominant readings have focused on the fact that Custance says nothing to protect herself. By quoting only the line "The theef fil over bord al sodeynly," Retallack switches attention to the sailor's dramatic dispatch.[38] She thus foregrounds the result of Custance's *active* struggle, the staging—even if for a brief moment—of Custance's independence. "HEREENDETHTHETALEOFTHEMAN-OFLAWE," Retallack declares later.[39] Elsewhere, she states, "Virginia said she likes the word *breach*." In asserting this, Retallack herself enacts a breach in the representation of Virginia in the "Physician's Tale," who is scripted as a chaste ideal, submissive in both word and body to her father's authority.

The picture of virtuous suffering that threatens to overwhelm the *Tales* is interrupted as Retallack does away with "moping virgins [*versions*] of all genders [*genres*]."[40] She suggests that this ideology of female self-sacrifice still circulates today, citing what could be a headline from any fashion magazine: "HOW TO eat a——and stay on a diet." "[W]htsthpntfvnshng" (what's the point of vanishing)," she asks. Images of femininity are themselves products of a consumer culture, inculcating uniformity and interchangeability. They deny the mess of women's actual lives. In shifting from "natures/rin/secycle" to "culturess/pin/cycle," Retallack humorously parallels the culture of the feminine to the wash cycle of laundry. Following the logic of the Edenic myth of female artifice and deception, she wonders: if appearances are deceptive, then what is the truth? Chaucer's masquerade as a female medieval character may reveal both truth and lie.

Although curiosity was considered a medieval sin, for Retallack it is a discipline of attention turned toward "shifts in perspective, those that might give us a chance to find newly productive silences in the noise of culture."[41] Apart from Sappho, Chaucer, and the atomic bomb, Retallack's lines cover environmental descriptions, numeric sequences, cultural categories, corporate training strategies, and everyday salutations like "Hi Vicki!"[42] While there may seem to be little rhyme *or* reason to it all, Retallack encourages the reader to reason laterally *through* rhyme, as well as to think through patterns of linguistic slippage, substitution, and association. The following sequence, for example, opens itself to multiple conceptual shifts:

> lurk   lucktool   ladlesaves
> non sexist naming of hurricanes (saves)
> any of various pigeon-like birds
> any of various pigeon-like lurk
> any of various pigeon-ladle saves
> pigeon lucktool sex various nonist[43]

A "non sexist naming of hurricanes" might save us from the traditional association of women with nature (although it will not save us from the destructive force of natural phenomena). This association is reinforced colloquially, as "birds" is a slang term for women. Retallack gives us what seems a fairly open category, "any of various pigeon-like birds." By having the word *pigeon* return in each consecutive line, Retallack reminds us that pigeons are "homing" birds. While we can imagine that a "pigeon-like bird" might be a kind of domesticated bird, a "pigeon-like lurk" or a "pigeon-ladle" are more difficult to imagine. Like the pigeons, we are left perched on a vertiginous ledge—the ledge of knowledge. By the last line, the words themselves are beginning to be emptied of cultural preconceptions.

Further references to birds are embedded in the text, whether this be "Buffalo wings," a "loose necked fowl," goose-stepping, or the famous line, "je ne regrette rien," by the Parisian singer Edith Piaf (popularly known as the Sparrow). Through aural slippage, Retallack moves from linguistics to desire to comedy in her conclusion. "[F]rom such signs whole cultures have been deduced," becomes "from such sighs even vultures have been seduced," which is transformed once more to "dumb luck thighs bring cultures home to roost."[44] Although one poem ends with the line, "'I' am afraid to fly," *Afterrimages* encourages a belief that if one can escape the centrifugal force of the ego, then all kinds of flight in meaning are possible.[45]

This is not to discount the real effects of history but to explode a singularity of view. *Afterrimages* reminds us that there is no originary or "native tongue," that different languages shape the future of Western civilization: Latin, Celtic, middle-English, French, modern English, and even contemporary street talk. Language itself comes to be seen as a site of violence, bearing the silencing processes of colonization as well as subversive force. While the unconscious may be disciplined ("sincetheEnglishhavebeenherewehavenodreamsanymore," she finds transformative power in local variants or reshapings of language such as rap with its unsubmissive salutation, "YO MAMA."[46]

In *Afterrimages*, the past becomes "thick."[47] Shifts in perspective jump between the wood and the trees, "thikket" and voice, thickness and textual density. Because correspondences become so diverse, the real is rendered much more complex. The reader is left "cruisin blue rien," where the nothing of "rien" elides the mourning of history's "ruin."[48] We move beyond the Romantic "Land-O-Lakes District" ego as dominating landscape, as well as the "Spitting Imagists" view of the world as consumer-friendly freeze frames of experience.[49] Rather, the poet is "O" (both void and surprise), and knowledge demands a "topological squeeze and stretch."[50] Page DuBois argues that "[t]he self constituted against a back ground of disorder can be a self of pleasure and authority that recognizes its construction of itself out of fragmentation, that acknowledges its own fictionality, its own historicity." In recognizing our implication in multiple versions of the past, we can try "to work them into a story about ourselves, a story that enables action in the present, for the future."[51] Joan Retallack's poethical perspective enables not only a multitude of stories, but projects an oblique angle of light over the unknown and culturally forgotten. Such a light might be perceived as both an affirmation and assertion of hope.

CHAPTER TWELVE

Cultural Recovery or Contractual Release: The Shadow-Show of Susan Howe's *The Liberties*

Liberty has been a potent motivational desire in the history of feminist politics. Even today we still speak of freeing ourselves from hegemonic structures, of being free to speak our difference. As Carole-Anne Tyler suggests, the wish for one's own terms and one's sovereign identity, perhaps the most deeply private property of all, is an impossible desire, since both are held in common with others in the community as an effect of the symbolic.[1] Susan Howe's *The Liberties* may largely be seen as a meditation on this philosophical ideal as she explores it in terms of poetic process.[2] Freedom, she holds, is "behavior toward risk."[3] In attempting to articulate the limits of the feminine and its representations, Howe proposes that "liberty" may not be universal or absolute but rather a dynamic that sounds out linguistic and cultural ambiguity.

Ostensibly, *The Liberties* reenvisages the stories of Jonathan Swift's Stella and William Shakespeare's Cordelia. Yet it is also a memorial, as the dedication suggests, to Howe's own Irish grandmother and namesake, Susan Manning. *The Liberties* links her matrilineal biography to the history of Stella and Cordelia as framed through the English literary tradition. Howe works on several thematic levels, focusing not only on the "nonnarratives" of Stella and Cordelia but also on questions of writing and its association with authority and the absolute. Often this involves interrogating the politics of the name, which she sees as underlying the agonistics of history. She explores not only the issue of how one can remember through writing (the desire to capture or mark a subject on paper, particularly given the culturally and temporally specific notion of subjectivity) but also who has the authority to undertake such a task and how one can escape from writing (absence or liberation from the word). For Howe, writing is ambivalent, a space for the infinite as well as an enclosure.

In a letter to Lyn Hejinian, Howe writes of the "terror I have always had—about words and their power." She wonders how much force they have over one's identity: "Did history make language or did language make history?" Furthermore, given their power, did "words have interlocked rules of their own—that we may not really understand?" Howe felt an affinity with Shakespeare and Swift, who "were also obsessed by words and reality and afraid at times of going mad."[4] Both wrote radical allegories of their own social periods. Yet they have since been read through canonical frameworks that, by their nature, consolidate hegemonies of cultural intercourse. In *The Liberties*, Howe attempts to rescue the innovative and dissident quality of Shakespeare's and Swift's work through reciting (and re-siting) it within her own. Recalling Emily Dickinson's Master Letters, she stages a communal intertext. Her task is complicated by her conflicting feelings for their writing. Like Samuel Johnson, she identified with Shakespeare's and Swift's obvious love of words but was distressed at the ends to which they sometimes used them. When compiling his dictionary of the English language, Johnson wrote that he was appalled by Swift's savagery and by the ending of *King Lear:* "I was . . . so shocked by Cordelia's death, that I know not whether I ever endured to read again the last scenes of the play till I undertook to revise them as an editor."[5] Howe also speaks of the author of *King Lear*, who "demonstrated his volcanic loathing for women . . . in a play tender beyond comparison."[6] For Howe, the innovative and magical tradition of Swift and Shakespeare comes at a price, namely in its representation of women.

Writing, then, is a multisubjective activity. Past historical figures are spectral to the writing self, in the sense of being echoes that demand a presence and act as doubles to a contemporary consciousness. In looking back through literary history, Howe senses "silenced factions waiting to be part of any expression."[7] Increasingly, she could see how women's voices within such a space were either elided or taken up and re-viewed within a culturally appropriate space of the feminine. This, in turn, affects Howe's own ability to speak for and of herself: "Identity and memory are crucial for anyone writing poetry. For women the field is still dauntingly empty. How do I, choosing messages from the code of others to participate in . . . Language, pull SHE from all the myriad symbols and sightings of HE?[8]"

Howe's genealogy in a sense had never been recorded. As she states, "I wish I could tenderly lift from the dark side of history, voices that are anonymous, slighted—inarticulate."[9] These voices were sites of memory but remained unilluminated. Taking Thoreau's comment as a starting point, she argues that maybe "exaggerated history is poetry."[10] This other discourse of poetry, however, is not a supplement to history but a writing that works within and against it. "If history is a record of survivors," Howe claims, then "poetry shelters other voices."[11] Poetry is both "collision or collusion with history."[12]

As such, it becomes a mode of translation, a continual interplay between the interpretation and representation of historical realities.[13] It looks toward the erroneous and the marginal, seeing these as still embedded in how we make sense of ourselves. Concerned with the violence of history through representation, Howe returns to the figures of Stella and Cordelia in order to explore what may be called an ethics of Antigone. She traces the connection of her own poetics to Antigone in her statement to the New Poetics Colloquium, quoting Creon's words to Antigone: "Go to the dead and love them."[14] Such an ethic is concerned with the relationship between the living and the dead, itself defined by a sharing of finitude. Such sharing cannot be communicated but is a *comparution*, meaning to be cited to appear together before judgment.[15]

Stella and Cordelia reflect Antigone's own position of marginality within the tradition of literature and philosophy. As Josette Féral argues, "[Antigone] is actually representative of the woman who refuses her condition as woman and pays for her transgression with death."[16] Both Stella and Cordelia are rendered exiles through heeding their duty of love over a duty to the State. They occupy the margins of excess, existing as border effects of social order and text. Rendered illegitimate as subjects, Stella and Cordelia can express themselves only through blanks and negation. They return to the narrative and are given existence as social or civil subjects but only through a confirmation by Swift and Lear.

In *The Liberties*, Stella's and Cordelia's stories are framed through the trope of Ireland, itself subjected and silenced as colonial margin to the British Empire. It is through Ireland that Howe begins to unravel the intersecting discourses of the proper, property, and civil duty, or propriety. She does this by opening and closing *The Liberties* with separate images. The closing image, entitled "Ireland's eye," is an archaic map of a small island near Howth in Dublin Bay, itself a margin to a margin (see fig. 8B). Lynn Keller points out that the drawing of the island resembles lips rather than an eye, reinforcing the double meaning of the island's name when voiced.[17] Howe plays on the slippage between "Ireland" and "island," as well as the slippage between the "eye" and "I." The subject of the gaze is also its object. Not only may this suggest that the writer is simultaneously a reader but also that "Ireland's eye" is symbolic of an ethical vision.

In contrast to this grounding or closure of *The Liberties*, the opening image is that of a postage stamp with a figure of liberty flying over a city and carrying a message that states "VOX HIBERNIAE" (the voice of Hibernia). Pictorially, it sets out Howe's grammatical and gestural strategies (see fig. 8A). The "voice" is signified by writing over any other visual signs. In contrast, a stamp is the official mark of a letter, yet it is not the letter itself. Beyond the actual letter or word, the text, as with the stamp, signals a ges-

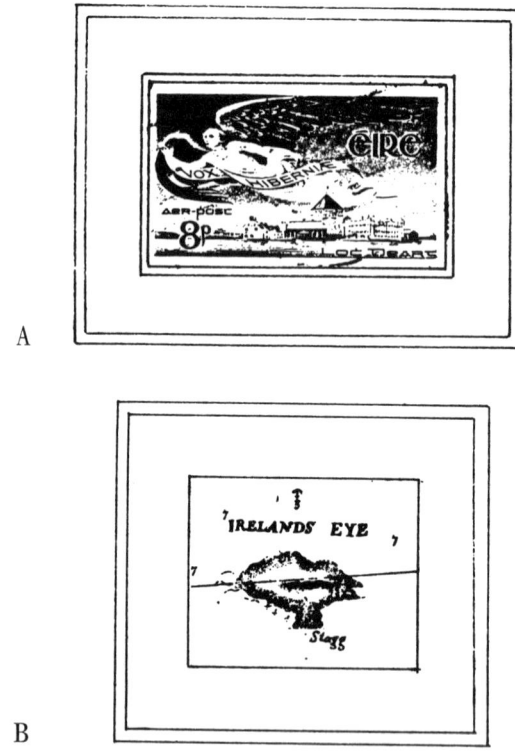

Fig. 8. Opening and closing graphics for Susan Howe's *The Liberties*, reprinted in *The Europe of Trusts* (Los Angeles: Sun & Moon Press, 1990). © Susan Howe. Used by permission of the author and publisher.

ture toward dialogue. It is, at once, a communication both with us as readers and with Swift and Shakespeare.

The stamp also illustrates Howe's method of using the marginalia of past documents to structure her own writing. Drawing on her background as an artist, Howe emphasizes the *process* of writing by foregrounding words and phrases as "found objects." Rather than write literary history anew, she selects and rearranges entries from Swift's *Journal to Stella* as well as Shakespeare's *King Lear*. This process of composition reinforces the constructedness of received history. Through this method of quotation, she uses the voices of Swift and Shakespeare to speak the testimony or "narratives in non-narrative" of Stella and Cordelia.[18]

To Howe, Ireland seemed a suitable backdrop to exploring a literary palimpsest. As she writes to Lyn Hejinian, "[A]ll Irish know there are ghosts. Ireland being the last outpost in the Atlantic before America and an island utterly under the influence of the sky and sea in a way hard to imagine until you experience it—is truly open to things of the air—or spirits."[19]

The Liberties is unusual for Howe in that it moves away from the New England setting in which most of her work is located. Yet it is within this particular work that Howe meditates on the various properties that construct her own voice, such as being female, a poet, and Irish American. The subject of Swift and Stella took on the status of cultural myth for Howe's Irish mother; but for Howe, brought up in America, it was merely "another Grimm's fairy tale."[20] For Howe, Ireland was a landscape of the imagination, signifying all that was magic, chaotic, and dramatic. As such, it is a place whose affect and memory challenge the contracting forces of a colonizing history, a history that forecloses rather than opens up a field of possibility. In an early interview, Howe talks of the shelves of Irish books that lined her father's study, stating that they provided an attractive alternative to those containing his American books, classics, and dictionaries.[21] In writing *The Liberties*, Howe attempts to move beyond the cultural differend that divides mother and daughter-writer, "trying to get to the place, a foreign place that was home to [her] mother, on paper."[22]

Howe begins the first section of *The Liberties* with a chronological account of Stella's life. Here I wish to stress the etymology of that term, *biographe*: the writing, mark, or inscription of self, for it is precisely the figure of Stella that is lost. Stella exists as a fabrication, a "hallucination in the mirror."[23] There is no authentic portrait of her, none of her letters were saved by Swift, and the authenticity of the poetry attributed to her is doubtful. Howe's biography of Stella is framed by the title, "Fragments of a Liquidation." Stylistically, there seems to be anything but fragments in this linear and explanatory historical record. The irony is further reinforced by an opening quotation from Swift's *Journal to Stella*, "Fais I don't conceal a bitt. as hope sav'd."[24]

Characterizing Stella as "a body of eyes in shadow," Howe recalls Swift's concern for Stella's problematic eyesight and her role as Swift's first reader. Yet it also suggests that Stella herself has been totally circumscribed by and through Swift's gaze and therefore is as much a fiction as Shakespeare's Cordelia. She exists historically as the addressee of Swift's letters, a role that was entirely regulated and foreclosed by Swift. Howe points out that Stella's duty to Swift is based on a paternal or proprietal line: he is at once father figure, lover, and keeper. Rachel Blau DuPlessis argues that Howe was attracted to the figure of Stella as the degree zero of femininity, as silence embodied.[25] She further suggests that *The Liberties* may be seen as itself an act of "liquidation," being the payment of a debt through an analysis of liabilities and assets in Swift's liquidation or account of Stella.[26] In contrast, I would contend that Howe attempts to escape just such a transaction, refusing an economy of duty based on exchange. Rather, Stella may be seen as a symbolic link to Howe's Irish past. Stella's history resembles in some small degree that of Howe's own mother, since both women chose exile from their country and its culture in a voluntary act of love.

In *The Liberties*, Howe parallels and synthesizes Stella's relationship to Swift with Cordelia's to Lear. Both are in a position of ex-centricity precisely because of the nature of their love. Both Stella and Cordelia figure love as being an outright gift, as being given freely, a concept that is incompatible within the economy in which they exist. Eventually, Swift forms an attachment with another woman while in England. Vanessa, as the other woman, operates within the logic of commodification, taking up Swift's long love poem to her and having it published posthumously. Lear, in turn, fails to recognize the value in Cordelia's love and rejects it. As he states in response to her inability to measure the value of her gift, "Nothing will come of nothing."[27]

Jean-Luc Nancy argues that freedom is not a property of the subject.[28] One could add that love, too, is not a property to be possessed. Nancy draws attention to the semantic equivalence of love and freedom—how they are intertwined linguistically and philosophically—by pointing out that the Anglo-Saxon root of *free* is "beloved" or "cherished."[29] As ethical concepts, both freedom and love mean to think against foundation. Nancy maintains that freedom must be a praxis of thought, the thing itself of thinking. As such, it cannot be appropriated but only pirated. Its seizure will always be illegitimate.[30] Howe herself sees Stella and Cordelia as freed particles, in the sense of being discursive sites of pure energy. Giorgio Agamben argues that ethics may come into being only when "the authentic and the proper have no other content than the inauthentic and the improper."[31] That is, when the civil can embrace the figuration of Antigone.

It is this ethical articulation of freedom that Howe traces. She seeks to construct Stella and Cordelia as liberties from and through literary history by thinking their voices into existence, by making language over into a site of "wild interiority."[32] For Howe and for Nancy, language has always been foreign to itself, overflowing its own grammar. It embodies innovation and invention as much as precedent. Nancy argues that "language withdraws into precisely the same position as freedom itself: it cannot be secured, least of all by impressions, sensations or 'lived experience.'"[33] As Howe suggests, it works against the authority of the name. Potentially, it is infinite.

Certainly, Swift's Stella is ambiguous in name. Baptized Hester Johnson, her own preference was for the name Esther, which ironically happened to be the given name of Swift's other woman, Vanessa. And of course there is "Stella," Swift's own name for her. Her slippage between names suggests that she falls outside the sphere of the proper. When Swift names Hester "Stella," he effectively territorializes her as his Other. She exists merely as his point of reflection, a property of desire. The proper name of Stella would seem to bring a halt to any metonymic sliding by stabilizing an identity within the space of the proper. Yet Howe argues against such a reading, positing that the shifting nature of what constitutes Stella's name (or who Stella is) is what enables her to have "no clear line" within the social order.[34] Names instead become "bridges to coast," a playful means of liberation.

Deleuze and Guattari support Howe's perception that the name is a point of possibility when they argue that "[t]he proper name does not designate an individual: it is on the contrary when the individual opens up to the multiplicities pervading him or her, at the outcome of the most severe operation of depersonalization, that he or she acquires his or her true proper name." The proper name, they suggest, "is the instantaneous apprehension of a multiplicity."[35] As Howe notes, words like *Mark* or *Swift* or *Sally* are both name and word, both proper and common. As such, the subject of their constitution is always ambivalent. In terms of function, they are a mobile space. Howe plays with the process of naming throughout *The Liberties* in order to undermine the citation of its referent as object under the letter of the law.

The final section of *The Liberties* contains a series of word squares or boxes, two titled "S" and two "C." Swift himself used alphabetical symbols as fond tokens to denote himself, Stella, or Rebecca Dingley. Thus, "MD" stood for my "My Dear," and "D" for Rebecca Dingley, Stella's lifetime companion. Rebecca Dingley was also represented as "Me," which Harold Williams argues may be Madam Elderly. "FW," he suggests, stands for both Farewell and Foolish Wenches. This cryptic language, a secret enclosure of thought and meaning known only to Stella and Swift, also played with a systematic substitution of these symbols. Thus *l* is often substituted for *r*, so "rove" stands for "love" and "vely" for "very." Because such language is often based on sound, "lele yet oo see" may mean "little yet you see."[36]

Swift often refers to Stella as "saucebox" or "sawcy" (phonetically, "saw-C"). In constructing her own boxes (fig. 9), Howe plays with the letters *S* and *C* as iconic ciphers of identity. She also plays with her own name and her grandmother's, Stella's and Cordelia's, as well as with the linguistic shifters of "I" and "you." In April 1979, Howe wrote to Bernadette Mayer: "I have just been reading much about Shakespeare's use of the punning 'eye aye I' in *Lear* and seeing without eyes."[37] Words such as *I, eye* and *you* map out various textual positions. What Howe does is emphasize the space between the subject who is spoken of (that is, the subject of biography or history) and the subject who speaks. She seems to suggest that this is a space of language and therefore never actually empty.

In the second square, Howe dissolves the construction of the "I" as speaking subject (see fig. 9B). In exhibiting the ambiguity of the homophone, she collapses its meaning with other words, such as *aye* and *eye*. She does the same for *you* with its aural equivalent *yew*. Another example of Howe's technique is the neologism of "estersnowe" with its combination of "Esther," "snow," "now," and "Howe." Swift himself was fond of neologisms, inventing terms such as "Stellakins," "slidikins," and "slids" for Stella. He also indulged in playful aural slippages, such as "Sollahs" for "sirrahs." Similarly, Howe works associatively, suggesting "Esther" by "Easter." She breaks words down into single letters such as *a* and *O* with their emphasis on singularity or "1-ness." The use of dates and brackets, not to mention the word *square* itself, further problematizes a system of reference. In doing this, Howe actively performs Nietzsche's sentiment: "Fundamentally, I am every name in history."[38]

This dispersion is liberating but still has constraints. On the one hand, Howe seems to suggest that feminine identity, while portrayed as concrete or static within the historical record, is, on closer inspection, aleatory and plural in nature. Following Kristeva's concept of *chora*, the feminine is closer to sound than grammar.[39] It is not oppositional to the paternal or patriarchal but rather undermines the codes that such structures are founded on. On the other hand, Howe's own identity is still framed and informed by the identities of past figures such as Stella and Cordelia. Quoting Nietzsche again, she suggests that tradition "comes towards us because we are its captives and are destined to it."[40] Although Howe's interrogations suppose a decentered self, she cannot completely escape the designations imposed on it by context, by language, and by others who position and "see" us in that context. In sharing the voices of Stella and Cordelia, Howe risks a similar fate.

The biographical narrative of Stella may be seen as a preface to the rest of *The Liberties*. In the "Travels" section, Howe departs from the record of tradition. This part contains both the "Book of Stella" and the "Book of Cordelia" under the subtitle "Their," a pronoun that suggests a sharing of properties. These are the books that were never written, that were perhaps not possible. Howe queries the effectiveness of such a project: "Is a poetics of intervening absence an oxymoron?"[41] This seeming dilemma of finding a voice within silence is what she goes on to explore. Howe argues that the communal vision of poetry is "one poem in another we haven't seen or thought."[42] The possibility of Stella's diary is likened to clouds, insubstantial, with Stella's voice being "wild geese in a stammered place."[43]

S

2.   only   fury   cleave   most   air

lovely   asymmetry   incline   light

lean   imagery   altus   x   soar   6

arc   hue   heraldic   puzzle   midhe

paradigm   bolt   motivic   prebendary

moor   breach   weir   tactile   spinster

herd   polyphonic   mathematic   madhouse

skip   cottage   easter   snow   homine

L   laracor   aye   yew   medb   heron

will   stirring   1668   bound   purely

(   )   aye   estersnowe   enclosure

prism

pennant

A   'nature of the future'

S

                    rebuke   boyne

          churn   alpha   bet   a   keep

1727   expose   blade   broken   hid

pierce   hang   sum

clear   hester   quay   Liberties   46

tense   whisper   here   libel   foam

print   pen   dot   i   still

B   hole   yew   skip   1.

Fig. 9. Word boxes in Susan Howe's *The Liberties*, reprinted in *The Europe of Trusts* (Los Angeles: Sun & Moon, 1990). © Susan Howe. Used by permission of the author and publisher.

The manuscripts of Swift's *Journal to Stella* have many erasures and crossed-out words. As in Howe's interpretation of the marks on Emily Dickinson's manuscripts, M. Emile Pons argues that these scrawls and blottings are as much a part of the original script as the written words. He believes not only that the scribbled obliterations were made by Swift when he wrote the letters but that the "secret enclosure of thought and meaning [between Swift and Stella] can only be understood if it be realized that the erasures are to be read as codes."[44] Much is made of an entry when Swift was ill: "so adieu deelest Md Md Md FW FW Me Me Me Me Lele I can say lele yet oo see—Fais I dont conceal a bitt. As hope sav'd." In another example, almost an entire line is blotted out, after which he writes, "that blot is a Blundr." Such lines appear to support Pons's interpretation. Alternatively, they may be read as cancellations made by Swift from motives of discretion.

The "Book of Cordelia" syntactically replicates gaps in the histories while also foregrounding an alternate layer of meaning that lies within marginalia, again through sound shifts and verbal patterns. Through a repetition of techniques such as assonance, rhythm and alliteration, the musicality of Howe's writing enables flight beyond a static mark or inscription. As Howe argues, "Sound is part of the mystery."[45]

WHITE FOOLSCAP

Book of Cordelia

heroine in ass-skin
mouthing O Helpful
=father revivified, waking when
nickname Hero men take pity spittle speak

only nonsense
my bleeding foot
I am maria wainscotted
cap o' rushes tatter-coat
common as sal salt sally
S (golden) no huge a tiny
bellowing augury

NEMESIS singing from cask
turnspit scullion the apples pick them   Transformation
wax forehead ash
shoe fits monkey-face oh hmm
It grows dark The shoe fits She stays a long something
Lent is where she lives shalbe shalbe
loving like salt (value of salt)[46]

This section plays with the central "O" that is Cordelia's voice—at once there and not there and existing as a hole or erratum. Howe foregrounds the hesitation it evokes in the reader, with the inclusion of the phrase "oh hmm." Cordelia here shifts between being a heroine in "ass-skin" (recalling Shakespeare's Bottom in *A Midsummer Night's Dream)* and being put to the question, as a heroine in the asking. It also recalls the letter *S,* the "S" skin that Cordelia wears as a tatter-coat, much like another Hester, the one who wears an *A* in Nathaniel Hawthorne's *The Scarlet Letter.* The letter *S* could be said to signify silence and (as Howe notes) is as common as "sal salt sally." Cordelia herself is the value of salt, doubled everywhere as the cultural feminine but nowhere as herself.

This passage illustrates the way Howe sieves through the multiple associations of words. In a letter to Hejinian, she writes:

Sometimes just the space between words and the shape of letters seem to carry a life of their own. Words as a law unto themselves. Space as another law. The space of a page, of the spaces between words and spaces of sounds and of silence. So much is involved. Memory metaphor shape silence suggestion echo.[47]

Later, she wrote again: "In fact one of the real difficulties in my 'dialogue' I have been working on between Swift's Stella and Shakespeare's Cordelia—is my utter inability to write a line of words—without zeroing in on each particular word as a world in itself."[48]

"The Book of Cordelia" is prefigured by the subtitle "White Foolscap." This suggests not only the color of salt and the blankness of a page but also a certain role-playing, namely, that Cordelia is wearing both fool's cap and heroine's dress in Lear's economy. Performance, then, is another strategy, alongside the phonic and physical properties of words, by which marginalia may yet say something. As history is based so much on event and generic procedure, Howe finds that performance is a preferable approach to engaging with it. Because history goes beyond the words on the page, the chaos and violence that constitute it must be matched visually. As such, Howe says that she feels that what she is doing on the page is very much like "moving people around on stage."[49]

This is perhaps why she has turned to actual dramatic material in her use of *King Lear.* Thus, the following section plays off elements of cross-dressing and role-playing, emphasizing how identity can be assumed as mere masquerade. Gender in particular is transgressed as a limitation. Stella, we are told, "must be traced through many dark paths as a boy."[50] She becomes refigured as "boy-bird of the air," an angel of alterity (recalling also the figure of liberty from the opening graphic).[51] Cordelia, too, is transformed into a swan or at least is winged. Howe continually repeats this trope of flight, perhaps proposing that Stella and Cordelia ultimately operate as what Nicole Brossard calls "aerial letters." The aerial vision that

Brossard outlines is of a feminine plural memory, one in which the gaze is never fixed on any one thing and where zones once made redundant through opacity or blankness can somehow appear clear.[52]

Finally, the third section of *The Liberties* represents Stella and Cordelia as existing beyond Swift's and Shakespeare's words by acting in a play entitled "God's Spies." Howe herself had "started life as an actress," and her mother had been a director of professional theater. This dramatic section proved the most challenging part for Howe to write. In a letter to Hejinian she noted that the staging of the section would require a "blending of sexes—where you can't tell what sex the voices are—and no-one could *see* Swift."[53] Howe seeks to register sexual and authorial ambivalency by both aural and visual means.

In "God's Spies," Cordelia and Stella are dressed as boys in their teens, and the setting is simply "a wilderness." It is within such a revolutionary space (no doubt influenced by Thoreau) that Cordelia can ask, "Did we survive at all?" and have Stella reply, "Left without regrets—tracing points—vertices—stages—flying swiftly—past fleecy stars."[54] Again, there are associations with the rest of the text, the drama of Lear, Swift ("swiftly"), and Stella ("stellar"). It is here, however, within the immediacy of the performative—of actually performing the impossible of female agency, that Howe overtakes history. As she argues elsewhere, "There are breaks in world-historical reason where forms of wildness brought up by memory become desire and multiply."[55] Howe stages subject effects in a Beckett-like gesture, foregrounding the question of the proper history only to enact its improper genealogy.

What Stella and Cordelia repeat more than anything else within this section is the phrase "They murder each other." This is the sovereign Necessity of history that Howe wishes to overcome, although she leaves it to the reader to decide whether it is possible to move beyond such boundaries. History is the truth, just as the name is also taken up as descriptive and prescriptive of a truth. Howe's poetics, then, strive like Antigone's toward antinomy, in the sense of moving against both name and governance. As Jean-Luc Nancy suggests, "Freedom must be the element or fundamental modality of being, as soon as being does not precede existence, or succeed it, but is at stake in it."[56] Only a free force can let incompatibilities persist, and that force is the imagination. For Howe as for Nancy, the imagination is a way of "making-possible, being-able."[57] It refigures the biographical as conversation and initiates a writing of community over and beyond the aporias of history.

CHAPTER THIRTEEN

Cutting Corners in Tina Darragh's American Pi

> This whole book now is going to be a detective story of how to write.
> A play of the relation of human nature to the human mind.
> And a poem of how to begin again.
> —Gertrude Stein, *The Geographical History of America*

Sharing an interest with Jackson Mac Low, John Cage, and Joan Retallack in process art, Tina Darragh's work is more about how to read than how to write. The title of her best-known volume, *Striking Resemblance* (1989), borrows from Wittgenstein's concept of "family resemblance" and takes the form of various language games or puzzles that explore the relationship between geography, language, and identity. This poetic game play is further strengthened by the association of Darragh's title with the word *pun*, which can mean alternatively to beat, strike, or pound, as well as its more common definition—to draw attention to words that have different meanings but resemble one another in sound.

Darragh's linguistic experiments resonate with her own genealogy, particularly the orientation of her knowledge through the respective roles of daughter, wife, and mother. Wittgenstein likewise saw language as a "form of life" connected with and contextualized by other forms of life. The term *striking* also refers to the political activism of Darragh and her partner, P. Inman, and suggests the potential limit-point or stoppage of resemblance. Finally, the title alludes to the writing community in which she situates herself. Besides the poetry of Inman, Darragh engages with the work of Susan Howe and Joan Retallack, two contemporaries whose writing has been pivotal to Darragh's own development.

Striking Resemblance is a collection of different procedural pieces, thematically linked by a spatial investigation of subjectivity. More specifically, there is a focus on the "I-in-error," which refers to the space that cannot be fitted into narrative logic.[1] Retallack notes of Darragh's work that "learning how to read in a new way has been incorporated in the experience of the work." This is because "certain guidelines are accessible . . . because there is the ability to identify with playful inquirer setting out on an investigation and leaving markers along the way."[2]

Darragh begins to measure the geographic location of her person in the first section, "Pi in the Skye." The very title brings together the initials of P. Inman, a geometric measure used to calculate a circle's boundary, and the old adage of "pie in the sky"—something promised but unreachable. While Gertrude Stein states that "[g]eography does not look like it does in relation to the human mind," Darragh tests whether, in fact, city structures might be reflected in language use.[3] Just as there are lines of construction, "factories, highways, homes/atop/lines of once freely flowing rivers," could there be similar constructions in grammar, "phrases, sentences, paragraphs.atop/ lines of once freely flowing sounds"?[4] Darragh's analogy between language and place parallels a psychoanalytic model of consciousness, in which the semiotic order embodies the linguistic depths and the symbolic order is associated with the surface technologies of society. Elsewhere, Darragh points out that Jacques Lacan was considering a mathematical model to theorize the psychology of embodied thought. She quotes from Sherry Turkle's *Psychoanalytic Politics:* "Lacan . . . was trying to 'invent another geometry,' the 'geometry of the chain'. . . he became preoccupied with 'little loops of string' in an attempt to think about body and psyche at the same time."[5]

In focusing on the idiom of place, Darragh wonders whether each person might have "[c]ertain sounds/ that repeat / that 'surface' / as parts of words preferred." These sounds might be thought of as clichés. Originating during the Industrial Revolution, the term was used to describe the noise of machinery as it shaped and processed material. It therefore has associations with both construction and sound. While *cliché* has since come to mean overuse, Darragh focuses on its sense as repeated sound. "[I]n thinking about cliché as sound," she wonders "whether these sound lines/ can be traced / to a particular geographic location / that PLACE/being 'home' for a person's voice?" Her procedure to find this place is to take "soundings" from "P's work," reading "fragments/that rise up in him / 'on line' at work / there scribbled on slips of paper / & later strung together."[6] By using the phrase "on line," Darragh emphasizes the relation between Inman's poetic and material practice. In the late seventies he worked briefly as a factory hand in the textile industry, surrounded quite literally by the cliché of the machine. At this time, he also became involved in the union movement.

Retallack argues that "[l]anguage, which saturates every aspect of being human, is always on the verge of invisibility that leads to its speaking itself as euphemisms, clichés, and set pieces."[7] Darragh's method is to make such language visible again and to foreground its cultural and historical specificity. In appearance and sound, Inman's work resembles Gaelic. His poetry is characterized by a dense clustering of words in which soft vowels occur with hard consonant blends. Darragh gives an example from "Number One Son," the first four lines of which read

> spodes dull glam) slud dry)
> jclaw) plab)gansett) klinge)
> lunmthened) tea wote (on ounced)
> cule drard) air culled omimm)[8]

Inman himself points to a kinship with Scotland in the title of his Tuumba book, *Ocker* (1982), a slang term for persons with surnames like O'Connell and O'Connor.[9] Darragh proceeds on the assumption that Skye, where there is a similar combination of soft vowels and hard consonants, might be the home for Inman's voice. Retallack, too, argues that Inman's work recalls the texture of old English pieces like *Beowulf*.[10] Yet the resulting experiment proves instead both a linguistic and a cultural separation from such landscapes.

In taking seventy examples from *A Linguistic Survey of the Gaelic Dialects of Scotland*, Darragh reveals that there is only one that is heard in Inman's work. Furthermore, she contrasts two lists. One is a Skye glossary. The other is a list of sounds that fall alongside the sounds within the word *Skye* itself. Out of this list come specifically American words or phrases: words like *skeadadle* (skedaddle), *skelp* (scalp), and *skat* (scat), and phrases like *yellow brick* (as in "Follow the yellow brick road"), *yellow streak* (coward), and *yellow stone* (geological formation specific to the United States).[11] Inman's work also has American words like *glam* (shortened from glamor) and *culled* (originally from the French, meaning "to collect"). *Ounced*, too, follows an American tendency to turn nouns into verbs.

Looking at the Skye glossary, there are recognizable words like *river, bush*, and *tube*. Yet in his extensive linguistics study, *The American Language*, H. L. Mencken points out that the meanings of such words have changed since their transfer across the Atlantic.[12] As the compiler of the first American dictionary, Noah Webster, states:

Numerous local causes, such as a new country, new associations of people, new combination of ideas in arts and sciences, and some intercourse with tribes wholly unknown in Europe, will introduce new words into the American tongue. These causes will produce, in a course of time, a language in North America as different from the future language of England as the modern Dutch, Danish and Swedish are from the German, or from one another: like . . . rays of light shot from the same center, and diverging from each other in proportion to their distance from the point of separation.[13]

Comparative studies have, in fact, shown that the common speech of the United States has a "striking *absence* of words and forms characteristic of Scotland, and of North and West of England."[14] The Old English that Retallack and Darragh hear is most likely a combination of archaisms from southern and eastern England. Inman's voice, then, is specifically American. Darragh contextualizes Inman's language use against other American word inventions, words such as *moola* and *razz-ma-tazz*. The American language is shown to be the product of both British colonialism and more recent immigration from countries around the world. It is characterized by processes of blending and mongrelization. *Moola* is the corruption of the Moslem, *mullah*, as well as a variation of *gool* (gold).[15] *Razz* has its roots in an Algerian expression, metamorphosing in its various uses as a slang term in football and in vaudeville. The factory would be a heightened site for such linguistic processes, its repetitive, manual work being one of the few options for immigrants who found English an unfamiliar or difficult language.

In the close of the first section, Darragh looks at the relationship between cliché and place, specifically the rainbow as a literal embodiment of pie in the sky (although Darragh alludes only indirectly to the mythical pot of gold—to America as a land of promise). As part of a circle, the curve of the rainbow also recalls the mathematical pi, an infinite number. Phenomena such as rainbows and pi are unfixed. She recalls Sir Isaac Newton's discovery that when light is bent by a prism, each frequency is deviated through a slightly different line or angle so that the emergent beam comes out of the prism as a fan of light and a spectrum of color. Yet Newton pretended to see orange and indigo when he made his first color scale, "so he could list seven colors—a lucky number."[16] Darragh notes that the discovery of this fact was equivalent to a religious experience: "Science as 'authority figure' was smashed, and I could lift Eden's curse of 'woman seeking knowledge destroys herself and others.'"[17]

Newton's stretching of the color spectrum is reflected in other rainbow associations, such as the Rainbow Tribe of Darragh's one-time idol, the singer Josephine Baker. Baker was said to have adopted a baby of every color; but instead of the original four, she compulsively brought more home until she had up to twelve children, "the number of the tribes of Israel." Like the tribes of Israel, Baker's family lived a life of displacement and exile after she lost both husband and home. Other figures whom Darragh associates with the rainbow are her namesake, St. Martin des Porres, and Jean Toomer, "both mulattoes / who felt they had all the colors / of the world's races in their blood."[18] Like Baker's, Toomer's story is one of migration and of a fall. Moving to the country's capital, he failed to continue his success after the innovative novel *Cane* established him as one of the foremost avant-garde writers of the day.

Both Baker and Toomer are emblematic of the American vision of itself as a new race—and also of its failure. America, like Baker, is no longer the "perfect international mother" who is able to care for all who turn to her. Darragh notes that although Washington is viewed as somewhere "where many scenes take place/people of mixed heritage/feeling at home," it can seem as if "all their colors combine/to make the omnipresent white/of the government buildings."[19] This recalls Newton's finding that white light is a compound of all the colors of the spectrum. In both cases, whiteness subsumes difference. Toomer eventually disavowed any African American identity. Darragh points out that this can be seen in the repetition of sounds in his life story. The names of his wives, "Margery/Marjorie," echo the meaning of "Margaret" as "pearl"—white luminance.[20]

Having mapped out a broad individual iconolatry of Newton, Baker, St. Martin des Porres, and Toomer, Darragh turns to a more intimate association. She recalls the photographs she took of "P. and D. building blocks/& in one shot/there is a small arc of light/to the right of their building."[21] The realization occurs that the rainbow is not a place but must be caught through looking in a particular direction. In "Error Message," Darragh confirms that she can explore meaning only as it appears from her own perspective. In living within conservative political and social structures in the eighties, she replaced the "story of the Revolution" with "the story of turning to words"—finding language structures to be a more subtle and ongoing kind of oppression.

Darragh's fascination with the relationship between sound, the subconscious, and independence of self is continued in "Raymond Chandler's Sentence." It is fittingly dedicated to "Susan Howe & her *The Liberties*." Like Darragh, Howe experiments with sounding out histories in the fragments and ruins of words, often turning to dictionaries as tools. Howe's work also has affinities with Inman's poetry, both in the scattering effect across the page and the use of dense, archaic linguistic clusters. Indeed, Howe gave a careful and appreciative reading of Inman's *Platin* in *L=A=N=G=U=A=G=E*, foregrounding its acoustic and visual levels as well as its shifts between kinship and contrast.[22] Like Darragh, Howe was intrigued by scientific frameworks, citing René Thom's *Mathematical Models of Morphogenesis* as instructive. Although there are these forms in space and time and in apparent chaos, "he seems to be saying maybe it's all a game. All you can do is move the chips around pretending there is some kind of order."[23]

In *The Liberties*, Howe explores the relationship of the American voice to the English by tracing her history and poetics back to Jonathan Swift and William Shakespeare. Darragh, however, focuses on a more recent influence: the gumshoe stories of Raymond Chandler. Just as Swift and

Shakespeare were particularly playful and innovative in their use of language, the criminal underworld has always been an area rich in invention. Chandler's stories are marked by their attention to the slang and speech patterns of American street talk between the wars. As H. L. Mencken points out, the cant of criminals seeks a constant movement of words. It is also characterized in its purpose to deceive or mystify the outsider.[24] Mencken himself co-founded the famous Black Mask imprint, which specialized in urban American detective fiction and featured Chandler's work. The chaos of language described by Mencken also attracted Darragh. After completing *on the Corner to off the Corner* (1981), she started reading police procedurals—literal transcriptions of the process of solving a crime. "[Y]ou really felt a part of the investigation," Darragh reflects. They motivated her to think about how to approach "a problem when you have all these very scattered bits of information."[25]

As Howe does in *The Liberties*, Darragh prefaces "Raymond Chandler's Sentence" with biographical background. Both texts focus on themes of exile and separation, as well as the attendant problems of communication. During the first seven years of his life, Chandler heard "small town" American and "frontier" American. After his father abandoned Chandler and his mother, they left for England, where he heard English spoken for the next sixteen years. For Chandler, English and American were two quite separate, distinct languages.

Upon returning to the United States as a young man, Chandler had to "learn American just like a foreign language."[26] He did this through imitating mystery writers like Erle Stanley Gardner: "Chandler would select a Gardner story, rewrite it, compare it with the original and rework it once more."[27] He attributed this practice to his training in the classics, where he learned to translate Cicero into English, then back again into Latin. His biographer, Frank MacShane, notes that when writing dialogue, Chandler carefully imitated American speech patterns. Accordingly, the word order was often switched to make the sentences sound realistic. Building on the creativity of the American language, he added numerous locutions of his own, as in a line Darragh cites as one of her favorites: "Get dressed, sweetheart—and don't fuss with your necktie. Places want us to go to them."[28] In contrast, the descriptive and narrative passages are written in standard British form.

Choosing words from Chandler's fiction, Darragh explores their various dictionary definitions, making them appear strange and unknown to the reader, much as Chandler might have seen them. *Deserted* is equated to being away from "a line" or "a series." *Country* is "that which lies opposite one's view." For "translate SEE 'transfer'—to bear, to carry across."[29] Many of the words she selects have particular meaning to Chandler's own life story. While the detective genre is usually distinguished by the predictability of its narrative conventions (the criminal act, the testing of alibis, and the denouement, for example), Chandler's distinction as a noir writer is his movement away from plot to a focus on affect. In her list, Darragh attempts to give the words a similar resonance.

Darragh's memory of Chandler's novels and other mysteries was of her mother "chain reading" in the afternoon, a memory similar to Inman's of his mother. Darragh notes that she too retires now to read mysteries, finding relief in reading "about someone / who knows what to do / when something goes wrong." The nonlinear, ongoing, and chaotic experiences of motherhood contrast sharply with the neat resolutions of detective fiction. While Darragh reflects on the cross-generational feminine habit of reading mysteries, Chandler's work also focuses specifically on familial patterns. In *The Big Sleep*, Chandler's detective takes a job for no money in the belief that a father has a right to remain ignorant of bad blood in his line. Darragh believes that this hides an underlying, more personal narrative. Using Chandler's translation procedure, she looks "for the verb / & if the rest of the sentence doesn't fall / into the usual subject / object sequence / the elusive construction / is probably a form of the ablative / something we don't have in our language / —a place case—." Psychologically significant elements in the novel's plot are linked with grammatical ablatives, which are structurally only able to be registered as absences in English:

> absence of the father—look for the verb
> dependence of the mother—the past participle used to express the future
> humiliation of a class system—place of separation
> marriage to an older woman—place of agent
> vice-presidential duties at Dabney Oil—place of instrument
> drunken binges ending in dismissal—place of means[30]

Darragh discovered that she and Chandler seek, at some level, a kind of Oedipal self-discovery by going after a lost father. In a similar way, Howe used Swift's letters to Cordelia in *The Liberties* to explore the childhood absence of her own father. In a "parting shot," Darragh finds that *abandon* comes from "to place" under "speak," "just where I've wanted to be / all along." Reading, then, becomes a kind of masquerade, enabling Darragh to step into imagined shoes. Like Chandler, Darragh is characterized by the detective in the story "Bay City Blues," who escapes by climbing into another room, dressing in someone else's clothes, and assuming another's voice.

In an early essay, called "Realism and Fairyland," Chandler attacked what he called "scientific realism." Science, he felt, seems to solve problems but only changes the circumstances. For Chandler, the subject should never control the author (as in social realism); the writer should control the subject. Writers who matter tend to be idealists rather than realists, be-cause "they exalt the sordid to a vision of magic; and create pure beauty out of plaster and vile dust."[31] The idealistic view, according to Chandler, deals with human possibility. It does not merely record facts as in a sociological catalog. Rather than failing to register unpleasant phenomena, writing should record them so that the reader can feel them emotionally, in terms of human joy and sorrow. Darragh's investigations follow Chandler's, then, in displacing language from order.

"Raymond Chandler's Sentence" is complemented by another section of *Striking Resemblance*, "'a perfect one of those . . .'/name weigh day." In this piece, Darragh turns to Chandler's peer, James M. Cain, and his novel *Mildred Pierce*. Like Chandler, Cain normally assumed a first-person voice "of someone he'd pretend to be." Yet *Mildred Pierce* was written in "the pretentious /(a.k.a. "straight") third person." It was his first serious novel about that "great American Institution that never gets mentioned on the Fourth of July—a grass widow with two small children to support."[32] His story focuses on Mildred Pierce, an ordinary housewife, who throws her weak husband out and attempts to raise two girls at the beginning of the Depression. Selling pies and working as a waitress, she builds on her suc-cess until she owns a whole chain of restaurants. Each afternoon, she re-turns home to listen to her daughter, Veda, play the piano, particularly a piece by Chopin "because it reminds [her] of that song about rainbows."[33] Mildred's "pie in the sky" is that one day Veda—whose highly flexible voice enables her to become a famous coloratura soprano—will return her love.

Darragh identifies with Mildred in her attempt to juggle the demands of home and work and in the feeling of total exhaustion at the end of the day. She points out that as voluntary working mothers, neither she nor Mildred Pierce are true grass widows. In "Error Message," Darragh argues that "I format my writing to go in and out of narrative to coincide with the way I respond to any worlded activity—that is, I follow a prescribed set of rules that produces a sense of 'numbness' which in turn redefines the prescrip-tion." The prescription in *Striking Resemblance* is the lack of options for working mothers like herself and Mildred. Faced with this problem in Cain's novel, Mildred utters, "I'll——!" For Darragh, the liberatory "numbness" is also a blank. "I've always liked the 'blank,'" she argues, "be-cause it suggests that the inarticulate void is not a mass of random particles per se, but [there is] some sort of structure [to] them—a hidden narra-tive."[34] In *Mildred Pierce* the blank comes to represent pride. Just as it takes twenty-nine lines for Cain to have "her give a value/to this blank," Dar-ragh goes on to list twenty-nine phrases from the lines surrounding "pride" in *A Dictionary of the Underworld*.[35]

Cain wrote colorfully about violence, sex, and greed and reveled in the use of clichés. "My clichés are more or less deliberate," he stated. "Many of life's most moving things are banal . . . I try in using a cliché, to set it up so perhaps it gains its own awkward, pathetic eloquence."[36] Clichés sometimes take a form similar to slang in their sensitivity to alliteration, rhythm, and rhyme. Making particular use of slang, Chandler stated that "there are only two kinds that are any good: slang that has established itself in the language, and slang that you make up yourself."[37] In feeling an affinity with the main character, Darragh decided to write with and alongside Cain and Chandler to explore the "weigh" (in the sense of "a measure of heaviness" as well as "way") of being a grass widow—what it means to occupy such a term. She therefore put together lists of her own rhyming slang as well as invented nursery rhymes about mothering. Recalling Mildred's mistakes, Darragh warns against losing dignity in the process of teaching etiquette or overly preparing the child. Her rhyming slang describes domestic objects through arresting compound images, like "toe rug" for "slug" and "biscuit rust" for "dust." Bringing together two otherwise unrelated words, she creates a vivid single image-complex.

Further descriptive compounds are generated in "Scale Sliding," which is dedicated to "Joan Retallack and her own slide rule." Retallack constructed a text ("Slide Rule") made to operate like the mathematician's slide rule: it consists of words that literally slide alongside each other. As a mathematical tool, the slide rule made it possible for complex mathematical problems to be read as the mechanical equivalent of addition or subtraction.

In her response to Retallack, Darragh disrupts the habitual cues used to distance self from other. Distance is usually signaled to the eyes by the angle of convergence. In Western culture we surround ourselves with a visual environment rich in cues to distance. Roads and railways present long parallel lines converging by perspective. Rooms, boxes, books, and other objects are generally rectangular, leading to a proliferation of right-angled corners. Yet distortions may still occur in perspective. Darragh recounts how she was a slow reader as a child, transposing letters and numbers when tired. She was diagnosed with "eyes which don't work together—'wide divergence at near and far.'"[38] Apart from this physiological theory, cognitive theories suggest that such errors occur when knowledge or strategies of seeing are misapplied. Other physiological theories argue that distortion occurs when there is disturbance in the information channels or in the functional units handling signs, rather than in how the information is applied to the perceptual situation.

Darragh discerns an analogy between the divergence of her eyes and the punning of words, in which sounds are used "so they can move /more than one way." One is "seeing double"; the other is "double talk."[39] She decides to "set [herself] straight" by focusing on corners, breaking down *corner* into its various definitions and creating ambiguous figures with the words that surround them in the dictionary. As R. L. Gregory writes in *Eye and Brain:*

Ambiguous figures put our perceptual system at a curious disadvantage; because they give no clue of which bet to make, and so it never settles for one bet. But the great advantage of an active . . . system of this kind is that it can often function in the absence of adequate information by postulating alternative realities.[40]

Her first example makes use of a visual illusion known as the Necker cube, in which alternative realities transpose in figure/ground relief. In breaking "corner" down into its various associations, Darragh selects the term *horn*, which creates a "rough corner" through its projecting angle:

```
face front            back face
      round dance            tortoise corns
face front            back face
      spike bowsprit            sembling flint
face front            back face
      mark length            varying cross
face front            back face
      leaves & small                oven-shaped mound
face front            back face
      out a horizon            glacial cinques
face front            back face
      mitted by such            out of (the) work
face front            back face
      guard pin            bearant part[41]
```

The word square is composed of parts of various definitions of *horn* from the *Random House Dictionary of the English Language*.[42] In terms of radio, the horn is "a tube of *varying cross* section used in some loudspeakers," whereas in geology, a horn is "a mountain peak formed by the intersection of three or more *glacial cinques*"(italics added). In horology, the horn is "either of the two prongs at the end of the lever fork guarding against overbanking when the *guard pin* is in the crescent"(italics added). Darragh also uses definitions of words where *horn* is a syllable or part of a phrase. So the definition for the nautical term "horn bowsprit" has "see spike bowsprit." *Hornito* is defined as "a low *oven-shaped mound*, which is common in the volcanic districts of South America"(italics added). She also fragments the definition according to the way it is presented on the page, borrowing part of the second line in the definition of *hornstone:* "a variety of quartz re/sembling flint."

Furthermore, she makes up neologisms like "tortoise corns," which brings together the words *horn-rimmed* ("frames that are made of horn, tortoise shell or plastic") and *corns* (the hard or hornlike growths on feet).

In a newly rendered term like "tortoise corns," Darragh shifts between transparent semantic depth and opaque phonemic surface.[43] We understand each part of the phrase but overall it defies comprehension. Alternatively, terms like "varying cross" or "guard pin" sound familiar but require further context for the reader to assign any meaning. Meanings may partly arise from the exercise of switching attention between phrases, moving back and forth between pairs, such as "leaves & small" and "oven-shaped mound" or "out a horizon" and "glacial cinques." This method provokes new images, such as a pile of leaves in fall or a frozen edge.

Aside from the Necker cube, Darragh makes use of the Ponzo/railroad track illusion, in which lines of equivalent length appear to be of different size when placed between two converging lines (the Ponzo visual illusion creates a hollow angle or false corner). She takes similar scraps of definitions from the words, *fragment* and *frame*, drawing attention to the elements of the illusion itself. She also excises fragments from the definitions of surrounding words on the dictionary page, such as *fraction* and *fractable*. "[W]hat interests me," Darragh states, "is the coincidence and juxtaposition of the words on the page in their natural formation (alphabetical order). In reference to each other, they have a story of their own." She continues: "The technical aspect (scientific and philosophical terminology as distinct from the conversational forms) of the language can be intriguing, too. Reading the definitions is like reading a foreign language developed specifically for English."[44]

In *The American Language*, H. L. Mencken argues that a proliferation of neologisms—chiefly compounds—arose with the new landscape and the new mode of life. Darragh refers to one of these, "fox grapes," in her variation of the Ponzo illusion. Other phrases, like "sembling flint," follow the shortening that also occurred with some words. She notes that neologisms can be "both a comfort and a challenge" because they "embody the strength and beauty of multiple, simultaneous measurements." They suggest that the world, generally viewed as a unified environment, "can be rearranged a different way, not as a retreat or as a false hope, but as a case in point."[45]

To further deconstruct the corner, Darragh moves from puzzle squares to the Ames Room. The Ames Distorted Room uses two straight lines and a sloping line to create a false corner. If a viewer stations herself at a fixed point just outside, two strangers of equal height standing at the far end look different in size. By positioning a two-dimensional template of the Ames Room over a dictionary page, fragments are generated randomly (see fig. 10).

Although the Ames Room is a three-dimensional illusion, Darragh translates it to invoke alternative directions in reading. The example of "ludicrous stick" has various definitions of *lick*. "Ludicrous stick" sounds conceivably ludicrous stick

to
clean
over: T
formal.
whip. b.
or surpass
completion or
etc.: They need
into shape. 6. 1
19) 7. lick the d
stroke of the tongue
be taken up by one str
cream cone. 10. See salt
b. a brief, brisk burst of ac
pace or clip; speed. 12. Jazz.
in swing music. 13. lick and a
perfunctory manner of doing some
time to clean thoroughly, but gave
promise. (ME lick (e), OE liccian; c.
akin to Goth (bi) laigon, L lingere, Gk
(up) — licker, n.

Lick (lik), n. a ring formation in the fi
the face of the moon: about 21 miles in
lick er-in (lik er in), n. a roller on
chine, esp. the roller that opens the st
the card and transfers the fibers to the
Also called taken-in. (n. use of v. phr
licking (lik ing), n. 1. Informal. a. a
thrashing. b. a reversal or disappointm
2. the act of one who or that which lick
licorice (lik e   ish, lik rish).

viewing
point

Fig. 10. Ames Room experiment from Tina
Darragh's *Striking Resemblance* (Provi-
dence, RI: Burning Deck, 1989).

like rhyming slang for *lick*. The first meaning of *lick*, "to clean over," can be
connected back to the opening passage of "Scale Sliding":

> each had a room
> the little by each roomed away from the rest, own to each
> in every room sunk: water   wash   paste   strays
> no matter, the fullness of a corner—it was clean
> of this course a one was not[46]

Darragh's writing works away from a "spick and span" order. Alhough *licking* can mean "taken in," Darragh's work relies on the reader to spot the joke. *Lick* is associated with repetition ("whip," "thrashing") as well as regular movement ("speed," "swing music," "roller"),[47] both recalling the cliché of the machine in "Pi in the Skye."

Darragh points out that even from a single viewing point or perspective, word fragments can be read either way. While the Ames Room experiments may seem artificial or forced, Darragh reminds the reader that similar reading experiences can happen in everyday environments. She recalls how a recent snowfall on her car hid some letters on the hood, so that the message (from the remaining letters of *o*, *t* and *s* and the distance between them) could be read either as "go to hell, fatso" or "hold fast to dreams."[48]

In reading *Striking Resemblance*, it becomes apparent that our sense of self and our unconscious desires are integrally tied to place. Identities such as gender and race are constructed spatially, often around the failed desire to be close to the Other. Darragh's experiments could be said to cognitively map a new kind of spatial imagination that reads less visible meanings on the template of words. Furthermore, she links meaning to both public use and private value, showing words to be liminal spaces between the national and the local. More specifically, Darragh's work foregrounds what she calls a "sputter plot," a constant negotiation of different variables.[49] She believes that women's lives are marked by irregular patterns and ambiguous figures. As *Striking Resemblance* reveals, mothers, in particular, are called upon to accommodate different narratives surrounding work, home, sexuality, and nurture. Rather than offer a solution, Darragh's puzzles present us with what Joan Retallack calls a geographical edge, the point at "which our present store of information is no longer useful."[50] It is at this point that we have to make an "each way" bet and begin to approach the real as a fractal and fragile form.

CHAPTER FOURTEEN

"I See Words": Hannah Weiner as a Tribal *Spoke* Person

In the sixties, Hannah Weiner took workshops with Kenneth Koch and Bill Berkson but found herself unable to write in the style encouraged by the New York school. Alienated by words, she turned instead to performance art. Along with John Perreault and Eduardo Costa, she organized "The Fashion Show Poetry Event," in which artists like Andy Warhol and Deborah Hay were paid to make costumes for a poetry parade. In "Streetworks," coast guards used flares to signal messages in Central Park. This would later be elaborated in her *Code Poems* (1982), where Weiner replaces language with the international code of signals.[1] In 1970 she suddenly became psychic and began seeing energy fields and pictures. Two years later, she also started to have visitations from "silent teachers." As Jackson Mac Low notes on the back of *Clairvoyant Journal* (1978), "She [was] . . . the only person on record . . . to have experienced the particular phenomenon . . . of being 'spoken to' by several persons, most of them seemingly external to herself, by means of printed words in various colors & sizes that appear both on other persons & objects & on her own forehead (in such a way that she can perceive them from within)."[2] In a sense, these visual cues may be seen as subliminal, emerging from the unconscious—over and despite any conscious relation to language.

Ron Silliman, who corresponded for many years with Weiner, points out that most of her books are fragmentary compilations from much larger writings.[3] He cites the example of *Clairvoyant Journal*, which, when published as a chapbook, contained all three pages for May 9, 1974, whereas the Angel Hair edition omitted the first page. Another example is *The Fast*, only a small section of a body of writing that amounts to almost one hundred notebooks.[4] Taken together, her clairvoyant books—*The Fast, Clairvoyant Journal, Spoke*, and *Silent Teachers Remembered Sequel*—show the development of Weiner's plurivocal poetic method.

They also constitute an intriguing record of the various communities of voices through which Weiner moved over the years, from those of Bernadette Mayer, John Perreault, Kathy Acker, and Jerry Rothenberg to the Language writers and then to a new generation of poets, including Jessica Grim, Melanie Neilson, and Andrew Levy. In addition to her ongoing commitment to the Jewish community, Weiner identified symbolically with the Native American community. This changing social formation is perhaps best explained by Weiner herself:

the words began to appear in 1972 and led to the *clairvoyant journal* a . . . performance poetry book about learning   explaining instructions/and the counter voice   years passed   the language group moved in/and so did the indians . . . *sixteen* and *spoke* begin to introduce the teaching   now she is reaching her ultimate achievement/learned first at her grandmother's knee TEACHING SILENT/she has dragged several poets into this with her gosh ma shes a/real female tarpsichordist.[5]

The word *tarpsichordist* is perhaps a neologism of *harpsichordist* and *tarpaulin*.[6] As a figure, then, she is both an instrument through which extralinguistic notes sing and a covering that stretches across the years, articulating the community and bearing its signs of weathering. Weathering, as Mohsen Mostafavi and David Leatherbarrow have pointed out, is part of the process by which human landscapes are "re-formed" gradually over time.[7] The weathering of a *community* would thus emphasize its construction through a discursive space that is constantly changing. As a tarpsichordist, Weiner is a psychic instrument, materializing into words her relationship to the marginal or the repressed.

In her work she seeks to foreground the disjunctive and nonsequential elements of writing. For Weiner, such heteroglossia is "a result of heightened states of consciousness and is nonpolitical, like other effects of heightened consciousness such as telepathy, out of body travel, clairvoyance, healing." She argues that "[t]he work is to make the consciousness political."[8] To do so, the process of thinking must be contextualized. The subject is not simply hearing voices but listening to what is otherwise thought to be noise. Unlike sound, noise is that which registers as unintelligible within the real. Weiner receives such cultural excesses as "overheard." Her "inner ear" is overdetermined, not only by present noises to be found in advertising, media, and everyday speech but also by noise from the past that has been denied or repressed.

Such a process dissociates Weiner from the Romantic structure of the artist as dispenser of the divine or Hegelian spirit. She is also distanced from the traditional role of the medium, whose ability as ventriloquist of the dead mobilizes much of modernist literature.[9] Finally, Weiner's voices, or "teachers," would seem to undermine the ideology of the feminine that generally grounds any figure informing or motivating poetry. As Rachel Blau DuPlessis points out, the muse has traditionally been used to interpret the dynamics of writing and desire. Historically, the muse has been gendered female and is either a fantasized object of the imagination or an actual person supportive of the writer.[10] While the muse remains "outside" writing itself, the female writer exists in a constitutionally ambivalent position. Yet Weiner's framework of clairvoyance seems to escape such inscription, opening up the activity of writing to further subject positions.

In *Clairvoyant Journal*, Weiner signals that Bernadette Mayer "is a/big influence."[11] In applying many of Mayer's workshop experiments, Weiner takes them literally and to extremes. When Mayer advises her students to "Rewrite someone else's writing" and "Experiment with theft & plagiarism in any form that occurs to you," Weiner repeats this as "Experiment with OK plagiarism in any form that occurs to Jackson."[12] Following Mayer's advice, she also works by association, deranges the language systematically, uses cut-ups, creates fill-in-the-blank situations, and engages in "tape recorder work, that is, speaking directly into the tape, perhaps at specific times." Weiner taped *Clairvoyant Journal* and also produced a version on video. She thus parallels Mayer in her cross-media explorations of textuality and consciousness. Weiner also adheres to Mayer's injunction, "Write exactly as you think, as close as you can come to this, that is, put pen to paper & don[']t stop.[13] In her essay, "The Radical Nature of Experience," Leslie Scalapino states that "Restatement adjusting perspective . . . to an ordered sense, rather than imitation continually in the perspective's moment—is psychic imperialism." In this respect, Weiner's inclusion of everything (asides, double-thinks, and hesitations) frees the psyche.

Weiner notes that her clairvoyant writing is structured by the three voices that she hears constantly. The voice represented by capital letters or dictating caps gives instructions. The italicized voice makes comments, and the voice in a standard font represents her own thoughts of "just getting through the day."[14] The effect of these three voices competing for space on the page is to convey the multilayered and conflicting process of thought. Nothing is censored as Weiner's journal shows symptoms of particular anxieties, drives, and compulsions. An example may be seen in the following passage:

3/10
How can I describe anything when all these interruptions keep arriving and then tell me I dont describe it well WELL forgive them big ME   COUNTDOWN got that for days and yesterday it didn't stop GO TO COUNTDOWN GO TO COUNTDOWN CALL DAVIDs get COUNTDOWN finally GO TO COUNT-
he isn't home

DOWN at the door so OK I go see these maroon velvet pants I'm not BUY $40 pants BLOOMINGDALES all over again I leave GO TO COUNTDOWN: refuge, get in a taxi, start for home, no peace, get out GO TO COUNTDOWN ok it's only money go back and buy the pants it's better than seeing GO TO COUNTDOWN for the rest of my life peace so they fit well   UNTIL   MICHAEL COOPER[15]

Here, Weiner reveals the overpowering effects of consumer culture on decision making. The words from an advertisement, "GO TO COUNT-DOWN," keep flashing across her mind. Resistant at first, she then succumbs to the message and visits the department store. Even though she is aware that the pants are too expensive, the advertisement continues to focus her attention on them. When she eventually buys the pants, she rationalizes her purchase with the cliché "it's only money."[16] The episode is illustrative of contrary interpellation, in that while her desires are constructed ideologically, Weiner can still recognize and understand the processes by which the ideology of capitalism works.

Written in 1981, *Spoke* follows a similar journal format to *Clairvoyant Journal* and expresses overlapping concerns. Its title refers most explicitly to the words that Weiner hears in their written form on various surfaces. But it also puns these psychic powers in the slippage between *spoke* and *spook*. Furthermore, the title suggests the spoke of a wheel as well as the past tense of *speak*. Taken together, these latter associations may gesture toward Weiner's engagement with Language writing and its poetics. Weiner could be seen as exploring the Language writing poetics that Silliman saw heralded by Robert Grenier's phrase, "I HATE SPEECH." In approaching this emergent community, she reflects on its construction as a "GROUP MIND" (as she calls it), and particularly on her own role as a representative and spokesperson of its psychic vibrations.[17] She further contrasts the concept of belonging with the resistance she feels to any larger mechanics of consensus. As John Rodden notes, group structures are formed as either "wheels" (where one person functions as the hub for all group members) or "chains," in which persons are situated in relation to one another without a center.[18] In its more negative reception, Language writing was often viewed as a wheel, with *L=A=N=G=U=A=G=E* depicted as its center. Being one spoke among many within a poetic circle, Weiner's writing position is simultaneously alienated and circumscribed. She would confess to Mayer, "I hate cliques, and closed groups SINCE I WAS A CHILD."[19]

The naming of Language writing as such shows how the machinery of canonization assimilates different writers into a single identity. Weiner herself refers to the people who see the Language group as those "who speak only general." She further suggests that the encompassing name is not altogether unwanted by some whose work it describes: "they want to be mentioned make it clear by name but they want the most publicity they can get also by name included signed."[20] Weiner's journal—a meditation on self, name, and signature—would seem, at first instance, to be in direct contrast to the group ethics and collaboration that defines Language writing.

Since Weiner claims that she can see group words, the idea of the group operates both socially and linguistically. Following the format of *Clairvoyant Journal*, *Spoke* moves outside traditional blocks of text. Words or phrases are often interrupted or displaced into other spaces. While the language itself may seem flat, its typography registers crisis points rising and falling across the page. Attention is drawn to the spaces between phrases or the asides written above or below the line. As with the work of Susan Howe or Tina Darragh, Weiner visually challenges official frames, her textual interruption paralleling a thematic intervention into habit and history. What occurs is a kind of double-talk, including not only metatextual commentary but also silences and incomprehension. Weiner's text therefore plays with edges of consciousness, caught in the confusions of language itself. To read such a text is to experience rupture, as words are displaced and meaning is caught only in snatches. In this respect, reading becomes a process in which loss of meaning is foregrounded.

In *Spoke*, the subject of writing is known by her own hesitancy and by the intrusion of other voices. The loss of a definitive first person structures the text. Maria Damon sees this as a kind of traumatic utterance.[21] There are incomplete strands of thought, often broken off or, alternatively, overdetermined. As such, Weiner turns to the process of writing itself. She writes: "Hannah its unbelievable that im thinking/twice around/in the impossible page where the secrets are information."[22] The self of *Spoke* is a second "after the first was failed."[23] Weiner writes a narrative of witness that foregrounds its own logic, namely that words can no longer witness, and that the "I" who speaks is no longer whole or reliable. Damon suggests that the trauma is postmodernity, marked in Weiner's case by the destruction of her culture through the Holocaust and its effect on a Jewish American girlhood. Yet an additional trauma is the gendering of modern subjectivity, particularly its impact on the process of writing. DuPlessis states:

What happens when you are a female poet wandering in . . . the mausoleums of poetry, given that the most poetical subject was—fairly recently—said to be the death of a beautiful woman . . . ? Do you turn away? Does turn away mean stop writing? Or just become unreadable, become hysterical . . . ? Is "hysterical" a powerful rhetoric and diction, or a cause for rejection . . .[24]

Weiner's clairvoyance is a writing of the body that collapses the distinction between discourses of the body and discourses of knowledge. "I can't make the words appear by willing them to," Weiner admits. "If I concentrate on projecting 'I think' I see 'I see words' and if I concentrate on 'I see words' I see 'I think.'"[25] In the Angel Hair edition of *Clairvoyant Journal* (1978), Weiner appears on the front cover with the phrase "I see words" marked on her forehead. Charles Bernstein has pointed out that this may be seen in light of *tfellin*, the small case containing scripture that orthodox Jewish men bind to their foreheads. Not only are the words marked on her head, but the taking of the photograph of her looking into the camera inverts the subject "I see" into an object seen by the viewer of the photograph. In this respect, "I see words" presents a conundrum of materiality (see fig. 11A). The very title of *Spoke* emphasizes the physical *énonciation* of words over and above the *énoncé* or meaning-content. Their value as a speech-act is greater than their value as reference (their possession by a single subject).

Fittingly then, her early journal is entitled *The Fast*. A fast is performative, a ritual act of deprivation inscribed *onto* the body as a literal sign of spirituality. This theme is continued in *Spoke*, where the term "line" is associated with the average mean of one's body weight. There are frequent references to a diet plan, to being thin, underweight, or under the line: "I wont be fat until May."[26] Weiner also writes of the woman's period as a performative marker of sexual difference: "I was bleedin   until I have no comments." Weiner constantly returns to the term "period" and its temporal associations, both in terms of syntax and as a way of fragmenting her own life into episodes. It also becomes a marker of gendered authorship. Whereas a "he" refers to periods as merely "points," for Weiner "WRITING IS INTERRUPTIONS."[27] A period, as Weiner suggests, has a split meaning for a woman writer as it may mean alternatively "stop" and "flow." As such, writing is not simply abstraction or prophecy. It is an embodied, lived experience.

Femininity, too, is repeated sayings that interlace to form one's identity and includes characterizations such as being a good girl or a mother's girl. The emotional becomes blurred with the grammatical, as illustrated by phrases like "Tempest tea old phrase in the pot."[28] Weiner suggests that there is nothing beneath such phrases—these are what have always already spoken for her. The irregularity of her period (which is matched by its grammatical absence) in *Spoke* is a physical sign of her denial of gender boundaries.[29] Both stylistic and material cues are symptomatic of anorexia. As Leslie Heywood has pointed out, modern culture is understood through a logic of anorexia, a logic that imposes control over emotion, the masculine over the feminine, the heroic over the fearful, and the transcendent over the everyday.[30] Through this logic, *Spoke* reveals how female subjectivity implodes and agency can only be expressed as contradiction. As

Weiner notes: "I feel terrible almost was picture   sulfish/sufish brave coward instant lead into words above."[31]

The irregularity of periods also heralds the onset of menopause. As Weiner's writing illustrates, both anorexia and menopause highlight social prescriptions of feminine worth. Fascinated by the physical and linguistic boundaries of femininity, Weiner repeatedly emphasizes her position on its edge, as well as her sense of lack. The effect of an anorexic logic on women writers is what Hélène Cixous would call a hysterical text. Yet in embracing such a position ("I am hysterical," she cheerfully declares at one stage), Weiner undermines any fall into absolute abjection.[32] An acute sense of the blackly comic or the ironic instills a subtle and continuing resistance of her gendered positioning.

What occurs, then, is a textual pressure rather than complete estrangement or erasure. Abjection in Weiner's text is mirrored linguistically, as she emphasizes what a statement or word is without. In addition, words may be contracted, like "Rosm," which can be "filled" in as "Rosmarie" by any reader familiar with the poetic community that Weiner refers to. Other names—like Maureen (Owen), Charles (Bernstein), Bernadette (Mayer), and Douglas (Messerli)—point to a real beyond the text. Damon notes that, for the Jewish community, unnaming, naming, and renaming have a history as acts of violence.[33] Weiner's writing, then, sets up an interesting opposition between the "familiar" reader (who knows or can construct narratives in the text) and the alienated or fragmented subject (the disentitled subject) of the writing. Naming becomes a mark of the tribe, with recognition of a name authorizing one's admittance. Yet at the same time, Weiner's autobiographic gestures suggest that it is the reader, rather than any "author" behind the words, who reenacts this ritual of community in being obliged to negotiate its chain of name, speech, and recognition.

A longing for kindred or community is also found in the symptomatic linking of her own personal history to the history of the Sioux tribe. As Jackson Mac Low points out, Weiner was friends with Henry Crow Dog, a jailed Oglala Sioux, and his family. Mac Low notes that Weiner's concerns for her own and the Crow Dog families blend into one, such that words like *mother* or *grandmother* may refer equally to members of either family.[34] As a result of such ambivalence, familial lines collapse, and self is identified with Other in an imaginary bond. Of the writing of the Fort Laramie Treaty, Weiner states:

ted states of america drove us crazy w

              i   i

          n   join us   t

      the u   h them[35]

The "join us"—protected under the preceding line—refers not only to the national identity of the United States but also to a more regional "us," the "GROUP ENTITY" that subsumes everything else. "I was also second class citizen," she writes.[36] Referring to herself as "sis" or "sister," Weiner foregrounds the intrafamilial appellation of herself as part of a larger unit.[37] Damon thinks that Weiner's interest in Native American political issues is one way in which to address explicitly such public traumas as ethnocide and genocide.[38] I would suggest that distinctions between public and private or collective and individual are, for Weiner, continually broken or crossed over by the very instance of writing.

An example of this may be seen in the following passage:

> in this article are my period pieces all my periods are
> pieces . . .
> The period piece over my illustration over my inbound book
>   ERAS
> make a note stupid you smalled letter and erased above
> at this ending page of my historical article finished by the
> letting of the pen run out somewhat on my next page. I am
> somewhat clean and I am writing another article about my
> hide hidden in the past ten years[39]

Weiner shifts paratactically between the "article" in its grammatical sense and its sense as an academic essay. Here, the indefinite article, *a,* a "smalled letter," is implicitly an address to her subjectivity, which is undergoing textual erasure. Later, she elides this with another form of erasure in exploring the term *article* as a clause in a treaty about territory. *Article,* in the form of the indefinite *a* thus becomes associated with the cultural loss of identity and property rights.

She speaks of Native Americans not being approved in an "official list" and of being denied a grant "for some reason as I was working underground."[40] This loss of rights is translated into the act of publishing. Weiner writes of Rosmarie Waldrop; "shes going/to publish an article about me without telling me without/permission thats all because she is very hard on mother/myname she wants to do a great big article stupid/breakdown."[41] The use of a journal format forcibly demonstrates the separation between signature, authorship, and authority. The voices and overheard phrases that fill Weiner's book constitute a forgery of ownership, such that it cannot be her name that assumes copyright for the material within the pages.

At the same time, Weiner seems to enact her agency by writing the journal through a continuous present. As a result, she states: "embarrass only sign it HANNAH/SUN late DOUGLAS IMPRINTED SOME sad publishing immediate errors."[42] The errors themselves appear on the next page as the misalignment of hand to keyboard: "just send Douglas cirrected nabyscruot befire/ge screans styroud." This physical or human fault is it-self "corrected" in the following line as "corrected manuscript before he screams stupid."[43] These errors mostly bear upon her identity as both pro-fessional writer and female: "I ams imprinted lucky girl incorrectly." In this frame of mind, Weiner tries to convince herself, "im like the language boys."[44] By repeating the terms "stupid" and "embarrassed," Weiner em-phasizes a lack of confidence that is out of kilter with the professional suc-cess of the "language boys." There is a marked lack of control as well as failure. "I CANT WIN THEM ALL DEARIE," she writes, echoing her mother's clichés about achievement.[45] Weiner's success cannot erase either the social conditioning of gender or the strictures that femininity is second-rate. Nor can it conceal her class and Jewish ethnicity within upper class WASP enclaves synonymous with Radcliffe, from which she gradu-ated in 1950 magna cum laude.

So *Spoke* deals with errors and representations that cannot be corrected, like names and histories. Significantly, the only handwritten word in *Spoke* is her signature, "Hannah."[46] Being Jewish and female, she cannot be cor-rected: "im like the language boys should be girls obey orders of course."[47] In replacing Hannah with the formulaic and generic blankness of "My name," Weiner experiences conflict:

> instead   My name the whole Israel country is up in arms
> stupid   My name its just two days in some place stupid . . .[48]

Weiner's history—perhaps embodied in the figure of her mother (since Jewish identity is determined through the matrilineal rather than the patri-lineal)—forever intercepts the present, informing it and constraining it. Weiner's "my name" is itself changed into many variations, including "my-name," "hymname," "noname," "sirname," "somename," "whoname," and "Hanasoname." All these variations suggest a self that exists in radical al-terity to the language and the social that defines her. In a sense, the proper name becomes overwhelmed by the improper. "Mynameis" aurally blurs into "my nemesis."[49] As Weiner suggests in *Clairvoyant Journal*, she is over-whelmed by guilt about her "living" relation to the dissolution—even "death"—of community.

Weiner notes her insecurity with the poetic community: "sis I used to/ be NEGLECTED a very angry unenlightened person/with the same group of   BECAUSE I CAN BE FELT MOTHE / STUPID AND THEY KNOW IT." She adds, "think how hard it is to be an intellectual" but rallies: "I CAN BE FUNNY ALL BY ITSELF SOMETIME."[50] Fur-ther on, she writes, "spot people laugh when you enjoy the sentence syn-tax/some courage."[51]

Weiner does not limit her exploration of gender effects to herself but keeps returning to the distinction between community roles and sexual difference. Her text looks at Alice Notley and Bernadette Mayer, seeing Notley as "Ted's/apostrophe simple Alice wife including interruptions."[52] She also refers to Bernadette Mayer's *Studying Hunger,* noting that "as hunger strikers/persist they grow blind always underline Bernadette's philosophy/ as a the leader." She adds that Bernadette "left us behind and married so her children would succeed/as important children on the front page."[53] This marks Mayer's move away from New York and the Poetry Project as well as her shift to a more intimate community, namely the immediate family. In *Spoke,* Mayer's name is mentioned far less often than in *Clairvoyant Journal,* where it is, at one stage, celebrated in large bold letters: "BERNADETTE TAKES A CHANCE."[54]

Alternatively, the "language boys" are seen to be drawn by the "money imperative" and Marxist ideologies: "BRUCE is incited exited/over the value of the money problem."[55] She sees her writing as distanced also from the poetics of the New Sentence: "some spell/INCOMPLET/e or isnt that the sentence formedand periodRon Silliman." She asks, "am I writing making sense across the page but in a pickle with some sentence form."[56] Weiner's lines are not written in recognizable sentences. To a degree, then, she seems to undermine Language writing interests, at least those of the "language boys." She writes: "MY NAME / I WISH I WERE GREAT BIG LINGUIST STUPID" and

> much courage reading across my name I'M READING LANGUAGE
> ARTICLES some space intend   my name I'M READING Russian
> BOLSHEVIST LITERATURE I am only working only on the
> steps
> I AM ONLY A . . .[57]

Here, Weiner puns on the contemporary relation between space, marginality, and illegality in replacing "steppes" with "steps.[58] The unfinished sentence leaves the cause of such domestic and theoretical exile open. But it becomes filled in as "I AM ONLY A GIRL" when she later writes: "poor girl was a second choice."[59] The "I" that writes is really an "o," "o silent being o prose continue I was a troubleshooter," or a "big circle O."[60]

Ultimately, however, Weiner does not produce a poetics of negation. Although some critics have argued that she writes specifically of and against gender encodings in the editing and publishing practices of Language writing, Weiner focuses on a broader and more invasive production of cultural meaning.[61] While elsewhere in *Spoke* she sometimes writes harshly of the poets around her, she refers nevertheless to Charles Bernstein as "charles a friend" and Bruce Andrews as "bruce darling."[62] Walt Whitman once wrote: "He most honors my style who learns under it to destroy the teacher."[63] In this vein, Weiner wonders whether "my darling Bernadette closes this bo/ok or did i."[64] Crossed out as the confusion of identity is resolved temporarily, the name "Bernadette" remains a visible palimpsest to Weiner's own writing project. This constant shifting between emotional and empirical poles makes the reader feel simultaneously intimate with and distant from the text. Expressing both insult and endearment, expulsion and need, Weiner's text performs a healing ritual. According to Damon, poetry originates in such rituals, being used as "invocations to the powers that govern material (epidemiological, meteorological, nutritional, anatomical) conditions and was intimately connected to the bodily and spiritual life of communities."[65]

Weiner's desire for community would be just as evident a decade later in *Silent Teachers Remembered Sequel*, which is motivated by the imperative "we must integrate into the next generation."[66] As Weiner writes, "forgodsakes the/children know more than me."[67] The photograph at the beginning of the book also shows a recognition of her role in the poetic community. The picture of Weiner on the cover of *Clairvoyant Journal* reveals a rather casual young woman, smiling and looking directly into the camera lens, wearing no makeup but with "I SEE WORDS" painted across her forehead (see fig. 11A). In contrast, the photograph in *Silent Teachers* presents a more formal version of the young Hannah Weiner, sitting down, eyes cast to somewhere beyond the camera, heavily made up, and with a serious expression on her face (see fig. 11B). Furthermore, the only word that appears in the photograph, significantly above her head in a college pennant pinned to the wall, is the word "CLASSICAL." Unlike the *Clairvoyant Journal* shot, this photograph embodies tradition and establishment and perhaps implies Weiner's changing position as elder of the poetic community.[68] Indeed, *Silent Teachers* has the epigraph "Published in honor of the author's 65th birthday, November 4, 1993." Kenneth Burke argues that "'[t]ribally,' one inherits *status*."[69] Speaking of the picture, Lee Ann Brown notes that the banner was incorporated into the photograph to enable the articulation of such cultural values.[70]

In *Silent Teachers*, Weiner maps a different poetic formation again, mentioning further teachers such as Barrett Watten and P. Inman, as well as Brown, who is part of a younger generation of East Coast writers. As with the artifice of the photograph (and following Mayer's mock blurbs in *Utopia*), the reviews on the cover of the book are "made up" by Weiner. "Well we all consider it quite remarkable that we hear each other almost entirely in her mind," the double of Watten states ventriloquially. W. C. Fields is quoted as saying: "And how do you transfer your intelligence. You think like the other person thinks and summon up their indiscretion."

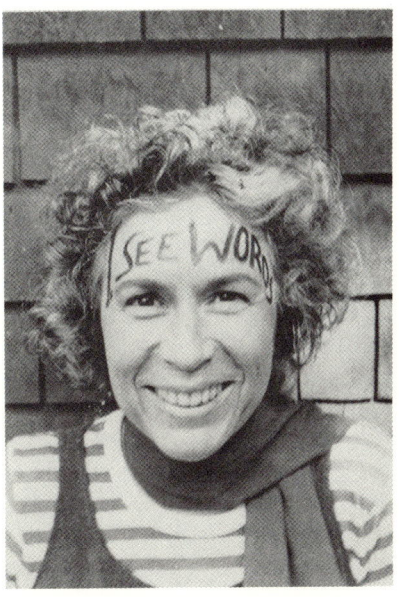 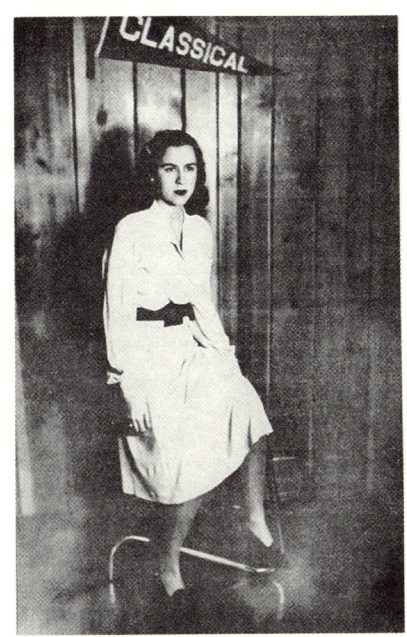

Fig. 11. (A) Hannah Weiner on front cover of *Clairvoyant Journal* (Lenox, MA: Angel Hair Books, 1978). Photo copyright © Tom Ahern. (B) Hannah Weiner as frontispiece for *Silent Teachers Remembered Sequel* (Providence, RI: Tender Buttons, 1994). Used with the permission of the Estate of Hannah Weiner.

Weiner's work remains hermetic insofar as it still works best with a limited audience that is familiar with the background she cites. Other in-house jokes include Weiner's reference to "barr/much luckier history content," a satiric allusion to Watten's recent work, *Bad History*.[71] Also mentioned by name are "asa" (Watten and Carla Harryman's child) and Brown's Tender Buttons Press ("press tender").[72] Weiner writes, then, a history not so much of poetry or of herself but rather of a family. This history spans almost four decades, responding to and incorporating the new voices who asked her, "hann please hann please write another."[73] In her final books, Hannah Weiner seems less anxious about her own position. Instead, she presents us with a picture of community that embraces and thus defies generationalism.

Toward the end of her life she began to be visited by a new silent teacher called "paw." Paw was an astral vision who appeared in various bear forms and eventually made himself at home with Weiner. In Native American culture the bear sometimes represents the healer. Besides paw, she was also visited by an ancient Mexican teacher:

who wanted to say certain things before he died to pass on some of his knowledge he kept flipping his blanket . . . the blanket was sort of like in squares of different colors with a black outline now the black outline always remained the same but the patterns and colors of the squares kept changing so the lesson learned from that you could create an image but you couldn't keep it constant, you had to keep changing the image.[74]

In combining numerous cultural histories of North America with her own experiences of the everyday, Weiner's writing creates just such a shifting image. In joining the venerable, if sometimes irreverent tribe of silent teachers, Weiner continues to provoke those who follow with her complex psychosocial vision.

CHAPTER FIFTEEN

Attention and Alterity in the Poetry of Rae Armantrout and Fanny Howe

The passing of the Romantic imagination and its attendant belief in the sublime corresponds with modernity's crisis in representation. In *Stanzas: Word and Phantasm in Western Culture*, Giorgio Agamben contends that "almost all modern poems since Mallarmé are fragments in that they allude to something (the totality of the poem) that can never be invoked in its integrity, but only rendered present through its negation."[1] Responding to the Language debates in *Sulfur*, Rachel Blau DuPlessis argues that, for her, the most limiting aspect of Language writing is its focus on the word or sentence to the exclusion of any further horizon. "[I]s there mystery?" she asks. "What happens to the quest of pleasure and passion? Or with strangeness?" Missing from Language writing is "the release of rhetoric from the thrall of the incessant = = = = = so allegorically registered in the name of one notable journal."[2] In a similar vein, Susan Howe notes that Language writers tend to "get the brilliance—the structure but they miss the terror—or the sense of MAGIC."[3] Poetry foregrounded this phenomenological impasse—the limits of language in describing the world and one's relation to it. In translating experience, the poem performs a risky crossing, putting us beside ourselves and rendering us strangers.

For many modern writers the task was to find and fight for some sort of wholeness outside conventional forms and forces. "I tried to make a paradiso/terrestre," wrote Ezra Pound in the final pages of *The Cantos*.[4] Others, like Louis Zukofsky, searched for a "rested totality" in the poem.[5] As DuPlessis rightly points out, projects like Pound's engaged in a masculine show of force. Pound saw himself "'bursting thru' to what were otherwise completely traditional versions of images of paradise, which "cohere, even if my notes (ie. metonymic registers) do not cohere."[6] Even Zukofsky's statement has an authorial arrogance in its presumption of a measured completeness.

Contrary to DuPlessis's suspicions, Language writers have been among a number of contemporary poets to negotiate knowledge beyond the strictures of grammar. Rae Armantrout, for example, sees her poetry as exploring "mysteries without boundaries."[7] Fanny Howe also investigates the "shock of the invisible," or consciousness.[8] Both write in a minimalist lyric that has much in common with the Objectivists. Presented without judgment but balancing apparent contradictions, their poetic observations engage with issues of ethics and justice in the contemporary world. Yet their subtle feminist orientation is less typical of Objectivism, save for the poetry of Lorine Niedecker. Rather, Armantrout's and Howe's writings seem to be more in line with the social philosophies of Simone Weil (whose work occasionally influences and overlaps with George Oppen's).[9] Their poetry also recalls, to a lesser extent, the radical negativity of some medieval women mystics as well as the politics of Hannah Arendt. Like other Language writers, Armantrout and Howe transform poetry into a site of self-reflexivity. Yet in meditating on single, often stunningly simple images, their work can appear far removed from the lengthier serial writing of their peers.

Both poets are informed by a feminist epistemology that foregrounds the alterity of self. Never quite at the center of their world, women have either been "beside" knowledge or its object. This position of marginality has been refigured by both Simone Weil and the female mystics as stimulating difference and multiplicity. In two essays, "The Contemporary Logos" and "The Ecstatic," Howe acknowledges the influence of Simone Weil on her work. Weil's primary concern was the relation between the invisible and earthly existence. "The object of my research," she states," is not supernatural but this world. The supernatural is the light. One must not be so bold as to make an object of it, or else one degrades it."[10] Holding that we each have a fundamental responsibility for the Other, Weil grounded her own life in physical activities such as agricultural and factory work, unionism, and community participation. For Weil, the attempt to secure existence or one's place in the world was known through the category of gravity. In contrast, grace is a falling away of self. It fills empty spaces, "but it can only enter where there is a void to receive it."[11] Weil saw this void emerging from "decreation," the subject's movement toward disintegration and weightlessness. "We must take the feeling of being at home into exile," she advocated. "We must be rooted in the absence of a place."[12]

This absence or nothingness is found primarily in silence. Much of Armantrout's poetry draws to silence, as in the following example:

A Pulse

Find the place
in silence
that is a person

or like a person
or like not
needing a person.

After the heart attack
she fills her apartment
with designer accents—

. . . .

Light changes:

Separation
anxiety refers
to this

as next
tears itself off . . .

a quick trip back
to mark the spot
where things stop
looking familiar[13]

Bearing only a few words in each line, Armantrout's poem is sparse, even fragmentary. In drawing attention to the space surrounding and even threatening to overwhelm its words, the poem invites silence. Indeed, it offers a textual void that parallels the emotional one experienced by the lone female figure that it takes at its center. According to Weil, there must first be "a tearing out, something desperate has to take place" for the void to be created.[14] While the heart attack in Armantrout's poem draws attention to the physical fragility of human existence, the overwhelming force of the poem is in the disorienting effect of grief. It is significant that Armantrout records the aftermath of a disabling illness. Like the woman, the words of the poem register a pulse—both poem and woman go on in the face of not knowing.

In "The Contemporary Logos," Howe suggests that affliction renders the voice all but inaudible. This is "the point of affliction," as Weil postulates, "where we are no longer able to bear either that it should go on or that we should be delivered from it."[15] Affliction renders the familiar strange—the world is met with new eyes and without speech. Elsewhere, Armantrout characterizes silence as "The power to be irretrievably lost." Like Edmond Jabès, she locates the desert as the metaphoric space of absence and exile:

Travels

Going to the desert
is the old term

'landscape of zeros'

the glitter of edges
again catches the eye

to approach these swords!

lines across which
beings vanish/flare

the charmed verges of presence[16]

Howe, too, forgoes civilization. For her, detachment requires a renunciation of material possessions and comforts:

You can only go wild
in the away—tracking

your miles like words in the sky

Each act is extinct
As soon as invented

and each thing too
This way you know it's not fame
but a high

time you are hunting
for in the way of

I AM.[17]

In going "wild," Howe seems to return to a primordial self. In "February Four," she further writes, "the spirit unfolds to the animal /of its form."[18] What Howe is describing is an approach to language. To be bewildered is to lose one's sense of where one is and what one is. In many respects, wilderness is not evocative enough, for a "complete collapse of reference and reconcilability" "is more than getting lost in the woods."[19] When language is stripped of its sense making, identity is also questioned.

In both examples, Armantrout and Howe focus on a bareness of existence that gives a heightened sense of finitude. Weil states that, unlike the hero, the saint remains without armor to protect herself from the sword. Such passivity in the face of death was seen by female mystics like Saint Teresa of Avila to provide an opportunity, not of destruction but of expansion. Hélène Cixous has also written of this movement toward loss of the ego: "Through the same opening that is her danger, she comes out of herself to go to the other, a traveler in unexplored places; she does not refuse, she approaches, not to do away with the space between but to see it, to experience what she is not, what she is, what she can be."[20] In this light, grace is not so much nihilism as nonenclosure, providing an opportunity to go beyond what can be adequately comprehended. Both Cixous and Howe suggest not so much a withdrawal of subjectivity as a merging of one's own consciousness with the Other. The vanishing of "beings" in Armantrout's poem is also described in terms of a "flare," a brilliance of reaction rather than an unnoticed dissolution of self.

A further key to approaching a Weilian state of grace is *attention*, that is, the ability to hold "pincer-like" in the mind seemingly incompatible truths, as well as to face harsh facts. Weil posits that "[a]ttention consists in suspending thought, in making it available, empty, penetrable by the object."[21] It is a retreat from expectation, which Nathaniel Tarn characterizes as

assurance in a state of awaiting the coming about of a favorable or unfavorable circumstance arising out of a moment of "now." Attention, absolutely and complete open to the moment as it arises (i.e. defines itself) and to the quiddity of whatever then is, has no such assurance and does not desire it. In fact, it cannot know any desire or expectation.[22]

Weil's and Tarn's descriptions of attention are similar to Hannah Arendt's reading of "detachment" in *The Human Condition*.[23] Both are expressed as the act of waiting and not taking the place of the Other. Waiting, for Weil, is when we touch the absolute good. This state of attention can be found in Armantrout's short poem "Dusk":

> Spider on the cold expanse
> of glass, three stories high
> rests intently
> and so purely alone.
>
> I'm not like that.[24]

Solitary, the spider is in a state of both temporal and spatial suspension. It exists under extreme conditions, without home and warmth. Although the spider appears in a humble position, it is, in this very stance, higher and therefore closer to the light. This paradox is in line with Weil's levering of forces: "A going down," she argues, "the condition of rising up."[25] She further believed that a higher order could be introduced into a lower order "under the form of something infinitely small." Armantrout distances herself from the spider, announcing, "I'm not like that." Yet, in this disclaimer, Armantrout perhaps more fully approaches the spider's state of grace. As Weil discerns, "The virtue of humility is nothing more or less than the power of attention."[26]

In "Close Up," Fanny Howe explores whether the act of writing itself could be an act of attention:

The orange flower on the other side of the pane—
Paper or fate?

Put your finger in the light, eyes and draw
A white field. A lamb made of lambs.

Before the world is round
There's a line of traffic
Which shakes aside all sparrowings.

Triggers follow feeling but precedes acting on them,
A feeling triggers a feeling, then the heft
Of the hand to work.

A human face is pressed on glass; mirrors, like armor
Breaks shapes into targets,

The woman's face on the other side of this pane—
Paper or fate?
Written in light, in either case.[27]

Howe's poem could be called an analytic lyric, in that it turns in on itself and questions the limits of its own form. Given that the word *close*, can mean to shut or proximity, Howe's title reads both as giving an intimate perspective and exploring whether language is a closed system. The other side of the pane is seen but has a separate reality. The phrase "A lamb made of lambs," reinforces a Platonic representation of reality, that words express aspirations or ideas rather than actual objects. Using color as an example, Weil also argued that we do not experience shades passively. We sort and select colors, positioning them along a spectrum. Language, then, works through "triggers" or association. The whiteness of a field contrasts with the orange petals of the flower but may also be thought analogous to a blank page.

Howe directs the reader's attention to the violence of the artificial and the man-made. Traffic "shakes aside all sparrowings." The reflection of mirrors "[b]reaks shapes into targets." The use of the word *trigger* recalls the gun and representation's inevitable violence of the Other. This is reinforced by the repetition of the phrase "Paper or fate?" The poem forces the question: is social violence linked to linguistic violence? The sacrificial symbol of the lamb merges with the human face "pressed on glass." Following the poem's religious perspicacity, Christ's sacrifice as lamb of God informs and is rendered part of the everyday.

In "The Ecstatic," Howe argues that "[w]ords which consciously aspire to the future are heightened by the desire to rise above, be free of, the tyranny of history. They aim for a heightened place—a paradise."[28] For Howe, ecstatic poetry is necessarily involved in the process of experiment. In approaching paradise, poetry must move outside habitual grammar. Hypothesis, rather than metaphor, defines its premise. Her use of the neologism "sparrowings" echoes the syntactic shifts of one of her favorite poets, Gerard Manley Hopkins, who also transforms nouns into verbs. "Sparrowings" gives a sense of humble song, another target for violence by the paths of writing.

Following this, Rae Armantrout speculates on the violence of history, drawing out its links with fiction and the imagination:

> *It*
>
> How we came to be
>
> this many
> is the subject
>
> of our tale
> One story
>
> has been told
> in many ways
>
> In the beginning
> there was just one
>
> woman
> or one language
>
> or one jot
> of matter
>
> infinitely dense
>
> It must be so
> but who can believe it?[29]

It is significant that both Howe's "Close Up" and Armantrout's "It" reverse the philosophic standard and feature a woman rather than a man at the center of their epistemic investigations. Traditionally a figure of silence, the woman is placed in a new relation to language. Yet there remains an uneasy awareness of the possible elision between the specific being (historically located) and the timeless category of Woman. What happens to the tales of individual women? Are they condemned to silence through being subsumed in myth?

The archetypal story of origins, the story of the ark is simultaneously a story of survival, evolution, and faith. Yet the last line, "who can believe it?" raises the figure of the projected audience of the story. What if nobody is listening? Nathaniel Tarn has argued that "the poet can suffer pushing into an 'originality' which, in many ways, has already proved itself to be 'unoriginal' and as to what the individual and collective components in the making of poetry might be."[30] The poet puts her poem forward, knowing that it is doomed to an end in any event.

In a further poem, "You," Armantrout emphasizes the inability to communicate with the Other:

> *1*
>
> Simple identity of slack
> wires with shadows
> on a white wall,
> *god-like*
> in the long pause.
>
> *2*
>
> When the boy who
> sees a snapshot
> can't get in
> through remembering,
> he must ask his mom
> "What were *you* thinking?"[31]

Like Howe, Armantrout deliberately recalls Plato's allegory of the cave. The white walls may be associated with the blankness of the page; the figure behind the wire with the poet or photographer herself. In her authorial role, Armantrout occupies a godlike role. The other is unable to recognize the picture of himself, so the past, too, becomes an abstract ideal—a lost reality. The separateness of self, even between mother and son, is made apparent.

In one of a series of short poems called "The Lyrics," Howe writes:

> Strange in content,
> though not in form,
>
> the round world as I saw it
> change around the edges,
>
> Pallid waters, scummy at surface,
> produced a red sail,
>
> constant invention,
> like colored leaves you can see thru.
>
> What is shook down, shakes up again,
> artificial off the real,
>
> alot like wishful drinking.[32]

Language may resemble nature ("like colored leaves") and appear transparent, but on closer inspection the waters are "pallid" and "scummy at surface." The three-dimensional "round" world changes at the edges until it turns out to be one flat plane. The redness of the sail is "like" the fall leaves yet, when shaken, is found to be not the same. As in the work of Samuel Beckett, there is a heightened sense of language, with the wit of the last line lifting the poem, giving a linguistic sense of the floating alluded to in the rest of the poem. Because we expect to read "wishful thinking," Howe's final line, with its phonemic play, not only throws such thought into question but brings our attention back to the semantic error of the material word.

Howe's poetry engenders a Weilian paradox through this unsettling moment. Another strategy is that of irony, which provokes the reader into readjusting perspective. In her essay "Irony and Postmodern Poetry," Armantrout contends that a person can be both "in the know" as well as aware of her own state of ignorance. "Irony, in its broadest sense," she argues, "marks the consciousness of dissonance."[33]

> *View*
>
> Not the city lights. We want
>
> —the moon—
>
> The Moon
> none of our doing![34]

Here, Armantrout creates a temporary check through a judicious use of irony. The poem starts with a negative proposition, "Not the city lights," which then turns into a whimsical desire for the moon. The moon itself is elliptic, both in the sky (rendered less clear by the haze of city lights) and on the page (separated from the expression of desire by the two dashes that surround it). With the declaration of the last line, "none of our doing!" Armantrout undermines the poetic mood. Philosophically speaking, the moon still exists even if we cannot see it or, in Armantrout's words, have nothing to do with it. The phrase she uses is a commonly heard one, retracting individual responsibility for forces that seem invisible or beyond our control.

Howe also makes use of the ironic but gives a much darker example of social indifference:

> That's the break of a day's
> crime, what comes with a clang of pails
>
> and leaden scarves
> off the back of cars. Four bodies, fallen
>
> into an amalgam frieze,
> all young black girls, are felled

> by some clasp of a mean man's hand,
> while the day's men planned
>
> in smokey diners, and the kitchen
> of the Ritz hotel lights up.[35]

Poverty's "clang of pails" is presented against a backdrop of wealth, comfort, and security. Howe reinforces this contrast, by counterposing the "frieze" of bodies and the lights of the Ritz. The pun on "freeze" is supported by other suggestions of coldness, such as the image of exhaust pipes as "leaden scarves." While the Ritz "lights up," these four girls are fallen. By adding the word "crime" to the cliché "break of day," Howe sets up a string of associations: the routine nature of crime, the broken bodies, and the structural break in the body of the poem. Accordingly, the poem demonstrates how powerful irony may be as a strategy. "To the extent that it can foreground social dissonances," Armantrout has stated, "it can serve a political end by increasing people's discomfort."[36] Howe carefully alludes to unseen structures of masculine power, drawing a link between the "day's men" and the girls' anonymous murderer.

No explanation is provided for the deaths. There is little emotion as the girls remain unindividuated and distanced through the plastic nature of representation (the "amalgam frieze"). The city continues. Following Marx, it is possible to argue that the evil of capitalism lies precisely in such dehumanization—separating a community through socioeconomic hierarchies. In its lack of judgment, Howe's poem opens itself to both class-based and gendered readings of oppression, revealing connections between the two identities.

According to Simone Weil, alienated labor encourages *malheur*, a kind of living death. She saw the preindustrial worker as being in a kind of primitive balance with nature. Such a worker is fully aware of the structures pertaining to his or her work and can participate in them fully. Work becomes a liberating act. Yet while a worker may build with and therefore respect the natural weight of a stone, there is a temptation to forget nature, to increase power and disrupt both natural balance and the limits of control. *Malheur* occurs when the worker is overwhelmed by organization.

Howe explores this in "Scattered Light":

> White slides over
> rows of windowed eyes:
> > stone housing, that is, a hundred years snowed.
>
> Surrounded by more craft
> than need, the dross of winter:
>
> Weather inspection
> stations the day then passes on information.

See birds beat the ice off their wings
for bits dressed in white,

    how the world contains everything
    the mind has to live by.[37]

As the first stanza suggests, nature overwhelms human craft. As Howe
states in "The Ecstatic," nature is often found to be in opposition to
"human nature." The expanse of time embodied in the stone house is jux-
taposed against the immediacy of the birds, beating "the ice off their
wings." The seasonal nature of their migration is closer to infinity. In con-
trast to information passed on through the man-made weather station, the
weather itself shares its knowledge immediately. While human life sleeps,
the birds are active in their labor that comes from necessity. As with
phrases like "sparrowings" and "wishful drinking," the phrase "a hundred
years snowed" not only moves beyond conventions of "real time" ("a hun-
dred years old") but offers another measure of time. Time is understood
through the example of nature, the word *snow* being both noun and verb—
action and object.

The effect of human labor decreases over time, while nature develops in
rhythms and cycles. In another poem, Howe writes:

    Alchemy's product comes sight unseen,
    how a blue sapphire's outer stone

    is a gray mention of time.
    Pace, as it's slow, has made

    laborious morality. And the wall
    took years to build. Now I see

    the stones decrease, now the ice.
    It's a little tree! let me know

    honey-slow, the flow
    of affliction, that's why it can be
    a motion of grace, one way to wise up.[38]

As the poem suggests, there is grace in the smallest element of nature.
Through language, the presence of nature is best approached through
sound. The sound of the long *o* in "slow," "know," "flow," and "stone"
gives a sense of expanded time. There is also a more subtle repetition of
the *s*, producing a softening effect in "ice," "wise," "decrease," and "see."
In "The Ecstatic," Howe discerns that "the slow structures given to words
might be viewed as an imitation of our motion, showing us the way its
pace determines our perspectives, morals, and aspirations. Language is
structured like the unknown, but poetic language, in its rhythms, tells us

something about time which is hidden and only waiting to be restored to light."[39] The poem's motion helps to create a sense of permanence and harmony. Suffering is described as the sweetness and viscous depth of honey. There is a saturation of the senses, particularly of the ear.

Simone Weil distinguishes between desire (a force of gravity) and beauty (which enables a state of grace). As an appetite, desire is linked to instinct or expectation. In calling one of her collections *The Invention of Hunger*, Armantrout points to hunger or desire as an artificial limit. Hunger and need can be satisfied. How are they to be distinguished from love or beauty? The difference is perhaps found in duration. Weil states: "[O]ne does not grow tired of beauty. One grows tired of what is pleasing, of what only flatters the senses."[40] Beauty continually attracts attention. "Face to face with a work of beauty," she continues, "we forget our own existence."[41] Likewise, there is a distinction between a love that will sacrifice self and a mere need for the Other. Weil herself would starve herself to death in the hope that more food would find its way to the soldiers of France during World War II. For Howe, love is much more problematic. It is more difficult to separate from the physical:

> The dark night of the body
> delivers that soft blow to complacency
>
> which is swallowed alone later,
> like a story re outer space or ghosts.
>
> But with you it puts me up against
> your fortress, fast, where my limbs
>
> and heart swing onto yours,
> and I pray in a pair
>
> we will mount the arc
> to the void, and not be flooded apart.[42]

Howe is deliberately vague in her address. Is she referring to a divine "you" or a human "you"? Weil expounds: "Do not allow yourself to be imprisoned by affection. Keep your solitude. The day, if it ever comes, when you are given true affection, there will be no opposition between interior solitude and friendship, quite the reverse."[43] In Howe's poem, the material separation of body from body undoes a sense of security. Furthermore, there is a fortress of emotion between the lover and the narrator. By praying "in a pair," the narrator hopes that both will reach a state of grace and the cords of attachment will remain unbroken even in death. Weil also was concerned that the violence of her attachment to a few would blind her to a greater love—the love of God: "I think I must love wrongly: otherwise things would not seem like this to me. My love would not be attached to a few beings. It would be extended to everything which is worthy of love."[44]

In "Context," Armantrout sexualizes the waiting for death and the eventual meeting between self and supernatural Other:

> Circles of an old woman's
> fingers trace
> on the nubs of
> her chair arms.
>
> Waits for the word to come
> to her, tensed
> as if for orgasm
>
> Fear surrounds language.[45]

The image may seem shocking at first, for we are socially conditioned to think of the elderly as desexualized. Armantrout suggests that the old woman is still capable of desire but that it holds different meanings for her. The passage may also confront the reader in the relationship it presents between self and God. To some degree, it recalls the sexualization of spirituality to be found in the writings of medieval women mystics. A visionary's meeting with Christ was often described quite erotically through the language of romantic lyric. These visions were immediate and physical, sexualizing the female body.[46]

The final line, "Fear surrounds language," suggests a violence in passion's force. In exploring the nature of this strong emotion and its effect, Howe's and Armantrout's poems take a strongly feminist slant. They insist that such an issue must be viewed in broader social terms. Howe, for instance, writes:

> Love between a couple
> of men and women has a strange
>
> momentum, witness the long suffering
> of many children born
>
> in one flash. Significance
> gains with time, the way a raised
>
> fist grows bigger, and the risk
> inherent in domestic passion
>
> is all the more daring, fenced
> in the electric network
>
> of winter trees around
> Boston's red brick projects.[47]

For Howe, the dangers of passion extend to the children, the inno-
cents who are born out of long suffering and who then experience it for
themselves. Violence, Howe maintains, gathers momentum. Small inci-
dences grow in significance. Howe leaves it undecided as to whether the
violence comes from the circle of poverty or from the redirection of pas-
sion. In contrast to the "honey-slow" time of attention, passion here is
"electric."

Armantrout also draws a link between desire and domestic violence in
her poem, "The Garden":

> Oleander: coral
> from lipstick ads in the 50's.
>
> Fruit of the tree of such knowledge.
>
> To "smack"
> (thin air)
> meaning kiss or hit.
>
> It appears
> in the guise of outworn usages
> because we are bad?
>
> Big masculine threat,
> insinuating and slangy.[48]

Passion is commodified and "outworn." Armantrout shows how a word
like *smack* may be a sign of both passion and violence. Just as there is little
difference between the color and beauty of a flower compared to a cos-
metic, so too is there "thin air" between appearance and act. The mascu-
line threat to all women is the encoded presumption that a woman who
displays her sexuality is necessarily "bad" and invites violence.

The ambivalence expressed by Howe and Armantrout in the relation of
love to the corporeal is found again in relation to the maternal body. As
feminist critics like Iris Marion Young have elaborated, the birthing process
"entails the most extreme suspension of the bodily distinction between
inner and outer."[49] Howe writes of pregnancy:

> A daring blue heron
> Hops into place
> And a cloud
> Sends showers down
> Some moves
> Provoke endless patterns
> Each thing is sewn into time, then
> Having a child
> Is the most extreme caprice
> A smashing of space.[50]

Here childbirth threatens the very fabric and rhythms of nature. It violates the space between self and Other, creating a radical moment of connection. Howe, paradoxically, seems to suggest that there is also a denial of responsibility: the woman loses control at a time when she would seem to require it. Armantrout also explored the moment of childbirth in "The Dark":

> Particular
> figment
>   of flesh.
>
> Grasping.
>
> Lone. Firm. Felt. There.
>   Mindlessly?
>
> "When you feel the urge, bear down!"
>
> Great urge to rain.[51]

In calling her poem "The Dark," Armantrout echoes Weil's dark night of the void. Here, the Other is not imagined but of the flesh. There is attachment. The baby is "firm" and "felt" in an exact physical location— "There." Armantrout questions whether the traditional separation of the epistemic self from the ontologic self can be sustained in this moment of consciousness. Weil herself saw labor as being in partnership with nature, as counterbalancing the forces of nature. Yet her idea of labor is more associated with production than with reproduction. She is silent on the subject of motherhood. Both Armantrout and Howe, however, suggest that birth is a moment when the self becomes multiple and heterogeneous (Howe speaks of "showers down"; Armantrout of a "[g]reat urge to rain"). In "Natural History," Armantrout further writes:

> Discomfort marks the boundary.
> One early symptom was the boundary.
>
> The invention of hunger.
> "I could use energy."
>
> To serve.
>
> Elaborate systems in the service of
> far-fetched demands.[52]

Here, responsibility to the Other is *to have*. Although there is a boundary between mother and unborn child (the wall of the womb), the relationship creates a set of ethics different from the relationship between self and supernatural Other. As the appetite of the mother is increased by the child, there is an intimate balance between the body of the mother and the body of the child. The maternal state is one of both affliction and joy.

Where Armantrout and Howe most differ from Weil is on the subject of sexuality and motherhood. Their poetry adjusts Weil's concepts of attention and labor in light of female-oriented activities. An awareness of desire and the corporeal body can actually draw one closer to the Other. Armantrout and Howe were not the only Language writers to contemplate these relationships. Lyn Hejinian also was fascinated with "the effects of things— invisible but not imperceptible."[53] Like Weil, she kept a notebook of her daily thoughts, calling it "Language & 'Paradise.'" Many of Bernadette Mayer's poems have thematic concerns in common with Armantrout's and Howe's; her longer works such as *Utopia*, *Moving*, and *Midwinter Day* may be seen as extended acts of attention. In particular, Mayer's "Eve of Easter" explores the often gendered quest for paradise in literature. What all four writers show, in quite different ways, is that the poetic encounter is weighted with gravity. Rather than ignore any further horizon, their poems investigate the relation of word to world, critiquing the very boundaries we impose on the self.

CHAPTER SIXTEEN

The Person as Chronic Text: From Lyn Hejinian's *Gesualdo* to *My Life*

"What do I know?" (*Que scay-je?*)
   —Montaigne

Hejinian's work may be seen as a continuing investigation of the epistemic subject. She points out that, for Westerners like herself, the self or person is "the very context of my living—my life's trope as it were."[1] Yet once the self is put under erasure and atomized by the ascendance of modernity, there is no longer any "secure external vantage point from which one can see clearly and objectively" and thus "realize" the subject.[2] Hejinian therefore turns toward the *accidence* of subjectivity, a bending in or turning of the person toward its collective fictions.[3] In contrast to the unified personality, *accidence* suggests that the self is fashioned and executed both in and against the social. In refiguring the very ground on which Western knowledge has traditionally been based, Hejinian explores the possibility of self-composition or poetic agency against the already written.

In manufacturing a self through writing, both biography and autobiography produce a semblance. As Susan Howe notes, in addressing the "material object" of the text in all its flux and possibility, "the vexed question of authorship [keeps] intruding itself."[4] In works such as *Gesualdo*, *Writing Is an Aid to Memory*, and *My Life*, Hejinian shifts between biography and autobiography so as to approach the communal but ever ambivalent relation of self to Other. In 1977 she wrote an as yet unpublished work called "Chronic Texts," which may be seen as a precursor to the eventual form and concerns of *My Life*. One effect of the critical tendency to read texts in isolation is that *My Life* is rarely considered part of a larger "chronic" project. In this chapter, I wish to take a sequential turn myself and look at one or two of the "incurable" patterns that ground Hejinian's body of writing.

Whereas autobiography concerns a knowable self, biography inscribes the self as Other. In postmodernism the writer always already experiences the alterity of self, as one's agency in language is cast in a rhetoric of suspicion. As such, postmodern autobiography is best viewed as a form of biography or portraiture. Jurgen Schlaeger points out that biography demands

a radically hermeneutical and person-centered approach. Everything in biography and about biography is interpretation of individuals. There is no meaningful talk about a "life" beyond interpretation. For biographers and their subjects "life" is interpretation, not interpretation of a reality beyond.[5]

Biography is therefore a form of quotation, with the biographer as composer twice removed from the real. Schlaeger posits that ultimately "the autobiographical discourse is a discourse of anxiety," but for Hejinian, this is also true of biography.[6] With the advent of poststructuralism, particularly deconstruction, the traditional presumptions of the interpretative act—objectivity, control, distance—collapse. Biography comes to experience the same strain that autobiography does.

Postmodern biography is a mode of writing that self-consciously emphasizes the role of the social imaginary in constructing various narratives about the person. It has been called "artobiography"[7] by Fanny Howe and "bio-fiction" by Christie McDonald.[8] Postmodern biography may be viewed as attempting to focus on the writing rather than the written: the very act of describing a person proves the means by which the agency of subjectivity may be recouped. Its flagrant use of quotations and a continuous present is supported by two early arbiters, Michel de Montaigne and Gertrude Stein. Like Hejinian, both Montaigne and Stein were involved in exploring the epistemic boundaries of one's self through performative acts of construction and reconstruction. This relation to knowledge may be seen as the doubled-up enfolding of process as reflection, and vice versa.

Autobiography and biography traditionally follow a linear narrative, constructed "in terms of origins and finalities" and seeking to "disclose an original identity."[9] Although viewed as life writing, both are framed retrospectively. Their drive, as genres, is toward the denial or repression of death. In contrast, postmodern biography openly explores the death of the authoritative subject, as well as the crime that produces it. It is a genre of decomposition as much as it is of recomposition. In its linguistic shifts within the space of subjectivity, postmodern poetry often works a similar destabilization. In both *Gesualdo* and *My Life*, Hejinian examines the relationship between presenting a figure and textually disfiguring it, largely by deconstructing its mythic inscriptions.

Writing to Silliman, Hejinian describes "Mythopoesis," a work written during the summer of 1964: "As I remember, the idea was to make a language-bound history, that is a history in the language itself, of poetry and poet—the latter more or less me, though without gender." About four months later she began a series of poems influenced by John Berryman in two respects: "One, the peculiar grammatical arrangements (nothing more than word order and not very remarkable to me now, but at the time extremely interesting) seemed to open up various ways of meaning things; and second, having a 'persona' seemed one way one could allow certain non-literary kinds of information into poetry."[10]

In *Gesualdo* we see again this fascination with grammatical arrangements and their sequence in the construction of a subject. Form becomes the means for mobilizing the raw materials of biography and for reflecting conditions of continuous change. "[L]anguage and consciousness are simultaneous," she told Tyrus Miller, "and the writing is thinking about writing."[11] This echoes Foucault's theory that the authored text informs subjectivity: "This transformation of one's self by one's own knowledge is, I think, something rather close to the aesthetic experience. Why should a painter work if he is not transformed by his own painting?"[12] Hejinian adds in her letter to Miller:

I think that being a person is a compelling literary problem, because personhood (social, subjective, cognitive) is so closely and diversely bound up with language. My experience tells me that a person . . . using language for thinking and socializing, is a radically unstable, wide-ranging, discontinuous construct that is not safely predictable, but rather, within the bounds of mortality, open-ended.[13]

While it is unclear whether the self or language is the agent of a person's life, in Hejinian's writing, it is definitely the language: "The words it uses determines, or better discovers, where the 'life' . . . will go and what might be known about it."[14] As language is itself inaccurate, the person Hejinian constructs and the one that she experiences as herself are also decentered and ambiguous.

Whose Gesualdo?

In *Gesualdo* (1978), Hejinian allegorizes this process of writing by taking as her subject Carlo Gesualdo, a sixteenth-century madrigalist known as much for the murder of his wife and her lover as for the innovation of his music. Freely acknowledging his complicity in their deaths, Gesualdo shifts between acts of composition and decomposition. The murder becomes a trope for the "death" of the subject in postmodern biography and raises further questions concerning legitimacy and authorization. By collapsing the roles of musician and murderer, Gesualdo's reputation shifts continuously between chords and silence, presence and absence.

Hejinian does not presume an authoritative narrative to tell "what happened" in a series of events, or *fabula*, but concentrates instead on that act of description that Russian formalists have termed the *sjuzet*. She therefore looks to other biographies for plot details, borrowing substantially from Glenn Watkins's *Gesualdo: The Man and the Music*, which had been published only a few years earlier, in 1973.[15] Following Cecil Gray, her meditation on Gesualdo also shows signs of reflecting on Thomas De Quincey's proposal that murder be thought of as an art form. Gray had previously considered this in a biography he coedited with Philip Heseltine, called *Carlo Gesualdo, Prince of Venosa: Musician and Murderer*.[16] Using cut-ups or thematic threads from other biographies, Hejinian's text is really a biography about the act of biography. Her *Gesualdo* may be seen as a reflection on how a life is "known" through the interdependence of work and reputation, which involves studying the reception of both the textual body and the body of a social subject.

In relation to the self, the text is a bibliography. It is the framework of ready references through which the person is always already composed. Using the biography by Watkins, Hejinian suggests that the figure of Gesualdo is constructed through various cultural fictions. She argues that, in her own culture, to be other than new or original in writing is to be considered repetitive or banal; nevertheless, one invariably "plagiarizes the past."[17] As Gertrude Stein remarks in "Composition as Explanation," "Everything is the same except composition and as the composition is different and always going to be different everything is not the same."[18] Like Stein, Hejinian views composition as a complexly layered phenomenon that is both artwork and process.[19] Its grounding repetition constantly forces one into crime.

But the figure of Gesualdo also has been emblematic of the author as genius, a concept that Hejinian seeks to displace. As she points out, the special validity of the artist is often proved by a heightened suffering or intensity of experience, which enables him or her to transcend the sphere of the average person. Certainly, the emotions involved in the murder—characterized as a crime of passion—have been seen as transferred into Gesualdo's music. Igor Stravinsky, for instance, notes in his preface to Watkins's biography that Gesualdo "weights the traditional madrigal of poised sentiments with the heavy intensity of emotion," the "heavy intensity" being a murderer's remorse.[20] Hejinian argues otherwise: "It is simply that the suffering of the madman is endured in its own non-relational context; it may be no greater than ours."[21]

Glenn Watkins's biography, *Gesualdo: The Man and His Music*, follows the pattern advocated in Eliot's "Tradition and the Individual Talent" of separating the "life" of the man (or murderer) from the "work" (the music).[22] Hejinian collapses this distinction from the very first paragraph of *Gesualdo*. As in *My Life*, she uses an inset phrase to comment on or supplement the main paragraph. The opening phrase, "Gesualdo to / an introduction," leads readers to a brief summary of Gesualdo's life, which appears to be styled generically in the manner of a biographical entry:

Gesualdo, dead now, d, rests his life faithful, his, in pieces, are discontinuous and harm the use, who did not lack intensity. Circa, c, and highly individual the murder which was married between instances of workmanship and reduction. Their dramatic exclamations push the basic scale a time of the more true. Born, b, whose fame rests on her lover and between. The first vocal in the first four in the last two are discontinuous and harmonic to an introduction.[23]

Through such content Hejinian undermines the genre's aims. The narrative corpus of Gesualdo is not a containable chronology but is "in pieces" and "discontinuous." She thus raises the issue of fidelity in representing a "life." The contractions "d," "c," and "b" may be viewed as traditional ways of dating or circumscribing a person's life, but they also signify the musical notes that form the chords of Gesualdo's madrigals. Murder and marriage may thus be seen, like music, as events of "workmanship and reduction."

Hejinian was not the first to read Gesualdo's accomplishments in this manner. Following De Quincey's "On Murder, Considered as One of the Fine Arts," Cecil Gray proposed that the murder of Gesualdo's wife and lover is another masterpiece to consider alongside his many madrigals. As Gray argues, "What finally and decisively justifies the claim of murder to be considered an art is, as with all the other arts, its emotional appeal; its function is, in the Aristotelian phrase, to purge the soul by means of pity and terror."[24] Gray adds that Gesualdo's twin acts are emblematic of the emergence of modernity, in that they represent a shift between the aesthetics of everyday life and the life of an aesthetic text. He suggests that "the beginning of the decline of murder as an art dates from precisely the same period as the development of music as a personal expression."[25] Whereas music was still largely a craft in Gesualdo's time, Gray argues that murder required a "boldness of conception, . . . breadth of style, the absolute sureness of execution."[26] In translating these qualities from murder to music, Gesualdo could be said to have become a modernist. As Hejinian writes, "Passions . . . haunt the classic style and the master, who was a modernist, bold and complex, furthering the true expression of his life."[27]

Hejinian went on to transfer substantial phrases from Watkins's biography of Gesualdo into a narrative of her own making. By doing so, she implicitly undermined the ideology of the originary text as sited in individual inspiration. She thus parallels not only Gesualdo's own method of grafting his madrigals but also textual borrowings by writers such as Montaigne and Roland Barthes (notably *S/Z*, which had recently been translated into English).[28] Watkins's first chapter, "The Early Years: 1560–1590," opens with an account of family origins and connections. I italicize the words or phrases used by Hejinian:

The village of *Gesualdo sits lonely and isolated in the foothills* one hundred kilometers east of Naples. It is *not an unpleasant* country *and* the view which the castle commands is *impressive. This is no accident,* for the castle was built in its present position as early as the middle of the seventeenth century in order to serve as a fortress.[29] (Italics added)

Hejinian writes:

an unrelenting schedule in fascinating detail   Gesualdo sits lonely and isolated in the foothills, not unpleasant and impressive. This is no accident. Seven children played in the courtyard, sufficient signs of fecundity, in the chronicles, the subject of endless poems, of the tales contained therein, of writers are filled with it.[30]

Publishing her version of *Gesualdo* in 1978, Hejinian uses a process of repetition and condensation to displace such phrases from their original service in Watkins's narrative. Impressive in its detail, his representation of Gesualdo's life moves through a straightforward linear chronology, which contrasts with Hejinian's circular and often contrary narrative development. Although the "seven children" are the offspring of Carlo Gesualdo's grandfather, the phrase "sufficient signs of fecundity" refers to Gesualdo's wife, Donna Maria, who had given birth to two children in a previous marriage. Hejinian therefore fuses the two separate events. Other parts of this passage come from Watkins's own reflections on biography:

The story ... has been variously recounted in the chronicles, popularized, made *the subject of endless poems,* and later even fashioned into a novella. We have a myriad of details, but a considerable sorting out is required to get at the truth, and even then a few enigmas remain. Two sources in particular enable us to establish the basic facts of the case. The first of these has come down to us in a number of manuscript copies, varying slightly in detail from copy to copy. Referred to as the Corona manuscript, it is one of the most colorful of the "chroniques scandaleuses" of the period. Gesualdo's story is the most elaborate *of the tales contained therein.*[31] (Italics added)

Hejinian goes on to quote directly from Gesualdo's story in the Corona manuscript, which is fully repeated in Watkins's biography. Her paragraph reads:

occasions,   In dances of the uniformity of minds and to enjoy the beauty of
the equal   gazes, their glances, which on the tongue were written messages
desires   and faithful messengers, on the fields of love, an appropriate place,
                   lingered not for the first time alone, in the garden of Don Garzia of
Toledo, about in the garden, with a pain in her body, guided by the gardener, without wasting time, a thousand times, and she him, to enjoy, but many, many times, on end continued, as a sentinel, recurring, although privately.[32]

The Corona manuscript, as translated and reproduced in Watkins's text, records:

The lovers' *uniformity of mind,* the *occasions* presented by *dances* during festivities, *the equal desire* of both *to enjoy the beauty of* the other through their *gazes* were all so much fuel which burnt in their breasts. The first *messages* of their desires were *their glances* which with the *tongue* of the heart of love betrayed the fire which burnt in each other's breasts. From glances of love they proceeded to *written messages,* given to *and* received by *faithful messengers,* in which they invited each other to battle *on the fields of love. . . .*
They met *alone for the first time in the garden of Don Garzia of Toledo. . . .* While she was going *about in the garden,* pretending that she was afflicted *with a pain in her body,* she betook herself from the group of those waiting on her, entering, *guided by* the wife *of the gardener,* who had been well paid by the Duke, into the house where he was hiding. Seeing her approach, he came *without wasting time,* and taking her in his arms, kissed her *a thousand times*—as *she* did *him. . . .*
This was not the last time that they were together in their pleasures, *but many, many times* for months *on end* such usuance *continued* in the said house of Don Garzia as well as in other secret places according as to their wit and fortune provided the opportunity. Many times in the bedroom of the Princess, with the maid *as a sentinel,* did they dally amorously together."[33] (Italics added)

Hejinian again condenses the story. Her own snatched phrases are characterized by another of her insets, "Gesualdo, gathered." What becomes important is not the phrases that Hejinian has taken from Watkins's text but the movement from one unit to the next. A discontinuous narrative requires a different logic of reading. Hejinian points to its instability by the inset, which may be seen as a paratextual commentary on the adjacent paragraph:

the discovery   You should not have loved me. I have not the heart for this. You
reports when   would lose me forever. You have no eyes. The arrow has sped to
whispers   its mark.[34]

The Corona manuscript reports that the Prince's uncle, Don Guilio Gesualdo, sought to satisfy his own passion for Donna Maria. Rebuffed, he believed her to be truly chaste. "But *when whispers* came to his ears of her loves and pleasures with the Duke . . . without losing a moment's time, he went to *report* the matter to the Prince." Don Carlo "determined that which had come to his ears should be evident, too, to his eyes."[35] At the same time, the Duke, Donna Maria's lover, tells her, "*I have no heart for this.*" The Princess, in her turn, replies:

As for the reasons which you have expressed, you should have given consideration to them before and not now when *the arrow has sped to its mark*. . . . *You should not have loved me*, nor I you, if such fears were to present themselves. In short, I so wish and so command, and to my wish let there be no opposition unless *you would lose me forever*.[36] (Italics added)

Hejinian has thus changed the order of events. The phrase "You have no eyes" most likely refers to Don Carlo. As Hejinian writes in *A Thought Is the Bride of What Thinking*, "The poet plays with order, makes order of disorder, and disorder of order, intent upon confusing all the issues. He is unwilling to distinguish reality from veracity, and veracity from tale, and sees what he thinks to see."[37] In her essay "Manifests," Rachel Blau DuPlessis argues that segmentivity, "the ability to articulate and make meaning by selecting, deploying, and combining segments[,] is the underlying characteristic of poetry as a genre."[38] Hejinian uses the fragment to create a *poetic* life-writing, which emphasizes narrative gaps or interruptions.

Hejinian's appropriation of Watkins's words transforms them into a different versioning of Gesualdo's life, textually distinct from Watkins's. This is made doubly apparent by the appearance of a further text, *Differences for Four Hands*[39] which was written by Rosmarie Waldrop as a response to *Gesualdo*. In this poetic sequence, Waldrop uses the sentence structure of Hejinian's poem to produce "a kind of invocation of Clara and Robert Schumann."[40] John Cage has said that the best criticism of one piece of music is another piece of music.[41] Waldrop's text is therefore both a copy and a critique of Hejinian's. Waldrop says of the connection to *Gesualdo:* "In the finished version this is not all that easy to trace any more. Hejinian's sentence is much more quirky than what I ended up with, because I needed something closer to the tension between fluidity and stillness that's characteristic of Schumann's music."[42] Here is an example of the way Waldrop uses Hejinian's structure:

Gesualdo:

Two are extremes. You place on noble souls. The most important was an extraordinary degree. What has been chosen from this, but a regular process of communication, shortly implored for long life and forgiveness. You are a target of my persuasion. I am overlooking the city. At times I am most devout and at others most serene, and both pleasure and displeasure haunt me. My heart is not above the rooftops.[43]

Differences for Four Hands:

Any two are opposite. You walk on sound. The coldest wind blows from the edges of fear. Which has been written down. Passion's not natural. But body and soul are bruised by melancholy, fruit of dry, twisted riverbeds. Loss discolors the skin. At times you devour apples, at others bite into your hand.[44]

Waldrop's piece would be more accurately entitled "Differences for Six Hands," or even "Differences for Many Hands," if one counts Gesualdo's and Schumann's influences. While Hejinian has taken phrases and words from Watkins as *objets trouvés*, Waldrop derives both formal structure and theme from Hejinian. Both kinds of borrowings undermine the ideology of authorial individuality. In each case, the signatures of Hejinian and Waldrop remain their own, in the sense that they refashion the turn of phrase or idea to alternative ends.

The passage of Gesualdo's story—from various period manuscripts via Watkins's biography to Hejinian's poetic text and then Waldrop's—reveals not only the reader-oriented shaping of the narrative but also its many intertextual debts. Traditionally centered on the cult of personality, biography such as Watkins's gains authority through a citing of other texts as "evidence." Hejinian's poetic text, by contrast, is more aligned with the style of quotation in Montaigne's *Essais* or even with Walter Benjamin's notion of art. Benjamin outlined a rhetorical trope of plagiarism, which entailed a depreciation of presence or authority. Writing "On Some Motifs in Baudelaire," Benjamin suggested that the aura of an object is contingent on the *viewer's* perception.[45] Hejinian's *Gesualdo* is therefore illustrative of the modern text per se, as she uses a method of recitation to engender an alternative portrait of the man. She went on to turn this technique to the life-writing of herself and explored the ways in which her own person is as much known and patterned on cultural fictions and repetitions as Gesualdo's.

Reading "Chronic Texts" Writing

"Chronic Texts" is a transitional (still unpublished) piece worked on be-
tween *A Thought Is the Bride of What Thinking* and *My Life*. Whereas *My
Life* was written in her thirty-seventh year and alludes to the fact in its
thirty-seven sections, "Chronic Texts" mentions Hejinian's age directly:
"thirty-six years was a think beside."[46] In this it resembles *Writing Is an Aid
to Memory*, in which Hejinian echoes "the nature of my thirty-seven of
whom / my own astonished sequel."[47] Both *My Life* and *Writing Is an Aid to
Memory* were written in 1978, the same year in which *Gesualdo* was pub-
lished. Hejinian divides "Chronic Texts" into two parts, an "Initial" section
and "Texts." The two epigraphs quote Paul Valéry and Roland Barthes on
the desire for and pleasure of writing. These are followed by Hejinian's
own statement that writing instills a continuous present, and is more of a
compulsive drive than a pleasurable act:

> I think in time
> I am the first second and third persons of my ages
> and in the chronic texts is my freedom
> of which I write in order to be forgiven.[48]

Like the figure of Gesualdo, her own person is a shifting concept—
sometimes perceived as a "distinct initial clarity" and at other times "that
someone is another and together they become us all in time, when taken
together is all that is known." Hejinian seeks "harder reasons" than those
that constitute the traditional autobiography of a unified subjectivity. His-
tory too is a "special myth," "'that tale of coming-true without end,' of
what we touch." Alternatively, Hejinian wishes to develop a method that
might be called the "chronoquick," a "lively run." She writes: "We cut our
lines into the circle and call the rest context." Hejinian is clearly interested
in this movement of writing, which structures "eclectic thought" by associ-
ation: "It is a talent for connection and thence an art of connection."[49]

She begins with "the article," a scene lacking definition: "A prilling in-
fant drawn from a human distance made fierced." Memory is of fragments:
"her face . . . hug and lunch. . . . The warm and cold breeze. The laundry
line squeak all." In infancy, words are not yet "habit" and therefore are an
unexpected discovery. Remembering the past, Hejinian suggests that the look
and sound of words such as *hug* and *lunch* have been lost: "I afix a thought to a
word. The language is not a meaning but a welter of enunciable syllables raw
if ripe between my teeth." Meaning is a luxury that no other creature re-
quires. The attention of animals, Hejinian suggests, is more "curious than
romantic," because perception and language are "mutually irrelevant."[50]

Hejinian plays with a plurality of selves through the positional shifters of "I" and "you." After stating, "I meet you in your career and your ambition in real life," she adds: "If the artist is the hero someone else is always the artist."[51] Hejinian thinks of childhood as a longing for heroes. The artist as a child looks to "someone else" to be the hero. A chronic text of Hejinian's is her happy childhood: "You had a happy childhood and remember much of it vividly with a longing for heroes."[52] Narratives of the past, like rumors about the murder of Gesualdo's wife, threaten to overtake all else: "There were more storytellers than there were stories, so that everyone in the family had a version of history and it was impossible to get close to the original, or to know 'what really happened.'"[53] In *My Life*, she writes of memory as mythmaking: "I wanted to be both the farmer and his horse when I was a child, and I tossed my head and stamped with one foot as if I were pawing the ground before a long gallop. . . . It made for a sort of family mythology. The heroes kept clean, chasing dusty rustlers, tonguing the air."[54] In "Chronic Texts," Hejinian considers writing as an analogy: "The artist is the child as an adult realizing play; his or her art makes play real."[55]

In the course of writing "Chronic Texts," *Writing Is an Aid to Memory*, and *My Life*, Hejinian immersed herself in autobiographies (by Trollope, George Sand, and Trotsky) and biographies (of Charlotte Brontë). She told Susan Howe that working on an autobiographical prose piece involved recollecting "with my customary nostalgia my own privileged, wondrous childhood." In the margins, she relates Trostky's opening chapter of his autobiography:

Childhood is looked upon as the happiest time of life. Is that always true? No, only a few have a happy childhood. The idealization of childhood originated in the old literature of the privileged. A secure, affluent, and unclouded childhood, spent in a home of inherited wealth and culture, a childhood of affection and play, brings back to one memories of a sunny meadow at the beginning of the road of life.[56]

The next section of "Chronic Texts" is marked as "the cave." Referring to representation, and specifically to Plato's parable of the cave, it becomes the "hollow" or "concavity" in other instances. Hejinian explores the relation between language, memory, and history. This section is particularly reminiscent of the opening of *My Life*, as Hejinian recounts: "Then, later, when he came back from the blue war in the Pacific he looked younger: his face seemed as in photographs from his soft childhood. I return your pen."[57] In *My Life* the color has changed, but it is still used as a vivid description: "A moment yellow, just as four years later, when my father returned from the war, the moment of greeting him, as he stood at the bottom of the stairs, younger, thinner than when he had left, was purple—though moments are no longer so colored. . . . The better things were gathered in a pen."[58] In "Chronic Texts," Hejinian habitually foregrounds the act of writing, the materiality of the text at hand. She continues describing the memory of her father's return: "Reading the difficult text was like swimming in an opaque sea, the entire psyche a composition of memory; I was in it and wet but it was difficult to see."[59] This memory is as local and relational as a baby's.

Hejinian emphasizes different frameworks for language, recalling both Fredric Jameson and Wallace Stevens in the line "Now it is as if you were in prison with no guitar. You pace your mind a cell."[60] A private language is also suggested. Hejinian relates these theories back to her childhood experience:

One day the comic deities embarrass us: they bite and I scissor the lip of my disguise on the side with the light, and though it is too late for the phone to ring, the pages flutter. The sounds are more dense than particular in summer. The library, always of stone, and the books were of wood and still. The wind fluttered the pages down the middle, the dog would bark. I wish. I brave it. I take it, and seriously, though quite simple, in music but in conversation, difficult.[61]

Even in solitude, exchange is ever possible, simply by the presence of the telephone, the library, or even the dog. Furthermore, there is no one reflection or "cell" but many alternative frames for understanding personal experience. She states:

My confessions are of secrets passed, and hence no longer secrets. The present remains secret not only to you, but to me. Is anything more "real" than a poem? . . . At the same time, I am in love with several styles of life, which are reflective of lives of my own—they don't overlap. Each is autonomous but incomplete. Like you, I am incomplete from any single view. The trappings of some interests contradict the aesthetics of others, yet they are all mine. Resolution is impossible; hence I am confused. From that confusion comes a large measure of energy. Those sides of my personality are romantic. It is not so much my life as my liveliness.[62]

While such confessions presume an ethical turn, there is also an erotic aspect to knowledge. Hejinian notes the passion of an intellectual love. In autobiography, a stranger to the subject wanders "the old neighborhood 36 years later." Such writing has the "gloss of gossip" directed at oneself: "gossip is seduction in conversation. Candor the same. You ask me to explain myself what I felt when I meant."[63]

For Hejinian there can be no blame or guilt in writing autobiography; it is fictional enough that "today will happen tomorrow." In writing autobiography, "me" meets an "old friend," the "me" of the past. One enters dialogue with oneself: "Hello, there, how are you? What do you know?"[64] As Hejinian notes, memories are fragments of knowledge, contingent: "Other forms of the same idea are permissible, probable—extension, ramification, work again." In stating that "[o]nce a writing is published as if finally, it ought not thereby become a forbidden landscape," she envisages autobiography as something that one can do time and again, even though there will always be points of possible closure at which "there is nothing more to say, for a time."[65]

Hejinian considers the relation of childhood happiness to the present self. Is it something that one is forced to put away? "This is a difficult subject," she declares, "being subject to and subject of one's own writing." The ambition of writing one's life is a cruel thing to do to "myself." Knowledge does not so much change the person as become another chronic theme: "We beat with it as if it were a favorite song." By chronic themes she means "old ideas always new, historical and interesting, even pressing, and I mean that they recur over time and are a condition of which I cannot rid myself; the persistent cough and the itch. I've lived into them."[66]

Hejinian wonders whether, if there are chronic themes of the person (these "unforgivable noemes"), it is possible that "we never change, not much, and that we never learn anything fixed." Even if there is a meditation of oneself, the knowing self remains knowable through those chronic themes. Alternatively, she wonders if knowledge can be a process or technique "without being revolutionary within the self." She wonders if there is knowledge outside the self, a "proximate wing'd navigator" that remains mysterious.[67] Hejinian continued to explore this gnostic element in "Language and 'Paradise.'" In trying to find meaning in her past, Hejinian wonders "[w]hat is 'to understand' except 'to make relevant' or 'to find relevancy in.'" Her life becomes a "difficult text."[68]

In the final section, Hejinian compares the Elizabethan self with both the traditional self of Enlightenment and the modern self. This earlier self is a picaresque hero such as Gesualdo, master of his actions and able to shape his world in a vertical present. The modern self, however, lives in a different present, "obsessed more by language than by event." The sense of time is changed. Rather than being a spot on a linear graph, it becomes an "aperture, learned, referring, preferable, hourly." The modern self is able to be both present and absent. Yet in this privileging of thought over event, there is a presumption of intellectual inviolability: "Between body and soul you made break. No tool could touch it, that soul."[69]

"Better two needs it resembled": The Bi-textuality of *My Life* and *Writing Is an Aid to Memory*

In a more detailed portraiture of her person, Hejinian again focuses less on event than on the assemblage through which subjectivity is produced. This is made up of language, clichés such as "pretty is as pretty does," or allusions to other (and particularly autobiographical) texts. Chronic themes are now materially manifest in the seriality of sentences and sections. Thus, *My Life* (1978), written when she was thirty-seven, contains thirty-seven sections, each with thirty-seven sentences; and when a second version was released eight years later, it contained forty-five sections with forty-five sentences apiece. Hejinian's focus on Elizabethan musical forms such as Gesualdo's madrigals shifts to literary forms of the same era in the numerological ordering of *My Life*. The precise pattern of her text resembles similar structural devices used by Renaissance writers such as Edmund Spenser, whose *Epithalamion* contained precisely 365 lines to reflect the number of days in the year.[70] Following Alastair Fowler's study of "silent poetry," the painstaking order of *My Life* may, in fact, have symbolic meaning.[71] As many critics have pointed out, *My Life* does proceed according to a pattern of a life, moving from childhood through adolescence to marriage.

Writing Is an Aid to Memory may be viewed as a literal aid or supplement to *My Life*. It is likely that Hejinian was working on both at the same time. She told Susan Howe that she wrote "some short things, now and then, to break up the strain of the longer, concentrated works."[72] *Writing Is an Aid* explores the repetition of words and themes, not only intratextually but also as an intertextual exchange with *My Life* and "Chronic Texts." Words such as *dollar* are reiterated in *Writing* through different phrases: "dollar honey so all for fog," "to see the world sand dollars in one language," and "dollar them still thinner."[73] Following Stein's earlier reflections on money, Hejinian puns here on the fiscal and metamorphic senses of "change."[74] The phrase "this wallpaper I rose wrap" is also echoed in the opening passage of *My Life*: "A pause, a rose, something on paper. . . . Somewhere, in the background, rooms share a pattern of small roses."[75] Similarly, "pretty is as pretty does" is paralleled with "maybe a pretty pink dress" and "showed off pretty."[76] One phrase in *Writing Is an Aid* ("if one has struck love as an intellectual") itself echoes a line from "Chronic Texts" ("I have, from time to time, fallen in love intellectually").[77] As with *Gesualdo*, detached phrases and words become segments or units in themselves.

What distinguished *Writing Is an Aid* from both "Chronic Texts" and *My Life* is its nonchronological, open form. Like *Gesualdo*, it continues a form more indebted to music than to narrative. Making frequent mention to being "in time" or "quick time," it moves away from the sentence-based form to focus more attention on the sounds of words, which shift "scat"-like against one another.

Eight years after writing *My Life*, Hejinian revised it, adding eight more sections, each containing an additional eight sentences. While such a revision seems appropriate to the form of Hejinian's text, the idea was acted on only *after* she encountered problems with a reprint. When the first edition went out of print, its editor, Rosmarie Waldrop, suggested publishing a collection of Hejinian's work that would include a reissue of *My Life*. However, Hejinian felt that such a volume would be "aesthetically unbalanced," because "every one of my works seems (at least to me) radically different from all the others—in form, in tone, at least (although there are certain 'chronic' themes or issues, I know)."[78]

Hejinian then outlined her tentative plans for *My Life*. She has been keeping a notebook in order "to write a work of equivalent or even size, called The Supplement," which would add "some of the things that were left out" of *My Life*. Furthermore, it would update the numerological form: "say, when I was 50 (or whatever age I happened to be at the time) I would write 50 paragraphs of 50 sentences each." Such a project, Hejinian pointed out, would be an "obvious companion work for a reissue of *My Life*," although she was "not prepared to do such a project now."[79]

Hejinian suggested that Waldrop include instead a long poem called *The Person*, although she was only fifteen pages into it "and mov[ing] very slowly." Another alternative was a prose work focusing on how we respond to sounds: "It is, in that sense, about perception and the language and psychology of perception—though limited to hearing. (It gives me a chance to acknowledge my debt to Larry and, through him, my 'other' artistic world)."[80] However, as this project was even sketchier than *The Person*, the collection Waldrop envisaged did not eventuate.[81] A further possibility proposed by Hejinian was that she herself might raise money for a reissue of the original edition.

However, *any* reissue was going to be a much more expensive venture than originally realized. It seems that Burning Deck had accidentally thrown away the plates of *My Life*. Douglas Messerli offered to rescue the book by telling Hejinian that Sun & Moon Press would be pleased to reprint it.[82] Hejinian accepted his offer, suggesting in the process her idea of expanding and "updating" the original. Messerli encouraged her to go ahead with this second version and agreed to put the edition on hold until Hejinian had more time to focus on it. But instead of waiting until she was fifty, they agreed on a version pitched at forty-five years.

Early in 1986, Hejinian confirmed that she was one-third through the revision, although it was "much more difficult" than she had envisaged. "What has been most interesting, though slightly oppressive," Hejinian relates, "is that I find I am still plagued and excited about the same ideas as I was 8 or 9 years ago." As such, her additions are "not so much putting in new ideas as amplifying old ones—though hopefully putting new twists into them."[83] By November, Hejinian had completed the second version. Along with the manuscript, Hejinian sent along some slides of artwork by her sister-in-law, Diane Andrews Hall. She wrote: "Might one of those paintings, or some other work by her, be suitable for a cover?"[84] Messerli was receptive to the idea and chose quite appropriately a triptych of clouds, entitled *Broken Horizons, Shattered Dreams*, which gives the impression of a film rush. Hejinian wrote to Jacki Ochs: "I've always wanted to make a film of *My Life*—every sentence a different shot. Some color, some black & white—real patchy. . . . I guess it would be too pretty to be a film. Some day . . ."[85]

The division of the painting into three parts promised a further version of *My Life*, which Hejinian confirmed in a letter written to Susan Howe the following year, when the second edition was published: "I'm going to write a third version of *My Life* when I'm 60. I won't be twice as old then as I am now, but the book will be almost twice as long. I absolutely can't figure out why."[86] Part of this third version has been realized, some of it published in the anthology *Out of Everywhere*. Subtitled "The Nineties," it takes *My Life* into Hejinian's fiftieth year and makes a more manageable volume than the one projected for her sixtieth. In it, she echoes her words to Jacki: "Imagine the film equivalent of this, one shot per sentence, this one of . . ."[87]

Nancy Miller suggests that to read texts together, bitextually, is to remove each from its familiar or internal narratives of authority.[88] Certainly, by reading *My Life* as part of an ongoing "chronic" project of Hejinian's, it is possible to see it as "two parts or more, a capacity for patterns, for pairing."[89] *My Life* escapes textual singularity by being placed in further frameworks for reading it. Hejinian's epistemic project of the person is thus rendered ongoing, intertextual, and multiple.

Conclusion: Moving beyond the Language Maps in Feminist Collaborations

Given that the text becomes a site where two or more individuals meet, interact, and produce cooperative work, collaboration is uniquely emblematic of community. In undermining the heroic assumptions of the author as inspired, solitary genius, collaboration emphasizes the nontranscendental character of writing. Rather than a static text, writing is revealed as an action and function of communication. For many women writers, collaboration provided an imagined space in which identity could remain in flux. A collaborator, in one sense of the word, is a figure who works both with and against a cultural hegemony, a sort of double agent. For critics such as Janet Wolff and Judith Butler, this is the role of contemporary feminists whose desires may be complicit with the Law even as they avow resistance.[1] Following this, I want to explore how women Language writers deploy the tropes of traveling and feminist transgression in order to locate an erotic politics in poetry.

The term "erotic politics" emphasizes not only the relation between the pleasurable and political as critical sites of feminism but also the ambivalent relation of an individual to the body politic. In Hobbes's concept of the body politic, the State represents or speaks for the community as a whole. As such, it prohibits a thinking of the self as something that occurs either as a part (what Jean-Luc Nancy terms *partage*) or as an effect of multiple identifications.[2] As a liminal space of encounter, collaboration emphasizes the dissemblance of self and reveals the contradictions of an identity grounded on categories or enclosure. Collaboration explores the space on interdependency between self and Other. This formation is best realized as a process of desire, where the text is a site of ongoing affirmation as well as argument. It becomes, to use Jonathan Monroe's term, an "erotext."[3] As the narrator in Carla Harryman and Lyn Hejinian's "The Wide Road" suggests, "Desires are perceptions more than motives, mediating the interplay of sensation with knowledge. In this, desires are a medium of acknowledgment, a way of identifying ourselves in terms of others."[4]

Within the erotic tradition, an active female desire has largely been elided or read as scandalous, insofar as it has been reproduced through an economy of gender. Jean-Jacques Rousseau argued that women are prone to an excess of sensibility. The fluidity of female sexuality—its transitive nature and lack of limits—signifies a threat to the moral order of a body politic. In the allegory of *Emile*, Rousseau proposed that the feminine narcissism of Sophie be transformed into a maternal conduit for the nation. Woman was to become not only a cultural screen reflecting back the masculine but a measure of what sort of knowledge or pleasure is ethically and socially fit.

Many feminist writers have turned to collaboration as a practice that has the potential to evade the hegemony of the male gaze that aesthetically informs such narratives. Since language is itself a collaborative event, a shared text further complicates the order of authority that determines who is looking at whom and who is the origin of a speech act. An important step in figuring desire outside the traditional sex/gender system was the publication in 1989 of Wayne Koestenbaum's book, *Double Talk: The Erotics of Male Literary Collaboration*, which looks specifically at the mechanics of male literary collaboration and argues (perhaps now infamously) that "men who collaborate engage in a metaphorical sexual intercourse, and . . . the text they balance between them is alternately the child of their sexual union, and a shared woman."[5] Although this is scarcely a promising sentiment, Koestenbaum shows desire to be an identification outside the Freudian norm, as being narcissistic rather than differentiating. This skewed identification, Koestenbaum discerns, was continually repressed in modernist aesthetics, which privileges a heterosexual system. Collaboration reveals sites of hysteria or discontinuity that escape such hegemony.

While Koestenbaum radically problematizes the Oedipal narrative of sexuality, Woman remains for him merely part of the talking cure, a reflection of the male subject coming into being. She is still an enabling sign rather than an embodied difference. Centering on this very point and coming out of the fast and furious debates triggered by *Double Talk*, Carey Kaplan and Ellen Cronan Rose continue Koestenbaum's idea of a desire that, consciously or unconsciously, might transgress normative sexual coding. Introducing the idea that collaboration itself promotes "strange bedfellows" and that it is too ambivalent and open to be characterized through a single model, Kaplan and Rose propose that desire be thought of in terms of a broad continuum of female desire, ranging from friendship to the intensities of sexual intimacy.[6]

Kaplan and Rose argue that collaboration enables a self-fashioning that destabilizes the corporeal out of the visual. It confuses the thinking bodies of a "you" and an "I" so that " 'She' and 'I' metamorphose into 'we,' hypothetical, invisible, yet nonetheless articulate. 'We' emerges from the space between our individual, different voices, its meaning elusive, dispersed, always deferred, never unitary."[7] This seems to suggest that collaboration creates something in excess of the textual labors and desires of each writer involved. It thus becomes a third term to any joint thinking of sexuality. Georges Bataille has argued that the erotic is one such moment of transition, when the subject's own finitude or integrity is called into question.[8] Roland Barthes also declares that the subject's own interval is what is perverse.[9] In collaboration, each writer is also reader; being a subject split twice, each is therefore doubly perverse.

As such, literary collaboration always performs a potentially erotic act. Writing becomes at once a site of suspension (with its potential violence to the self) and of attention to the Other. It is this dynamics of desire that collaborations between women Language writers have focused on as potentially liberating, since such projects continually return to articulate the poetics of a *moving* imaginary. In *The Practice of Everyday Life*, Michel de Certeau argues that "every story is a travel-story—a spatial practice."[10] The space of the text becomes a site of *practiced* exploration or, in Deleuzian terms, a site of transitive becoming.

Hejinian notes that in collaborating on *Sight*, she and Leslie Scalapino had two initial rules: one was to write about things seen, and the other was that each "poem" or "installment" would consist of two "takes" to give a sense of binocular vision. In bringing the two perspectives together, they could find "new things and new ways to think and see."[11] Both Hejinian and Scalapino investigated the relationship between the perception and comprehension of sexual identity. Hejinian, for instance, foregrounds the paradox of multiple, private sensations within the one outwardly social body:

I was thinking of sex and of culture (both generating visibility) when I wrote of the mice "inside." Mice in "my" bed would brush not "my" entire body at once but places on it, its parts, and in doing so they would call "my" attention to them, disclosing their secrets: elbow, nipple, armpit, ribs, etc.—hence being on the inside they put the haystack on the outside. Its quiver is sexual, but outside, and therefore culture. (I am speculating that anything linking inside to outside is "culture"—guards are such links, and so (I am proposing) are confessions.[12]

In responding to one another, the poems form a disjointed meditation on the "I"/eye of the text. Scalapino saw the collaborative experience as analogous to travel "in the sense of dislocation of one's own perspective."[13] The result is a self-imposed culture shock. The gesture to the other culture that occurs as the act of writing is as important as (if not integrally bound to) the description or the idea of the writing. Scalapino suggests that writing is an emptying of cultural expectations: "one has to be a nomad to/continually engage one's decomposing self/without 'meaning' and so actual in existence."[14] Alternatively, Hejinian writes:

> We are in a predicament: we are in a foreign country (I
>   don't know where) and we are in theory.
> The only other figure is in an empty place and no one is in
>   the figure.
> To reach this neighbor and its neighborhood I must act in
>   defiance (casting the bit).[15]

In "These are the Gay Dissolute Streets of Yoshiwara," Joan Retallack and Phyllis Rosenzweig also locate their short collaboration in a foreign landscape:

> there is no contact with the outside world
> cold air passes over warmer air
> this is a cruel but reasonable justice
> this can be used in conversations
> a new class arises with vulgar cheerfulness
> the process of adjusting is much like zeroing-in[16]

In this new world, logic is reversed: cold air rises over warm air. The collaboration covers a period of cultural adjustment.

Another of Joan Retallack's collaborations, this time with Lyn Hejinian, required substantial adjustment, perhaps because they literally lived much farther apart. Originally, they tried a form of collaboration based on footnotes, in which a poem would provoke annotation rather than a completely separate response. Retallack speaks of becoming emissaries: "Our collaborating, our two poems and the different ways we went about annotating them seems to be in some sense—containing as it does elements of delight and trepidation—visiting across gaps (space time) and borders (irregular and permeable outlines of one anothers' [sic] minds)."[17] However, Hejinian admitted to finding the footnoting system difficult. But although she considered asking for a change in form, she decided to proceed with the next installment. Eventually, both realized that they enjoyed writing each other letters without the restrictive footnoting format. Retallack reflects, "[w]e decided that our impulse toward one another could best take form in an epistolary poetics of strange letters."[18] In the published version of the collaboration, "The Clouds: (This Is Not by Henrik Isbn)," it becomes harder to trace the meeting points in the writing. In one excerpt, the first version is written in the following structure:

this may be the only the to be the point of whats [1]

[1 The best words get said frequently like fertile pips]

the point of vanishing [2]

[2 The identified apples fall heavily to the ground considering the body as a phi-
losophy which cannot be perfect]

    a past which reveals itself   reversed in reputation
    (nature-rouge/mind-noire)
      reversed in quotation
    (mind-rouge/body-noire)
      reversed in repetition
    (body-rouge/nature-noire)   [3]

[3 Passion, as Nietzsche says, applies even playful expressions to serious matters'

    obscene but not pornographic see enclosure [4]

[4 It speaks disturbed]

    out of extremities of contemplation out on a limb or involving a limbic system [5]

[5 Sometimes it regrets and sometimes it rejoices at absurdity]

    perennial the of the prime cartographic problem [6]

[6 Passion itself is not repetitious but it can result in delicious reserves]

    & too   numbers that can no longer be divided by

      themselves

    into an in a too in what is seen to be the the the [7]

[7 The things said over and over are sensuous signs of memory]

    sprung logics concentric lines of in the we can now monitor
    each new level of self consciousness [8]

[8 But words say something more each time and sustain our reputation]

    Psittacus Paradisi ex Cuba [9]

[9 They are reputedly passionate]

    HeddaNora projections in a nineteenth century cartography of
      in
    exquisite detail of [10]

[10 Their unsatiated simplicity goes full to the ground]

    Also
    Helmer the lawyer   Rank the doctor   Krogstad the attorney
    Tesman the historian   Lovborg the genius [11]

[11 Passion is original to those who repeat it]

    fortuitous timing of the classical reference
    breaking the speed o time [12]

[12 Time then not life is incomplete][19]

In the published version the relation of call to response is displaced as the poems are unpacked and separated from one another. The effect of this is to lose part of the poetic meaning to be found in the original intertwined state. In this particular example, Hejinian's poem (the numbered lines) is clearly a response to Retallack's meditation on passion and writing. It interrogates not only the mind-body division but the performative reiteration of both acts, as well as whether such acts might be thought pornographic. Furthermore, her use of Ibsen's characters foreground precursors to their own passions as women writers—women who desire to escape from social constraints at the risk of their own reputations. Through transforming the male proper name "Ibsen" into "Isbn," the collaboration also rejects bibliographic encoding.

An unpublished but lengthy collaboration between Bernadette Mayer and Alice Notley similarly plays with past literary markers of desire, such as the Elizabethan courtly lyric.[20] These lyrics were transformed so as to convey a homosocial desire for one another as women writers. Described by Notley as "Brooklyn's bird full sweet," Mayer herself writes of Notley: "A woman's vision, your wall, the pallor of your face I'd rather see / Before my eyes every day than any one . . ." Later, she adds, "We can know a noun is a verb then or vice / Versa, as the vice is greater we can get the greater / Pleasure from our instinctual gossipy female notoriety."[21] To Hejinian, Mayer confessed to wanting to write an even more intimate and entangled form of collaboration:

[P]art of me wants to try to write a true collaboration, and by true I mean not just alternating lines or stanzas but really working with another person at writing. . . . It would be fascinating to do a cooperative analysis which would also be being written by both people & it would include certain set experiments, like going places or even maybe sex (oh dear, what am I proposing?).[22]

Collaboration, as Mayer views it, is an agreed-upon passing between. As she points out, this rejection of ego boundaries is viewed as particularly risky: "I find myself suggesting collaborative writing to people from time to time but . . . often there is little interest or even an immediately negative response."[23]

Hejinian and Carla Harryman focused specifically on the erotic in "The Wide Road." Hejinian suggested that they were "attempting a de-commodification or de-reification . . . of such categories as feminine, poem, and person," but Harryman saw their collaboration as creating an alternative "conceptual feminine reality."[24] In an interview with Megan Simpson, she stated:

We're trying to eroticize language, trying to see how far we can get with it. But I would say that this is also like public girl-talk, except that it's literally transformative. It's not real girl-talk, because it's just not exactly on or about girl-talk topics. We infuse other topics with the desire inherent in girl-talk. That is not permitted; you can't just do that.[25]

By doing something taken to be taboo (sharing female heterosexual fantasies), they enter a zone that is never articulated. This gives them a freedom to test the boundaries between social and private knowledge.

Written in the form of a travel journal, "The Wide Road" is a picaresque journey undertaken by a plural and female "we." In a radio interview, Hejinian revealed a long-term attraction to travel writing, having first been fascinated by her grandfather's collection of exploration journals. She was also intrigued by the way that Sir Francis Bacon described language through a language of exploration.[26] Initially recording heroic male narratives of discovery and conquest, the travel journal later became an occasional form of life-writing produced by women. During Victorian times, it was thought personal and unliterary, a domestic rather than a public form of writing. Self-consciously autobiographical, the travel journal stresses the subject's own fabulation through her shifting relation to an outside, to new environments. "When I'm traveling," Harryman noted, "everything that makes a striking impression on me seems . . . to open a door through which I disappear, so that keeping tabs on my self becomes a matter of remembering what I would think in an emergency—an emergency of confrontation."[27] As Homi Bhabha points out, travel across boundaries can produce new identities: "It is in this sense that the boundary becomes the place from which something begins its presencing." Travel also foregrounds other kinds of cultural difference, as societal contradictions become more apparent.

Harryman and Hejinian modeled their collaboration on a non-Western tradition of travel writing. In taking the title, "The Wide Road" they signal their indebtedness to the Japanese poet Matsuo Basho and his best-known work, *The Narrow Road to the Interior* (also translated as *The Narrow Road to the Far North*). Basho himself practiced a tradition of linked poetry known as *haikai*, a form of writing that recognized women not only as participants but as collaborative equals. In "The Wide Road," Harryman and Hejinian map out a purely fictional space that enables a free-floating and multiple subjectivity. The collection pronoun *we* enables them to have more than the usual number of body parts, as well as "to adventure across normal boundaries, or to blur them at the very least."[28]

Using Basho's method of writing in part prose and part lyric, they return to familiar tropes of sexuality and engage with them through a process of rediscovery. As Hejinian suggests, the travel narrative enables what are otherwise ordinary or expected details to be observed in a form that lends itself to imagination and curiosity.[29] Basho had earlier transformed the travel journal into what Earl Miner calls "plotless narrative," a story-practice that works in fragments rather than maintaining an overall unity.[30] His writing emphasizes the spiritual and physical significance of the journeying rather than its end point or destination. Basho also was well known for incorporating aspects of the everyday or inferior world into his aesthetic, as is evident in stanzas such as the one that records, "Nomi shirami/uma no pari suru/makura moto" (Fleas and lice/and the sounds of horses/pissing next to my pillow).[31] Harryman and Hejinian also write:

> our hum off a stiff horizon
> a captain came in with a can of nuts
> his wet ship was in
>
> its high fleas are fish
> one flea reached the end of a pubic hair

We thought the flea would belt us or scream, "You can't have him, he's mine!" We thought this because we'd been reading fables while watching TV in the fog.[32]

Later in the passage, the captain changes sex as casually as the fleas change into fish. "Fleas" itself is a phonic slippage of "seas," and the fantasized flea is of indeterminate gender, both aggressively violent and hysterically feminine. Not only do they turn a scene of high melodrama into one of farce, but Harryman and Hejinian present the body as holding multiple sexualities. While knowledge of the body may be gendered through language, the body with its knowledge may not. Through their collective imaginary, Harryman and Hejinian are "able to embody/sex even more than we might if we were only traveling through a land of singularly defined difference." "[T]here are ways of crossing distinctions which may or may not involve sex," they add, "but which create a liberated space through the blurring of identity—a blurring which collaboration emphasizes."[33]

   While using an Eastern form, Harryman and Hejinian also critique Western constructions of desire, particularly those of the Marquis de Sade. In *Geometry in the Boudoir: Configurations of French Erotic Narrative*, Peter Cryle argues that erotic education in eighteenth-century literature often took place not in the classroom or the bedroom, but "through adventure, on the open road." A picaresque narrative, Cryle points out, "shows the accumulation of worldly wisdom through a lifetime of inventive wandering."[34] Sade's narratives of instruction often featured such picaresque journeys. He posited that reason itself was a form of passion, undoing the dialectic of self-reflection in which a "sovereign subject" was believed separate from the object of his or her thought. Furthermore, Sade's staging of the struggle between mind and flesh may be read as an allegory of the body politic and the bourgeois revolution. His perversions are not just against individual taboos but against the system of social and moral values. Accordingly, his erotic philosophy strives to maintain a rigorous balance between law and impulse in order that laws may be transgressed as many times—and in as many ways—as possible. The ideal would be ongoing insurrection, a revolution that never exhausts itself.

Of course, Sade's education of women was generally toward self-destruction. Chantal Thomas argues that Sade's female libertine is a good schoolgirl "who learns with pleasure and enthusiastically repeats lessons which she doesn't really understand, except for the frenzy they produce."[35] As an embodied subject, a "fleshy I," Harryman thought that "one might speak back to and even parody Sade."[36] In "The Wide Road," Harryman and Hejinian's collective narrator heads north, where they come across "an Institute of Inquiry, though not of Measure." They parody the disciplined abstraction that informs Sade's pedagogy:

We lay about with some students who were discussing brute force. "This topic always makes people obvious," said the woman who was supporting herself with her right arm on our lap in order to lean more emphatically toward the splendid but rigid man. "We need immediate substitution," she added.[37]

This is a play on the Sadian representation of an object of desire (generally gendered as "she"), not as a distinct being but as an element that can be indefinitely substituted in an erotic equation. Yet in Harryman and Hejinian's example the men are the passive objects while the woman speaks. In another example, they write, "Measuring desire is never a quantifying of lovers; although, sometimes we imagine them all in the same room together as a substitute for a furnace in winter."[38] Besides Sade's endless sexual configurations, Harryman and Hejinian also parody traditional representations of female sexuality as either a rapacious monster or a fortress of virtue:

The toe was sucked into the Vagina Dentata. It tickled and came out just a little bloody.

> Dentata, conductor, vagina, a village
> our teeth measure length
> his conductor seeks desire
> and our vagina
> is an engine of strength.

There isn't anything we can't imitate. Sometimes this merely embarrasses us: "O dear, we did it again," we say remorsefully. "O.K.," we are forced to admit, "we didn't read the book." But we begin again and solicitously (in this, originally) imitate.[39]

In all these examples black comedy, with its edging of irony, is potentially as powerful a tool of subversion as Sade's erotics of violence. As Hejinian suggests, a failed logic also bears an erotic charge.[40] Through reiterative slippage, the ideological unity of identity may be ruptured:

> It is in the places where things
> don't fit
> together neatly
>
> that we can best insert our political will[41]

Aside from exploring the social mechanics of desire, Harryman and Hejinian also invoke animalistic or instinctual desires—desire as immediate, fluid, and unmediated. Hejinian states that "[b]y examining eroticism very closely, I feel its impulses binding me to very diverse kinds of materials and experiences—for example, car engines, babies in parks, the ramifications of local propositions on the ballot, storms and cold weather, the aftertaste of certain foods, the postal system, and so forth."[42] "The Wide Road" maps out regions of pleasure that are unusual or unexpected. Following Basho, Harryman and Hejinian include snippets from the radio or the way a bean is eaten or merely words otherwise unconnected but paratactically suggestive: "Peach juice/slut/tripple."[43]

This last phrase, as well as other parts of "The Wide Road," appear again in Carla Harryman's "Autonomy Speech." Harryman notes that "Autonomy Speech" was written to challenge the notion of textual autonomy. It deliberately weaves in "prior" texts as "a mimetic device used to dramatize its premise."[44] Collaboration, more generally, foregrounds the intertextual nature of writing. As with *Sight*, "The Wide Road" appeared as a series of exchanges in various journals and edited collections. The collaboration was written in various forms of intimacy, from the single-voiced "we" that narrates some sections to the double-voiced columns of essays that appear in the Canadian journal, *Tessera*. As with the ghosting effect of Harryman's "Autonomy Speech," Hejinian and Scalapino point out that parts of *Sight* overlap with *A Border Comedy* and *Front Matter, Dead Souls*.

Hejinian recalls that she wrote *A Border Comedy* as a kind of autocollaboration: after writing one line, she would wait long enough for it to be unfamiliar to her when she returned to the work.[45] The self became recognized as an Other. Alternatively, Leslie Scalapino began writing "As: All

Occurrence in Structure, Unseen—(Deer Night)" as part of an intended collaboration with Tina Darragh and Joan Retallack. In reflecting on friendship as occurring only in and of itself, Scalapino critiqued and re-wrote King Lear's reliance on love as a bond. The resulting text has one signature, but its subject is polyvocal as a past, present, and future person. As Scalapino writes:

I dreamt, when I was in fact traveling, that I met Carla—but having nothing to do with "traveling," happening to—and the sole thought, nothing said, as a revelation and alleviating, "there's no reason (that people can) not to enjoy people/that it's possible/enjoyment of people."
The dream about Carla is information.
Not 'As material *for* something therefore'—as it's not *for* words, this.
While traveling, I saw Bill Viola's video, *The Meeting*, where three women meet-ing and greeting, no words (the 'scene' taken from a 'prior scene,' of a painting, so they're dressed in sense as subliminal of earlier clothes)—are an original occur-rence of two seconds which is stretched and takes place in twelve minutes 'giving it?' the greeting a sense of being heavenly and intense, uncovering what occurs in actions.[46]

In both *A Border Comedy* and "As: All Ocurrence in Structure, Unseen—(Deer Night)," the writing act is seen to be itself erotic as well as having an estranging function. Thought becomes an action of the writing itself reaching out to the Other.

Jena Osman and Juliana Spahr emphasized the link between collabo-ration and poetic community in their inaugural issue of *Chain*. Seeking to provide a framework for collective practice, they hoped to feature collab-orations that continued beyond their editorial gaze. In their preface they state that they "conceived of an arbitrary spiral that spins loosely out from the work to include another—arbitrary in that a spiral's geometry is a fixed set of coordinates moving in a direction, but the nature of these coordinates is unknown."[47] By mobilizing a series of chain letters, Osman and Spahr hoped to move the journal away from its base in their author-ity and to activate a form of writing that attested to an open, unfixed poetic community.

While the chain letter is a potentially open-ended genre, it is neverthe-less already scripted with a particular ideological narrative. Traditionally, it promises profit if sent on to another, and implicitly threatens bad luck should its instructions not be carried out. It is therefore a fairly oppressive form of collaboration. An alternative chain form of writing is *haikai*, of which Basho was a skillful proponent. *Haikai* is quite flexible in form, since each stanza is connected only to the stanza before and the one after. Overall wholeness or coherency is not required. Linked poetry such as *haikai* also relies on a process of emotional affect. That is, it is based on the presumption that the recipient would be moved to reply with a poem of his or her own, which would in turn provoke a further response. Linked poetry is thus unhierarchical and cannot take place without a group effort. As such, it is a radically democratic form, based on equivalency while still promoting a practice of difference.

The resulting assemblage of chain poems in Osman and Spahr's journal approximate more closely the principles of *haikai* than those of the chain letter. Removed from an economy of obligation or repression, each poem is best viewed as a catena, a connected series of writings from different authors. Many of the catenas allude to travel, particularly the movement that collaborative writing entails. Lisa Houston ends the opening sequence, which passes between five women, with the words: "each life, then, being a degree of/gravity much like the candle lit occasionally/so as to be seen from the road."[48] In turn, Lee Ann Brown opens the subsequent one with:

> The whole shifts   the world that is
> written specifically every remembered
> for the chain   sequel
>   elegantly pursued.[49]

Abigail Child has the following chain or catena begin with "Bodies co-exist in motion"; later still, Tina Darragh opens another with the saying "may to meet the road you rise."[50] As is apparent from Darragh's playfully self-conscious slip of the tongue, many of these openings are ambiguously and sexually charged, intermingling intellect with the bodily. Furthermore, the poems bear witness to an intergenerational community of writers; older writers like Child and Darragh, both associated with Language writing, are presented alongside younger ones like Brown.

While most critiques of feminist collaboration foreground its positive and productive effects, studies of failed collaborations may reveal pressure points in a collective practice. An example is the *Raddle Moon* forum "Women/Writing/Theory," which revealed widely divergent poetic frameworks. Johanna Drucker believes that the fact that they were all women and believed themselves to be among friends led the participants to identify with one another and thus expect consensus.[51] When their individual responses revealed a lack of political agreement, communication failed, and the project ended in anger and resentment. The logic of collaboration exposed a women's writing community to be grounded more on a presumed continuation of self than on an engagement with the Other.

The collaborative process foregrounds, then, the cultural and textual limitations of a collective practice, as well as its liberatory possibilities. Hejinian states that collaboration invites—indeed, insists—that "one acknowledge the social impetus and impact of writing."[52] Steve Benson also argues that collaborations are more likely to occur when a lot of work is circulating in manuscript, when a writing community is discovering both its sociality and, at the same time, a possible language of exchange. Collaborations, he contends, spurt up "in periods when people are interested in experiment, where they are interested in the possibilities of risk and exchange, and in entertaining the unexpected."[53] In the thirties, for instance, the surrealists entered into blind collaboration through a children's game known as *cadavres exquis* (exquisite corpses). The game is played with folded paper, each person participating with a drawing or a sentence without knowing what the other two or three players have produced. As Renée Riese Hubert points out, the output was often not devoid of coherence due to the affinity of the participants.[54] Oddly enough, most of the *cadavres exquis* also represented an overdetermined sexuality. Aside from a focus on male and female anatomies, many contained figures with substituted sexual organs or androgynous characters that were capable of experiencing both male and female pleasure. A collaborative erotics, then, became a primary means of dispelling gender boundaries.

Collaboration was a common factor—indeed, a key element—in all three emergent Language writing communities. Rae Armantrout and Ron Silliman collaborated on "Engines."[55] Steve Benson, Bob Perelman, and Kit Robinson undertook a three-way surrealist-style collaboration involving what Perelman calls "automatic listening."[56] Lyn Hejinian collaborated with Robinson on *Individuals* and later, in the eighties and nineties, with numerous writers, including Carla Harryman, Harryette Mullen, Leslie Scalapino, and Joan Retallack.[57] The Washington community also collaborated on poetic projects, some of which subsequently appeared in magazines like *Dog City*. Tina Darragh, Lynne Dreyer, Joan Retallack, and Phyllis Rosenzweig conducted a nonpoetic collaboration, "Intraview," that undermined the formal division in the interview between call and response. During the seventies, Bernadette Mayer started *Unnatural Acts* and later worked with Alice Notley on a playful collaboration. In the late seventies, Bruce Andrews, Charles Bernstein, Ray DiPalma, Steve McCaffery, and Ron Silliman strengthened their emerging ties by writing *Legend* together.

In reading poetry like Tina Darragh's *Striking Resemblance* and Rosmarie Waldrop's *Difference for Four Hands*, it becomes apparent that many single-authored texts are also direct responses to the writing of peers. Only with anthologies like *Moving Borders: Three Decades of Innovative Writing by Women* can this dynamic of textual interaction begin to be mapped out and made visible. Acts of editing, counsel, reviewing, and publishing further shape the final published versions of poetry. The work of small presses like

Tuumba, magazine ventures like *HOW(ever)*, and radio programs like *Poetry* should not be underestimated for their role in generating a supportive context for poetic production. In considering such paratextual vehicles, collaboration is seen to merge with a broader concept of community practice. On one level, readings and talk series would provide feedback and attract new audiences. More informal discussions and improvisations would also generate a healthy atmosphere of exploration. Carla Harryman recalls a morning in which she and Erica Hunt read aloud from Barrett Watten's lyric work, "Silence," gaining pleasure in the triangulated conversation produced out of different textual readings. During the early eighties, she and Steve Benson would regularly work on improvisations, with Abigail Child coming to film their "voice."[58]

Michel de Certeau argues that "readers are travelers [who] move across lands belonging to someone else, like nomads poaching their way across fields they did not write."[59] In Language writing, the reader is transformed from being a tourist, voyeur, or nomad into a fellow traveler. The authority of distance is collapsed into an erotics of exchange. As a form, collaboration encourages spontaneity and promises a release from the habitual and the typical. Hejinian argues that the resultant "we" of collaboration "is not the we of a gang; instead it can be the we of supervention, the we of surprise."[60] The collaborator is both a stranger *and* inside the community. This double function foregrounds the tensions between self and Other. In terms of the poetic text, it emphasizes writing's own alterity. As collaboration illustrates, the citing of a subject—or of a community—must remain always a point of anxiety.

In itself, a genealogy is also collaborative, relying on encounters with writers, critics, poetic texts, and archives to discover further linkages, further travel stories. This example may be added to an increasing number of feminist engagements that are challenging reductive narratives of poetic community and testing the modes of history making. Through serially linking such work, it may be possible to move out of the self-perpetuating values or distinction assigned to poetry and to think about the space beyond. As Leslie Scalapino's final lines of *Sight* contend,

They *are* dismantled—

then.[61]

Appendix

ARCHIVES AND RESOURCES

Mandeville Special Collections Library
UCSD Libraries 0175-S
University of California, San Diego
La Jolla, California 92093–0175

The Poetry/Rare Books Collection
Lockwood Library
SUNY-Buffalo
420 Capen Hall
Box 602200
Buffalo, NY 14260–2200

Poetry Center and American Poetry Archives
San Francisco State University
1600 Holloway Avenue
San Francisco, CA 94132

HOW2
http://www.departments.bucknell.edu/stadler_center/how2/intro.html

Electronic Poetry Center, SUNY–Buffalo
http://wings.buffalo.edu/epc/

ARCHIVES ARE CITED USING THE FOLLOWING ABBREVIATIONS:

Lockwood	Poetry/Rare Books Collection, Lockwood Library, State University of New York at Buffalo
Mandeville	Archive for New Poetry, Mandeville Special Collections Library, University of California, San Diego
Hejinian Papers	Lyn Hejinian Papers (MSS 74), Mandeville Special Collections Library, University of California, San Diego
Howe Papers	Susan Howe Papers (MSS 201), Mandeville Special Collections Library, University of California, San Diego
Mayer Papers	Bernadette Mayer Papers (MSS 420), Mandeville Special Collections Library, University of California, San Diego

Silliman Papers   Ron Silliman Papers (MSS 75), Mandeville Special Collec-
                   tions Library, University of California, San Diego

Sun & Moon Papers Sun & Moon Archive (MSS 224), Mandeville Special Col-
                   lections Library, University of California, San Diego

The triple-numbered archival code following all the Archive for New
Poetry references represents the collection no., box no., and folder no., in
that order.

Notes

Introduction (pp. 3–19)

1. Johanna Drucker, *The Century of Artists' Books* (New York: Granary Books, 1995), 166.
2. Johanna Drucker, "'Through Light and the Alphabet:' An Interview with Johanna Drucker," conducted by Matthew G. Kirschenbaum *Postmodern Culture* 5 (1997): n. pag.
3. Johanna Drucker, *From A to Z: OUR AN (Collective Specific) an im partial bibliography* (San Francisco: Chased Press, 1977), n. pag.
4. Lynne Dreyer, "Tamoka," *Roof* 9 (1979): 53.
5. Bob Perelman, *The Marginalization of Poetry: Language Writing and Literary History* (Princeton, NJ: Princeton UP, 1996).
6. Dreyer, "Tamoka," 44.
7. Drucker, *From A to Z*, n. pag.
8. Perelman, *The Marginalization of Poetry*, 152–53.
9. Joan Retallack, "Intraview," with Tina Darragh et al., unpublished (1987), 11.
10. Charles Bernstein, *A Poetics* (Cambridge, MA: Harvard UP, 1992), 2.
11. Carla Harryman, interview, conducted by Megan Simpson, *Contemporary Literature* 37.4 (1996): 532.
12. Susan Howe, *My Emily Dickinson* (Berkeley, CA: North Atlantic, 1985), 11.
13. Charles Bernstein, *Content's Dream: Essays 1975–1984* (Los Angeles: Sun & Moon, 1986), 370.
14. Retallack is currently working on a collaborative composition, *And That's It*, an opera in two parts, with Andrew Culver. See <http://www.anarchicharmony.org/Opera/andthatsit.html>.
15. Lyn Hejinian, "The Rejection of Closure," *Writing/Talks*, ed. Bob Perelman (Carbondale: Southern Illinois UP, 1985), 285.
16. Retallack, "Intraview," 20.
17. Kim Whitehead, *The Feminist Poetry Movement* (Jackson: UP of Mississippi, 1996), xix.
18. Cynthia G. Franklin, *Writing Women's Communities: The Politics and Poetics of Contemporary Multi-Genre Anthologies* (Madison: U of Wisconsin P, 1997), 14.
19. Fanny Howe, rev. of *Midwinter Day*, by Bernadette Mayer, *American Book Review* 6 (1984): 16.
20. Rena Rosenwasser, "Chain/Kelsey St. Press," *Chain* 1 (spring/summer 1994): 92.
21. Quoted by Marcella Durand in "Publishing a Community: Women Publishers at the Poetry Project," paper presented at "Where Lyric Tradition Meets Language Poetry" Conference, 8–10 April 1999, Barnard College, New York.

22. Hannah Weiner, interview, conducted by Charles Bernstein, LINEbreak program, 1995. See <http://wings.buffalo.edu/epc/linebreak/programs/weiner>.

23. Harryette Mullen, interview, conducted by Cynthia Hogue, *Postmodern Culture* 9.2 (1999): n. pag.

24. Gloria Anzaldúa, *Borderlands/La Frontera: The New Mestiza* (San Francisco: Aunt Lute, 1987).

25. Charles Altieri, "What is Living and What is Dead in American Postmodernism: Establishing the Contemporaneity of Some American Poetry," *Critical Inquiry* 22 (summer 1996): 767.

26. Tina Darragh, "Intraview," with Joan Retallack et al., unpublished (1987), 12.

27. Naomi Schor, "Depression in the Nineties," *Bad Objects: Essays Popular and Unpopular* (Durham, NC: Duke UP, 1995), 163.

28. Tom Clark, "Stalin as Linguist," *Poetry Flash* (July 1985); rpt. in *Partisan Review* 54.2 (1987): 299–304.

29. Charles Bernstein, "The Conspiracy of 'Us,'" was originally part of a dialogue with Michael Lally in L=A=N=G=U=A=G=E 8 (1979); rpt. in *Content's Dream: Essays 1975–1984* (Los Angeles: Sun & Moon, 1986); 343–47.

30. See Ron Silliman et al., "Aesthetic Tendency and the Politics of Poetry: A Manifesto," *Social Text* 19–20 (fall 1988): 261–75.

31. Ann Lauterbach, "Misquotations from Reality," *Diacritics* 26.3–4 (fall–winter 1996): 152.

32. David Bottoms and Dave Smith, eds., *The Morrow Anthology of Younger American Poets* (New York: Quill, 1985), 19.

33. Rae Armantrout, "Mainstream Marginality," *Poetics Journal* 6 (1986): 143.

34. The anthology in question was *19 New American Poets of the Golden Gate*, ed. Philip Dow (San Diego: Harcourt Brace Jovanovich, 1984).

35. Michael Davidson, "Language Poetry," *The New Princeton Encyclopedia of Poetry and Poetics*, ed. Alex Preminger et al. (Princeton, NJ: Princeton UP, 1993).

36. Douglas Messerli, ed. *"Language" Poetries* (New York: New Directions, 1987); Ron Silliman, ed., *In the American Tree: Language, Realism, Poetry* (Orono, ME: National Poetry Foundation, 1986).

37. Jerome Rothenberg and Pierre Joris, eds. *Poems for the Millennium: The University of California Book of Modern and Postmodern Poetry*, vol. 2 (Berkeley: U of California P, 1998).

38. Whitehead, *Feminist Poetry Movement*.

39. Rachel Blau DuPlessis and Ann Snitow, eds., *The Feminist Memoir Project: Voices from Women's Liberation* (New York: Three Rivers, 1998).

40. Cynthia G. Franklin, *Writing Women's Communities: The Politics and Poetics of Contemporary Multi-Genre Anthologies* (Madison: U of Wisconsin P, 1997).

41. In a review of Maggie O'Sullivan's 1996 anthology, *Out of Everywhere: Linguistically Innovative Poetry by Women in North America and the UK* and Bob Perelman's *The Marginalization of Poetry*, Marjorie Perloff wonders, "Are women language poets coming into their own just when their male counterparts are flagging? Has second-stage language poetry abandoned some of the principles of its New York and San Francisco founding fathers?" As she points out, such questions are not easy to answer. See "The Coming of Age of Language Poetry," *Contemporary Literature* 38.3 (fall 1997): 559. In response, I would suggest that what is changing most radically is not the production but the *reception* of innovative writing. While the work of women Language writers increasingly attracts attention, there is a risk

that critical trends of the past will simply be reversed and challenging new volumes by male contemporaries elided.

42. Lyn Hejinian, *The Language of Inquiry* (Berkeley: U of California P, forthcoming); Joan Retallack, *The Poethical Wager* (Berkeley: U of California P, forthcoming).

43. Kathleen Fraser, *Translating the Unspeakable: Poetry and Innovative Necessity* (Tuscaloosa: U of Alabama P, 1999).

44. Maggie O'Sullivan, ed., *Out of Everywhere: Linguistically Innovative Poetry by Women in North America and the UK* (London: Reality Street Editions, 1996); Mary Margaret Sloan, ed., *Moving Borders: Three Decades of Innovative Writing by Women* (Jersey City, NJ: Talisman, 1998).

45. Mary Margaret Sloan, "Unfolding Boundaries: A Talk with Mary Margaret Sloan," conducted by Robin Tremblay-McGaw, *Poetry Flash* 278 (September–October 1998): 12.

46. Susan Stanford Friedman, "Making History: Reflections on Feminism, Narrative, and Desire," *Feminism beside Itself*, ed. Diane Elam and Robyn Wiegman (New York: Routledge, 1995) 12.

47. Marjorie Perloff, *Poetic License: Essays on Modernist and Postmodernist Lyric* (Evanston, IL: Northwestern UP, 1990), 2–3.

48. Judith Butler, "Sexual Ideology and Phenomenological Description: A Feminist Critique of Merleau-Ponty's Phenomenology of Perception," *The Thinking Muse: Feminism and Modern French Philosophy*, ed. Jeffner Allen and Iris Marion Young (Bloomington: Indiana UP, 1989), 86.

49. Johanna Drucker, "Response," in "Women/Writing/Theory" forum, *Raddle Moon* 6.2 (1994): 50–51.

50. Rachel Blau DuPlessis, *The Pink Guitar: Writing as Feminist Practice* (New York: Routledge, 1990), 5.

51. Charles Bernstein mentions some of these aspects in his preface to *The Politics of Poetic Form: Poetry and Public Policy* (New York: Roof, 1990), vii.

52. Kathy E. Ferguson, "Interpretation and Genealogy in Feminism," *Signs* 16.2 (1991): 324.

53. See Teresa de Lauretis for a more detailed discussion of contemporary feminism's double-edged practice of critique in "Eccentric Subjects: Feminist Theory and Historical Consciousness," *Feminist Studies* 16.1 (1990), esp. 137.

54. Andreas Huyssen, "Mapping the Postmodern," *Feminism/Postmodernism*, ed. Linda J. Nicholson (New York: Routledge, 1990), 271.

55. Ellen Rooney, "Discipline and Vanish: Feminism, the Resistance to Theory, and the Politics of Cultural Studies," *Differences* 2.3 (1990): 16.

56. Toril Moi, *Simone De Beauvoir: The Making of an Intellectual Woman* (Oxford: Blackwell, 1994), 5.

57. Moi, *Simone De Beauvoir*, 7.

58. I am grateful to Bett Miller for drawing attention to the term *neographer*, a neologism created during a two-day seminar in 1993 organized by Professor Stephanie H. Jed at the University of California at San Diego with the Italian paleographers Armando Petrucci and Fraca Nardelli. *Neographer* refers to a "paleographer" of "new" manuscripts and typescripts, such as those housed in the Mandeville Department of Special Collections, the Poetry Archive at San Francisco State University, and the Poetry/Rare Books Collection at State University of New York at Buffalo.

59. Quoted by Dodie Bellamy in "The Eternal Repository: Dodie Bellamy Interviews Lyn Hejinian," *Chain* 2 (spring 1995): 19.

60. Bellamy, "Eternal Repository," 19.

61. Allan Sekula, "Reading an Archive," *Blasted Allegories: An Anthology of Writings by Contemporary Artists*, ed. Brian Wallis (New York: The New Museum of Contemporary Art and MIT Press, 1987), 115.

62. Sekula, "Reading an Archive," 116.

63. Maryanne Dever, "Reading Other People's Mail," *Archives and Manuscripts: The Journal of the Australian Society of Archivists* 24.1 (May 1996): 118.

64. Significantly, Dodie Bellamy notes that many writers who have given their papers to an archive have subsequently regretted doing so. Lyn Hejinian also notes that some of her correspondents were unhappy with her decision to sell her papers to the Archive of New Poetry. For Bellamy and Hejinian's discussion of this topic, see Bellamy's "Eternal Repository," 19–25.

65. See Janet Malcolm, *The Silent Woman: Sylvia Plath and Ted Hughes* (New York: Alfred A. Knopf, 1994). For discussion of further issues and case histories, see *The Seductions of Biography*, ed. Mary Rhiel and David Suchoff (New York: Routledge, 1996), particularly the section titled "Whose Life Is It Anyway?"

66. Marta L. Werner, *Emily Dickinson's Open Folios: Scenes of Reading, Surfaces of Writing* (Ann Arbor: U of Michigan P, 1995), 2.

67. Michel Foucault, "Nietzsche, Genealogy, History," *The Foucault Reader*, ed. Paul Rabinow (New York: Pantheon, 1984), 76.

1. Cities and Communities (pp. 21–36)

1. Elizabeth Grosz, "Bodies-Cities," *Sexuality and Space*, ed. Beatriz Colomina et al. (New York: Princeton Architectural Press, 1992), 250.

2. Joan Retallack, "Local Ex-Centrisms: The Dupont Circle Circle," *Washington and Washington Writing*, ed. David McAleavey (Washington, DC: George Washington University, 1986), 87.

3. Michael Lally, ed., *None of the Above: New Poets of the USA* (Trumansburg, NY: Crossing, 1976).

4. Retallack, "Local Ex-Centrisms," 91.

5. P. Inman, letter to author, 22 May 1999.

6. Lee Lally, "You Were Burying Us Before We Were Dead," *These Days* (Washington, DC: Some of Us, 1971–72).

7. Retallack, "Local Ex-Centrisms," 88.

8. Retallack, "Local Ex-Centrisms," 91.

9. Phyllis Rosenzweig, "Intraview," by Tina Darragh et al., manuscript.

10. Diane Ward, "Home Plate," *Dog City* 1 (1977): n. pag.

11. Phyllis Rosenzweig, "Untitled," *Dog City* 2 (1980): n. pag.

12. Lynne Dreyer, e-mail to the author, 13 June 1999.

13. Nick Piombino, "The Aural Ellipsis and the Nature of Listening in Contemporary Poetry," *Close Listening: Poetry and the Performed Word*, ed. Charles Bernstein (New York: Oxford UP, 1998), 66.

14. P. Inman, letter to author, 22 May 1999.

15. Lynne Dreyer, e-mail to the author, 13 June 1999.

16. Barbara Baracks, letter to Ron Silliman, 10 May 1974, Silliman Papers, Mandeville (75, 2, 12).

17. Charles Bernstein, letter to Ron Silliman, n.d., Silliman Papers, Mandeville (75, 3, 11).

18. Lynne Dreyer, e-mail to the author, 13 June 1999.

19. Charles Bernstein, letter to Ron Silliman, 12 June 1979, Silliman Papers, Mandeville (75, 3, 11).

20. Diane Ward, e-mail to the author, 4 June 1999.

21. Bruce Andrews et al., *Legend* (New York: L=A=N=G=U=A=G=E / Segue, 1980).

22. "*L=A=N=G=U=A=G=E* Distributing Service," n.d., Silliman Papers, Mandeville (75, 3, 11).

23. Charles Bernstein, "Provisional Institutions: Alternative Presses and Poetic Innovation," *Arizona Quarterly* 51.1 (spring 1995): 142.

24. Bruce Andrews and Charles Bernstein, "*L=A=N=G=U=A=G=E* Flyer," Silliman Papers, Mandeville (75, 3, 11).

25. Andrews and Bernstein, "*L=A=N=G=U=A=G=E* Flyer."

26. Charles Bernstein, letter to Ron Silliman, 14 February 1977, Silliman Papers, Mandeville (75, 3, 10).

27. Charles Bernstein, letter to Ron Silliman, 14 February 1977, Silliman Papers, Mandeville (75, 3, 10).

28. Bee went on to coedit *M/E/A/N/I/N/G* with Mira Schor in the mid-eighties. In many ways, their journal maps fruitful intersections between contemporary art and Language writing. *M/E/A/N/I/N/G* would feature Bernstein, Johanna Drucker, Alan Davies, and Hannah Weiner. Bee notes that gender was crucial to its editorial practice. See her statement in *Chain* 1 (spring/summer 1994): 7.

29. Charles Bernstein, "Counting and Uncounting," *Poetry Project Newsletter* (July 1978); "Hejinian's Notes," *Reality Studios* 3.2 (1980); "Making Words Visible," *L=A=N=G=U=A=G=E* 5 (1978). These are reprinted in *Content's Dream: Essays 1975–1984* (Los Angeles: Sun & Moon, 1986).

30. Charles Bernstein, letter to Ron Silliman, 12 June 1979, Silliman Papers, Mandeville (75, 3, 11).

31. Lyn Hejinian, letter to Susan Howe, dated 5 November, Howe Papers, Mandeville (201, 1, 8).

32. Lyn Hejinian, letter to Susan Howe, n.d., Howe Papers, Mandeville (201, 1, 8).

33. Susan Howe, letter to Douglas Messerli, 15 September, 1980, Sun & Moon Papers, Mandeville (224, 45, 1).

34. Robert Grenier, rev. of *Writing is an Aid to Memory*, *L=A=N=G=U=A=G=E* 2.2 (June 1979): n. pag.

35. Lyn Hejinian, letter to Susan Howe, 13 August 1980, Howe Papers, Mandeville (201, 1, 8).

36. Bernstein, "The Conspiracy of 'Us,'" in *Content's Dream: Essays, 1975–1984* (Los Angeles: Sun & Moon, 1986), 343.

37. Sandra Kumamoto Stanley, *Louis Zukofsky and the Transformation of a Modern American Poetics* (Berkeley: U of California P, 1994), 149.

38. Kit Robinson, letter to Lyn Hejinian, 21 December 1978, Hejinian Papers, Mandeville (74, 6, 24).

39. Charles Bernstein, letter to Ron Silliman, 31 December 1979, Silliman Papers, Mandeville (75, 3, 10).

40. Bernstein, "Conspiracy of 'Us,'" 344.

41. Charles Bernstein, letter to Bruce Andrews and Ron Silliman, 4 March 1977, Silliman Papers, Mandeville (75, 3, 11).

42. Barrett Watten, "The Bride of the Assembly Line: From Material Text to Cultural Poetics," *The Impercipient Lecture Series* 1.8 (October 1997): 17.

43. Carla Harryman, "Belief," manuscript, n. pag.

44. Bruce Boone, "Writing, Power and Activity," *L=A=N=G=U=A=G=E* 9–10 (October 1979): n. pag.

45. Robert Glück, "Baucis and Philemon," *Poetics Journal* 5 (May 1985): 111.

46. Ibid., 113.

47. Harryman relates this in "Belief," n. pag.

48. Harryman, "Belief," n. pag.

49. Harryman, "Belief," n. pag.

50. Rae Armantrout, interview, conducted by Anne Brewster, *Southern Review* 31.2 (1998): 238.

51. Joan Retallack, e-mail to the author, 7 May 1999.

52. Phyllis Rosenzweig, "Intraview," with Tina Darragh et al., unpublished, 13.

53. Joan Retallack, "Intraview," with Tina Darragh et al., unpublished, b.

54. Tina Darragh, e-mail to the author, 11 May 1999.

55. Lynne Dreyer, e-mail to the author, 13 June 1999.

56. Phyllis Rosenzweig, "Intraview," with Tina Darragh et al., unpublished, d.

57. Douglas Messerli, letter to Charles Bernstein, 11 April 1987, Sun & Moon Papers, Mandeville (224, 18, 5).

58. Charles Bernstein, "Poetry and (Male?) Sex," *Sulfur* 24 (1989): 192.

59. Bernstein, "Poetry and (Male?) Sex," 190.

60. Bruce Andrews, "Be Careful Now You Know Sugar Melts in Water (On Sexuality)," *Paradise and Method: Poetics and Praxis* (Evanston, IL: Northwestern UP, 1996), 125–33.

61. Joan Retallack, e-mail to the author, 7 May 1999.

2. *Poetic Fields and the "Painted Birds" of Language Writing (37–48)*

1. The feminist method of collective consciousness raising is discussed in Catherine Mackinnon's "Feminism, Marxism, Method and the State: An Agenda for Theory," *Signs* 7.3 (1982): 515–44.

2. Florence Howe and Ellen Bass, eds., *No More Masks!: An Anthology of Poetry by Women* (Garden City, NY: Anchor, 1973).

3. Erica Hunt, "Notes for an Oppositional Poetics," *The Politics of Poetic Form: Poetry and Public Policy*, ed. Charles Bernstein (New York: Roof, 1990), 204.

4. Rae Armantrout, '"Why Don't Women Do Language-Oriented Writing?"' *In the American Tree: Language, Realism, Poetry*, ed. Ron Silliman (Orono, ME: National Poetry Foundation, 1986), 544.

5. Kathleen Fraser, "Partial Local Coherence: Regions with Illustrations," *Ironwood* 20 (1982): 137. Caroline Bergvall echoes Fraser's concerns in her question: "Can female poets in fact afford to dispense with identity-seeking when positive female identification is still culturally and politically so vulnerable?" Caroline Bergvall, "No Margins to This Page: Female Experimental Poets and the Legacy of Modernism," *Fragmente* 5 (1993): 33. In their common use of the term *afford*, both Fraser and Bergvall frame feminist practice within a restrictive rather than an open economy.

6. Adrienne Rich, *What Is Found There: Notebooks on Poetry and Politics* (New York: W. W. Norton, 1993), 167–68.

7. Responding to Hejinian's concerns about appearing in a women's issue of a magazine, Susan Howe writes:

They are self-defeating in that they isolate you into a preciousness of category. ... My case is typical in a "point of view" issue. ... The poem was dealing with my own childhood memories of ... fears and how they live on in us especially at night. Out of the series [the editor] plucked three that might be concerned with "women's problems," thus giving them meaning they were never meant to have.

See Susan Howe, letter to Lyn Hejinian, n.d., Hejinian Papers, Mandeville (74, 4, 18). However, as Rosmarie Waldrop points out, such publications were sometimes the only means through which to open up access to the writing. See Rosmarie Waldrop, postcard to Hejinian, 20 May 1979, Mandeville (74, 7, 16).

8. These two poles merged as gynocentric poetry became increasingly popular. By 1974 the National Book Award was accepted by Adrienne Rich (other women nominees included Audre Lorde and Alice Walker) "in the name of all the women whose voices have gone and still go unheard in a patriarchal world" and in light of "the struggle for self-determination of all women, of every color, identification or derived class." Quoted by Rachel Blau DuPlessis in "Contemporary Women's Poetry," *The Oxford Companion to Women's Writing in the United States*, ed. Cathy N. Davidson et al. (New York: Oxford UP, 1995), 674.

9. Rae Armantrout, "Feminist Poetics and the Meaning of Clarity," *Sagetrieb* 11.3 (winter 1992): 9.

10. See Gayatri Chakravorty Spivak, *In Other Worlds: Essays in Cultural Politics* (New York: Methuen, 1987), particularly "A Literary Representation of the Subaltern: A Woman's Text from the Third World," at 241–68.

11. Nicole Brossard explores this point in "Poetic Politics," *The Politics of Poetic Form: Poetry and Public Policy*, ed. Charles Bernstein (New York: Roof, 1990), 75–78.

12. See Leslie Scalapino and Ron Silliman's subsequent discussion of Silliman's article in "What/Person: From an Exchange," *Poetics Journal* 9 (June 1991): 51–68.

13. Leslie Scalapino, interview, conducted by Elisabeth A. Frost, *Contemporary Literature* 37.1 (1996): 12.

14. Cora Kaplan, *Sea Changes: Essays on Culture and Feminism* (London: Verso, 1986), 71.

15. Susan Howe, "Encloser," *The Politics of Poetic Form: Poetry and Public Policy*, ed. Charles Bernstein (New York: Roof, 1990), 193.

16. Susan Howe, interview, conducted by Edward Foster, *Postmodern Poetry: The Talisman Interviews* ed. Edward Foster (Hoboken, NJ: Talisman House, 1994), 58.

17. Marianne DeKoven, "Male Signature, Female Aesthetic: The Gender Politics of Experimental Writing," *Breaking the Sequence: Women's Experimental Fiction*, ed. Ellen G. Friedman and Miriam Fuchs (Princeton, NJ: Princeton UP, 1989), 73.

18. Marianne DeKoven, "Gertrude's Granddaughters," *The Women's Review of Books* 4.2 (November 1986): 12.

19. Mary Daly, *Gyn/Ecology: The Metaethics of Radical Feminism* (London: Women's Press, 1979), 333–36.

20. DeKoven, "Male Signature, Female Aesthetic," 76.

21. Meaghan Morris, *The Pirate's Fiancée: Feminism, Reading, Postmodernism* (London: Verso, 1988), 43–45, 50.

22. Linda Kinnahan, *Poetics of the Feminine: Authority and Literary Tradition in William Carlos Williams, Mina Loy, Denise Levertov, and Kathleen Fraser* (Cambridge: Cambridge UP, 1994), 184.

23. Linda Kinnahan, "'Look for the Doing Words': Carol Ann Duffy and Questions of Convention," *Contemporary British Poetry: Essays on Theory and Criticism*, ed. James Acheson and Romana Huk (Albany: SUNY, 1996), 247.

24. Anne Waldman, "Sexifesto," *Writing for Bernadette*, ed. William Corbett and Michael Gizzi (Great Barrington, The Figures, 1995), n. pag.

25. Ellen G. Friedman and Miriam Fuchs, "Contexts and Continuities: An Introduction to Women's Experimental Fiction in English," *Breaking the Sequence: Women's Experimental Fiction*, ed. Ellen G. Friedman and Miriam Fuchs (Princeton, NJ: Princeton UP, 1989), 3–51.

26. Furthermore, such maps reinforce a cultural identity along nationalist lines, maintaining the closure of a specifically American innovative tradition.

27. Christine Brooke-Rose, "Illiterations," *Breaking the Sequence: Women's Experimental Fiction*, ed. Ellen G. Friedman and Miriam Fuchs (Princeton, NJ: Princeton UP, 1989), 67.

28. See the discussion following Rosmarie Waldrop's "Alarms and Excursions," *The Politics of Poetic Form: Poetry and Public Policy*, ed. Charles Bernstein (New York: Roof, 1990), 66.

29. See Brooke-Rose, "Illiterations," 67.

30. See Rae Armantrout, letter to Lyn Hejinian, 8 September 1990, Hejinian Papers, Mandeville (74, 11, 1).

31. See Rae Armantrout, letter to Lyn Hejinian, 3 July 1992, Hejinian Papers, Mandeville (74, 11, 1).

32. Joan Retallack, ":Re:Thinking:Literary:Feminism: (three essays onto shaky grounds)," *Feminist Measures: Soundings in Poetry and Theory*, ed. Lynn Keller and Christanne Miller (Ann Arbor: U of Michigan P, 1994), 344–77.

33. Harryette Mullen, "Poetry and Identity," *West Coast Line* 30.1 (spring 1996): 95–99. For further discussion of race and formally innovative writing, see Nathaniel Mackey, *Discrepant Engagement: Dissonance, Cross-Culturality and Experimental Writing* (Cambridge: Cambridge UP, 1993).

34. Maggie O'Sullivan, "To the Reader," *Out of Everywhere: Linguistically Innovative Poetry by Women in North America and the UK*, ed. Maggie O'Sullivan (London: Reality Street Editions, 1996), 9.

35. Nina Baym, ed., *The Norton Anthology of American Literature*, vol. 2, "1865 to the Present," 5th ed. (New York: W. W. Norton, 1998).

36. Apart from DuPlessis and Fraser, Ann Lauterbach also characterizes herself as "a sort of second cousin / by marriage . . . a cross between disinterested onlooker and advocate or fan." See "Lines Written to Bob Perelman in the Margins of *The Marginalization of Poetry*," *The Impercipient Lecture Series* 1.4 (May 1997): 14.

37. Rachel Blau DuPlessis, "On the Davidson/Weinberger Exchange," *Sulfur* 22 (1988): 189.

38. Rachel Blau DuPlessis, "On the Davidson/Weinberger Exchange," 190.

39. Rae Armantrout, letter to Lyn Hejinian, n.d., Hejinian Papers, Mandeville (74, 2, 1).

40. Rachel Blau DuPlessis and Members of Workshop 9, "For the Etruscans: Sexual Difference and Artistic Production: The Debate over a Female Aesthetic," *The Future of Difference*, ed. Hester Eisenstein and Alice Jardine (Boston: G. K. Hall, 1980), 132.

41. Rachel Blau DuPlessis, "Otherhow," *The Pink Guitar: Writing as Feminist Practice* (New York: Routledge, 1990), 153.

42. Quoted by Carla Harryman in "Open Letter to Kathleen Fraser," Hejinian

Papers, Mandeville (74, 4, 11). The form that it eventually appeared in reads: "Silliman is here interpreting Lyn Hejinian's work to an audience that he has very systematically worked to help create for writers now identified with this movement. Hejinian had been writing beautifully and publishing in 'modernist' magazines for years before she was claimed as a Language writer." Fraser, "Partial Local Coherence," 132.

43. Kathleen Fraser, "Partial Local Coherence," 137.

44. Carla Harryman, "Open Letter to Kathleen Fraser," Hejinian Papers, Mandeville (74, 4, 11).

45. Harryman, "Open Letter to Kathleen Fraser."

46. Harryman, "Open Letter to Kathleen Fraser."

47. Kathleen Fraser, letter to Carla Harryman, 12 August 1982, Hejinian Papers, Mandeville (74, 3, 25).

48. Fraser, letter to Carla Harryman, 12 August 1982.

49. Fraser put together a detailed list of bookstores, cafés, and conferences that could feature Tuumba books. She also wrote to thank Hejinian for having distributed *Magritte Series* so well. Recalling a friend's son who had said that the book was "nicely displayed" at a Harvard bookstore and that "everyone" was buying or being really excited about it, Fraser states: "I'm so pleased [with the direct feedback]. It seemed real, for the first time since I've been writing." See Kathleen Fraser, letter to Lyn Hejinian, 23 January 1977, Hejinian Papers, Mandeville (74, 3, 25).

50. Kathleen Fraser, letter to Carla Harryman, 12 August 1982, Hejinian Papers, Mandeville (74, 3, 25).

51. Fraser, letter to Carla Harryman, 12 August 1982.

52. Fraser, letter to Carla Harryman, 12 August 1982.

3. In the Middle of Writing (pp. 50–62)

1. Walter Kalaidjian, *American Culture between the Wars: Revisionary Modernism and Postmodern Critique* (New York: Columbia UP, 1993), 194.

2. An excellent example of such mapping is Joan Retallack's ":Re:Thinking:Literary:Feminism: (three essays onto shaky grounds)," *Feminist Measures: Soundings in Poetry and Theory*, ed. Lynn Keller and Christanne Miller (Ann Arbor: U of Michigan P, 1994), 344–77.

3. Kate Millett, *Sexual Politics* (New York: Doubleday, 1970); Hester Eisenstein and Alice Jardine, eds., *The Future of Difference* (Boston: G. K. Hall, 1980); Elaine Marks and Isabelle de Courtivron, eds., *New French Feminisms: An Anthology* (Amherst: U of Massachusetts P, 1980).

4. Frances Jaffer, "Procedures for Having Lunch," unpublished manuscript; quoted in Rachel Blau DuPlessis and Members of Workshop 9, "For the Etruscans," *The Future of Difference*, ed. Hester Eisenstein and Alice Jardine (Boston: G. K. Hall, 1980), 128.

5. Frances Jaffer, "Working Notes," *Mirage* 3 (1989): 90.

6. Joan Retallack, interview, conducted by P. Inman, *Washington Review* 13.2 (1987): 26.

7. Kathleen Fraser, "this.notes.new.year," *il cuore: Selected Poems 1970–1995* (Hanover, NH: UP of New England for Wesleyan UP, 1997), 39–40.

8. Kathleen Fraser, "Partial Local Coherence: Regions with Illustrations," *Ironwood* 20 (1982): 139.

9. Kathleen Fraser, "How Did Emma Slide? Or the Gestate: A New Poem Form for Women," *Trellis* 3 (1979): 14.

10. Kathleen Fraser, interview, conducted by Cynthia Hogue, *Contemporary Literature* 39.1 (spring 1998): 14.

11. Bob Perelman, "Facing the Surface: Representations of Representation," *North Dakota Quarterly* 55.4 (fall 1987): 302.

12. Beverly Dahlen, *A Reading 1–7* (San Francisco: Momo's Press, 1985), 85.

13. Dahlen, *A Reading 1–7*, 76.

14. Dahlen, *A Reading 1–7*, 76–77.

15. Lyn Hejinian, letter to Rae Armantrout, 1 June 1982, Hejinian Papers, Mandeville (74, 2, 1).

16. Lyn Hejinian, letter to Susan Howe, dated 1 June, Hejinian Papers, Mandeville (74, 4, 18).

17. Lyn Hejinian, letter to Susan Howe, 4 February 1983, Howe Papers, Mandeville (201, 1, 8).

18. Michael Davidson, *The San Francisco Renaissance: Poetics and Community at Mid-Century* (Cambridge: Cambridge UP, 1989), 212.

19. Johanna Drucker, "Women/Writing/Theory: What Is at Stake?" *Raddle Moon* 11 (1992): 18.

20. Johanna Drucker, "Women and Language," *Poetics Journal* 4 (May 1984): 58.

21. Denise Riley, *"Am I That Name?": Feminism and the Category of "Women" in History* (Basingstoke, UK: Macmillan, 1988).

22. Judith Butler, "Gender Trouble: Feminist Theory and Psychoanalytic Discourse," *Feminism/Postmodernism*, ed. Linda Nicholson (New York: Routledge, 1990), 329.

23. Riley, *"Am I That Name?"* 3.

24. Riley, *"Am I That Name?"* 6.

25. Riley, *"Am I That Name?"* 7.

26. Judith Butler, *Gender Trouble: Feminism and the Subversion of Identity* (New York: Routledge, 1990), 148.

27. Lynne Dreyer, "Intraview," with Tina Darragh et al., unpublished (1987), 8.

28. Johanna Drucker, *Figuring the Word: Essays on Books, Writing, and Visual Poetics* (New York: Granary, 1998), 274.

29. Lyn Hejinian, letter to Susan Howe, 20 September 1985, Howe Papers, Mandeville (201, 1, 8).

30. Bruce Robbins, "Introduction: The Grounding of Intellectuals," *Intellectuals: Aesthetics, Politics, Academics*, ed. Bruce Robbins (Minneapolis: U of Minnesota P, 1990), xvii.

31. Robbins, "Introduction," xvii–xviii.

32. Robbins, "Introduction," xviii.

33. Lyn Hejinian, letter to Susan Howe, dated 16 June, Howe Papers, Mandeville (201, 1, 8).

34. Lyn Hejinian, letter to Ron Silliman, 14 October 1981, Hejinian Papers, Mandeville (74, 7, 6).

35. Joan Riviere, "Womanliness as a Masquerade," *Formations of Fantasy*, ed. Victor Burgin et al. (London and New York: Methuen, 1986), 38.

36. Lyn Hejinian, letter to Rae Armantrout, 22 April 1984, Hejinian Papers, Mandeville (74, 2, 1).

37. Fanny Howe, *For Erato: The Meaning of Life* (Berkeley, CA: Tuumba, 1984), n. pag.

38. Rae Armantrout, letter to Lyn Hejinian, n.d., Hejinian Papers, Mandeville (74, 2, 1).

39. Tina Darragh, interview conducted by Joan Retallack, *Aerial* 5 (1989): 77.

40. Tina Darragh, interview conducted by Joan Retallack, 77.

41. Diane Ward, "The Narration," *Poetics Journal* 5 (May 1985): 95.

42. Donna Haraway, "A Manifesto for Cyborgs: Science, Technology, and Socialist Feminism in the 1980s," *Coming to Terms: Feminism, Theory, Politics*, ed. Elizabeth Weed (New York: Routledge, 1989), 173. Rosmarie Waldrop points out that irony also appears in her work as a way through which a feminist consciousness may be articulated. See "Alarms and Excursions," *The Politics of Poetic Form: Poetry and Public Policy*, ed. Charles Bernstein (New York: Roof, 1990), 65.

43. Rae Armantrout, *Necromance* (Los Angeles: Sun & Moon, 1991), 7.

44. Bob Perelman further links the poppy and the siren through their narcotic propensities. See *The Marginalization of Poetry: Language Writing and Literary History* (Princeton, NJ: Princeton UP, 1996), 139.

45. Lyn Hejinian, *The Cell* (Los Angeles: Sun & Moon, 1992).

46. Armantrout, *Necromance*, 8.

47. Armantrout, *Necromance*, 8.

48. See Rae Armantrout's "Attention," *Necromance*, 39.

49. Donna Haraway, "A Manifesto for Cyborgs," 173.

50. Kathy E. Ferguson, "Interpretation and Genealogy in Feminism," *Signs* 16.2 (1991): 338.

51. Rae Armantrout, interview, conducted by Manuel Brito, *A Suite of Poetic Voices: Interviews with Contemporary American Poets*, ed. Manuel Brito (Santa Brigida, Canary Islands: Kadle, 1992), 21.

52. Lyn Hejinian, letter to Rae Armantrout, 7 December 1983, Hejinian Papers, Mandeville (74, 2, 1).

53. Carla Harryman, *The Middle* (San Francisco: Gaz, 1983), 9–10.

54. Carla Harryman, "Toy Boats," *There Never Was a Rose without a Thorn* (San Francisco: City Lights, 1995), 2.

55. Joan Retallack, interview, conducted by P. Inman. 26.

56. Joan Retallack, introduction, John Cage, *Musicage: Cage Muses on Words, Art, Music* ed. Joan Retallack (Hanover, NH: UP of New England for Wesleyan UP, 1996), xxxii.

57. Gillian Rose, *The Broken Middle: Out of Our Ancient Society* (Oxford: Blackwell, 1992), xii.

58. Rose, *Broken Middle*, 155.

4. *Supporting a Scene (pp. 63–76)*

1. Karen Burke LeFevre, *Invention as a Social Act* (Carbondale: Southern Illinois UP, 1987), 65.

2. Lyn Hejinian, "Lyn Hejinian/Andrew Schelling: An Exchange," *Jimmy & Lucy's House of K* 6 (1986): 8.

3. Lyn Hejinian, "Lyn Hejinian/Andrew Schelling," 3.

4. Alice Notley, e-mail to Marcella Durand, March 1999. Living in the Midwest, Tom Beckett saw *The Difficulties* as "a tool I use to get people to talk to me." See Tom Beckett, statement, "Patterns/Contexts/Time: A Symposium on Contemporary Poetry," ed. Phillip Foss and Charles Bernstein, *Tyuonyi* 6/7 (1990): 11.

Rosmarie Waldrop also states that running a magazine or press "can act as an anti-dote to isolation." See Rosmarie Waldrop, statement, *Chain* 1 (spring/summer 1994): 112.

5. Jerome McGann, *Black Riders: The Visible Language of Modernism* (Princeton, NJ: Princeton UP, 1993), 168.

6. Clark Coolidge, *The Maintains* (Oakland, CA: This, 1974).

7. Quoted in Geoffrey Soar and R. J. Ellis, "Little Magazines in the British Isles Today," *British Books News* (December 1983), 732.

8. Angel Hair Books was later renamed United Artists Books.

9. Susan Albertine, introduction, *A Living of Words: American Women in Print Culture*, ed. Susan Albertine (Knoxville: U of Tennessee P, 1995), xi.

10. Lyn Hejinian, letter to Susan Howe, n.d., Howe Papers, Mandeville (201, 1, 8).

11. Nigel Wheale, "Uttering Poetry: Small-Press Publication," *Poets on Writing: Britain, 1970–1991*, ed. Denise Riley (Basingstoke, UK: Macmillan, 1992), 9.

12. Charles Bernstein, "Provisional Institutions: Alternative Presses and Poetic Innovation," *Arizona Quarterly* 51.1 (spring 1995): 138.

13. Jennifer Moxley, letter to the author, 27 January 1997.

14. Lyn Hejinian, letter to Susan Howe, 1 June 1982, Howe Papers, Mandeville (201, 1, 8).

15. See Susan Howe's interview with members of the collective on WBAI "Poetry," ANP Tapes Listening Series L-1128, Mandeville. Mary Biggs notes that the cooperative or collective was a popular variation in the seventies of small-press publishing (*A Gift That Cannot Be Refused*, 54). Apart from distribution groups, there were many collective presses specializing in women's writing and oriented by feminist policies. The seventies also saw the emergence of specialist bookstores, many of which had greater success than those with a broad focus. Both Kathleen Fraser and Barbara Baracks advised Hejinian to market Tuumba in women's bookstores because they had a healthy record in poetry sales. See Kathleen Fraser, letter to Lyn Hejinian, 23 January 1977, Hejinian Papers, Mandeville (74, 3, 25); and Barbara Baracks, letter to Lyn Hejinian, 3 July 1977, Hejinian Papers, Mandeville (74, 2, 4).

16. Mary Biggs, *A Gift That Cannot Be Refused: The Writing and Publishing of Contemporary American Poetry* (Westport, CT: Greenwood, 1990), 101.

17. Lyn Hejinian, interview conducted by Vicki Hudspith, *Poetry Project Newsletter* (December 1979): n. pag.

18. Susan Coultrap-McQuin, *Doing Literary Business: American Women Writers in the Nineteenth Century* (Chapel Hill: U of North Carolina P, 1990).

19. Jed Rasula, rev. of Tuumba Press, *Jimmy & Lucy's House of K* 6 (May 1986):163–64.

20. Lyn Hejinian, letter to Susan Howe, dated 6 September, Howe Papers, Mandeville (201, 1, 8).

21. Lyn Hejinian, letter to Susan Howe, dated 6 September.

22. Lyn Hejinian, letter to Susan Howe, dated 29 August, Howe Papers, Mandeville (201, 1, 8).

23. Lyn Hejinian, letter to Susan Howe, n.d., Howe Papers, Mandeville (201, 1, 8).

24. Lyn Hejinian, letter to Susan Howe, 9 February 1977, Howe Papers, Mandeville (201, 1, 7).

25. Lyn Hejinian, flyer for Tuumba Press, received 19 July 1976, Tuumba Papers, Lockwood.

26. Lyn Hejinian, letter to Susan Howe, 21 August 1976, Howe Papers, Mandeville (201, 1, 7).

27. In a response to Hejinian's flyer, Beverly Ruth Vander Kooy of the Poetry/ Rare Books Collection states the library's policy is to only collect poetry and prose by poets. See Beverly Ruth Vander Kooy, letter to Lyn Hejinian, 18 August 1976, Tuumba Papers, Lockwood. Given the difficulty of the generic classification, the collection ordered individual issues in a piecemeal fashion but did not include Tuumba works like Dick Higgins's *Cat Alley: A Long Short Novel* or Barbara Baracks's *No Sleep.*

28. Susan Howe, rev. of *Extremities*, by Rae Armantrout, *The L=A=N=G=U=A=G=E Book*, ed. Bruce Andrews and Charles Bernstein. (Carbondale: Southern Illinois UP, 1984), 211.

29. Susan Howe, *Secret History of the Dividing Line* (New York: Telephone, 1978); rpt. in *Frame Structures: Early Poems, 1974–1979* (New York: New Directions, 1996), 96.

30. Susan Howe, letter to Lyn Hejinian, 23 December 1977, Hejinian Papers, Mandeville (201, 1, 7).

31. Kathleen Fraser, letter to Lyn Hejinian, 23 January 1977, Hejinian Papers, Mandeville (74, 3, 25).

32. Fanny Howe, *For Erato: The Meaning of Life* (Berkeley, CA: Tuumba, 1984), n. pag.

33. Michael Palmer, interview, conducted by Lee Bartlett, *Talking Poetry: Conversations in the Workshop with Contemporary Poets*, ed. Lee Bartlett. (Alberquerque: U of New Mexico P, 1987), 137.

34. Another example is the cover of Rae Armantrout's *Invention of Hunger* (Berkeley, CA: Tuumba, 1979). In keeping with Armantrout's suggestions, the cover simply featured the title in red ink on a beige cover. See Rae Armantrout, letter to Lyn Hejinian, n.d., Hejinian Papers, Mandeville (74, 2, 1).

35. Lyn Hejinian, letter to Susan Howe, dated "Saturday after Thanksgiving, 1977," Howe Papers, Mandeville (201, 1, 7).

36. Claire Hoertz Badaracco, *Trading Words: Poetry, Typography and Illustrated Books in the Modern Literary Economy* (Baltimore: Johns Hopkins UP, 1995), 197.

37. Johanna Drucker, "Experimental, Visual, and Concrete Poetry: A Note of Historical Context and Basic Concepts," *Avant-Garde Critical Studies* 10 (1996): 55.

38. Johanna Drucker, "'Through the Light and the Alphabet': An Interview with Johanna Drucker," conducted by Matthew G. Kirschenbaum, *Postmodern Culture* 5 (1997): 31.

39. Tim Woods, letter to Lyn Hejinian, 18 June 1994, Hejinian Papers, Mandeville (74, 37, 21).

40. Rasula, rev. of Tuumba Press, 161.

41. Barbara Baracks, letter to Lyn Hejinian, 23 April 1976, Hejinian Papers, Mandeville (74, 2, 4).

42. Baracks, letter to Lyn Hejinian, 23 April 1976, Hejinian Papers, Mandeville (74, 2, 4).

43. Barbara Baracks, letter to Lyn Hejinian, 3 July 1977, Hejinian Papers, Mandeville (74, 2, 4).

44. Barbara Baracks, letter to Lyn Hejinian, 22 September [1976], Hejinian Papers, Mandeville (74, 2, 4).

45. Lyn Hejinian, letter to Susan Howe, 9 February 1977, Howe Papers, Mandeville (201, 1, 7).

46. For a discussion of this tradition, see Jerome McGann, *Black Riders: The Visible Language of Modernism* (Princeton, NJ: Princeton UP, 1993).

47. Hejinian bought the press a week after she moved from Willits to Berkeley.
48. Holly A. Laird, "Editing Feminist Journals: Report on the October 1993 Conference, 'Publishing Feminist Scholarship,'" *Chain* 1 (spring/summer 1994): 73.
49. Fanny Howe, letter to Lyn Hejinian, n.d., Hejinian Papers, Mandeville (74, 4, 17).
50. Lyn Hejinian, letter to Fanny Howe, 12 April 1984, Hejinian Papers, Mandeville (74, 4, 17).
51. Rasula, rev. of Tuumba Press, 161.
52. Rasula, rev. of Tuumba Press, 163.
53. Rasula, rev. of Tuumba Press, 163.
54. Lyn Hejinian, letter to Rae Armantrout, 22 April 1984, Hejinian Papers, Mandeville (74, 2, 1).
55. Charles Bernstein, in "Poetry, Community, Movement: A Conversation," conducted between Charles Bernstein, Ann Lauterbach, Jonathan Monroe, and Bob Perelman, *Diacritics* 26.3–4 (fall-winter 1996): 209
56. Rasula, rev. of Tuumba Press, 164.
57. Lyn Hejinian, letter to Erica Hunt, 13 February 1983, Hejinian Papers, Mandeville (74, 5, 1).
58. Lyn Hejinian, letter to Rae Armantrout, 13 December 1982. Hejinian Papers, Mandeville (74, 2, 1).
59. Lyn Hejinian, letter to Rae Armantrout, 25 April 1980, Hejinian Papers, Mandeville (74, 2, 1). Rosmarie Waldrop also notes that the slowness of letterpress printing made her "extremely aware of any unnecessary 'fat,'" with the result that her own poems had become "leaner." See Rosmarie Waldrop, statement, *Chain* 1 (spring/summer 1994): 112.
60. Douglas Messerli, letter to Joyce Jenkins, 31 January 1989, Sun & Moon Papers, Mandeville (224, 65, 15).
61. Bernstein, "Provisional Institutions," 141.
62. Lee Ann Brown, "From CUZ to zuk," *Chain* 1 (spring/summer 1994): 17.
63. Tender Buttons is also informed by Brown's feminist orientation. Brown's policy of publishing only women writers seeks to redress what she sees as a continuing underrepresentation of women in innovative writing. In this respect, the logo of the press is emblematic of her poetics. Picturing double pansies in a dress-coat, it performatively blurs the division between nature and artifice that traditionally inscribes the cultural modes of femininity as well as its singularity.

5. *Making Waves (pp. 77–87)*

1. Harriet Monroe, "The Radio and the Poets," *Poetry* (April 1930): 35.
2. Adalaide Morris, ed., *Sound States: Acoustical Technologies and Modern and Postmodern Writing* (Chapel Hill: U of North Carolina P, 1997); Charles Bernstein, ed., *Close Listening: Poetry and the Performed Word* (New York: Oxford UP, 1998).
3. Rudolf Arnheim, *Radio*, trans. Margaret Ludwig and Herbert Read (1936; rpt. New York: Arno and the *New York Times*, 1971), 18.
4. Joseph Harrington, "Why American Poetry Is Not American Literature," *American Literary History* 8.3 (fall 1996): 504–5.
5. The relation between mass markets and gender in modernity has been explored in Janice Radway's "The Scandal of the Middlebrow: The Book-of-the-Month Club, Class Fracture, and Cultural Authority," *South Atlantic Quarterly* 89.4

(fall 1990): 703–36. For a discussion of the modernist gendering of poetic taste, see Suzanne Clark's *Sentimental Modernism: Women Writers and the Revolution of the Word* (Bloomington: Indiana UP, 1991).

6. For a discussion of the involvement of Bloomsbury writers with radio, see Kate Whitehead, "Broadcasting Bloomsbury," *Yearbook of English Studies* 20 (1990): 121–31.

7. Anne Waldman, introduction, *Out of this World: An Anthology of the St. Mark's Poetry Project, 1966–1991*, ed. Anne Waldman (New York: Crown, 1991), 3.

8. Susan Stewart, "Letter on Sound," *Close Listening: Poetry and the Performed Word*, ed. Charles Bernstein (New York: Oxford UP, 1998), 45.

9. Roman Jakobson, *On Language*, ed. Linda R. Waugh and Monique Monville-Burston (Cambridge, MA: Harvard UP, 1995), 172.

10. Susan Howe, letter to Lyn Hejinian, n.d., Hejinian Papers, Mandeville (74, 4, 18).

11. Susan Howe, letter to Lyn Hejinian, 19 August 1977, Hejinian Papers, Mandeville (74, 4, 18).

12. In April 1980, Hejinian wrote to Howe that Erica Hunt was now running the KPFA radio show that she and Robinson started. See Lyn Hejinian, letter to Susan Howe, 12 April 1980, Howe Papers, Mandeville (201, 1, 8).

13. Susan Howe, letter to Lyn Hejinian, 26 December 1978, Hejinian Papers, Mandeville (74, 4, 18).

14. Virginia Woolf, letter to Vita Sackville-West, 15 July 1927, *Letters of Virginia Woolf*, ed. Nigel Nicholson (London: Chatto & Windus, 1977), 3:397.

15. Susan Howe, letter to Lyn Hejinian, n.d., Hejinian Papers, Mandeville (74, 4, 18).

16. Susan Howe, letter to Lyn Hejinian, 19 August 1977, Hejinian Papers, Mandeville (74, 4, 18).

17. Susan M. Schultz, "Exaggerated History," rev. of *The Nonconformist's Memorial* and *The Birth-Mark: Unsettling the Wilderness in American Literary History*, by Susan Howe, *Postmodern Culture*, 4.2 (January 1994): n. pag.

18. Susan Howe, letter to Lyn Hejinian, 19 August 1977, Hejinian Papers, Mandeville (74, 4, 18).

19. Susan Howe, letter to Lyn Hejinian, 6 November 1977, Hejinian Papers, Mandeville (74, 4, 18).

20. Susan Howe, letter to Lyn Hejinian, 23 December 1977, Hejinian Papers, Mandeville (74, 4, 18).

21. Erving Goffman, *Forms of Talk* (Philadelphia: U of Pennsylvania P, 1981), 230.

22. Susan Howe, letter to Bernadette Mayer, 8 April 1979, Mayer Papers, Mandeville (420, 9, 22).

23. Susan Howe, letter to Lyn Hejinian, 6 November 1977, Hejinian Papers, Mandeville (74, 4, 18).

24. Susan Howe, letter to Lyn Hejinian, 26 December 1978, Hejinian Papers, Mandeville (74, 4, 18).

25. Susan Howe, letter to Bernadette Mayer, 24 June 1980, Mayer Papers, Mandeville (420, 9, 22).

26. Susan Howe, letter to Lyn Hejinian, 19 August 1977, Hejinian Papers, Mandeville (74, 4, 18).

27. Susan Howe, letter to Lyn Hejinian, 17 January 1979, Hejinian Papers, Mandeville (74, 4, 18).

28. Howe, letter to Lyn Hejinian, 17 January 1979.

29. ANP Tapes Listening Series, SPL L-1030, Mandeville.

30. Bruce Andrews and Charles Bernstein, "The Pacifica Interview," conducted by Susan Howe, *L=A=N=G=U=A=G=E* Supplement No. 3 (October 1981): n. pag.

31. Susan Howe, letter to Ron Silliman, 27 December 1985, Silliman Papers, Mandeville (75, 9, 27).

32. ANP Tapes Listening Series, SPL L-1067, Mandeville.

33. Claire Moses, "Made in America: 'French Feminism' in United States Academic Discourse," *Australian Feminist Studies* 11.23 (April 1996): 17. Moses argues that Burke in particular conflated French women writers like Cixous with the women's movement, namely, the *mouvement de libération des femmes* (MLF). In doing so, Burke fashioned for American readers a more literary than sociological version of French feminism. However, it was this version that writers like Susan Howe, Lyn Hejinian, Kathleen Fraser, and Beverly Dahlen took up and enthusiastically investigated in their own explorations of language and gender. Indeed, had Marks and Burke been anything other than French-language *literature* specialists, American Language writing might well have developed a very different formation.

34. Susan Howe, letter to Lyn Hejinian, 26 August 1979, Hejinian Papers, Mandeville (74, 4, 18).

35. Susan Howe, letter to Lyn Hejinian, 20 September 1979, Hejinian Papers, Mandeville (74, 4, 18).

36. In a letter to Douglas Messerli, Howe suggests that the program she and Bernstein envisaged was a series of interviews with philosophers and critics. See Susan Howe, letter to Douglas Messerli, 9 May 1980, Sun & Moon Papers, Mandeville (224, 45, 2).

37. Susan Howe, letter to Lyn Hejinian, 30 November 1982, Hejinian Papers, Mandeville (74, 4, 18). Howe was referring to the end of Maureen Owen's *Telephone* magazine and press, which, like "Poetry," had stopped because of loss of funding.

6. *Kathleen Fraser's Feminist Alternative (pp. 88–99)*

1. Kathleen Fraser directed the Poetry Center at San Francisco State University from 1972 to 1975; in 1974 she founded the American Poetry Archives, also housed at the Center.

2. Kathleen Fraser, "The Tradition of Marginality," *Where We Stand: Women Poets on Literary Tradition*, ed. Sharon Bryan (New York: W. W. Norton, 1993), 60.

3. Fraser, "Tradition of Marginality," 60.

4. Fraser, "Tradition of Marginality," 60.

5. Frances Jaffer, rev. of *Literary Women*, by Ellen Moers, *Chrysalis: A Magazine of Women's Culture* 1 (1977): 136.

6. Hester Eisenstein and Alice Jardine, eds., *The Future of Difference* (Boston: G. K. Hall, 1980).

7. Mira Schor went on to become co-editor with Susan Bee of *M/E/A/N/I/N/G*, a feminist journal focusing on art issues rather than literature.

8. Kathleen Fraser, e-mail to the author, 17 June 1999.

9. Kathleen Fraser, interview, conducted by Cynthia Hogue, *Contemporary Literature* 39.1 (spring 1998): 15.

10. Fraser, "Tradition of Marginality," 61.

11. Kathleen Fraser, interview conducted by the author, 2 September 1996.

12. Frances Jaffer, "Why *HOW(ever)*?" *HOW(ever)* 1.1 (May 1983): 1.

13. Kathleen Fraser, "*trans*figuring," response to Annie Finch's "The Sonnet Transfigured," *HOW(ever)* 6.3 (summer, 1991): 16.

14. Kathleen Fraser, "Why *HOW(ever)*?" *HOW(ever)* 1.1 (May 1983): 1.

15. Kathleen Fraser, "The Jump: Editing *HOW(ever)*," *Chain* 1 (spring/summer 1994): 43.

16. Fraser, "The Jump," 43.

17. Fraser, "The Jump," 45.

18. Jaffer, "Why *HOW(ever)*?" 1.

19. Fraser, "The Jump," 43–44.

20. Fraser, "Why *HOW(ever)*?" 1.

21. In *HOW(ever)* 3.1 (January 1986): 13, the editors also state that they "intentionally think of these comments as not complete in the scholarly sense, with the hope of removing prohibitions linked with thinking/writing critically."

22. Fraser, "The Jump," 44–45.

23. Fraser, "The Jump," 46.

24. Fraser, "Why *HOW(ever)*?" 1.

25. Fraser, "Why *HOW(ever)*?" 1.

26. Annie Finch, "The Sonnet Transfigured," *HOW(ever)* 6.2 (October 1990): 13.

27. Rachel Blau DuPlessis, "Thinking about Annie Finch: On Female Power and the Sonnet," *HOW(ever)* 6.3 (summer 1991): 16. Taking her *HOW(ever)* response as a springboard, these arguments would be further developed in "Manifests," *Diacritics* 26.3–4 (fall-winter 1996): 31–53.

28. DuPlessis, "Thinking about Annie Finch," 16.

29. Fraser, "*trans*figuring," 15.

30. Fraser, "*trans*figuring," 15.

31. Norma Cole, "Whose Mouth? Cole on Quotation, "*HOW(ever)* 6.3 (summer 1991): 15.

32. Eliot Weinberger, "A Final Response," *Sulfur* 22 (1988): 201.

33. Adrienne Rich, *Adrienne Rich's Poetry and Prose*, ed. Barbara Charlesworth Gelpi and Albert Gelpi (New York: W. W. Norton, 1994), 270.

34. It is unclear why the "Women and Modernism" issue was delayed for so long that it appeared one year after the first issue of *HOW(ever)*. The clash of schedules between the two would not have helped matters.

35. Lyn Hejinian, letter to Susan Bee, 26 February 1983, Hejinian Papers, Mandeville (74, 2, 10). Although Carla Harryman, Erica Hunt, and Diane Ward proposed papers on Jane Bowles, Louis Zukofsky, and Bernadette Mayer, respectively, none would reach publication. Hejinian also wanted to expand the focus of the *Poetics Journal* issue to include articles on art and film. A primary distinction between *HOW(ever)* and the "Women and Modernism" issue was that one-third of the eventual contributors to the latter were male. Like Fraser, Hejinian and Watten hoped to attract an academic readership for the issue. She told Susan Bee that they planned to distribute the issue to women's studies programs. See Lyn Hejinian, letter to Susan Bee, 23 March 1983, Hejinian Papers, Mandeville (74, 2, 10).

36. See Rae Armantrout, "Through Walls," *HOW(ever)* 1.4 (May 1984): 6–7; rev. of *The Guard*, by Lyn Hejinian, *HOW(ever)* 2.2 (February 1985): 13–14.

37. See Armantrout, rev. of *The Guard, HOW(ever)*; draft rev. of *The Guard*, Hejinian Papers, Mandeville (74, 2, 1).

38. Kathleen Fraser, letter to Rae Armantrout, 21 November 1984, Hejinian Papers, Mandeville (74, 3, 25).

39. Fraser, letter to Rae Armantrout, 21 November 1984.
40. Rae Armantrout, "Poems," *Feminist Studies* 11.1 (spring 1985): 127–28, and Lyn Hejinian, "Poem," Feminist Studies 11.1 (spring 1985): 129.
41. Jane Miller, letter to Kathleen Fraser, *HOW(ever)* 2.2 (February 1985): 15.
42. Quoted by Susan Gevirtz in "Doctor Editor," *Chain* 1.1 (spring/summer 1994): 54.
43. Wayne Koestenbaum argues that "men who collaborate engage in a metaphorical sexual intercourse, and that the text they balance between them is alternatively the child of their sexual union and a shared woman." See *Double Talk: The Erotics of Male Literary Collaboration* (New York and London: Routledge, 1989), 3.
44. In a postcard to *HOW(ever)*, Daphne Marlatt states that "*HOW(ever)* has been a model for *(f.)Lip*" See "Why?" *HOW(ever)* 5.2 (January 1989): 13.
45. Angela Hryniuk, interview conducted by the author, 31 July 1994.
46. Kathleen Fraser, letter to Daphne Marlatt, *HOW(ever)* 5.2 (January 1989): 14.
47. Kathleen Fraser, "Editor's Notes," *HOW2* 1.1 (March 1999).

7. *Models, Manifestoes, and Morphogenesis (pp. 101–116)*

1. Barbara Johnson, *A World of Difference* (Baltimore: Johns Hopkins UP, 1987), 33.
2. Jacques Derrida, "The Law of Genre," *Glyph* 7 (spring 1980); rpt. in *Critical Inquiry* (autumn 1980): 55–81.
3. Ann Lauterbach, "Lines Written to Bob Perelman in the Margins of *The Marginalization of Poetry*," *The Impercipient Lecture Series* 1.4 (May 1997): 17.
4. Mary Margaret Sloan, "Unfolding Boundaries," interview, conducted by Robin Tremblay-McGaw, *Poetry Flash* 278 (September–October 1998): 17.
5. Sloan, "Unfolding Boundaries," 17.
6. This quote is borrowed from the title of Lyn Hejinian's early poetic collection, *A Thought Is the Bride of What Thinking* (Willits, CA: Tuumba, 1976).
7. See Slavoj Zizek's stereotypic characterization of theory and poeticism in *The Sublime Object of Ideology* (London: Verso, 1989), 155.
8. Charles Bernstein, *Content's Dream: Essays 1975–1984* (Los Angeles: Sun & Moon, 1986); Alan Davies, *Signage* (New York: Roof, 1987); Steve McCaffery, *North of Intention: Critical Writings, 1973–1986* (New York: Roof, 1986); Ron Silliman, *The New Sentence* (New York: Roof, 1987); and Barrett Watten, *Total Syntax* (Carbondale: Southern Illinois UP, 1985). It is perhaps significant that Alan Davies's *Signage*, which is the most playful and adventurous of these texts, fails to be mentioned in most critiques of Language writing.
9. Bob Perelman, *The Marginalization of Poetry: Language Writing and Literary History* (Princeton, NJ: Princeton UP, 1996), 79.
10. Joan Retallack, "The Meta-Physick of Play: L=A=N=G=U=A=G=E U.S.A.," *Parnassus* 12.1 (1984): 217. Like Perelman, Retallack named Ron Silliman, Steve McCaffery, Bruce Andrews, and Charles Bernstein "[t]he leading theoreticians of the Language group" in the early eighties.
11. Lyn Hejinian, letter to Erica Hunt, dated 13 February 1983, Hejinian Papers, Mandeville (74, 5, 1).
12. Lyn Hejinian, letter to Susan Howe, dated 16 June, Howe Papers, Mandeville (201, 1, 8).
13. Kathleen Fraser, letter to Carla Harryman, 12 August 1982, Hejinian Papers, Mandeville (74, 3, 25).

14. Fraser, letter to Carla Harryman, 12 August 1982.

15. Fraser, letter to Carla Harryman, 12 August 1982.

16. Rasula argues, "Language poets have insisted that we know the prescription that our linguistic lenses have been made to fill." See *The American Poetry Wax Museum: Reality Effects, 1940–1990* (Urbana, IL: National Council of Teachers of English, 1996), 406.

17. Rasula, *American Poetry Wax Museum*, 458.

18. Rasula, *American Poetry Wax Museum*, 403–4. In *The Marginalization of Poetry*, Bob Perelman would follow Rasula's lead by not only singling out Scalapino on the issue of women theorizing but doing so via a footnote.

19. Jed Rasula notes that Language writing is repeatedly and favorably singled out in prestigious journals, including *Critical Inquiry, New Literary History, South Atlantic Quarterly, Boundary 2, American Literary History* and *The Southern Review* (*The American Poetry Wax Museum* 459). Although three books to date have focused solely on Language writing, it is appearing more frequently as a topic within books. See, most recently, Alan Golding's *From Outlaw to Classic: Canons in American Poetry* (Madison: U of Wisconsin P, 1995), Hank Lazer's *Opposing Poetries*, pts. 1 and 2 (Evanston, IL: Northwestern UP, 1996), and Marjorie Perloff's *Wittgenstein's Ladder: Poetic Language and the Strangeness of the Ordinary* (Chicago: U of Chicago P, 1996).

20. John Guillory, *Cultural Capital: The Politics of Literary Canon Formation* (Chicago: U of Chicago P, 1993), xii.

21. See Barbara Christian, "The Race for Theory," *Cultural Critique* 6 (1987): 51–63.

22. William Lavender, "Disappearance of Theory, Appearance of Praxis: Ron Silliman, *L=A=N=G=U=A=G=E*, and the Essay," *Poetics Today* 17.2 (summer 1996): 194.

23. Lavender, "Disappearance of Theory," 196.

24. The poem was not written specifically with Fraser's letter in mind although the issue it raised seems to have been a continuing concern for Harryman.

25. Carla Harryman, "There Is Nothing Better Than a Theory," *Animal Instincts* (Oakland, CA: This, 1989), 94–95, 105.

26. Catherine Lutz, "The Gender of Theory," *Women Writing Culture*, ed. Ruth Behar and Deborah A. Gordon (Berkeley: U of California P, 1995), 251.

27. Elaine Showalter, "Feminist Criticism in the Wilderness," *The New Feminist Criticism: Essays on Women, Literature and Theory*, ed. Elaine Showalter (London: Virago, 1985), 243–70.

28. Lutz, "Gender of Theory," 252

29. Ron Silliman, Carla Harryman, Lyn Hejinian, Steve Benson, Bob Perelman, and Barrett Watten, "Aesthetic Tendency and the Politics of Poetry: A Manifesto," *Social Text* 19–20 (fall 1988): 261–75.

30. Silliman, *New Sentence* 88.

31. Charles Bernstein, letter to Ron Silliman, n.d., Silliman Papers, Mandeville (75, 3, 11). Silliman seems to have directly addressed Bernstein's criticisms in his final version of *The New Sentence*. In its published form, he briefly responds to the East Coast writers that Bernstein lists as doing sentence exploration. Silliman notes Weiner's particular use of the New Sentence and further discusses why Coolidge's work (such as *Weathers*) does not fit within the parameters of the New Sentence.

32. Charles Bernstein, letter to Ron Silliman, n.d., Silliman Papers, Mandeville (75, 3, 11).

33. Lutz, "Gender of Theory," 253.

34. Perelman, *Marginalization of Poetry*, 61.

35. Watten, *Total Syntax*, xi.

36. Watten, *Total Syntax*, x.

37. Susan Howe, *My Emily Dickinson* (Berkeley, CA: North Atlantic, 1985).

38. Retallack, "Meta-Physick of Play," 243.

39. Trinh T. Minh-ha, *Woman, Native, Other: Writing Postcoloniality and Feminism* (Bloomington: Indiana UP, 1989), 41.

40. Bernstein, *A Poetics*, 153.

41. Bernstein, *A Poetics*, 157.

42. Rosmarie Waldrop, "Alarms and Excursions," The Politics of Poetic Form: Poetry and Public Policy, ed. Charles Bernstein (New York: Roof, 1990), 65.

43. Rosmarie Waldrop, "Thinking of Follows," *Onward: Contemporary Poetry and Poetics*, ed. Peter Baker (New York: Peter Lang, 1996), 78.

44. Lutz, "Gender of Theory," 254.

45. Susan Howe, letter to Lyn Hejinian, 30 November, 1982, Hejinian Papers, Mandeville (74, 4, 18).

46. Leslie Scalapino, "What/Person: From an Exchange," conducted between Leslie Scalapino and Ron Silliman, *Poetics Journal* 9 (June 1991): 52.

47. Lutz, "Gender of Theory," 254.

48. Bernstein, *A Poetics*, 175.

49. Lutz, "Gender of Theory," 254.

50. Clark Coolidge, interview, conducted by Lee Bartlett, *Talking Poetry: Conversations in the Workshop with Contemporary Poets*, ed. Lee Bartlett (Albuquerque: U of New Mexico P, 1987), 13.

51. Barrett Watten, "Reinventing Community: A Symposium on/with Language Poets," *Minnesota Review* 32 (summer 1989): 32.

52. See Andrew Levy, "The Existence of the Writer—the Unthought Known," *A Poetics of Criticism*, ed. Juliana Spahr et al. (Buffalo: Leave, 1994), particularly at 204.

53. Robert Creeley, interview, conducted by Alan Riach, *Australasian Journal of American Studies* 15.1 (July 1996): 42.

54. The degree to which formalities of genre are adhered to may also vary within the work of one writer. As with the difference between Bernstein's "Artifice of Absorption" and the surrounding essays in *A Poetics*, Susan Howe's *My Emily Dickinson* is quite different from some of the work collected in *The Birth-Mark: Unsettling the Wilderness in American Literary History*.

55. Carla Harryman, *There Never Was a Rose without a Thorn* (San Francisco: City Lights, 1995) n. pag.

56. Abigail Child, "Active Theory," *Raddle Moon* II (1992): 47–54.

57. Rachel Blau DuPlessis, "f-Words: An Essay on the Essay," *American Literature* 68.1 (1996): 15–45.

58. Derrida, "Law of Genre," 55.

59. This is the term John Taggart uses in describing the shifting reputation of poets and poetry. See his review of *My Emily Dickinson* by Susan Howe in *Conjunctions* 11 (1987): 264.

60. David Lehmann, *Signs of the Times: Deconstruction and the Fall of Paul de Man* (New York: Poseidon, 1991), 32.

61. Lehmann, *Signs of the Times*, 33

62. Johanna Drucker, "Women/Writing/Theory: What Is at Stake?" *Raddle Moon* 11 (1992): 18.

63. Quoted by Susan Clark in her preface to the forum of "Women/Writing/Theory," *Raddle Moon* 11 (1992): 16.

64. Susan Clark, preface, "Women/Writing/Theory," 16.

65. Johanna Drucker, "Response," *Raddle Moon* 13 (1994): 48.

66. Drucker, "Response," 50.

67. Call for papers for *Tessera* 6 as printed in *Tessera/CV* 2 11.23 (1988). As quoted by Pamela Banting in "S(m)other Tongue?: Feminism, Academic Discourse, Translation," *Collaboration in the Feminine: Writings on Women and Culture from Tessera*, ed. Barbara Godard (Toronto: Second Story, 1994), 171.

68. Janice Williamson, "*(f.)Lip* Sides," letter to the editors *(f.)Lip* 1.1 (1987): 22.

69. Drucker, "Response," 51.

70. Chris Tysh, "Critical Theory, or Tooling That Thing," *Raddle Moon* 13 (1994): 45.

71. Drucker, "Response," 52.

72. Drucker, "Women/Writing/Theory: What Is at Stake?" 18.

73. In a more recent interview, Drucker notes a shift in her relation to theory: "Having initially believed that 'writing could save me from being a woman' . . . I had, not surprisingly, come to believe that theory could do the same. I think women in academia in the 1980s were intent on proving they could 'do theory with the boys' as a way of asserting their intellectual credentials." Today she is more interested in how visual art or writing might function as a cultural practice and in exploring a more fluid relation between theory and praxis. See "'Through Light and the Alphabet': An Interview with Johanna Drucker," conducted by Matthew G. Kirschenbaum, *Postmodern Culture* 5 (1997): n. pag.

74. Jean Day, "Response," *Raddle Moon* 13 (1994): 57.

75. Abigail Child, "Active Theory," *Raddle Moon* 13 (1994): 16.

76. Abigail Child, "Cross Referencing the Units of Sight and Sound/Film and Language," *The L=A=N=G=U=A=G=E Book*, ed. Bruce Andrews and Charles Bernstein (Carbondale: Southern Illinois UP, 1984), 94.

77. Janet Lyon, "Transforming Manifestoes: A Second-Wave Problematic," *Yale Journal of Criticism* 5.1 (1991): 102.

78. Abigail Child, "Active Theory," *Raddle Moon* 11 (1992): 47.

79. Rachel Blau DuPlessis, "For the Etruscans," *The Pink Guitar: Writing as Feminist Practice* (New York and London: Routledge, 1990), 15.

80. Lyon, "Transforming Manifestoes," 105.

81. Child, "Active Theory," *Raddle Moon* 11 (1992): 53.

82. Lyon, "Transforming Manifestoes," 121.

83. Tina Darragh, "The Best of Intentions," *Moving Borders: Three Decades of Innovative Writing by Women*, ed. Mary Margaret Sloan (Jersey City, NJ: Talisman House, 1998), 702.

84. Barrett Watten, *Bad History* (Berkeley, CA: Atelos, 1998).

8. *"I Hate Speech"* (pp. 117–133)

1. See Katharyn Howd Machan: "Breath into Fire: Feminism and Poetry Readings," *Mid-American Review* 12.2 (1992): 120.

2. Charles Bernstein, "Provisional Institutions: Alternative Presses and Poetic Innovation," *Arizona Quarterly* 51.1 (spring 1995): 135.

3. See Allen Ginsberg, "Foreword," *Out of This World: An Anthology of the St. Mark's Poetry Project 1966–1991*, ed. Anne Waldman (New York: Crown, 1991), xxiv.

4. Anne Waldman, Introduction, *Out of This World*, 1.

5. Carla Harryman, "Belief," unpublished manuscript.

6. See, generally, Erving Goffman, "The Lecture," in *Forms of Talk* (Philadelphia: U of Pennsylvania P, 1981).

7. Linda Alcoff, "The Problem of Speaking for Others," *Feminist Nightmares, Women at Odds: Feminism and the Problem of Sisterhood*, ed. Susan Ostrov Wesser and Jennifer Fleischner (New York: New York UP, 1994), 285, 291.

8. Carla Harryman, "Belief."

9. Bob Perelman, preface, *Writing/Talks*, ed. Bob Perelman (Carbondale: Southern Illinois UP, 1985) viii.

10. See Richard Rorty, *Philosophy and the Mirror of Nature* (Princeton, NJ: Princeton UP, 1979).

11. Nancy Hartsock, "Rethinking Modernism: Minority vs. Majority Theories," *Cultural Critique* 7 (fall 1987): 199, 201.

12. Bob Perelman, "Language Writing and Literary History," *Aerial* 8 (1995): 132.

13. Wystan Curnow recalls his experience as a marginal figure at such talks in San Francisco in 1981: "I went to several readings a place called Intersection, including one called 'An Evening with The Figures.' The Figures being, it turned out, a small press. . . . Most of it was very puzzling to me. Equally so were Barrett Watten's lectures, also at Intersection, which kept referring, it turned out, to writers who were there in the audience." See "Interview: Roger Horrocks and Friends Talk with Wystan Curnow," *Landfall* 45.1 (March 1991), 12.

14. Bob Perelman, "Speech Effects: The Talk as a Genre," *Close Listening: Poetry and the Performed Word*, ed. Charles Bernstein (New York: Oxford UP, 1998), 205.

15. Perelman, "Speech Effects," 206. A copy of the taped talk is available in the Archive for New Poetry.

16. Perelman, "Speech Effects," 206.

17. Cited by Bob Perelman in "Speech Effects," 206.

18. Alcoff, "Problem of Speaking for Others," 291.

19. Elizabeth Aries has recently argued that popularized beliefs about gender differences significantly shape our perceptions and evaluations of speakers. As Aries suggests, men and women use both masculine and feminine styles of interaction in terms of their status, role, gender identity, and objectives. She proposes that as greater variation in behavior is encouraged, the less force such stereotypical divisions in speech patterns will have over actual speech patterns. See *Men and Women in Interaction: Reconsidering the Differences* (New York: Oxford UP, 1996).

20. Jennifer Coates, *Women, Men and Language* (London: Longman, 1986), 154.

21. Candace West and Don H. Zimmerman, "Small Insults: A Study of Cross-Sex Conversations between Unacquainted Persons," *Language, Gender and Society*, ed. Barrie Thorne et al. (Rowley, MA: Newbury House, 1983), 103.

22. Lyn Hejinian, letter to Susan Howe, n.d., Howe Papers, Mandeville (201, 1, 8).

23. Robin Lakoff, *Language and Woman's Place* (New York: Octagon, 1976), esp. 51–73.

24. See "Talks," *Hills* (1980): 6–7.

25. Bob Perelman, informal discussion with the author, 31 March 1998.

26. Carla Harryman, "Rules and Restraints in Women's Experimental Writing," paper presented at The New Modernisms Conference, Penn State University, 8 October 1999.

27. Susan Howe, letter to Lyn Hejinian, 13 July 1980, Hejinian Papers, Mandeville (74, 4, 18).

28. Lyn Hejinian, letter to Susan Howe, 13 August 1980. Howe Papers, Mandeville (201, 1, 8).

29. Lyn Hejinian, letter to Susan Howe, 13 August 1980, Howe Papers, Mandeville (201, 1, 8).

30. Susan Howe, letter to Lyn Hejinian, 20 August 1980, Hejinian Papers, Mandeville (74, 4, 18).

31. Lyn Hejinian, letter to Susan Howe, 10 September 1980, Howe Papers, Mandeville (201, 1, 8).

32. Howe noted that Bernstein and Bee read the publishing of Notley's talk as a "direct reaction" to the *Hills* issue. See Susan Howe, letter to Lyn Hejinian, 6 September 1980, Hejinian Papers, Mandeville (74, 4, 18).

33. Lyn Hejinian, letter to Rae Armantrout, 27 February 1983, Hejinian Papers, Mandeville (74, 2, 1).

34. Perelman, "Speech Effects," 215.

35. Lyn Hejinian, letter to Rae Armantrout, 27 February 1983, Hejinian Papers, Mandeville (74, 2, 1).

36. Lyn Hejinian, letter to Susan Howe, 4 February 1983, Susan Howe Papers, Mandeville (201, 1, 8).

37. Lyn Hejinian, letter to Erica Hunt, 13 February 1983, Hejinian Papers, Mandeville (74, 5, 1).

38. Lyn Hejinian, letter to Susan Howe, 4 February 1983, Susan Howe Papers, Mandeville (201, 1, 8).

39. Lyn Hejinian, letter to Susan Howe, 4 February 1983, Susan Howe Papers, Mandeville (201, 1, 8).

40. Lyn Hejinian, letter to Susan Bee and Charles Bernstein, 13 February 1983, Hejinian Papers, Mandeville (74, 2, 10).

41. Lyn Hejinian, letter to Susan Bee and Charles Bernstein, 13 February 1983, Hejinian Papers, Mandeville (74, 2, 10).

42. Lyn Hejinian, letter to Susan Bee, 26 February 1983, Hejinian Papers, Mandeville (74, 2, 10).

43. Lyn Hejinian, letter to Susan Howe, 29 May 1983, Howe Papers, Mandeville (201, 1, 8).

44. Lyn Hejinian, "Language and 'Paradise,'" *Line* 6 (spring 1985): 83–99.

45. Lyn Hejinian, letter to Susan Bee, 23 March 1983, Hejinian Papers, Mandeville (74, 2, 10).

46. Harryman, "Belief."

47. Fanny Howe, letter to Bernadette Mayer, n.d., Mayer Papers, Mandeville (420, 9, 21). Mayer discussed the Langton Street residency with the program's organizers at the end of April 1983.

48. Lyn Hejinian, letter to Rae Armantrout, 7 December 1983, Hejinian papers, Mandeville (74, 2, 1).

49. Hejinian, letter to Rae Armantrout, 7 December 1983. Armantrout also found the women writers group that she attended supportive.

50. See Anne Ruggles Gere, "Common Properties of Pleasure: Texts in Nineteenth Century Women's Clubs," *The Construction of Authorship: Textual Appropriation*

in Law and Literature, ed. Martha Woodmansee and Peter Jaszi (Durham, NC: Duke UP, 1994), 383–99.

51. Armantrout is also careful about the specificity of her comments, stating, "Always in this talk I was only talking about the passages I was talking about, not the person's work as a whole." See Rae Armantrout, "Poetic Silence," *Writing/ Talks*, ed. Bob Perelman (Carbondale: Southern Illinois UP, 1985), 41.

52. Barrett Watten's "Russian Formalism and the Present" was also replaced by his talk, "Olson in Language: Part II." As "Russian Formalism and the Present" was being published in *Total Syntax*, the decision was probably made to replace it with an unpublished paper.

53. Robert Glück, "Who Speaks for Us: Being an Expert," *Writing/Talks*, ed. Bob Perelman (Carbondale: Southern Illinois UP, 1985), 2–3.

54. George Lakoff, "On Whose Authority?" *Poetry Flash* 147 (June 1985): 5.

55. Charles Bernstein, "Characterization," *Writing/Talks*, ed. Bob Perelman (Carbondale, IL: Southern Illinois UP, 1985), 8.

56. Charles Bernstein, "Characterization," 20.

57. Charles Bernstein, "Characterization," 25.

58. Michael Palmer, response to "Characterization," 25.

59. Armantrout, "Poetic Silence," 31–32.

60. Armantrout, "Poetic Silence," 34–35.

61. Armantrout, "Poetic Silence," 40.

62. Beverly Dahlen, "From *The Tradition of Marginality*," *Poetics Journal* 6 (1986): 72.

63. Diane Ward, e-mail to the author, 4 June 1999.

64. The proceedings of the conference were published as *In the Feminine: Women and Words*, ed. Ann Dybikowski et al. (Edmonton, Alberta: Longspoon, 1985).

65. Di Brandt, "letting the silence speak," *Language in Her Eye: Writing and Gender*, ed. Libby Scheier et al. (Toronto: Coach House, 1990), 55.

66. See Janice Williamson, "Citing Resistance: Vision, Space, Authority and Transgression in Canadian Women's Poetry," diss., York (1987), 65.

67. Williamson, "Citing Resistance," 65.

68. See Paulette Jiles, "Hustling at the New Poetics Colloquium," *Brick* 27 (spring 1986): 45–50.

69. See Smaro Kamboureli, "Theory: Beauty or Beast? Resistance to Theory in the Feminine," *Open Letter* 7.8 (summer 1990): 5–26.

70. Diane Ward, e-mail to the author, 4 June 1999.

71. Ward, e-mail to the author, 4 June 1999.

72. Lyn Hejinian, letter to Susan Howe, 20 September 1985, Howe Papers, Mandeville (201, 1, 8).

73. Williamson, "Citing Resistance," 66.

74. Bob Perelman, "Notes on The First World," *Line* 6 (1985): 100–12. Being placed in the final space of the program, Charles Bernstein's paper, while flexible in form, nevertheless served as an overview or response to issues raised by the colloquium. Its eventual form was published as "Artifice of Absorption" in *A Poetics* (Cambridge, MA: Harvard UP, 1992) 9–89. Apart from Silliman's and Howe's, other papers included Bruce Andrews's "Total Equals What: Poetics and Practice," published in expanded form in *Poetics Journal* 6 (1986): 48–61. Nicole Brossard spoke on the concept of the "intimate journal" as a feminist form, with reference to her own *Journal Intime* (Montreal: Editions Herbes Rouges, 1984). Barrett Watten read excerpts from *Plasma/Parallels*, *X* and *Total Syntax*. Lyn Hejinian discussed

her writing of *The Guard*, subsequently published as "Language and 'Paradise,'" *Line* 6 (1985): 83– 99.

75. Ron Silliman's "'Postmodernism': Sign for a Struggle, the Struggle for the Sign" was published in *Conversant Essays: Contemporary Poets on Poetry*, ed. James McCorkle (Detroit: Wayne State UP, 1990), 79– 98. Susan Howe's "There Are Not Leaves Enough to Crown to Cover to Crown to Cover" was published in *Jimmy and Lucy's House of K* 5 (1985): 13– 17; rpt. in *The Europe of Trusts* (Los Angeles: Sun & Moon, 1990), 9– 14. Although Ron Silliman's statement for the colloquium was informal, the history he relates is not as intimate as Howe's. See "Statement for the New Poetics Colloquium, Vancouver 1985," *Jimmy and Lucy's House of K* 5 (1985): 17– 19.

76. Susan Howe, "The Captivity and Restoration of Mrs. Mary Rowlandson," *Temblor* 2 (1985): 113– 21.

77. Lyn Hejinian, letter to Susan Howe, 20 September 1985, Howe Papers, Mandeville (201, 1, 8).

78. Williamson, "Citing Resistance," 66.

79. Williamson, "Citing Resistance," 70– 74.

80. Lyn Hejinian, letter to Susan Howe, 20 September 1985, Howe Papers, Mandeville (201, 1, 8).

81. Daphne Marlatt, "Magazining: Interview with Daphne Marlatt," conducted by Pauline Butling, *Open Letter* 8.5– 6 (1992): 120.

82. Janice Williamson cites this line as an epigraph to her criticism of the colloquium.

83. See Jeff Derksen's comments in "Jeff Derksen and Ron Silliman," *Philly Talks* 6 (1998): 14.

9. *Cabinets, Closets, and Consumption (134– 148)*

1. John Yau, "Neither Us Nor Them," *American Poetry Review* 23.2 (1994): 48.

2. Jed Rasula, *The American Poetry Wax Museum: Reality Effects, 1940–1990* (Urbana, IL: National Council of Teachers of English, 1996), 466.

3. Maggie O'Sullivan, ed., *Out of Everywhere: Linguistically Innovative Poetry by Women in North America and the UK* (London: Reality Street Editions, 1996).

4. Rosmarie Waldrop, "Alarms and Excursions," *The Politics of Poetic Form*, ed. Charles Bernstein (New York: Roof, 1990), 66.

5. Mary Margaret Sloan, ed., *Moving Borders: Three Decades of Innovative Writing by Women* (Jersey City, NJ: Talisman, 1998).

6. Ellen Bass and Florence Howe, eds., *No More Masks! An Anthology of Poems by Women* (New York: Anchor, 1973); Sharon Barba and Laura Chester, eds., *Rising Tides: Twentieth Century American Women Poets* (New York: Simon & Schuster, 1973).

7. Louise Bernikow, ed., *The World Split Open: Women Poets 1552– 1956* (London: Women's Press, 1974).

8. Laura Chester, introduction to *Deep Down: The New Sensual Writing by Women*, ed. Laura Chester (Boston: Faber and Faber, 1988), 1.

9. Mary Margaret Sloan, "Of Experience to Experiment: Women's Innovative Writing, 1965– 1995," draft chapter in *The World in Space and Time: Towards a History of Innovative American Poetry, 1970– 2000*, ed. Edward Foster and Joseph Donahue (Jersey City, NJ: Talisman, forthcoming).

10. Sharon Olds, "First Boyfriend," *Deep Down* 31.

11. Leslie Scalapino, "From *Floating Series*," *Deep Down: The New Sensual Writing by Women*, ed. Laura Chester (Boston and London: Faber and Faber, 1988), 176.

12. Marge Piercy, introduction to *Early Ripening: American Women's Poetry Now*, ed. Marge Piercy (New York: Pandora, 1987), 1.

13. Piercy, introduction, *Early Ripening*, 2.

14. Joel Lewis, "Dreamers That Remain," *American Book Review* (March–April 1987): 9.

1515. Michael Lally, *None of the Above: New Poets of the U.S.A.* (Trumansburg, NY: Crossing, 1976).

16. Marjorie Perloff, "What 'Les Jeunes' Are Up To," *Washington Post*, 26 December 1976.

17. Ron Silliman, ed., *In the American Tree: Language, Realism, Poetry* (Orono, ME: National Poetry Foundation, 1986).

18. Helen Vendler, ed., *The Harvard Book of Contemporary American Poetry* (Cambridge, MA: Belknap, 1985); A. Poulin Jr., ed., *Contemporary American Poetry*, 4th ed. (Boston: Houghton Mifflin, 1985); Dave Smith and David Bottoms, eds., *The Morrow Anthology of Younger American Poets* (New York: Quill, 1985).

19. Douglas Messerli, ed., *"Language" Poetries* (New York: New Directions, 1987). Michael Greer, "Ideology and Theory in Recent Experimental Writing, or, The Naming of 'Language Poetry,'" *Boundary2* 16 (winter–spring 1989): 336.

20. Hank Lazer, *Opposing Poetries* (Evanston, IL: Northwestern UP, 1996), 1:37. Lazer originally made the statement in 1989, well before the publication of *Out of Everywhere* and *Moving Borders*.

21. Paul Hoover, ed., *Postmodern American Poetry* (New York: W. W. Norton, 1994); Pierre Joris and Jerome Rothenberg, eds., *Poems for the Millennium*, vols. I and II (Berkeley: U of California P, 1995, 1998).

22. Ron Silliman, statement, "Reinventing Community: A Symposium On/With Language Poets," *Minnesota Review* 32 (summer 1989): 41.

23. Donald M. Allen, ed., *The New American Poetry* (New York: Grove, 1960); William Carlos Williams, *In the American Grain* (New York: New Directions, 1956).

24. Bob Perelman, *The Marginalization of Poetry: Language Writing and Literary History* (Princeton, NJ: Princeton UP, 1996), 20.

25. Douglas Messerli, letter to Ron Silliman, 28 September 1985, Sun & Moon Papers, Mandeville (224, 71, 6).

26. Douglas Messerli, introduction to *"Language" Poetries*, ed. Douglas Messerli (New York: New Directions, 1987), 8.

27. Leslie Scalapino, interview, conducted by Anne Brewster, unpublished.

28. Joan Retallack, e-mail to the author, 28 April 1999.

29. Douglas Messerli, e-mail to the author, 15 September 1999.

30. Linda Reinfeld, *Language Poetry: Writing as Rescue* (Baton Rouge: Louisiana State UP, 1992), 25.

31. Lyn Hejinian, letter to Ron Silliman, 16 November 1982, Silliman Papers, Mandeville (74, 7, 6).

32. Susan Howe, "From *Pythagorean Silence*," *In the American Tree: Language, Realism, Poetry* (17).

33. Susan Howe, letter to Ron Silliman, 3 November 1985, Silliman Papers, Mandeville (75, 9, 27).

34. Dennis Barone and Peter Ganick, eds., *The Art of Practice: 45 Contemporary Poets* (Elmwood, CT: Potes & Poets, 1994).

35. Douglas Messerli, "To the Reader," *From the Other Side of the Century: A New American Poetry 1960–1990* (Los Angeles: Sun & Moon, 1994), 31.

36. Douglas Messerli, "To the Reader," 32.

37. Carla Harryman, letter to Douglas Messerli, 5 October 1985, Sun & Moon Papers, Mandeville (224, 40, 11).

38. Lyn Hejinian, letter to Ron Silliman, 16 November 1982, Silliman Papers, Mandeville (74, 7, 6).

39. Susan Howe, letter to Douglas Messerli, 25 October 1985, Sun & Moon Papers, Mandeville (224, 45, 1).

40. Tina Darragh, letter to Ron Silliman, dated "end of January 1986," Silliman Papers, Mandeville (75, 5, 1).

41. Douglas Messerli, *From the Other Side of the Century: A New American Poetry 1960 – 1990* (Los Angeles: Sun & Moon, 1994).

42. *Mirage* 3 (1989).

43. Linda France, introduction to *Sixty Women Poets*, ed. Linda France (Newcastle-upon-Tyne: Bloodaxe, 1993), 16.

44. Andrew Crozier and Tim Longville, eds., *A Various Art* (Carcanet, 1987); London: Paladin, 1990).

45. Iain Sinclair, ed., *Conductors of Chaos* (London: Picador, 1996).

46. Gillian Allnutt et al., eds., *The New British Poetry, 1968 – 1988* (London: Paladin, 1988).

47. Silliman, statement, "Reinventing Community," 41.

48. Mary Margaret Sloan, e-mail to the author, 21 May 1999.

49. Mary Margaret Sloan, introduction to *Moving Borders*, 8.

50. Mary Margaret Sloan, e-mail to the author, 7 January, 2000.

51. Mary Margaret Sloan, "Unfolding Boundaries: A Talk with Mary Margaret Sloan," conducted by Robin Tremblay-McGaw, *Poetry Flash* 278 (September – October 1998): 12.

52. Mary Margaret Sloan, e-mail to the author, 21 May 1999.

53. Mary Margaret Sloan, paper presented at the "How to Survive the Canon" panel, Page Mothers Conference, San Diego, 5 – 6 March 1999.

54. Sloan, "Unfolding Boundaries," 17.

55. Sloan, introduction to *Moving Borders*, 7.

56. Mary Margaret Sloan, e-mail to the author, 21 May 1999.

57. Marjorie Perloff, "Whose New American Poetry: Anthologizing in the Nineties" *Diacritics* 26 (fall 1997): 111– 12.

58. Susan Bee helped with the design and editorial production of Susan Howe's *Kulchur Book, Defenestration of Prague* (1983). See Lynn Keller and Cristanne Miller, "Gender and Avant-Garde Editing: Comparing the 1920s with the 1990s," *HOW2* 1.2 (1999). Susan Howe discussed her publishing history in an interview with Lynn Keller.

10. Desire Not a Saint (150–166)

1. Quoted by Peggy Phelan in *Unmarked: The Politics of Performance* (London: Routledge, 1993), 19.

2. Recent work by critics such as Stephen Cope and Juliana Spahr is redressing this lack.

3. Linda Reinfeld, *Language Poetry: Writing as Rescue* (Baton Rouge: Louisiana State UP, 1992) 44.

4. Bernadette Mayer, *Memory* (Plainfield, VT: North Atlantic, 1975), 182.

5. Bernadette Mayer, letter to Lyn Hejinian, 1 September 1983, Hejinian Papers, Mandeville (74, 6, 1).

6. Bernadette Mayer, interview with Bill Berkson, dated February 1981, Mayer Papers, Mandeville (420, 4, 16).

7. Bernadette Mayer, *Studying Hunger* (Big Sky, 1976); rpt. in *In the American Tree*, ed. Ron Silliman: (Orono, ME: The National Poetry Foundation), 413.

8. Pierre Nora, "Between Memory and History: *Les Lieux de Mémoire*," *History and Memory in African American Culture*, ed. Genevieve Fabre and Robert O'Meally (New York: Oxford UP, 1994), 285.

9. Bernadette Mayer, *Studying Hunger*, rpt. in *In the American Tree*, 410.

10. Bernadette Mayer, "From: A Lecture at the Naropa Institute, 1989," *Disembodied Poetics: Annals of the Jack Kerouac School*, ed. Anne Waldman and Andrew Schelling (Albuquerque: U of New Mexico P, 1994), 101.

11. Mayer, *Studying Hunger*, rpt in *In the American Tree*, 413.

12. Mayer, "From," 98.

13. David Rubinfine, introduction to *Memory*, n. pag.

14. Quoted by Richard Bridgman in *Gertrude Stein in Pieces* (New York: Oxford UP, 1970), 13.

15. Gertrude Stein, *Selected Writings of Gertrude Stein*, ed. Carl van Vechten (New York: Random House, 1972), 249.

16. Stein, *Selected Writings of Gertrude Stein*, 243.

17. Mayer, "From," 98.

18. Mayer, *Memory*, 152.

19. Mayer, *Memory*, 88.

20. Mayer, *Memory*, 50.

21. Mayer, *Memory*, 89.

22. Mayer, *Memory*, 55–56.

23. Mayer, *Memory*, 14.

24. Mayer, *Memory*, 93, 99.

25. Mayer, *Memory*, 81.

26. Mayer, *Memory*, 7.

27. Mayer, *Memory*, 189.

28. Mayer, *Memory*, 195.

29. Clark Coolidge, letter to Peter Baker, 28 June 1994, *Onward: Contemporary Poetry and Poetics*, ed. Peter Baker (New York: Peter Lang, 1996), 257. Mayer quoted by Peter Baker in "Bernadette Mayer," *Dictionary of Literary Biography*, vol. 165, "American Poets Since World War II," ed. Joseph Conte (Detroit: Gale, 1996), 167

30. Quoted by Peter Baker in "Bernadette Mayer," 167.

31. Baker, "Bernadette Mayer," 167.

32. Ron Padgett and David Shapiro, eds., *An Anthology of New York Poets* (New York: Random House, 1970).

33. Marcella Durand, "Publishing a Community: Women Publishers at the Poetry Project," paper presented at "Where Lyric Tradition Meets Language Poetry" Conference, 8–10 April 1999, Barnard College, New York. The anthology's blatant bias caused unrest among many New York women writers, even motivating Eileen Myles to start her own press, Dodgems.

34. Clark Coolidge, letter to Peter Baker, 28 June 1994, *Onward: Contemporary Poetry and Poetics*, 256.

35. Douglas Messerli, letter to Bernadette Mayer, 8 January 1985, Mayer Papers, Mandeville (420, 14, 35).

36. Lynne Dreyer, "I Started Writing," *In the American Tree: Language, Realism, Poetry*, ed. Ron Silliman (Orono, ME: National Poetry Foundation, 1986), 521.

37. Bernadette Mayer, quoted by Marcella Durand in "Publishing a Community: Women Publishers at the Poetry Project," paper presented at "Where Lyric Tradition Meets Language Poetry" Conference, 8–10 April 1999, Barnard College, New York.

38. Diana Hume George, "'How Many of Us Can You Hold to Your Breast?':' Mothering in the Academy," *Listening to Silences: New Essays in Feminist Criticism*, ed. Elaine Hedges and Shelley Fisher Fishkin (New York: Oxford UP, 1994), 227.

39. Bernadette Mayer, "The Colors of Consonance," interview conducted by Ken Jordan, *The Poetry Project Newsletter* 146 (October–November 1992): 7.

40. Mayer, "The Colors of Consonance," 8.

41. Bernadette Mayer, "Experimental Writing, or Writing the Long Work," *Onward: Contemporary Poetry and Poetics*, ed. Peter Baker (New York: Peter Lang, 1996), 6.

42. Mayer, *Studying Hunger*, rpt. in *In the American Tree*, 412.

43. Bernadette Mayer, "The Obfuscated Poem," *Code of Signals: Recent Writings in Poetics*, ed. Michael Palmer (Berkeley, CA: North Atlantic, 1983), 166.

44. Susan Howe, letter to Lyn Hejinian, 13 July 1980, Hejinian Papers, Mandeville (74, 4, 18).

45. Susan Howe, letter to Lyn Hejinian, 4 March 1983, Hejinian Papers, Mandeville (74, 4, 18).

46. Jerome McGann, "Contemporary Poetry, Alternate Routes," *Critical Inquiry* 13.3 (spring 1987), rpt. in *Politics and Poetic Value*, ed. Robert von Hallberg (Chicago: U of Chicago P, 1987),265.

47. Charles Bernstein, "Experiments," *Boundary 2* 23.3 (1996) 67–72. While Mayer is credited in a footnote, her name is absent from the table of contents and title.

48. Mayer, "Experimental Writing," 8.

49. Bernadette Mayer, "The Complete Introductory Lectures on Poetry," *Onward: Contemporary Poetry and Poetics*, ed. Peter Baker (New York: Peter Lang, 1996), 20–21.

50. ANP Tapes Listening Series, SPL 1–1021, Mandeville.

51. Fanny Howe, rev. of *Midwinter Day*, *American Book Review* 6 (1984): 16.

52. Lyn Hejinian, letter to Susan Howe, n.d., Howe Papers, Mandeville (201, 1, 8).

53. Lyn Hejinian, letter to Rae Armantrout, 22 April 1984, Hejinian Papers, Mandeville (74, 2, 1).

54. Barrett Watten, *Total Syntax* (Carbondale: Southern Illinois UP, 1985), 56–57.

55. Toril Moi, *Simone de Beauvoir: The Making of an Intellectual Woman* (Oxford: Blackwell, 1994), 7.

56. The term *compromise* is Ashbery's own to describe his change of style. See John Ashbery, "An Interview in Warsaw," conducted by Pietr Sommer, *Code of Signals: Recent Writings in Poetics*, ed. Michael Palmer (Berkeley, CA: North Atlantic, 1983), 302. Jerome McGann discusses the "two Ashberys" in "Contemporary Poetry, Alternate Routes," 256–57. As McGann suggests, Ashbery's nonpolitical stance has enabled his work to be embraced by institutional and avant-garde forces.

57. Bernadette Mayer, *The Desires of Mothers to Please Others in Letters* (West Stockbridge, MA: Hard Press, 1994), 221.

58. Bernadette Mayer, letter with Alice Notley collaboration, Mayer Papers, Mandeville (420, 18, 9– 10).

59. Lyn Hejinian, letter to Fanny Howe, 20 September 1983, Hejinian Papers, Mandeville (74, 4, 17).

60. Lola Lemire Tostevin, *Subject to Criticism* (Stratford, ON: Mercury, 1995), 16.

61. Carroll Smith-Rosenberg, "The Female World of Love and Ritual: Relations between Women in Nineteenth-Century America," *Signs* 1.1 (1975): 1– 29.

62. Mayer, *Desires of Mothers*, 91.

63. Mayer, *Desires of Mothers*, 91.

64. Mayer, *Desires of Mothers*, 118.

65. Susan Howe, letter to Lyn Hejinian, 13 July 1980, Hejinian Papers, Mandeville (74, 4, 18).

66. Mayer, *Desires of Mothers*, 16.

67. Mayer, *Desires of Mothers*, 190.

68. Mayer, *Desires of Mothers*, 155.

69. Mayer, *Desires of Mothers*, 53.

70. Mayer, *Desires of Mothers*, 153.

71. Mayer, *Desires of Mothers*, 208.

72. Mayer, *Desires of Mothers*, 59– 60.

73. In *The Waves*, for example, the narrator observes: "[M]y imagination is too feeble. But some doubt remained. A shadow flitted through my mind like moths' wings." Virginia Woolf, *The Waves* (London: Hogarth, 1931; 1990), 179.

74. Mayer, *Desires of Mothers*, 53. In an interview with Janet Ruth Falon, Howe revealed that, like Mayer, she read Woolf as a young mother living in isolation and mostly alone. Like Mayer, Howe also was divided over her desire to write and her responsibilities as a mother. She states: "When you reach that point where no concessions in art are possible, you face true power, *alone*. But if you have young children you will make all sorts of concessions. Writing still seems more threatening to me than painting because it becomes so self-absorbing. I saw my desire as a threat to my children" (34).

75. Mayer, excerpt from *Studying Hunger*, 414.

76. Mayer, *Desires of Mothers*, 169.

77. Mayer, *Desires of Mothers*, 26.

78. Mayer, *Desires of Mothers*, 27.

79. Mayer, *Desires of Mothers*, 146.

80. Mayer, *Desires of Mothers*, 181.

81. Mayer, *Desires of Mothers*, 58.

82. William Corbett and Michael Gizzi, eds. *Writing for Bernadette* (Great Barrington: The Figures, 1995).

83. The passage may be read (out of the context of the rest of the poem) as an allegory about Bernadette Mayer. Not only did Mayer become interested in conceptual art in the late seventies, but in *The Desires of Mothers*, she writes of coming "from the saintly stodgy Germans with . . . no tragedy or drama . . . and little fragility among our nerves." Mayer, *Desires of Mothers*, 166. "Histoire de Florida" has also been published in Robert Greeley's *Life and Death* (New York: New Directions, 1998).

84. See *The Poetry Project Newsletter* 146 (October/November, 1992).

85. Baker, "Bernadette Mayer," 170.
86. Gertrude Stein, *Four Saints in Three Acts*, in *Selected Writings of Gertrude Stein*, ed. Carl Van Vechten (New York: Vintage, 1962), 581.

11. Taking a Poethical Perspective (167–178)

1. Joan Retallack, "The Poethical Wager" *Onward: Contemporary Poetry and Poetics*, ed. Peter Baker (New York: Peter Lang, 1996), 301–2.
2. Joan Retallack, "Blue Notes on the Know Ledge," *Poetics Journal* 10 (June 1998): 43.
3. R. G. H. Siu, *The Tao of Science* (Cambridge MA: MIT, 1957).
4. Joan Retallack, "Introduction: Conversations in Retrospect," *Musicage: Cage Muses on Words, Art, Music* (Hanover, NH: UP of New England for Wesleyan UP, 1996), xxii.
5. Retallack, "Poethical Wager," 294.
6. Retallack, "Poethical Wager," 304.
7. Retallack, "Poethical Wager," 305.
8. Joan Retallack, *WESTERN CIV CONT'D, AN OPEN BOOK* (Riverdale: Pyramid Atlantic, 1995).
9. Joan Retallack, "WESTERN CIV CONT'D: A Brief Experiment in Linguistics," *How To Do Things with Words* (Los Angeles: Sun & Moon, 1998), 85–92.
10. Hank Lazer, "Partial to Error: Joan Retallack's *Errata 5uite*," *Opposing Poetries*, vol. 2 (Evanston: Northwestern UP, 1996), 72.
11. Quoted by Joan Retallack in *Afterrimages* (Hanover, NH: UP of New England for Wesleyan UP, 1995): n. pag.
12. Jacques Derrida, *Memoires for Paul de Man* (New York: Columbia UP, 1986), 66.
13. Homer, *The Illiad* 1.21.108. Translated by Simon Goldhill in "Refracting Classical Vision: Changing Cultures of Viewing," *Vision in Context: Historical and Contemporary Perspectives on Sight*, ed. Teresa Brennan and Martin Jay (New York: Routledge, 1996), 17.
14. Simon Goldhill, "Refracting Classical Vision," 20.
15. Walter Benjamin, "Theses on the Philosophy of History," *Illuminations: Essays and Reflections*, ed. Hannah Arendt, trans. Harry Zohn (London: Jonathan Cape, 1970), 265.
16. Joan Retallack, "Secnahc Gnikat: Taking Chances," *Moving Borders: Three Decades of Innovative Writing by Women*, ed. Mary Margaret Sloan (Jersey City, NJ: Talisman, 1998), 713.
17. Retallack, "Blue Notes on the Know Ledge," 43.
18. In *Metaphysics*, Aristotle relies on epistemological dualisms to define and schematize meaning, including "limit and unlimited, odd and even, one and plurality, right and left, male and female, resting and moving, straight and curved, light and darkness, good and bad, square and oblong." See *The Complete Works of Aristotle*, trans. W. D. Ross, ed. Jonathan Barnes (Princeton, NJ: Princeton UP, 1984), I(A).5.9.986a1.
19. Retallack, *Afterrimages* 15, 22.
20. Retallack, "Secnahc Gnikat: Taking Chances," 713.
21. Retallack, *Afterrimages*, 5.
22. Retallack, "Blue Notes on the Know Ledge," 50.

23. Joan Retallack, *Afterrimages* 6.

24. Page DuBois, *Sappho Is Burning* (Chicago: U of Chicago P, 1995), 3.

25. DuBois, *Sappho Is Burning*, 79.

26. DuBois, *Sappho Is Burning*, 6.

27. Retallack, *Afterrimages*, 6.

28. Sappho, *The Poems and Fragments*, ed. and trans. C. R. Haines (London: George Routledge, 1926), 199.

29. Retallack, "Blue Notes on the Know Ledge," 45.

30. DuBois, *Sappho Is Burning*, 3.

31. Retallack, *Afterrimages*, 7.

32. Retallack, "Blue Notes on the Know Ledge," 44.

33. Retallack, *Afterrimages*, 7.

34. Anne Laskaya, *Chaucer's Approach to Gender in* The Canterbury Tales, Chaucer Studies, vol. 23 (Cambridge: D. S. Brewer, 1995), 45.

35. Joan Retallack, interview conducted by P. Inman, *Washington Review* 13.2 (1987): 26.

36. Retallack, *Afterrimages*, 10.

37. Alice Jardine, *Gynesis: Configurations of Woman and Modernity* (Ithaca, NY: Cornell UP, 1985), 93.

38. Retallack, *Afterrimages*, 9.

39. Retallack, *Afterrimages*, 17.

40. Retallack, *Afterrimages*, 21.

41. Retallack, "Blue Notes on the Know Ledge," 47.

42. Retallack, *Afterrimages*, 26.

43. Retallack, *Afterrimages*, 13.

44. Retallack, *Afterrimages*, 29.

45. Retallack, *Afterrimages*, 22.

46. Retallack, *Afterrimages*, 9.

47. Retallack, *Afterrimages*, 11.

48. Retallack, *Afterrimages*, 27.

49. Retallack, *Afterrimages*, 33.

50. Retallack, *Afterrimages*, 33, 32.

51. DuBois, *Sappho Is Burning*, 75.

12. *Cultural Recovery or Contractual Release (pp. 179–190)*

1. Carole-Anne Tyler, "Passing: Narcissism, Identity, and Difference," *Differences* 6.2– 3 (1994): 215.

2. *The Liberties* was originally published as a pamphlet (Guilford, CT: Loon, 1980). It has been reprinted in *Defenestration of Prague* (New York: Kulchur Foundation, 1983) and in *The Europe of Trusts* (Los Angeles: Sun & Moon, 1990). I have used this last reprint for all references in this chapter.

3. Susan Howe, "Scattering as Behavior toward Risk," *Singularities* (Hanover, NH: UP of New England for Wesleyan UP, 1990).

4. Susan Howe, letter to Lyn Hejinian, 26 August 1979, Hejinian Papers, Mandeville (74, 4, 18).

5. Samuel Johnson, "*King Lear*," *Johnson on Shakespeare*, ed. Arthur Sherbo, vol. 2 (New Haven, CT: Yale UP, 1968), 704.

6. Susan Howe, *My Emily Dickinson* (Berkeley, CA: North Atlantic, 1985), 107.

7. Susan Howe, *The Difficulties* interview, conducted by Tom Beckett, *The Difficulties* 3.2 (1989): 24.

8. Howe, *My Emily Dickinson* 17–18.

9. Susan Howe, "There Are Not Leaves Enough to Crown to Cover to Crown to Cover," *The Europe of Trusts* (Los Angeles: Sun & Moon, 1990), 14.

10. Susan Howe, "The Captivity and Restoration of Mrs. Mary Rowlandson," *The Birth-Mark: Unsettling the Wilderness in American Literary History* (Hanover, NH: UP of New England for Wesleyan UP, 1993), 96.

11. Howe, *The Difficulties* interview, 25.

12. Susan Howe, "Articulation of Sound Forms in Time," *Singularities*, 33.

13. Henry Sayre, *The Object of Performance: The American Avant-Garde since 1970* (Chicago: U of Chicago P, 1989), 18.

14. Howe, "There Are Not Leaves Enough," 13.

15. Georges Van Den Abbeele, introduction, *Community at Loose Ends*, ed. Miami Theory Collective (Minneapolis: U of Minnesota P, 1991), xiv.

16. Josette Féral, "Antigone, or the Irony of the Tribe," *Diacritics* (September 1978): 2.

17. Lynn Keller, *Forms of Expansion: Recent Long Poems by Women* (Chicago: U of Chicago P, 1999), 237.

18. Susan Howe, "Thorow," *Singularities*, 41.

19. Susan Howe, letter to Lyn Hejinian, n.d., Hejinian Papers, Mandeville (74, 4, 18).

20. Susan Howe, "Talisman Interview," conducted by Edward Foster, *The Birth-Mark*, 166.

21. Janet Ruth Falon, "Speaking with Susan Howe," *Difficulties* 3.2 (1989): 40.

22. Howe, "Talisman Interview," 166.

23. Howe, "Talisman Interview," 169.

24. Susan Howe, *The Liberties*, 149.

25. Rachel Blau DuPlessis, *The Pink Guitar: Writing as Feminist Practice* (New York: Routledge, 1990), 136.

26. DuPlessis, *Pink Guitar*, 136.

27. William Shakespeare, *King Lear* (1.1.92). As quoted by Howe in *The Liberties*, 170.

28. Jean-Luc Nancy, *The Experience of Freedom*, trans. Bridget McDonald (Stanford, CA: Stanford UP, 1993), 21.

29. Nancy, *The Experience of Freedom*, 154.

30. Nancy, *The Experience of Freedom*, 20.

31. Giorgio Agamben, *The Coming Community*, trans. Michael Hardt (Minneapolis: Routledge, 1993), 14.

32. Howe, *The Difficulties* interview, 26.

33. Quoted by Peter Fenves in foreword to Jean-Luc Nancy's *Experience of Freedom*, xxxi.

34. Howe, *The Difficulties* interview, 20.

35. As quoted by Howe in "Thorow," 42.

36. Harold Williams, introduction, *Journal to Stella*, by Jonathan Swift, ed. Harold Williams (Oxford: Clarendon, 1948), lvi.

37. Susan Howe, letter to Bernadette Mayer, 18 April 1979, Mayer Papers, Mandeville (420, 9, 22).

38. As quoted by Howe in *The Difficulties* interview, 18.

39. Julia Kristeva, *Revolution in Poetic Language*, trans. Margaret Waller (New York: Columbia UP, 1984), 25–30.

40. Howe, *The Difficulties* interview, 18.

41. Susan Howe, "Submarginalia," *Birth-Mark* 27.

42. Howe, *The Difficulties* interview, 20.

43. Howe, *Liberties*, 158.

44. Quoted by Harold Williams in the introduction to *Journal to Stella*, liii–iv.

45. Howe, *The Difficulties* interview, 21.

46. Howe, *Liberties*, 171.

47. Susan Howe, letter to Lyn Hejinian, 17 January 1979, Hejinian Papers, Mandeville (74, 4, 18).

48. Susan Howe, letter to Lyn Hejinian, 26 August 1979, Hejinian Papers, Mandeville (74, 4, 18).

49. Susan Howe, interview, conducted by Lynn Keller, *Contemporary Literature* 36.1 (spring 1995): 13.

50. Howe, *Liberties*, 162.

51. Howe, *Liberties*, 163. The image also inverts the Elizabethan custom of having boys act out the female roles of stage drama.

52. Nicole Brossard, *The Aerial Letter*, trans. Marlene Wildeman (Toronto: Women's Press, 1988), 85.

53. Susan Howe, letter to Lyn Hejinian, n.d., Hejinian Papers, Mandeville (74, 4, 18).

54. Howe, *Liberties*, 184.

55. Howe, *The Difficulties* interview, 20.

56. As quoted by Peter Fenves, foreword to Nancy, *Experience of Freedom*, xix.

57. As quoted by Peter Fenves, foreword to Nancy, *Experience of Freedom*, xix.

13. Cutting Corners in Tina Darragh's American Pi (191–203)

1. Tina Darragh, quoted in Tina Darragh and Jena Osman, *Philly Talks* 4 (1998): n. pag.

2. Joan Retallack in Tina Darragh, interview, conducted by Joan Retallack, *Aerial* 5 (1989): 80.

3. Gertrude Stein, *The Geographical History of America or the Relation of Human Nature to the Human Mind* (Baltimore: Johns Hopkins UP, 1936, 1973), 112.

4. Tina Darragh, *Striking Resemblance* (Providence, RI: Burning Deck, 1989), 13, 14.

5. Sherry Turkle, quoted by Tina Darragh in *a(gain)²st the odds* (Elmwood, CT: Potes & Poets Press, 1989), n. pag.

6. Tina Darragh, *Striking Resemblance*, 15.

7. Joan Retallack, "Post-Scriptum-High-Modern," *Postmodern Genres*, ed. Marjorie Perloff (Norman: U of Oklahoma P, 1989), 266.

8. P. Inman, quoted by Tina Darragh in *Striking Resemblance*, 16.

9. P. Inman, *Ocker* (Berkeley, CA: Tuumba, 1982).

10. Joan Retallack, "The Meta-Physick of Play: *L=A=N=G=U=A=G=E* U.S.A.," *Parnassus* 12.1 (1984): 226.

11. Darragh, *Striking Resemblance*, 16.

12. H. L. Mencken, *The American Language: Supplement 1* (New York: Alfred A Knopf, 1945), 217.

13. Noah Webster, *Dissertations on the English Language* (Boston, 1789), 22–23. Quoted in H. L. Mencken, *The American Language*, 25–26.

14. Rev. Edward Gepp, quoted by H. L. Mencken, *The American Language* (New York: Alfred A. Knopf, 1945), 129.

15. Darragh, *Striking Resemblance*, 18.

16. Darragh, *Striking Resemblance*, 20.

17. Tina Darragh, "'s the any ME *finel mes:* A Reflection on Donna Haraway's 'Cyborg Manifesto,'" *Moving Borders: Three Decades of Innovative Writing by Women*, ed. Mary Margaret Sloan (Jersey City, NJ: Talisman House, 1998), 699.

18. Darragh, *Striking Resemblance*, 21.

19. Darragh, *Striking Resemblance*, 22.

20. Darragh, *Striking Resemblance*, 22.

21. Darragh, *Striking Resemblance*, 23–24.

22. Susan Howe, "P. Inman, *Platin*," *L=A=N=G=U=A=G=E* (1980): n. pag.

23. Susan Howe, *Talisman* interview, conducted by Edward Foster, rpt. in *The Birth-mark: Unsettling Wilderness in American Literary History* (Hanover, NH: UP of New England for Wesleyan UP, 1993), 173.

24. Mencken, *The American Language*, 463.

25. Tina Darragh, interview conducted by Joan Retallack, *Aerial* 5 (1989):70.

26. Quoted by Frank MacShane in *The Life of Raymond Chandler* (London: Hamish Hamilton, 1976; 1986), 49.

27. Darragh, *Striking Resemblance*, 27.

28. Quoted by Tina Darragh in *Striking Resemblance*, 32.

29. Darragh, *Striking Resemblance*, 28.

30. Darragh, *Striking Resemblance*, 31.

31. Quoted in MacShane, *Life of Raymond Chandler*, 19.

32. James M. Cain, *Mildred Pierce* (Feltham, UK: Hamlyn, 1943, 1982), 13.

33. Cain, *Mildred Pierce*, 167.

34. Tina Darragh, "Error Message," *Poetics Journal* 5 (1985): 120.

35. Darragh, *Striking Resemblance*, 56.

36. Quoted in David Madden, *Cain's Craft* (Metuchen, NJ: Scarecrow, 1985), 138.

37. Quoted in MacShane, *Life of Raymond Chandler*, 58.

38. Darragh, *Striking Resemblance*, 37.

39. Darragh, *Striking Resemblance*, 38.

40. R. L. Gregory, *Eye and Brain: The Psychology of Seeing*, 4th ed. (Princeton, NJ: Princeton UP, 1966; 1990), 230.

41. Tina Darragh, *Striking Resemblance*, 40.

42. Jess Stein, ed. *Random House Dictionary of the English Language* (New York: Random House, 1981), 684.

43. Joan Retallack also points to this simultaneous opacity and transparency in terms of P. Inman's work, referring specifically to the Necker cube. See "Post-Scriptum-High-Modern," 265.

44. Tina Darragh, "Procedure," *The L=A=N=G=U=A=G=E Book* (Carbondale: Southern Illinois UP, 1984), 107–8.

45. Tina Darragh, quoted in Jena Osman, "Tina Darragh and Jena Osman," *Philly Talks* 4 (February 1998): n. pag.

46. Darragh, *Striking Resemblance*, 35.
47. Darragh, *Striking Resemblance*, 48.
48. Darragh, *Striking Resemblance*, 49–50.
49. Tina Darragh, interview conducted by Joan Retallack, *Aerial* 5 (1989): 76.
50. Joan Retallack, "Post-Scriptum-High-Modern," 265.

14. "I See Words" (204–216)

1. Hannah Weiner, *Code Poems* (Barrytown, NY: Station Hill, 1982).
2. Hannah Weiner, *Clairvoyant Journal* (New York: Angel Hair, 1978).
3. Ron Silliman, *The New Sentence* (New York: Roof, 1989), 188.
4. See Hannah Weiner, endnote, *Silent Teachers Remembered Sequel* (Providence, RI: Tender Buttons, 1994), n. pag.
5. Weiner, endnote, *Silent Teachers*, n. pag.
6. "Tarpsichordist" also could be associated with dancing, given that Terpsichore was the muse of dance.
7. Joseph Grigely applies this to the "work" of literature in *Textualterity: Art, Theory, and Textual Criticism* (Ann Arbor: U of Michigan P, 1995), 2–3. See Mohsen Mostafavi and David Leatherbarrow, *On Weathering: The Life of Buildings in Time* (Cambridge, MA: MIT, 1993), 64, 69.
8. Hannah Weiner, "Forum," with P. Inman, James Sherry, and Nick Piombino, *The Politics of Poetic Form: Poetry and Public Policy*, ed. Charles Bernstein (New York: Roof, 1990), 227.
9. See Helen Sword's "Modernist Mediumship" in *Modernism, Gender, and Culture: A Cultural Studies Approach*, ed. Lisa Rado (New York: Garland, 1997), 65–77.
10. Rachel Blau DuPlessis, "Manifests," *Diacritics* 26.3–4 (fall–winter 1996): 35.
11. Weiner, *Clairvoyant Journal*, entry dated 3/1.
12. Weiner, *Clairvoyant Journal*, entry dated 3/1.
13. Bernadette Mayer and the Members of the St. Mark's Church Poetry Project Writing Workshop, 1971–75, "Experiments," *In the American Tree: Language, Realism, Poetry*, ed. Ron Silliman (Orono, ME: National Poetry Foundation, 1986), 558.
14. Bernadette Mayer et al., "Experiments," 558.
15. Hannah Weiner, interview, conducted by Charles Bernstein, LINEbreak program, 1995. See <http://wings.buffalo.edu/epc/linebreak/programs/weiner>.
16. Weiner, *Clairvoyant Journal*, n. pag.
17. Charles Bernstein quotes Weiner's phrase of "group mind" in "Making Words Visible/Hannah Weiner" in *Content's Dream: Essays 1975–1984* (Los Angeles: Sun & Moon, 1986), 269.
18. John Rodden, The Politics of Literary Reputation: *The Making and Claiming of "St. George" Orwell* (New York: Oxford UP, 1989), 418.
19. Hannah Weiner, letter to Bernadette Mayer, n.d., Mayer Papers, Mandeville (420, 16, 12–13).
20. Hannah Weiner, *Spoke* (Washington, DC: Sun & Moon, 1984), 7.
21. Maria Damon, "Hannah Weiner Beside Herself: The Trauma of Clairvoyance," Draft of paper presented at the 1996 MLA Convention.
22. Weiner, *Spoke*, 80.
23. Weiner, *Spoke*, 81.

24. DuPlessis, "Manifests," 36.

25. Hannah Weiner, letter to Bernadette Mayer, 27 August 1975, Mayer Papers, Mandeville (420, 16, 12–13).

26. Weiner, *Spoke*, 88.

27. Weiner, *Spoke*, 103.

28. Weiner, *Spoke*, 94.

29. See Weiner, *Spoke*, particularly at 35: "I get my period twice Aug again."

30. Leslie Heywood, *Dedication to Hunger: The Anorexic Aesthetic in Modern Culture* (Berkeley: U of California P, 1996).

31. Weiner, *Spoke*, 95.

32. Weiner, *Spoke*, 104.

33. Maria Damon, *The Dark End of the Street: Margins in American Vanguard Poetry* (Minneapolis: U of Minnesota P, 1993), 37–38.

34. Jackson Mac Low, rev. of *Persia, Sixteen*, and *Code Poems*, by Laura Moriarty and Hannah Weiner, *Poetics Journal* 4 (May 1984): 92.

35. Weiner, *Spoke*, 53.

36. Weiner, *Spoke*, 79.

37. Jackson Mac Low points this out in his review of *Persia, Sixteen*, and *Code Poems*, 92.

38. Damon, "Hannah Weiner beside Herself."

39. Weiner, *Spoke*, 63.

40. Weiner, *Spoke*, 21.

41. Weiner, *Spoke*, 10.

42. Weiner, *Spoke*, 8.

43. Weiner, *Spoke*, 9.

44. Weiner, *Spoke*, 8.

45. Weiner, *Spoke*, 8.

46. Weiner, *Spoke*, 20.

47. Weiner, *Spoke*, 9.

48. Weiner, *Spoke*, 9.

49. Weiner, *Spoke*, 100.

50. Weiner, *Spoke*, 15.

51. Weiner, *Spoke*, 17.

52. Weiner, *Spoke*, 12.

53. Weiner, *Spoke*, 81.

54. Weiner, *Clairvoyant Journal*, entry dated May 12.

55. Weiner, *Spoke*, 92.

56. Weiner, *Spoke*, 92.

57. Weiner, *Spoke*, 23, 21.

58. As Kate Fagan pointed out in conversation, "steps" could also refer to Ron Silliman's *Sitting Up, Standing, Taking Steps* (Berkeley, CA: Tuumba, 1978).

59. Weiner, *Spoke*, 82.

60. Weiner, *Spoke*, 104.

61. See Linda Kinnahan, "'this/lyric forever error': Female Subjectivity and the Feminist Community in American and British Women's Poetry," paper presented at the Assembling Alternatives Conference, Durham, NH, 30 August 1996.

62. Weiner, *Spoke*, 97, 94.

63. Walt Whitman, *Leaves of Grass*, vol. 1 of *The Works of Walt Whitman*, 2 vols. (New York, Funk and Wagnalls, 1968), 109.

64. Weiner, *Spoke*, 40.

65. Damon, *Dark End of the Street*, 21.

66. Weiner, *Silent Teachers*, 33. Weiner undermines this notion of history with an addendum: "the next generation could be the one that is done and gone and who is teaching you now."

67. Weiner, *Silent Teachers*, 15–16.

68. It also echoes the line in *Spoke:* "WHAT IS THE STYLE PREVALENT IN OUR OWN AGE CLASSICAL," 31.

69. As quoted by John Rodden in *The Politics of Literary Reputation*, 59.

70. Lee Ann Brown, "From CUZ to zuk," *Chain* 1 (spring/summer 1994): 18.

71. Weiner, *Silent Teachers*, 16; Barrett Watten, *Bad History* (Berkeley, CA: Atelos, 1998).

72. Weiner, *Silent Teachers*, 16, 15.

73. Hannah Weiner, *Silent Teachers*, 17.

74. Hannah Weiner, "Astral Visions," *Mr. Knife, Miss Fork: Performances* (Los Angeles: Sun & Moon, forthcoming). For preview, see <http://wings.buffalo.edu/epc/authors/weiner/astral.html>.

15. Attention and Alterity in the Poetry of Rae Armantrout and Fanny Howe (217–232)

1. Giorgio Agamben, *Stanzas: Word and Phantasm in Western Culture*, trans. Ronald L. Martinez (Minneapolis: U of Minnesota P, 1993), 32.

2. Rachel Blau DuPlessis, "On the Davidson/Weinberger Exchange," *Sulfur* 22 (1988): 191.

3. Susan Howe, letter to Lyn Hejinian, 26 August 1979, Hejinian Papers, Mandeville (74, 4, 18).

4. Ezra Pound, *The Cantos of Ezra Pound* (London: Faber and Faber, 1954, 1975), 802.

5. Louis Zukofsky, *Prepositions: The Collected Critical Essays of Louis Zukofsky* (Berkeley: U of California P, 1967, 1981), 13.

6. DuPlessis, "On the Davidson/Weinberger Exchange," 192.

7. Rae Armantrout, interview, conducted by Manuel Brito, *A Suite of Poetic Voices* (Santa Brigida, Canary Islands: Kadle, 1992), 22.

8. Fanny Howe, "The Contemporary Logos," *Code of Signals: Recent Writings in Poetics*, ed. Michael Palmer (Berkeley, CA: North Atlantic, 1983), 47.

9. See in particular George Oppen's *Seascape: Needle's Eye* (Fremont, MI: Sumac, 1972).

10. Quoted as an epigraph in Dorothy Tuck McFarland, *Simone Weil* (New York: Frederick Ungar, 1983).

11. Simone Weil, *Gravity and Grace*, trans. Emma Craufurd (London and New York: Ark, 1952; 1987), 10.

12. Simone Weil, *Gravity and Grace*, 34.

13. Rae Armantrout, *Made to Seem* (Los Angeles: Sun & Moon, 1995), 21–22.

14. Weil, *Gravity and Grace*, 10.

15. Weil, *Gravity and Grace*, 73.

16. Rae Armantrout, "Travels," *Extremities* (Great Barrington, MA: The Figures, 1978), 7.

17. Fanny Howe, "The Tunnel Is a Lung," *The End* (Los Angeles: Littoral Books, 1992), 58.

18. Fanny Howe, *O'Clock* (London: Reality Street Editions, 1995), 51.

19. Fanny Howe, "Bewilderment," *HOW2* 1.1 (March 1999).

20. Hélène Cixous, "Sorties," in Hélène Cixous and Catherine Clement, *The Newly Born Woman*, trans. Betsy Wing (Minneapolis: U of Minnesota P, 1986), 86.

21. Simone Weil, *Waiting for God*, trans. Emma Craufurd (New York: Harper & Row, 1973), 92.

22. Nathaniel Tarn, "Voice Politics/Body Politic," *Talus* 10 (1997): 44.

23. Hannah Arendt, *The Human Condition* (Chicago: U of Chicago P, 1958). Arendt's unfinished *The Life of the Mind* investigates issues previously touched upon by Weil (New York: Harcourt Brace Jovanovich, 1978), vols. 1 and 2.

24. Rae Armantrout, *The Invention of Hunger* (Berkeley, CA: Tuumba, 1979), n. pag.

25. Weil, *Gravity and Grace*, 84.

26. Weil, *Gravity and Grace*, 116.

27. Fanny Howe, *The End* (Los Angeles: Littoral Books, 1992), 5.

28. Fanny Howe, "The Ecstatic," *Ironwood* 24 (1984): 18.

29. Rae Armantrout, "It," *Boxkite* 1 (1997): 135–36.

30. Nathaniel Tarn, *Views from the Weaving Mountain: Selected Essays in Poetics and Anthropology* (Albuquerque: U of New Mexico P, 1991), 346.

31. Armantrout, *Made to Seem*, 56.

32. Fanny Howe, "The Lyrics," *The End* (Los Angeles: Littoral Books, 1992), 49.

33. Rae Armantrout, "Irony and Postmodern Poetry," *Moving Borders: Three Decades of Innovative Writing by Women*, ed. Mary Margaret Sloan (Jersey City, NJ: Talisman, 1998), 674.

34. Armantrout, *Extremities*, 25.

35. Fanny Howe, "The Lyrics," 36.

36. Armantrout, "Irony and Postmodern Poetry," 675.

37. Fanny Howe, "Scattered Light," *The Vineyard*, 1988; rpt. in *Moving Borders*, 140.

38. Fanny Howe, "The Lyrics," 48.

39. Fanny Howe, "The Ecstatic," 18.

40. Weil, *Gravity and Grace*, 184.

41. Weil, *Gravity and Grace*, 185.

42. Fanny Howe, "The Lyrics," 33.

43. Weil, *Gravity and Grace*, 60.

44. Weil, *Gravity and Grace*, 131.

45. Rae Armantrout, *Necromance* (Los Angeles: Sun & Moon, 1991), 10.

46. Elizabeth Alvilda Petroff discusses this eroticism in *Body and Soul: Essays on Medieval Women and Mysticism* (New York: Oxford UP, 1994).

47. Fanny Howe, "The Lyrics," 52.

48. Armantrout, *Necromance*, 11.

49. Iris Marion Young, "Pregnant Embodiment: Subjectivity and Alienation," *Throwing Like a Girl and Other Essays in Feminist Philosophy and Social Theory* (Bloomington: Indiana UP, 1990), 163.

50. Fanny Howe, *The Vineyard*, 1988; rpt. in *Moving Borders*, 141.

51. Armantrout, *Invention of Hunger*, n. pag.

52. Armantrout, *Invention of Hunger*, n. pag.

53. Lyn Hejinian, interview, conducted by Andrew Schelling, *Jimmy & Lucy's House of K* 6 (1986): 5.

16. The Person as Chronic Text (233–248)

1. Lyn Hejinian, "The Quest for Knowledge in the Western Poem," *Disembodied Poetics: Annals of the Jack Kerouac School*, ed. Anne Waldman and Andrew Schelling (Albuquerque: U of New Mexico P, 1994), 175.
2. Marjorie Garber, "Introduction: Postmodernism and the Possibility of Biography," *The Seductions of Biography*, ed. Mary Rhiel and David Suchoff (New York and London: Routledge, 1996), 169.
3. Lyn Hejinian, "If Written Is Writing," *The L=A=N=G=U=A=G=E Book*, ed. Bruce Andrews and Charles Bernstein (Carbondale: Southern Illinois UP, 1984), 29.
4. Susan Howe, *A Bibliography of the King's Book or, Eikon Basilike* (Providence, RI: Paradigm, 1989); rpt. in *The Nonconformist's Memorial* (New York: New Directions, 1993), 50.
5. Jurgen Schlaeger, "Biography: Cult as Culture," *The Art of Literary Biography*, ed. John Batchelor (Oxford: Clarendon, 1995), 58.
6. Schlaeger, "Biography," 59.
7. Fanny Howe, "Artobiography," *Writing/Talks*, ed. Bob Perelman (Carbondale: Southern Illinois UP, 1985), 192.
8. Christie McDonald, "Personal Criticism: Dialogue of Differences," *Feminism beside Itself*, ed. Diane Elam and Robyn Wiegman (New York: Routledge, 1995), 239.
9. Toril Moi, *Simone de Beauvoir: The Making of an Intellectual Woman* (Oxford: Blackwell, 1994), 7.
10. Lyn Hejinian, letter to Ron Silliman, 14 October 1981, Silliman Papers, Mandeville (75, 9, 14).
11. Lyn Hejinian, "Lyn Hejinian and Tyrus Miller: An Exchange of Letters," *Paper Air* 4.2 (1989): 34.
12. Michel Foucault, *Politics, Philosophy, Culture: Interviews and Other Writings, 1977–1984*, trans. A. Sheridan et al., ed. L. Kritzman (New York: Routledge, 1988), 14.
13. Hejinian, "Lyn Hejinian and Tyrus Miller," 35.
14. Hejinian, "Lyn Hejinian and Tyrus Miller," 35.
15. Glenn Watkins, *Gesualdo: The Man and His Music*, 2nd ed. (Oxford: Clarendon, 1971, 1991).
16. Cecil Gray, "Carlo Gesualdo considered as a Murderer," *Carlo Gesualdo, Prince of Venosa: Musician and Murderer*, ed. Cecil Gray and Philip Heseltine (London: Kegan Paul, 1926; rpt. Westport, CT: Greenwood, 1971).
17. Lyn Hejinian, *A Thought Is the Bride of What Thinking* (Willits, CA: Tuumba, 1976) n. pag.
18. Gertrude Stein, "Composition as Explanation," *Selected Writings of Gertrude Stein*, ed. Carl Van Vechten (New York: Vintage, 1962), 516.
19. Charles Caramello, *Henry James, Gertrude Stein, and the Biographical Act* (Chapel Hill: U of North Carolina P, 1996), 11.
20. Igor Stravinsky, "Gesualdo di Venosa: New Perspectives," preface to Glenn Watkins's *Gesualdo*, vii–viii.

21. Hejinian, *A Thought Is the Bride*, n. pag.

22. T. S. Eliot argues "the more perfect the artist, the more completely separate in him will be the man who suffers and the mind which creates." See "Tradition and the Individual Talent," *Selected Prose of T. S. Eliot*, ed. Frank Kermode (London: Faber and Faber, 1975), 41.

23. Lyn Hejinian, *Gesualdo* (Berkeley, CA: Tuumba Press, 1978), n. pag.; rpt. in Hejinian, *The Cold of Poetry* (Los Angeles: Sun & Moon, 1994), 63.

24. Gray, "Carlo Gesualdo Considered as a Murderer," 65.

25. Gray, "Carlo Gesualdo Considered as a Murderer," 73.

26. Gray, "Carlo Gesualdo Considered as a Murderer," 72.

27. Hejinian, *Gesualdo*, 66

28. Watkins, *Gesualdo*, 130–31.

29. Watkins, *Gesualdo*, 3.

30. Hejinian, *Gesualdo*, 64.

31. Watkins, *Gesualdo*, 7.

32. Hejinian, *Gesualdo*, 74–75.

33. Watkins, *Gesualdo*, 9.

34. Hejinian, *Gesualdo*, 75.

35. Watkins, *Gesualdo*, 10.

36. Watkins, *Gesualdo*, 11.

37. Hejinian, *A Thought Is the Bride*, n. pag.

38. Rachel Blau DuPlessis, "Manifests," *Diacritics* 26.3–4 (fall-winter 1996): 51.

39. Rosmarie Waldrop, *Differences for Four Hands* (Philadelphia: Singing Horse, 1984); rpt. in *Denver Quarterly* 31.1 (summer 1996): 123–34.

40. Rosmarie Waldrop, "Thinking of Follows," *Onwards: Contemporary Poetry and Poetics*, ed. Peter Baker (New York: Peter Lang, 1996), 81.

41. Quoted by Susan Clark in "To See, or Theory," *Raddle Moon* 13 (1994): 38.

42. Waldrop, "Thinking of Follows," 81.

43. Hejinian, *Gesualdo*, 71.

44. Waldrop, *Differences for Four Hands*, 125.

45. Walter Benjamin, "On Some Motifs in Baudelaire," *Illuminations*, ed. Hannah Arendt, trans. Harry Zohn (London: Jonathan Cape, 1970), 190.

46. Lyn Hejinian, "Chronic Texts," Hejinian Papers, Mandeville (75, 9, 14) 1.

47. Lyn Hejinian, *Writing Is an Aid to Memory* (Berkeley, CA: The Figures, 1978; Los Angeles: Sun & Moon, 1996), n. pag.

48. Hejinian, "Chronic Texts," 1.

49. Hejinian, "Chronic Texts," 2.

50. Hejinian, "Chronic Texts," 3.

51. Hejinian, "Chronic Texts," 3.

52. Hejinian, "Chronic Texts," 3.

53. Lyn Hejinian, *My Life*, 2nd ed. (Los Angeles: Sun & Moon, 1987), 21.

54. Hejinian, *My Life*, 22.

55. Hejinian, "Chronic Texts," 4.

56. Lyn Hejinian, letter to Susan Howe, dated 29 August Tuesday, Howe Papers, Mandeville (201, 1, 8).

57. Hejinian, "Chronic Texts," 4–5.

58. Hejinian, *My Life*, 7.

59. Hejinian, "Chronic Texts," 5.

60. It is also one of the earliest references to the "cell," which she would later

use to again meditate on thought and language in *The Cell* (Los Angeles: Sun & Moon, 1992).

61. Hejinian, "Chronic Texts," 5.

62. Hejinian, "Chronic Texts," 6.

63. Hejinian, "Chronic Texts," 6.

64. Hejinian, "Chronic Texts," 6–7.

65. Hejinian, "Chronic Texts," 7.

66. Hejinian, "Chronic Texts," 8.

67. Hejinian, "Chronic Texts," 7.

68. Hejinian, "Chronic Texts," 8.

69. Hejinian, "Chronic Texts," 8.

70. Spenser's *Epithalamion* has many other structural details. These are examined by A. Kent Hieatt in *Short Time's Endless Monument: The Symbolism of Numbers in Edmund Spenser's "Epithalamion"* (New York: Columbia UP, 1960; rpt. London: Kennikat, 1972).

71. Alastair Fowler, *Triumphal Forms: Structural Patterns in Elizabethan Poetry* (Cambridge: Cambridge UP, 1970). I am grateful to Ken Ruthven for drawing the numerological aspects of Hejinian's *My Life* to my attention.

72. Lyn Hejinian, letter to Susan Howe, dated 29 August Tuesday, Howe Papers, Mandeville (201, 1, 8).

73. Hejinian. *Writing Is an Aid to Memory*, n. pag.

74. Stein wrote a series of short pieces about money that were published in *How Writing Is Written*, vol 2 of *Previously Uncollected Writings of Gertrude Stein*, ed. Robert Bartlett Haas (Santa Barbara, CA: Black Sparrow, 1977), 106–112.

75. Hejinian. *Writing Is an Aid to Memory*, n. pag; *My Life*, 7.

76. Hejinian, *My Life*, 7; *Writing Is an Aid to Memory*, n. pag.

77. Hejinian, "Chronic Texts," 6.

78. Lyn Hejinian, letter to Rosmarie Waldrop, 30 September 1984, Hejinian Papers, Mandeville (74, 7, 16).

79. Lyn Hejinian, letter to Rosmarie Waldrop, 30 September 1984.

80. Hejinian, letter to Rosmarie Waldrop, 30 September 1984.

81. While the collection did not eventuate at that stage, a similar collection was put together by Douglas Messerli and published as *The Cold of Poetry* (Los Angeles: Sun & Moon, 1994).

82. Douglas Messerli, letter to Lyn Hejinian, 20 December 1984, Hejinian Papers, Mandeville (224, 42, 7).

83. Lyn Hejinian, letter to Douglas Messerli, 20 March 1986, Sun & Moon Papers, Mandeville (224, 42, 7).

84. Lyn Hejinian, letter to Douglas Messerli, 18 November 1986, Sun & Moon Papers, Mandeville (224, 42, 7).

85. Lyn Hejinian, letter to Jacki Ochs, 8 November 1983, Hejinian Papers, Mandeville (74, 6, 9).

86. Lyn Hejinian, letter to Susan Howe, 21 November 1987, Howe Papers, Mandeville (201, 1, 8).

87. Lyn Hejinian, "From My Life (The Nineties)," *Out of Everywhere: Linguistically Innovative Poetry by Women in North America and the UK*, ed. Maggie O'Sullivan (London: Reality Street Editions, 1996), 63.

88. Nancy K. Miller, "Men's Reading, Women's Writing: Gender and the Rise of the Novel," *The Politics of Tradition: Placing Women in French Literature*, ed. Joan DeJean and Nancy K. Miller, Yale French Studies 75 (New Haven, CT: Yale UP

1988), 49. She further develops this concept in *French Dressing: Women, Men and Ancien Regime Fiction* (New York: Routledge, 1995), particularly in the opening chapter, "Repairing the Tradition."

89. Hejinian, *Gesualdo*, 69.

Conclusion (249–262)

1. See Janet Wolff, "The Female Stranger: Marginality and Modes of Writing," *Resident Alien: Feminist Cultural Criticism* (Cambridge: Polity, 1995), and Judith Butler, *Gender Trouble: Feminism and the Subversion of Identity* (New York: Routledge, 1990), particularly 2–3.

2. Jean-Luc Nancy, *The Inoperative Community*, trans. Peter Connor et al., ed. Peter Connor (Minneapolis: U of Minnesota P, 1991), 25.

3. See Jonathan Monroe's notes to "Syntextural Investigations," *Diacritics* 26.3–4 (fall-winter 1996): 135.

4. Carla Harryman and Lyn Hejinian, "The Wide Road," *Tessera* 15 (winter 1993): 56.

5. Wayne Koestenbaum, *Double Talk: The Erotics of Male Literary Collaboration* (New York: Routledge, 1989), 3.

6. Carey Kaplan and Ellen Cronan Rose, "Strange Bedfellows: Feminist Collaborations," *Signs* 18 (1993): 551.

7. Kaplan and Rose, "Strange Bedfellows," 549.

8. See, generally, Georges Bataille, *Eroticism: Death and Sensuality*, trans. Mary Dalwood (San Francisco: City Lights, 1986).

9. See, generally, Roland Barthes, *The Pleasure of the Text*, trans. Richard Miller (New York: Noonday, 1975).

10. Michel De Certeau, *The Practice of Everyday Life*, trans. Steven F. Rendall (Berkeley: U of California P, 1984), 115.

11. Lyn Hejinian, letter to Karen Kahn, 5 January 1994, Hejinian Papers, Mandeville (74, 23, 13).

12. Lyn Hejinian, *Sight*, by Lyn Hejinian and Leslie Scalapino (Washington, DC: Edge, 1999), 32.

13. Leslie Scalapino, "Experience," *Sight*, n. pag.

14. Scalapino, *Sight*, 36.

15. Hejinian, *Sight*, 58.

16. Joan Retallack and Phyllis Rosenzweig, "These Are the Gay Dissolute Streets of Yoshiwara," *Dog City* 2 (1980): n. pag.

17. Joan Retallack, letter to Lyn Hejinian, 10 October 1993, Hejinian Papers, Mandeville (74, 32, 6).

18. Joan Retallack, epilogue, "The Clouds: (This Is Not by Henrik Isbn)," by Lyn Hejinian and Joan Retallack, *Chain* 6 (1999): 119.

19. Lyn Hejinian, letter to Joan Retallack, 10 August 1993, Hejinian Papers, Mandeville (74, 32, 6).

20. In its debt to different styles, the collaboration also made Alice Notley think about a genealogy of American poetry. She wrote *Dr Williams' Heiresses* as a "pre-collaboration event." See Alice Notley, letter to Bernadette Mayer, 22 January 1980, Mayer Papers, Mandeville (420, 18, 9–10).

21. Bernadette Mayer, poem to Alice Notley, 8 August 1980, Mayer Papers, Mandeville (420, 18, 9–10).

22. Bernadette Mayer, letter to Lyn Hejinian, 1 September 1983, Hejinian Papers, Mandeville (74, 6, 1).

23. Mayer, letter to Lyn Hejinian, 1 September 1983.

24. Lyn Hejinian, letter to Peter Middleton, 2 February 1994, Hejinian Papers, Mandeville; (74, 26, 25); Carla Harryman, interview, conducted by Megan Simpson, *Contemporary Literature* 37.4 (1996): 525.

25. Harryman, interview, *Contemporary Literature*, 524–25.

26. Lyn Hejinian, interview, conducted by Charles Bernstein, LINEbreak program, 1996. See <http://wings.buffalo.edu/epc/linebreak/programs/hejinian>.

27. Carla Harryman, "Dialogue: Museo de Antropología, Mexico," by Steve Benson and Carla Harryman, *Poetics Journal* 8 (June 1989): 47.

28. Carla Harryman and Lyn Hejinian, "A Comment on 'The Wide Road' for O," *Subliminal Time*, ed. Leslie Scalapino (Oakland, CA: O Books, 1993), 83.

29. Lyn Hejinian, quoted by Barrett Watten in *Total Syntax* (Carbondale: Southern Illinois UP, 1985), 147.

30. Earl Miner, *Japanese Linked Poetry: An Account with Translations of Renga and Haikai Sequences* (Princeton, NJ: Princeton UP, 1979), x.

31. Matsuo Basho, "The Narrow Road to the Interior," trans. Earl Miner, *Japanese Linked Poetry*, 16.

32. Harryman and Hejinian, "Comment on 'The Wide Road,'" 84.

33. Harryman and Hejinian, "Comment on 'The Wide Road,'" 83.

34. Peter Cryle, *Geometry in the Boudoir: Configurations of French Erotic Narrative* (Ithaca, NY: Cornell UP, 1994), 147.

35. Chantal Thomas, "Fantasizing Juliette," *Sade and the Narrative of Transgression*, ed. David B. Allison et al. (Cambridge: Cambridge UP, 1995), 257.

36. Carla Harryman, interview, conducted by Chris Tysh, *Poetics Journal* 10 (June 1998): 211.

37. Carla Harryman and Lyn Hejinian, "The Wide Road," *Aerial* 5 (1989): 53.

38. Carla Harryman and Lyn Hejinian, "The Wide Road," *Tessera* 15 (winter 1993): 57.

39. Carla Harryman and Lyn Hejinian, "The Wide Road," *Avec* 4 (1991): 30.

40. Lyn Hejinian, "A Correspondence from 'The Wide Road,'" conducted by Carla Harryman and Lyn Hejinian, *Aerial* 5 (1989): 83.

41. Carla Harryman and Lyn Hejinian, "The Wide Road," *Everyday Life* 2 (1988): 4.

42. Hejinian, "Correspondence from 'The Wide Road,'" 39.

43. Harryman and Hejinian, "The Wide Road," *Aerial* 5 (1989): 52.

44. Carla Harryman, footnote to "Autonomy Speech," *There Never Was a Rose without a Thorn* (San Francisco: City Lights, 1995), 40.

45. Quoted by Leslie Scalapino in *The Public World/Syntactically Impermanence* (Hanover, NH: UP of New England for Wesleyan UP, 1999) 3.

46. Leslie Scalapino, "As: All Occurrence in Structure, Unseen—(Deer Night)," *The Public World/Syntactically Impermanence*, 126.

47. Jena Osman and Juliana Spahr, "Editors' Notes: Frameworks," *Chain* 1 (spring/summer 1994): 133.

48. Lisa Houston, "Domestic Bliss/Dominus Patrus," *Chain* 1 (spring/summer 1994): 156.

49. Lee Ann Brown, "Deep Gossip Not," *Chain* 1 (spring/summer 1994): 158.

50. Abigail Child, "Two Countries," *Chain* 1 (spring/summer 1994): 164; Tina Darragh, untitled, *Chain* 1 (spring/summer 1994): 190.

51. Johanna Drucker, "Statement for Editorial Forum," *Chain* 1 (spring/summer 1994): 37.

52. Lyn Hejinian, letter to Karen Kahn, 5 January 1994, Hejinian Papers, Mandeville (74, 23, 13).

53. Steve Benson, "On Collaboration," *Jimmy & Lucy's House of K* 9 (1989): 88.

54. Renée Riese Hubert, *Magnifying Mirror: Women, Surrealism and Partnership* (Lincoln: U of Nebraska P, 1994), 9.

55. "Engines" was published in Ron Silliman's *Demo to Ink* (Tucson, AZ: Chax, 1992).

56. This would subsequently appear in three separate publications: Steve Benson, *As Is* (Berkeley, CA: The Figures, 1978); Bob Perelman, *7 Works* (Berkeley, CA: The Figures, 1979); and Kit Robinson, *Down and Back* (Berkeley, CA: The Figures, 1978).

57. Lyn Hejinian and Kit Robinson, *Individuals* (Tucson, AZ: Chax, 1988).

58. Carla Harryman, "Belief," unpublished, n. pag.

59. Michel de Certeau, *The Practice of Everyday Life*, 174.

60. Lyn Hejinian, letter to Karen Kahn, 5 January 1994, Hejinian Papers, Mandeville (74, 23, 13).

61. Scalapino, *Sight*, 112.

Works Cited

Abbeele, Georges Van Den. "Introduction." *Community at Loose Ends*. Ed. Miami Theory Collective. Minneapolis: U. of Minnesota P, 1991. ix–xxvi.

Agamben, Giorgio. *The Coming Community*. Trans. Michael Hardt. Minneapolis: U of Minnesota P, 1993.

———. *Stanzas: Word and Phantasm in Western Culture*. Trans. Ronald L. Martinez. Minneapolis: U of Minnesota P, 1993.

Albertine, Susan, ed. *A Living of Words: American Women in Print Culture*. Knoxville: U of Tennessee P, 1995.

Alcoff, Linda. "The Problem of Speaking for Others." *Feminist Nightmares, Women at Odds: Feminism and the Problem of Sisterhood*. Ed. Susan Ostrov Wesser and Jennifer Fleischener. New York and London: New York UP, 1994. 285–309.

Allen, Donald M., ed. *The New American Poetry*. New York: Grove, 1960.

Allnutt, Gillian et al., ed. *The New British Poetry 1968–1988*. London: Paladin, 1988.

Altieri, Charles. "What is Living and What is Dead in American Postmodernism: Establishing the Contemporaneity of Some American Poetry." *Critical Inquiry* 22.4 (summer 1996): 764–89.

Andrews, Bruce. "Total Equals What: Poetics and Praxis." *Poetics Journal* 6 (1986): 48–61.

———. *Paradise & Method: Poetics & Praxis*. Evanston: Northwestern UP, 1996.

Andrews, Bruce, Charles Bernstein, Ray DiPalma, Steve McCaffery, and Ron Silliman. *Legend*. New York: L=A=N=G=U=A=G=E /Segue, 1980.

Andrews, Bruce, and Charles Bernstein, "The Pacifica Interview," Conducted by Susan Howe. *L=A=N=G=U=A=G=E* supplement No. 3 (October 1981): n. pag.

Andrews, Bruce, and Charles Bernstein, eds. *The L=A=N=G=U=A=G=E Book*. Carbondale: Southern Illinois UP, 1984.

Anzaldúa, Gloria. *Borderlands/La Frontera: The New Mestiza*. San Francisco: Aunt Lute, 1987.

Arendt, Hannah. *The Human Condition*. Chicago: U of Chicago P, 1958.

———. *The Life of the Mind*. Vols. 1 and 2. New York: Harcourt Brace Jovanovich, 1978.

Aries, Elizabeth. *Men and Women in Interaction: Reconsidering the Differences*. New York: Oxford UP, 1996.

Aristotle. *The Complete Works of Aristotle*. Ed. Jonathan Barnes. Trans. W. D. Ross. Princeton, NJ: Princeton UP, 1984.

Armantrout, Rae. *Extremities*. Great Barrington, MA: The Figures, 1978.

———. *The Invention of Hunger*. Berkeley: Tuumba, 1979.

———. "Through Walls." *HOW(ever)* 1.4 (May 1984): 6–7.

———. Rev. of *The Guard* by Lyn Hejinian. *HOW(ever)* 2.2 (February 1985): 13–14.

———. "Poems." *Feminist Studies* 11.1 (spring 1985): 127–28.

———. "Poetic Silence." *Writing/Talks* Ed. Bob Perelman. Carbondale: Southern Illinois UP, 1985. 31–47.

———. "Why Don't Women Do Language-Oriented Writing?" *In the American Tree: Language, Realism, Poetry* Ed. Ron Silliman. Orono, ME: National Poetry Foundation, 1986. 544–46.

———. Statement. "Patterns/Contexts/Time: A Symposium on Contemporary Poetry." Eds. Charles Bernstein and Phillip Foss. *Tyuonyi* 6/7 (1990): 10.

———. *Necromance*. Los Angeles: Sun & Moon, 1991.

———. Interview. Conducted by Manuel Brito. *A Suite of Poetic Voices: Interviews with Contemporary American Poets*. Ed. Manuel Brito. Santa Brigida, Canary Islands: Kadle, 1992. 13–22.

———. "Feminist Poetics and the Meaning of Clarity." *Sagetrieb* 11.3 (Winter 1992): 7–16.

———. *Made to Seem*. Los Angeles: Sun & Moon, 1995.

———. "It." *Boxkite* 1 (1997): 135–36.

———. Interview. Conducted by Anne Brewster. *Southern Review* 31.2 (1998): 231–43.

———. "Irony and Postmodern Poetry." *Moving Borders: Three Decades of Innovative Writing by Women*. Ed. Mary Margaret Sloan. Jersey City, NJ: Talisman, 1998. 674–79.

Arnheim, Rudolph. *Radio*. Trans. Margaret Ludwig and Herbert Read. 1936; New York: Arno Press and The New York Times, 1971.

Ashbery, John. "An Interview in Warsaw." Conducted by Piotr Sommer *Code of Signals: Recent Writings in Poetics*. Ed. Michael Palmer. Berkeley, CA: North Atlantic, 1983. 294–314.

Badaracco, Claire Hoertz. *Trading Words: Poetry, Typography and Illustrated Books in the Modern Literary Economy*. Baltimore: Johns Hopkins UP, 1995.

Baker, Peter. "Bernadette Mayer." *Dictionary of Literary Biography* 165. "American Poets Since World War II." Detroit: Gale, 1996. 165–72.

Banting, Pamela. "S(m)other Tongue?: Feminism, Academic Discourse, Translation." *Collaboration in the Feminine: Writings on Women and Culture from Tessera*. Ed. Barbara Godard. Toronto: Second Story, 1994. 171–81.

Barba, Sharon, and Laura Chester, eds. *Rising Tides: Twentieth Century American Women Poets*. New York: Simon & Schuster, 1973.

Barone, Dennis and Peter Ganick, eds. *The Art of Practice: 45 Contemporary Poets*. Elmwood, CT: Potes & Poets, 1994.

Barthes, Roland. *The Pleasure of the Text*. Trans. Richard Miller. New York: Noonday, 1975.

———. *The Rustle of Language*. Trans. Richard Howard. New York: Hill and Wang, 1986.

Bartlett, Lee. "What is 'Language Poetry'?" *Critical Inquiry* 12 (1986): 741–52.

Bataille, Georges. *Eroticism: Death and Sensuality*. Trans. Mary Dalwood. San Francisco: City Lights, 1986.

Baym, Nina, ed. *The Norton Anthology of American Literature*. 2 vols. 5th ed. New York: W. W. Norton, 1998.

Beckett, Tom. Statement. "Patterns/Contexts/Time: A Symposium on Contemporary Poetry." Eds. Charles Bernstein and Philip Foss. *Tyuonyi* 6/7 (1990): 11–12.

Bee, Susan. Statement. *Chain* 1 (Spring/Summer 1994): 7–8.

Benjamin, Walter. *Illuminations*. Ed. Hannah Arendt. Trans. Harry Zohn. London: Jonathan Cape, 1970.

Benson, Steve. *As Is*. Berkeley, CA: The Figures, 1978.

———. "Views of Communist China." *Hills* 6/7 (spring 1980): 74–103.

———. "On Collaboration." *Jimmy & Lucy's House of K* 9 (January 1989): 85–90.

Benson, Steve, and Carla Harryman. "Dialogue: Museo de Antropología, Mexico." *Poetics Journal* 8 (June 1989): 46–54.

Bergvall, Caroline. "No Margins to This Page: Female Experimental Poets and the Legacy of Modernism." *Fragmente* 5 (1993): 30–38.

Berkson, Bill. "Talk" *Hills* 6/7 (Spring 1980): 7–24.

Bernstein, Charles. "The Conspiracy of 'Us,'" *L=A=N=G=U=A=G=E* 8 (1979): n. pag. Rpt. in *The L=A=N=G=U=A=G=E Book.* Ed. Bruce Andrews and Charles Bernstein. Carbondale: Southern Illinois UP, 1984, 185–88 and in *Content's Dream: Essays 1975–1984.* Los Angeles: Sun & Moon, 1986. 343–47.

——. Interview. Conducted by Tom Beckett. *The Difficulties* 2.1 (1981): 29.

——. "Characterization." *Writing/Talks* Ed. Bob Perelman. Carbondale: Southern Illinois UP, 1985. 7–30.

——. *Content's Dream: Essays 1975–1984.* Los Angeles: Sun & Moon, 1986.

——. "Poetry and (Male?) Sex." *Sulfur* 24 (1989): 189–93.

——. *The Politics of Poetic Form: Poetry and Public Policy.* New York: Roof, 1990.

——. *A Poetics.* Cambridge, MA: Harvard UP, 1992.

——. "Provisional Institutions: Alternative Presses and Poetic Innovation." *Arizona Quarterly* 51.1 (spring 1995): 133–46.

——. "Community and the Individual Talent." *Diacritics* 26.3–4 (fall-winter 1996): 176–95.

——. "An Autobiographical Interview with Charles Bernstein." Conducted by Loss Pequeño Glazier. *Boundary* 2 23.3 (1996): 21–43.

——. "Experiments." *Boundary* 2 23.3 (1996): 67–72.

——. ed. *Close Listening: Poetry and the Performed Word.* New York: Oxford UP, 1998.

Bernstein, Charles, and Susan B. Laufer. "Style." *L=A=N=G=U=A=G=E* 1.6 (December 1978): n. pag.

Bernstein, Charles et al. "Poetry, Community, Movement: A Conversation." *Diacritics* 26.3–4 (fall-winter 1996): 196–210.

Biggs, Mary. *A Gift That Cannot Be Refused: The Writing and Publishing of Contemporary American Poetry.* Westport, CT: Greenwood, 1990.

Boone, Bruce. "Writing, Power and Activity." *L=A=N=G=U=A=G=E* 9–10 (October 1979): n. pag.

Bottoms, David, and Dave Smith, eds. *The Morrow Anthology of Younger American Poets.* New York: Quill, 1985.

Brandt, Di. "letting the silence speak." *Language in Her Eye: Views on Writing and Gender by Canadian Women Writing in English.* Ed. Libby Scheier et al. Toronto: Coach House, 1990. 54–58.

Brennan, Sherry, et al. "Domestic Bliss, Dominus Patrus." *Chain* 1 (spring/summer 1994): 138–56.

Bridgman, Richard. *Gertrude Stein in Pieces.* New York: Oxford UP, 1970.

Brooke-Rose, Christine. "Illiterations." *Breaking the Sequence: Women's Experimental Fiction.* Ed. Ellen G. Friedman and Miriam Fuchs. Princeton, NJ: Princeton UP, 1989. 55–71.

Brossard, Nicole. *The Aerial Letter.* Trans. Marlene Wildeman. Toronto: Women's Press, 1988.

——. "Poetic Politics." *The Politics of Poetic Form: Poetry and Public Policy.* Ed. Charles Bernstein. New York: Roof, 1990. 73–86.

——. Statement. "Patterns/Contexts/Time: A Symposium on Contemporary Poetry." Eds. Charles Bernstein and Philip Foss. *Tyuonyi* 6/7 (1990): 32.

Brown, Lee Ann. Statement. *Chain* 1 (Spring/Summer 1994): 16–23.
——. "Deep Gossip Not." *Chain* 1 (Spring/Summer 1994): 158.
Butler, Judith. "Sexual Ideology and Phenomenological Description: A Feminist Critique of Merleau-Ponty's Phenomenology of Perception," *The Thinking Muse: Feminism and Modern French Philosophy*. Eds. Jeffner Allen and Iris Marion Young. Bloomington: Indiana UP, 1989. 85–100.
——. "Gender Trouble, Feminist Theory, and Psychoanalytic Discourse." *Feminism/ Postmodernism*. Ed. Linda J. Nicholson. New York: Routledge, 1990. 324–40.
——. *Gender Trouble: Feminism and the Subversion of Identity*. New York: Routledge, 1990.
Byrd, Don. "Language Poetry, 1971–1986." *Sulfur* 20 (fall 1987): 149–57.
Cain, James M. *Mildred Pierce*. Feltham: Hamlyn, 1943; 1982.
Caramello, Charles. *Henry James, Gertrude Stein, and the Biographical Act*. Chapel Hill: U of North Carolina P, 1996.
Chester, Laura, ed. *Deep Down: The New Sensual Writing by Women*. Boston and London: Faber & Faber, 1988.
Child, Abigail. "Cross Referencing the Units of Sight and Sound/Film and Language." *The L=A=N=G=U=A=G=E Book*. Eds. Bruce Andrews and Charles Bernstein. Carbondale: Southern Illinois UP, 1984. 94–96.
——. "Active Theory." *Raddle Moon* 11 (1992): 47–54.
——. "Active Theory." *Raddle Moon* 13 (1994): 12–33.
——. "Two Countries." *Chain* 1 (spring/summer 1994): 164–71.
Child, Abigail and Sally Silvers. "Rewire//Speak in Disagreement." *Poetics Journal* 4 (May 1984): 69–76.
Christian, Barbara. "The Race for Theory." *Gender and Theory: Dialogues on Feminist Criticism*. Ed. Linda Kauffman. Oxford: Blackwell, 1989. 225.
Cixous, Hélène. "Sorties." *The Newly Born Woman*, by Hélène Cixous and Catherine Clement. Trans. Betsy Wing. Minneapolis: U of Minnesota P, 1986.
Clark, Susan. Preface to "Women/Writing/Theory" Symposium, *Raddle Moon* 11 (1992): 16.
Clark, Suzanne. *Sentimental Modernism: Women Writers and the Revolution of the Word*. Bloomington: Indiana UP, 1991.
Clark, Tom. "Stalin as Linguist." *Poetry Flash* (July 1985). Rpt. in *Partisan Review* 54.2 (1987): 299–304.
Coates, Jennifer. *Women, Men and Language*. London: Longman, 1986.
Cole, Norma. "Whose Mouth? Cole on Quotation." *HOW(ever)* 6.3 (summer 1991): 15.
Coolidge, Clark. *The Maintains*. Oakland, CA: This: 1974.
——. Interview. Conducted by Lee Bartlett. *Talking Poetry: Conversations in the Workshop with Contemporary Poets*. Ed. Lee Bartlett. Albuquerque: U of New Mexico P, 1987. 1–18.
——. "[From] Letter to Peter Baker." *Onward: Contemporary Poetry and Poetics*. Ed. Peter Baker. New York: Peter Lang, 1996. 256–58.
Corbett, William and Michael Gizzi, eds. *Writing for Bernadette*. Great Barrington: The Figures, 1995.
Coultrap-McQuin, Susan. *Doing Literary Business: American Women Writers in the Nineteenth Century*. Chapel Hill: U of North Carolina, 1990.
Coward, Rosalind. *Female Desires*. London: Paladin Grafton, 1984.
Creeley, Robert. Interview. Conducted by Alan Riach. *Australasian Journal of American Studies* 15.1 (July 1996): 31–43.

———. *Life & Death.* New York: New Directions, 1998.

Crozier, Andrew, and Tim Longville, eds. *A Various Art.* Carcanet, 1987; London: Paladin, 1990.

Cryle, Peter. *Geometry in the Boudoir: Configurations of French Erotic Narrative.* Ithaca, NY: Cornell UP, 1994.

Curnow, Wystan. "Interview: Roger Horrocks and Friends Talk with Wystan Curnow." *Landfall* 45.1 (March 1991): 7–26.

———. *A Reading 1–7.* San Francisco: Momo, 1985.

Dahlen, Beverly. "From the Tradition of Marginality." *Poetics Journal* 6 (1986): 72–73.

Daly, Mary. *Gyn/Ecology: The Metaethics of Radical Feminism.* London: Women's Press, 1979.

Damon, Maria. *At the Dark End of the Street: Margins in American Poetry Vanguards.* Minneapolis: U of Minnesota P, 1993.

———. "Hannah Weiner Beside Herself: The Trauma of Clairvoyance." Draft of MLA paper, 1996.

Darragh, Tina. "Error Message." *Poetics Journal* 5 (1985): 120–21.

———. *Striking Resemblance, Work 1980–1986.* Providence, RI: Burning Deck, 1989.

———. Interview. Conducted by Joan Retallack *Aerial* 5 (1989): 69–85.

———. *a(gain)²st the odds.* Elmwood, CT: Potes and Poets, 1989.

———. Untitled Poem. *Chain* 1 (spring/summer 1994): 190–91.

———. "s the any ME finel mes: A Reflection on Donna Haraway's 'Cyborg Manifesto.'" *Moving Borders: Three Decades of Innovative Writing by Women.* Ed. Mary Margaret Sloan. Jersey City, NJ: Talisman House, 1998. 696–701.

———. "The Best of Intentions." *Moving Borders: Three Decades of Innovative Writing by Women.* Ed. Mary Margaret Sloan. Jersey City, NJ: Talisman House, 1998. 702–3.

Darragh, Tina and Jena Osman. *Philly Talks* 4 (1998): n. pag.

Davidson, Michael. "The Prose of Fact." *Hills* 6/7 (1980): 166–83.

———. *The San Francisco Renaissance: Poetics and Community at Mid-Century.* Cambridge: Cambridge UP, 1989.

———. "Language Poetry." *The New Princeton Encyclopedia of Poetry and Poetics.* Ed. Alex Preminger et al. Princeton, NJ: Princeton UP, 1993. 675–76.

Davies, Alan. *Signage.* New York: Roof, 1987.

Day, Jean. "Response." *Raddle Moon* 13 (1994): 56–61.

De Certeau, Michel. *The Practice of Everyday Life.* Trans. Steven Randall. Berkeley: U of California P, 1984; 1988.

DeKoven, Marianne. "Gertrude's Granddaughters." *The Women's Review of Books* 4.2 (1986): 12–14.

———. "Male Signature, Female Aesthetic: The Gender Politics of Experimental Writing." *Breaking the Sequence: Women's Experimental Fiction.* Eds. Ellen G. Friedman and Miriam Fuchs. Princeton, NJ: Princeton UP, 1989. 72–81.

De Lauretis, Teresa. "Eccentric Subjects: Feminist Theory and Historical Consciousness." *Feminist Studies* 16.1 (1990): 115–50.

Derksen, Jeff, and Ron Silliman. *Philly Talks* 6 (1998), n. pag.

Derrida, Jacques. "The Law of Genre." *Glyph* 7 (spring 1980). Rpt. in *Critical Inquiry* (Autumn 1980): 55–81.

———. *Memoires for Paul de Man.* New York: Columbia UP, 1986.

Dever, Maryanne. "Reading Other People's Mail," *Archives and Manuscripts: The Journal of the Australian Society of Archivists* 24.1 (May 1996): 116–29.

Dow, Philip, ed. *19 New American Poets of the Golden Gate*. San Diego, CA: Harcourt Brace Jovanovich, 1984.

Dreyer, Lynne. "Tamoka." *Roof* 9 (1979): 42–57.

———. *The White Museum*. New York: Segue, 1986.

Drucker, Johanna. *From A to Z: OUR AN (Collective Specific) an im partial bibliography*. San Francisco: Chased Press, 1977.

———. "Women & Language." *Poetics Journal* 4 (May 1984): 56–68.

———. "Women/Writing/Theory: What Is at Stake?" *Raddle Moon* 11 (1992): 17–19.

———. "Response." *Raddle Moon* 13 (1994): 48–55.

———. Statement. *Chain* 1 (spring/summer 1994): 37.

———. *The Century of Artists' Books*. New York: Granary Books, 1995.

———. "Experimental, Visual, and Concrete Poetry: A Note on Historical Context and Basic Concepts." *Avant-Garde Historical Studies* 10 (1996): 39–61.

———. "Through Light and the Alphabet." Interview, conducted by Matthew G. Kirschenbaum. *Postmodern Culture* 5 (1997): n. pag.

———. *Figuring the Word: Essays on Books, Writing, and Visual Poetics*. New York: Granary Books, 1998.

DuBois, Page. *Sappho Is Burning*. Chicago: U of Chicago P, 1995.

DuPlessis, Rachel Blau. "Draft #1: It." *Temblor* 5 (1987): 22–28.

———. "On the Davidson/Weinberger Exchange." *Sulfur* 22 (1988): 188–93.

———. *The Pink Guitar: Writing as Feminist Practice*. New York: Routledge, 1990.

———. "Thinking about Annie Finch, On Female Power and the Sonnet." *HOW(ever)*.6.3 (summer 1991):16.

———. "Contemporary Women's Poetry." *The Oxford Companion to Women's Writing in the United States*. Ed. Cathy N. Davidson et al. New York: Oxford UP, 1995. 672–76.

———. "f-Words: An Essay on the Essay." *American Literature* 68.1 (1996): 15–45.

———. "Manifests." *Diacritics* 26.3–4 (fall-winter 1996): 31–53.

DuPlessis, Rachel, and Ann Snitow, eds. *The Feminist Memoir Project: Voices from Women's Liberation*. New York: Three Rivers, 1998.

DuPlessis, Rachel Blau, and Members of Workshop 9. "For the Etruscans: Sexual Difference and Artistic Production—The Debate Over a Female Aesthetic." *The Future of Difference*. Eds. Hester Eisenstein and Alice Jardine. Boston: G. K. Hall, 1980. 128–56.

Durand, Marcella. "Publishing a Community: Women Publishers at the Poetry Project." Paper presented at "Where Lyric Tradition Meets Language Poetry" Conference, 8–10 April 1999, Barnard College, New York.

During, Simon. *Foucault and Literature: Toward a Genealogy of Writing*. London: Routledge, 1992.

Dybikowski, Ann, et al., ed. *In the Feminine: Women and Words*. Edmonton, AB: Longspoon, 1985.

Eisenstein, Hester and Alice Jardine, eds. *The Future of Difference*. Boston: G. K. Hall, 1980.

Eliot, T. S. *Selected Prose of T. S. Eliot*. Ed. Frank Kermode. London: Faber and Faber, 1975.

Falon, Janet Ruth. "Speaking with Susan Howe." *The Difficulties* 3.2 (1989): 28–42.

Féral, Josette. "Antigone, or the Irony of the Tribe." *Diacritics* (September 1978): 2–14.

Ferguson, Kathy E. "Interpretation and Genealogy in Feminism." *Signs* 16.2 (1991): 322–39.

Finch, Annie. "The Sonnet Transfigured." *HOW(ever)* 6.2 (October 1990): 13.

Firestone, Shulamith. *The Dialectic of Sex: The Case for Feminist Revolution*. New York: Morrow, 1970.

Foster, Edward. *Postmodern Poetry: The Talisman Interviews*. Hoboken, NJ: Talisman, 1994.

Foucault, Michel. *The Foucault Reader*. Ed. Paul Rabinow. New York: Pantheon Books, 1984.

———. *Politics, Philosophy, Culture: Interviews and Other Writings 1977–1984*. Ed. Lawrence Kritzman. Trans. Alan Sheridan et al. New York: Routledge, 1988.

Fowler, Alastair. *Triumphal Forms: Structural Patterns in Elizabethan Poetry*. Cambridge: Cambridge UP, 1970.

France, Linda, ed. *Sixty Women Poets*. Newcastle-upon-Tyne: Bloodaxe, 1993.

Franklin, Cynthia G. *Writing Women's Communities: The Politics and Poetics of Contemporary Multi-Genre Anthologies*. Madison: U of Wisconsin P, 1997.

Fraser, Kathleen. "How Did Emma Slide? Or the Gestate: A New Poem Form for Women." *Trellis* 3 (1979): 12–14.

———. "Partial Local Coherence: Regions with Illustrations, Some Notes on Language Writing." *Ironwood* 20 (1982): 122–39.

———. "Why *HOW(ever)*?" *HOW(ever)* 1.1 (May 1983): 1.

———. Letter to Daphne Marlatt. *HOW(ever)* 5.2 (January 1989):14.

———. "*trans*figuring," Response to *The Sonnet Transfigured* by Annie Finch." *HOW(ever)* 6.3 (summer 1991):15–16.

———. "The Tradition of Marginality." *Where We Stand: Women Poets on Literary Tradition*. Ed. Sharon Bryan. New York: W. W. Norton, 1993. 52–65.

———. "The Jump: Editing *HOW(ever)*." *Chain* 1 (Spring/Summer 1994): 42–46.

———. *il cuore: Selected Poems 1970–1995*. Hanover, NH: UP of New England for Wesleyan UP, 1997.

———. Interview, conducted by Cynthia Hogue. *Contemporary Literature* 39.1 (Spring 1998): 1–26.

———. "Editor's Notes." *HOW2* 1.1 (March 1999).

Friedman, Ellen G., and Miriam Fuchs. "Contexts and Continuities: An Introduction to Women's Experimental Fiction in English." *Breaking the Sequence: Women's Experimental Fiction*. Eds. Ellen G. Friedman and Miriam Fuchs. Princeton, NJ: Princeton UP, 1989. 3–51.

Friedman, Susan Stanford. "Making History: Reflections on Feminism, Narrative, and Desire," *Feminism Beside Itself*. Eds. Diane Elam and Robyn Wiegman. New York and London: Routledge, 1995. 11–53.

Gannett, Cinthia. *Gender and the Journal: Diaries and Academic Discourse*. Albany: SUNY P, 1992.

Garber, Marjorie. "Introduction: Postmodernism and the Possibility of Biography." *The Seductions of Biography*. Eds. Mary Rhiel and David Suchoff. New York and London: Routledge, 1996. 169–71.

Gelpi, Albert. "The Genealogy of Postmodernism: Contemporary American Poetry." *Southern Review* 26 (summer 1990): 517–41.

George, Diana Hume. "'How Many of Us Can You Hold to Your Breast?': Mothering in the Academy." *Listening to Silences: New Essays in Feminist Criticism*. Eds. Elaine Hedges and Shelley Fisher Fishkin. New York: Oxford UP, 1994. 225–44.

Gere, Anne Ruggles. "Common Properties of Pleasure: Texts in Nineteenth Century Women's Clubs." *The Construction of Authorship: Textual Appropriation in*

Law and Literature. Eds. Martha Woodmansee and Peter Jaszi. Durham, NC: Duke UP, 1994. 383–99.

Gevirtz, Susan. "Doctor Editor." *Chain* 1 (spring/summer 1994): 47–55.

Ginsberg, Allen. Foreword to *Out of This World: An Anthology of the St. Mark's Poetry Project 1966–1991*. Ed. Anne Waldman. New York: Crown, 1991. xxiv-xxx.

Glück, Robert. "Who Speaks for Us: Being an Expert." *Writing/Talks*. Ed. Bob Perelman. Carbondale: Southern Illinois UP, 1985. 1–6.

———. "Baucis and Philemon." *Poetics Journal* 5 (May 1985): 110–13.

Godard, Barbara, with Daphne Marlatt, Kathy Mezei, and Gail Scott. "Theorizing Fiction Theory." *Collaboration in the Feminine: Writings on Women and Culture from* Tessera. Ed. Barbara Godard. Toronto: Second Story, 1994. 53–62.

Goffman, Erving. *Frame Analysis: An Essay on the Organization of Experience*. New York: Harper & Row, 1974.

———. *Forms of Talk*. Philadelphia: U of Pennsylvania P, 1981.

Goldhill, Simon. "Refracting Classical Vision: Changing Cultures of Viewing." *Vision in Context: Historical and Contemporary Perspectives on Sight*. Ed. Teresa Brennan and Martin Jay. New York: Routledge, 1996. 17–28.

Golding, Alan. *From Outlaw to Classic: Canons in American Poetry*. Madison: U of Wisconsin P, 1995.

Gray, Cecil, and Philip Heseltine. *Carlo Gesualdo; Prince of Venosa: Musician and Murderer*. London: Kegan Paul, 1926; rpt. Westport, CT: Greenwood, 1971.

Greer, Michael. "Ideology and Theory in Recent Experimental Writing or, The Naming of 'Language Poetry.'" *Boundary* 2 41.2–3 (spring 1989): 335–55.

Gregory, R. L. *Eye and Brain: The Psychology of Seeing*. 4th ed. Princeton, NJ: Princeton UP, 1966; 1990.

Grenier, Robert. Rev. of *Writing Is an Aid to Memory*, by Lyn Hejinian. *L=A=N=G=U=A=G=E* 2.2 (June 1979): n. pag.

Grigely, Joseph. *Textualterity: Art, Theory, and Textual Criticism*. Ann Arbor: U of Michigan P, 1995.

Grosz, Elizabeth. "Bodies-Cities." *Sexuality and Space*. Ed. Beatriz Colomina et al. New York: Princeton Architectural Press, 1992. 241–54.

Guillory, John. *Cultural Capital: The Problem of Literary Canon Formation*. Chicago and London: U of Chicago P, 1993.

Haraway, Donna. "A Manifesto for Cyborgs: Science, Technology and Socialist Feminism in the 1980s." *Coming to Terms: Feminism, Theory, Politics*. Ed. Elizabeth Weed. New York: Routledge, 1989.

Harrington, Joseph. "Why American Poetry Is Not American Literature." *American Literary History* 8.3 (Fall 1996): 496–515.

Harryman, Carla. *The Middle*. San Francisco: GAZ, 1983.

———. *Animal Instincts*. Oakland, CA: This, 1989.

———. "Letter to Rod Smith." *Aerial* 5 (1989): 25–26.

———. *There Never Was a Rose without a Thorn*. San Francisco: City Lights, 1995.

———. Interview. Conducted by Megan Simpson. *Contemporary Literature* 37.4 (Winter 1996): 510–32.

———. Interview. Conducted by Chris Tysh. *Poetics Journal* 10 (June 1998): 207–17.

———. "Belief." Unpublished manuscript, n. pag.

———. "Rules and Restraints in Women's Experimental Writing." Paper presented at the New Modernisms Conference, Penn State University, 8 October 1999.

Harryman, Carla, and Lyn Hejinian. "From 'The Wide Road.'" *Everyday Life* 2 (1988): 2–11.

——. Harryman, Carla, and Lyn Hejinian. "A Correspondence from 'The Wide Road.'" *Aerial* 5 (1989): 27–43.

——. Harryman, Carla, and Lyn Hejinian. "From 'The Wide Road.'" *Aerial* 5 (1989): 44–53.

——. Harryman, Carla, and Lyn Hejinian. "From 'The Wide Road.'" *Aerial* 6/7 (1991): 163.

——. Harryman, Carla, and Lyn Hejinian. "From 'The Wide Road.'" *Avec* 4 (1991): 26–30.

——. Harryman, Carla and Lyn Hejinian. "The Wide Road." *Tessera* 15 (winter 1993)

——. Harryman, Carla and Lyn Hejinian. "A Comment on 'The Wide Road' for O." *Subliminal Time*. Ed. Leslie Scalapino. Oakland, CA: O Books, 1993. 83–91.

Hartley, George. *Textual Politics of the Language Poets*. Bloomington: Indiana UP, 1989.

Hartsock, Nancy. "Rethinking Modernism: Minority vs. Majority Theories." *Cultural Critique* 7 (fall 1987): 201.

Hejinian, Lyn. *A Thought Is the Bride of What Thinking* Willits, CA: Tuumba, 1976.

——. *Gesualdo*. Berkeley, CA: Tuumba, 1978.

——. "Smatter." *L=A=N=G=U=A=G=E* 8 (June 1979): n. pag.

——. Interview, conducted by Vicki Hudspith, *Poetry Project Newsletter* (December 1979): n. pag.

——. "If Written Is Writing." *The L=A=N=G=U=A=G=E Book*. Eds. Bruce Andrews and Charles Bernstein. Carbondale: Southern Illinois UP, 1984. 29–30.

——. "Poem." *Feminist Studies* 11.1 (spring 1985): 129.

——. "Language and 'Paradise.'" *Line* 6 (fall 1985): 83–99.

——. "The Rejection of Closure." *Writing/Talks*. Ed. Bob Perelman. Carbondale: Southern Illinois UP, 1985. 270–91.

——. "Lyn Hejinian and Andrew Schelling: An Exchange." *Jimmy & Lucy's House of K* 6 (1986): 1.

——. *My Life*, 2nd ed. Los Angeles: Sun & Moon, 1987.

——. *The Cell*. Los Angeles: Sun & Moon, 1992.

——. *The Cold of Poetry*. Los Angeles: Sun & Moon, 1994.

——. "The Quest for Knowledge in the Western Poem." *Disembodied Poetics: Annals of the Jack Kerouac School*. Eds. Anne Waldman and Andrew Schelling. Albuquerque: U of New Mexico P, 1994. 171–89.

——. "From *A Border Comedy*." *Abacus* 93 (1995): 1–16.

——. "The Eternal Repository: Dodie Bellamy Interviews Lyn Hejinian." *Chain* 2 (spring 1995): 19–25.

——. *Writing Is an Aid to Memory*. Berkeley: The Figures, 1978: Los Angeles: Sun & Moon, 1996.

——. Interview. Conducted by Charles Bernstein, LINEbreak program, 1996. Available at <http://wings.buffalo.edu/epc/linebreak/programs/hejinian>.

——. *The Language of Inquiry*. Berkeley: U of California P, forthcoming.

Hejinian, Lyn, and Tyrus Miller. "An Exchange of Letters." *Paper Air* 4.2 (1989): 33–40.

Hejinian, Lyn, and Joan Retallack, "The Clouds: (This Is Not by Henrik Isbn)" *Chain* 6 (1999): 111–19. .

Hejinian, Lyn, and Kit Robinson. *Individuals*. Tuscon: Chax, 1988.

Hejinian, Lyn, and Leslie Scalapino. "From 'Sight.'" *Raddle Moon* 13 (1994): 71–83.
——. *Sight.* Washington, DC: Edge Books, 1999.
Heywood, Leslie. *Dedication to Hunger: The Anorexic Aesthetic in Modern Culture.* Berkeley: U of California P, 1996.
Hieatt, A. Kent. *Short Time's Endless Monument: The Symbolism of the Numbers in Edmund Spenser's "Epitalamion."* New York: Columbia UP, 1960; rpt. London and Port Washington, NY: Kennikat, 1972,
Hoover, Paul, ed. *Postmodern American Poetry: A Norton Anthology.* New York: W. W. Norton, 1994.
Howe, Fanny. "The Contemporary Logos." *Code of Signals: Recent Writings in Poetics.* Ed. Michael Palmer. Berkeley, CA: North Atlantic, 1983. 47–55.
——. "The Ecstatic." *Ironwood* 24 (1984): 17–20.
——. *For Erato: The Meaning of Life.* Berkeley, CA: Tuumba, 1984.
——. Rev. of *Midwinter Day*, by Bernadette Mayer. *American Book Review* 6 (1984): 16.
——. "Artobiography." *Writing/Talks.* Ed. Bob Perelman. Carbondale: Southern Illinois UP, 1985. 192–206.
——. "Scattered Light." *The Vineyard,* 1988. Rpt. in *Moving Borders: Three Decades of Innovative Writing by Women.* Ed. Mary Margaret Sloan. Jersey City, NJ: Talisman, 1998. 140.
——. *The End.* Los Angeles: Littoral Books, 1992.
——. *O'Clock.* London: Reality Street Editions, 1995.
——. "Bewilderment." *HOW2* 1.1 (March 1999): n. pag.
Howe, Florence, and Ellen Bass, eds. *No More Masks! An Anthology of Poems by Women.* Garden City, NY: Anchor, 1973.
Howe, Susan. "P. Inman, *Platin.*" *L=A=N=G=U=A=G=E* 12 (1980): n. pag.
——. *The Liberties.* Guilford, CT: Loon Books, 1980. Rpt. in *The Europe of Trusts.* Los Angeles: Sun & Moon, 1990. 147–217.
——. Rev. of *Extremities*, by Rae Armantrout. *The L=A=N=G=U=A=G=E Book.* Ed. Bruce Andrews and Charles Bernstein. Carbondale: Southern Illinois UP, 1984. 208–11.
——. *My Emily Dickinson.* Berkeley, CA: North Atlantic, 1985.
——. Statement for the New Poetics Colloquium, Vancouver, 1985. *Jimmy & Lucy's House of K* 5 (1985): 13–17.
——. "The Captivity and Restoration of Mrs. Mary Rowlandson." *Temblor* 2 (1985): 113–21.
——. *The Difficulties* Interview, Conducted by Tom Beckett. *The Difficulties* 3.2 (1989): 17–27.
——. *The Europe of Trusts.* Los Angeles: Sun & Moon, 1990.
——. *Singularities.* Hanover, NH: UP of New England, 1990.
——. "Encloser." *The Politics of Poetic Form: Poetry and Public Policy.* Ed. Charles Bernstein. New York: Roof, 1990. 175–96.
——. *The Nonconformist's Memorial.* New York: New Directions, 1993.
——. *The Birth-Mark: Unsettling the Wilderness in American Literary History.* Hanover, NH: UP of New England for Wesleyan UP. 1993.
——. Interview. Conducted by Lynn Keller. *Contemporary Literature* 36.1 (spring 1995): 1–34.
——. *Frame Structures: Early Poems 1974–1979.* New York: New Directions, 1996.
Hryniuk, Angela. Interview. Conducted by the author. 31 July 1994.

Hubert, Renée Riese. *Magnifying Mirrors: Women, Surrealism and Partnership*. Lincoln: U of Nebraska P, 1994.

Hunt, Erica. "Notes for an Oppositional Poetics." *The Politics of Poetic Form: Poetry and Public Policy*. Ed. Charles Bernstein. New York: Roof, 1990. 197–212.

Huyssen, Andreas. "Mapping the Postmodern." *New German Critique* 33 (1984): 5–52. Rpt. in *Feminism/Postmodernism*. Ed. Linda J. Nicholson. New York: Routledge, 1990. 234–80.

Inman, P. *Ocker*. Berkeley, CA: Tuumba, 1982.

Jaffer, Frances. Rev. of *Literary Women* by Ellen Moers. *Chrysalis: A Magazine of Women's Culture* 1 (1977): 136.

———. "Why HOW(ever)?" *HOW(ever)* 1.1 (May 1983): 1.

———. "Working Notes." *Mirage* 3 ("The Women's Issue." ed. Dodie Bellamy). (1989): 90.

Jakobson, Roman. *On Language*. Ed. Linda R. Waugh and Monique Monville-Burston. Cambridge, MA: Harvard UP, 1995.

Jardine, Alice. *Gynesis: Configurations of Woman and Modernity*. Ithaca, NY: Cornell UP, 1985.

Jiles, Paulette. "Hustling at the New Poetics Colloquium." *Brick* 27 (spring 1986): 45–50.

Johnson, Barbara. *A World of Difference*. Baltimore: Johns Hopkins UP, 1987.

Johnson, Samuel. Vol. 2 of *Johnson on Shakespeare*. 2 vols. Ed. Arthur Sherbo. New Haven, CT: Yale UP, 1968.

Joris, Pierre, and Jerome Rothenberg, eds. *Poems for the Millennium: The University of California Book of Modern & Postmodern Poetry*. 2 vols. Berkeley: U of California P, 1995.

Kalaidjian, Walter. *American Culture between the Wars: Revisionary Modernism and Postmodern Critique*. New York: Columbia UP, 1993.

Kamboureli, Smaro. "Theory: Beauty or Beast? Resistance to Theory in the Feminine." *Open Letter* 7.8 (summer 1990): 5–26.

Kaplan, Caren, and Ellen Cronan Rose. "Strange Bedfellows: Feminist Collaboration." *Signs* 18 (1993): 547–61.

Kaplan, Cora. *Sea Changes: Essays on Culture and Feminism*. London: Verso, 1986.

Keller, Lynn. *Forms of Expansion: Recent Long Poems by Women*. Chicago: U of Chicago P, 1997.

Keller, Lynn, and Cristanne Miller. "Gender and Avant-Garde Editing: Comparing the 1920s with the 1990s." *HOW2* 1.2 (1999): n. pag.

Kinnahan, Linda. *Poetics of the Feminine: Authority and Literary Tradition in William Carlos Williams, Mina Loy, Denise Levertov, and Kathleen Fraser*. Cambridge: Cambridge UP, 1994.

———. " 'Look for the Doing Words': Carol Ann Duffy and the Question of Convention." *Contemporary British Poetry: Essays in Theory and Criticism*. Eds. James Acheson and Romana Huk. Albany: SUNY P, 1996. 245–68.

———. " 'this/lyric forever error': Feminist Poetics and Female Subjectivity in American and British Innovative Poetries." Paper presented at the Assembling Alternatives Conference, U of New Hampshire, 30 August 1996.

Koestenbaum, Wayne. *Double Talk: The Erotics of Male Literary Collaboration*. New York: Routledge, 1989.

Kristeva, Julia. *Revolution in Poetic Language: A Semiotic Approach to Literature and Art*. Trans. Margaret Waller. New York: Columbia UP, 1984.

Laird, Holly A. "Editing Feminist Journals: Report on the October 1983 Conference, 'Publishing Feminist Scholarship,'" *Chain* 1 (spring/summer 1994): 70–79.

Lakoff, George. "On Whose Authority?" *Poetry Flash* 147 (June 1985): 5–7.

Lakoff, Robin. *Language and Woman's Place*. New York: Octagon, 1976.

Lally, Lee. *These Days*. Washington, DC: Some of Us, 1971–72.

Lally, Michael, ed. *None of the Above: New Poets of the USA*. Trumansburg, NY: Crossing, 1976.

Laplanche, Jean, and Jean-Bertrand Pontalis. "Fantasy and the Origins of Sexuality." *Formations of Fantasy*. Ed. Victor Burgin et al. London: Methuen, 1986. 5–34.

Laskaya, Anne. *Chaucer's Approach to Gender in* The Canterbury Tales. Chaucer Studies, vol. XXIII. Cambridge: D. S. Brewer, 1995.

Lauterbach, Ann. "Misquotations from Reality." *Diacritics* 26.3–4 (fall-winter 1996): 143–57.

———. "Lines Written to Bob Perelman in the Margins of *The Marginalization of Poetry*." *The Impercipient Lecture Series* 1.4 (May 1997).

Lavender, William. "Disappearance of Theory, Appearance of Praxis: Ron Silliman, *L=A=N=G=U=A=G=E*, and the Essay." *Poetics Today* 17.2 (summer 1996) 181–202.

Lazer, Hank. *Opposing Poetries*. 2 vols. Evanston, IL: Northwestern UP, 1996.

LeFevre, Karen Burke. *Invention as a Social Act*. Carbondale: Southern Illinois UP, 1987.

Lehmann, David. *Signs of the Times: Deconstruction and the Fall of Paul de Man*. New York: Poseidon, 1991.

Levy, Andrew. "The Existence of the Writer – the Unthought Known." *A Poetics of Criticism*. Ed. Juliana Spahr et al. Buffalo, NY: Leave, 1994. 201–7.

Lewis, Joel. "Dreamers That Remain." *American Book Review* (March-April 1987): 9.

Lutz, Catherine. "The Gender of Theory." *Women Writing Culture*. Eds. Ruth Behar and Deborah A. Gordon. Berkeley: U of California P, 1995. 249–66.

Lyon, Janet. "Transforming Manifestoes: A Second-Wave Problematic." *Yale Journal of Criticism* 5.1 (1991): 101–27.

Machan, Katharyn Howd. "Breath into Fire: Feminism and Poetry Readings." *Mid-American Review* 12.2 (1992): 120–26.

Mackey, Nathaniel. *Discrepant Engagement: Dissonance, Cross-Culturality, and Experimental Writing*. Cambridge: Cambridge UP, 1993.

Mackinnon, Catherine. "Feminism, Marxism, Method and the State: An Agenda for Theory." *Signs* 7.3 (1982): 512–44.

Mac Low, Jackson. Rev. of *Persia, Sixteen, Code Poems*, by Laura Moriarty and Hannah Weiner. *Poetics Journal* 4 (May 1984): 88–97.

MacShane, Frank. *The Life of Raymond Chandler*. London: Hamish Hamilton, 1976, 1986.

Madden, David. *Cain's Craft*. Metuchen, NJ: Scarecrow, 1985.

Malcolm, Janet. *The Silent Woman: Sylvia Plath and Ted Hughes*. New York: Alfred A. Knopf, 1994.

Marks, Elaine, and Isabelle de Courtivron, eds. *New French Feminisms: An Anthology*. Amherst: U of Massachusetts P, 1980.

Marlatt, Daphne. "Why?" *HOW(ever)* 5.2 (January 1989): 13–14.

———. "Magazining: Interview with Daphne Marlatt." Conducted by Pauline Butling. *Open Letter* 8.5–6 (1992): 113–24.

Mayer, Bernadette. *Memory*. Plainfield, VT: North Atlantic, 1975.

———. "The Obfuscated Poem." *Code of Signals: Recent Writings in Poetics*. Ed. Michael Palmer. Berkeley, CA: North Atlantic, 1983. 166.

———. "From *Studying Hunger*." *In the American Tree: Language, Realism, Poetry*. Ed. Ron Silliman. Orono, ME: National Poetry Foundation, 1986. 410–24.

———. *A Bernadette Mayer Reader*. New York: New Directions, 1992.

———. "The Colors of Consonance." Interview, conducted by Ken Jordan. *The Poetry Project Newsletter* 146 (October-November 1992): 5–9.

———. *The Desires of Mothers to Please Others in Letters*. West Stockbridge, MA: Hard Press, 1994.

———. "From: A Lecture at Naropa." *Disembodied Poetics: Annals of the Jack Kerouac School*. Albuquerque: U of New Mexico P, 1994. 95–102.

———. "Experimental Writing, or, Writing the Long Work." *Onward: Contemporary Poetry and Poetics*. Ed. Peter Baker. New York: Peter Lang, 1996. 6–8

———. "The Complete Introductory Lectures on Poetry." *Onward: Contemporary Poetry and Poetics*. Ed. Peter Baker. New York: Peter Lang, 1996. 20–21.

———. *Proper Name and Other Stories*. New York: New Directions, 1996.

———. *Midwinter Day*. Berkeley, CA: Turtle Island Foundation, 1982. Rpt. New York: New Directions, 1999.

Mayer, Bernadette, and the Members of the St. Mark's Church Poetry Project Writing Workshop, 1971–75. "Experiments." *In the American Tree: Language, Realism, Poetry*. Ed. Ron Silliman. Orono, ME: National Poetry Foundation, 1986. 557–60.

McCaffery, Steve. *North of Intention: Critical Writings, 1973–1986*. New York: Roof, 1986.

McDonald, Christie. "Personal Criticism: Dialogue of Differences," *Feminism beside Itself*. Eds. Diane Elam and Robyn Wiegman. New York: Routledge, 1995. 237–59.

McFarland, Dorothy Tuck. *Simone Weil*. New York: Frederic Ungar, 1983.

McGann, Jerome. "Contemporary Poetry, Alternate Routes." *Critical Inquiry* 13 (spring 1987). Rpt. in *Politics and Poetic Value*. Ed. Robert von Hallberg. Chicago: U of Chicago P, 1987. 253–76.

———. *Black Riders: The Visible Language of Modernism*. Princeton, NJ: Princeton UP, 1993.

Mencken, H. L. *The American Language*. New York: Alfred A. Knopf, 1945.

———. *The American Language: Supplement 1*. New York: Alfred A. Knopf, 1945.

Messerli, Douglas. "Anatomy of Self." Rev. of *Eruditio ex Memoria* by Bernadette Mayer. *The L=A=N=G=U=A=G=E Book*. Eds. Bruce Andrews and Charles Bernstein. Carbondale: Southern Illinois UP, 1984. 247–49.

———, ed. *"Language" Poetries*. New York: New Directions, 1987.

———, ed. *From the Other Side of the Century: A New American Poetry 1960–1990*. Los Angeles: Sun & Moon, 1994.

Miller, Bett. "Dancing the Divide: Reading *au féminin* and the Work of Nicole Brossard." Diss. U of California at San Diego, 1993.

Miller, Jane. Letter to Kathleen Fraser. *HOW(ever)* 2.2 (February 1985): 15.

Miller, Nancy K. "Men's Reading, Women's Writing: Gender and the Rise of the Novel." *The Politics of Tradition: Placing Women in French Literature*. Eds. Joan DeJean and Nancy K. Miller. Yale French Studies 75. New Haven, CT: Yale UP, 1988. 40–55.

Millett, Kate. *Sexual Politics*. New York: Doubleday, 1970.

Miner, Earl. *Japanese Linked Poetry: An Account with Translations of Renga and Haikai Sequences.* Princeton, NJ: Princeton UP, 1979.

Minh-ha, Trinh T. *Woman, Native, Other: Writing Postcoloniality and Feminism.* Boomington: Indiana UP, 1989.

Moi, Toril. *Simone De Beauvoir: The Making of an Intellectual Woman.* Oxford: Blackwell, 1994.

Monroe, Harriet. "The Radio and the Poets." *Poetry* (April 1935): 35.

Monroe, Jonathan. "Syntextural Investigations." *Diacritics* 26.3–4 (fall-winter 1996): 126–41.

Morris, Adalaide, ed. *Sound States: Acoustical Technologies and Modern and Postmodern Writing.* Chapel Hill: U of North Carolina P, 1997.

Morris, Meaghan. *The Pirate's Fiancée: Feminism, Reading, Postmodernism.* London: Verso, 1988.

Moses, Claire. "Made in America: 'French Feminism' in United States Academic Discourse." *Australian Feminist Studies* 11.23 (April 1996): 17–31.

Mostafavi, Mohsen, and David Leatherbarrow. *On Weathering: The Life of Buildings in Time.* Cambridge, MA: MIT, 1993.

Mullen, Harryette. "Poetry and Identity," *West Coast Line* 30.1 (spring 1996) 85–89.

———. Interview, conducted by Cynthia Hogue. *Postmodern Culture* 9.2 (1999): n. pag.

Nancy, Jean-Luc. *The Inoperative Community.* Trans. Peter Connor et al. Ed. Peter Connor. Minneapolis: U of Minnesota P, 1991.

———. *The Experience of Freedom.* Trans. Bridget McDonald. Stanford, CA: Stanford UP, 1993.

Nora, Pierre. "Between Memory and History: *Les Lieux de Mémoire.*" *History and Memory in African-American Culture.* Eds. Genevieve Fabre and Robert O'Meally. New York: Oxford UP, 1994. 284–300.

Notley, Alice. *Doctor Williams' Heiresses.* Berkeley, CA: Tuumba, 1980.

Oppen, George. *Seascape: Needle's Eye.* Fremont, MI: Sumac, 1972.

Osman, Jena, and Juliana Spahr. "Editors' Notes: Frameworks." *Chain* 1 (spring/summer 1994): 129–34.

O'Sullivan, Maggie, ed. *Out of Everywhere: Linguistically Innovative Poetry by Women in North America and the UK.* London: Reality Street Editions, 1996.

Owen, Maureen. *Amelia Earheart.* San Francisco: Vortex Editions, 1984.

Padgett, Ron, and David Shapiro, eds. *An Anthology of New York Poets.* New York: Random House, 1970.

Palmer, Michael, ed. *Code of Signals: Recent Writings in Poetics.* Berkeley, CA: North Atlantic, 1983.

———. Interview. Conducted by Lee Bartlett. *Talking Poetry: Conversations in the Workshop with Contemporary Poets.* Albuquerque: U of New Mexico P, 1987. 125–48.

———. Interview. Conducted by Peter Gizzi. *Exact Change Yearbook No. 1* Boston: Exact Change; Manchester: Carcanet, 1995. 161–79.

Perelman, Bob. *7 Works.* Berkeley, CA: The Figures, 1979.

———, ed. *Writing/Talks.* Carbondale: Southern Illinois UP, 1985.

———. "Notes on *The First World.*" *Line* 6 (1985): 100–12.

———. "Facing the Surface: Representations of Representation." *North Dakota Quarterly* 55.4 (1987): 301–11.

———. "Language Writing and Literary History." *Aerial* 8 (1995): 123–40.

———. *The Marginalization of Poetry: Language Writing and Literary History.* Princeton, NJ: Princeton UP, 1996.

———. "The Manchurian Candidate: A Remake." *Onward: Contemporary Poetry and Poetics.* Ed. Peter Baker. New York: Peter Lang, 1996. 372–86.

———. "Speech Effects: The Talk as a Genre." *Close Listening: Poetry and the Performed Word.* Ed. Charles Bernstein. Oxford: Oxford UP, 1998. 200–16.

Perloff, Marjorie. "What 'Les Jeunes' Are Up To." *Washington Post,* 26 December 1976.

———. *Poetic License: Essays on Modernist and Postmodernist Lyric.* Evanston, IL: Northwestern UP, 1990.

———. *Radical Artifice: Writing Poetry in the Age of Media.* Chicago: U of Chicago P, 1991.

———. *Wittgenstein's Ladder: Poetic Language and the Strangeness of the Ordinary.* Chicago: U of Chicago P, 1996.

———. "Whose New American Poetry? Anthologizing in the Nineties." *Diacritics* 26.3–4 (fall-winter 1996): 104–23.

———. "The Coming of Age of Language Poetry." *Contemporary Literature* 38.3 (fall 1997): 558–68.

Petroff, Elizabeth Alvilda. *Body and Soul: Essays on Medieval Women and Mysticism.* New York: Oxford UP, 1994.

Phelan, Peggy. *Unmarked: The Politics of Performance.* London: Routledge, 1993.

Piercy, Marge, ed. *Early Ripening American Women's Poetry Now.* New York: Pandora, 1987.

Piombino, Nick. "The Aural Ellipsis and the Nature of Listening in Contemporary Poetry." *Close Listening: Poetry and the Performed Word.* Ed. Charles Bernstein. New York: Oxford UP, 1998. 53–72.

Poulin A., Jr., ed. *Contemporary American Poetry.* 4th ed. Boston: Houghton Mifflin, 1985.

Pound, Ezra. *The Cantos of Ezra Pound.* London: Faber and Faber, 1954; 1975.

Radway, Janice. "The Scandal of the Middlebrow: The Book-of-the-Month Club, Class Fracture, and Cultural Authority." *South Atlantic Quarterly* 89.4 (fall 1990): 703–36.

Random House Dictionary of the English Language. New York: Random House, 1981.

Rasula, Jed. "Tuumba." *Jimmy & Lucy's House of K* 6 (1986): 160.

———. *The American Poetry Wax Museum: Reality Effects, 1940–1990.* Urbana: National Council of Teachers of English, 1995.

Reinfeld, Linda. *Language Poetry: Writing as Rescue.* Baton Rouge: Louisiana State UP, 1992.

Retallack, Joan. "The Metaphysick of Play *L=A=N=G=U=A=G=E* U.S.A." *Parnassus* 12.1 (1984): 213.

———. "Local Excentrisms: The Dupont Circle Circle." *Washington and Washington Writing.* Ed. David McAleavey. Washington, DC: George Washington University, 1986.

———. Interview, conducted by P. Inman. *Washington Review* 13.2 (1987): 25–56.

———. "Intraview" with Tina Darragh, Lynne Dreyer and Phyllis Rosenzweig. Unpublished manuscript, 1987.

———. "Post-Scriptum-High-Modern." *Postmodern Genres.* Ed. Marjorie Perloff. Norman: U of Oklahoma P, 1989. 248–73

———. ":Re:Thinking:Literary:Feminism: (three essays onto shaky grounds)." *Feminist Measures: Soundings in Poetry and Theory*. Eds. Lynn Keller and Christanne Miller. Ann Arbor: U of Michigan P, 1994. 344–77.

———. *Afterrimages*. Hanover, NH: UP of New England for Wesleyan UP, 1995.

———. *WESTORN CIV CONT'D, AN OPEN BOOK*. Riverdale: Pyramid Atlantic, 1995.

———. "Introduction: Conversations in Retrospect." *Musicage: Cage Muses on Words, Art, Music*, by John Cage. Ed. Joan Retallack. Hanover: Wesleyan UP, 1996.

———. "The Poethical Wager." *Onward: Contemporary Poetry and Poetics*. Ed. Peter Baker. New York: Peter Lang, 1996. 293–306.

———. "Secnāhc Gnikāt: Taking Chances." *Moving Borders: Three Decades of Innovative Writing by Women*. Ed. Mary Margaret Sloan. Jersey City, NJ: Talisman, 1998. 708–14.

———. "Blue Notes on the Know Ledge." *Poetics Journal* 10 (June 1998): 39–54.

———. *How to Do Things with Words*. Los Angeles: Sun & Moon, 1998.

———. *The Poethical Wager*. Berkeley, U of California P, forthcoming.

Rhiel, Mary, and David Suchoff, eds. *The Seductions of Biography*. New York: Routledge, 1996.

Rich, Adrienne. *What Is Found There: Notebooks on Poetry and Politics*. New York: W. W. Norton, 1993.

———. *Adrienne Rich's Poetry and Prose*. Eds. Barbara Charlesworth Gelpi and Albert Gelpi. New York: W. W. Norton, 1994.

Riley, Denise. *Am I That Name? Feminism and the Category of 'Women' in History*. Minneapolis: U of Minnesota P, 1988.

Riviere, Joan. "Womanliness as a Masquerade." *Formations of Fantasy*. Ed. Victor Burgin et al. London: Methuen, 1986. 35–44.

Robbins, Bruce, ed. *Intellectuals: Aesthetics, Politics, Academics*. Minneapolis: U of Minnesota P, 1990.

Robertson, Lisa. "My Eighteenth Century: Draft Towards a Cabinet." Paper presented at the Assembling Alternatives Conference, U of New Hampshire, 2 September 1996.

Robinson, Kit. *Down and Back*. Berkeley, CA: The Figures, 1978.

Rodden, John. *The Politics of Literary Reputation: The Making and Claiming of "St. George" Orwell*. New York: Oxford UP, 1989.

Rooney, Ellen. "Discipline and Vanish: Feminism, the Resistance to Theory, and the Politics of Cultural Studies." *Differences* 2.3 (1990): 14–28.

Rorty, Richard. *Philosophy and the Mirror of Nature*. Princeton, NJ: Princeton UP, 1979.

Rose, Gillian. *The Broken Middle: Out of our Ancient Society*. Oxford: Blackwell, 1992.

Rosenwasser, Rena. "Chain/Kelsey St. Press." *Chain* 1 (spring/summer 1994): 92–97.

Rosenzweig, Phyllis. "Untitled." *Dog City* 2 (1980): n. pag.

Ross, Andrew. "Reinventing Community: A Symposium on/with Language Poets." *The Minnesota Review* 32 (summer 1989): 27–29.

Rothenberg, Jerome, and Pierre Joris, eds. *Poems for the Millennium: The University of California Book of Modern & Postmodern Poetry*. 2 vols. Berkeley: U of California P, 1998.

Rubinfine, David. Introduction, *Memory*, by Bernadette Mayer. Plainfield, VT: North Atlantic, 1975.

Sappho. *The Poems and Fragments*. Ed. and trans. C. R. Haines. London: George Routledge, 1926.

Sayre, Henry. *The Object of Performance: The American Avant-Garde since 1970*. Chicago: U of Chicago P, 18.

Scalapino, Leslie. Interview. Conducted by Elisabeth A. Frost. *Contemporary Literature* 37.1 (1996): 1–23.

——. *The Public World/Syntactically Impermanence*. Hanover, NH: UP of New England for Wesleyan UP, 1999.

——. Interview, conducted by Anne Brewster, unpublished.

——, ed. *Subliminal Time*. Oakland, CA: O Books, 1993.

Scalapino, Leslie, and Ron Silliman. "What/Person: From an Exchange." *Poetics Journal* 9 (June 1991): 51–68.

Schjeldahl, Peter. "Poetry: A Job Description." *The L=A=N=G=U=A=G=E Book*. Eds. Bruce Andrews and Charles Bernstein. Carbondale: Southern Illinois UP, 1984. 184.

Schlaeger, Jürgen. "Biography: Cult as Culture." *The Art of Literary Biography*. Ed. John Batchelor. Oxford: Clarendon, 1995. 57–71.

Schor, Naomi. *Bad Objects: Essay, Popular and Unpopular*. Durham, NC: Duke UP, 1995.

Schultz, Susan M. "Exaggerated History." Rev. of *The Nonconformist's Memorial* and *The Birth-Mark: Unsettling the Wilderness in American Literary History*, by Susan Howe. *Postmodern Culture* 4.2 (January, 1994): n. pag.

Sekula, Allen. "Reading an Archive." *Blasted Allegories: An Anthology of Writings by Contemporary Artists*. Ed. Brian Wallis. New York: New Museum of Contemporary Art, 1989. 114–28.

Showalter, Elaine. "Feminist Criticism in the Wilderness." *The New Feminist Criticism: Essays on Women, Literature, and Theory*. Ed. Elaine Showalter. London: Virago, 1985. 243–70.

Silliman, Ron. *Sitting Up, Standing, Taking Steps*. Berkeley, CA: Tuumba, 1978.

——. "For Charles Bernstein Has Such a Spirit . . ." *The Difficulties* 2.1 (1981): 98.

——. "Realism." *Ironwood* 20 (1982): 62–69.

——. *Paradise*. Providence, RI: Burning Deck, 1985.

——. "Statement for the New Poetics Colloquium, Vancouver 1985." *Jimmy & Lucy's House of K* 5 (1985): 17–19.

——. *The New Sentence*. New York: Roof, 1989.

——. "Reinventing Community: A Symposium On/With Language Poets." *Minnesota Review* 32 (1989): 39–44.

——. "'Postmodernism': Sign for a Struggle, The Struggle for the Sign." *Conversant Essays: Contemporary Poets on Poetry*. Ed. James McCorkle. Detroit: Wayne State UP, 1990. 79–98.

——. *Demo to Ink*. Tucson: Chax, 1992.

——, ed. *In the American Tree: Language, Realism, Poetry*. Orono, ME: National Poetry Foundation, 1986.

Silliman, Ron, et al. "Aesthetic Tendency and the Politics of Poetry: A Manifesto." *Social Text* 19–20 (fall 1988): 261–75.

Sinclair, Iain, ed. *Conductors of Chaos*. London: Picador, 1996.

Siu, R.G.H. *The Tao of Science*. Cambridge, MA: MIT, 1957.

Sloan, Mary Margaret. "Unfolding Boundaries." Interview. Conducted by Robin Tremblay-McGaw. *Poetry Flash* 278 (September-October 1998): 1–17.

——. Paper presented in the "How to Survive the Canon" panel, PageMothers Conference, 5–6 March, 1999, San Diego.

———. "Of Experience to Experiment: Women's Innovative Writing 1965–1995." Draft in *The World in Space and Time: Towards a History of Innovative American Poetry, 1970–2000*. Ed. Edward Foster and Joseph Donahue. Jersey City, NJ: Talisman, forthcoming.

———, ed. *Moving Borders: Three Decades of Innovative Writing by Women*. Jersey City, NJ: Talisman, 1998.

Smith-Rosenberg, Carroll. "The Female World of Love and Ritual: Relations Between Women in Nineteenth-Century America." *Signs* 1.1 (1975): 1–29.

Soar, Geoffrey and R. J. Ellis. "Little Magazines in the British Isles Today." *British Book News* (December 1983): 728–33.

Spivak, Gayatri Chakravorty. *In Other Worlds: Essays in Cultural Politics*. New York: Methuen, 1987.

———. "A Response to 'The Difference Within: Feminism and Critical Theory,'" *The Difference Within: Feminism and Critical Theory*. Ed. Elizabeth Meese and Alice Parker. Amsterdam: John Benjamin, 1989. 207–19.

Stanley, Sandra Kumamoto. *Louis Zukofsky and the Transformation of a Modern American Poetics*. Berkeley: U of California P, 1994.

Stein, Gertrude. *The Geographical History of America or The Relation of Human Nature to the Human Mind*. 1936; London: Johns Hopkins UP, 1973.

———. *Selected Writings of Gertrude Stein*. Ed. Carl Van Vechten. New York: Random House, 1972.

Stewart, Susan. "Letter on Sound." *Close Listening: Poetry and the Performed Word*. Ed. Charles Bernstein. New York: Oxford UP, 1998. 29–52.

Swift, Jonathan. *Journal to Stella*. 2 vols. Ed. Harold Williams. Oxford: Clarendon, 1948.

Sword, Helen. "Modernist Mediumship." *Modernism, Gender, and Culture: A Cultural Studies Approach*. Ed. Lisa Rado. New York: Garland, 1997. 65–77.

Taggart, John. "Letter to the Editor." *L=A=N=G=U=A=G=E* 1.2 (April 1978): n. pag.

———. Rev. of *My Emily Dickinson* by Susan Howe. *Conjunctions* 11 (1987): 264–74.

Tarn, Nathaniel. *Views from the Weaving Mountain: Selected Essays in Poetics and Anthropology*. Albuquerque: U of New Mexico P, 1991.

———. "Voice Politics/Body Politic." *Talus* 10 (1997): 43–47.

Thomas, Chantal. "Fantasizing Juliette." *Sade and the Narrative of Transgression*. Ed. David B. Allison et al. Cambridge: Cambridge UP, 1995. 251–64.

Tostevin, Lola Lemire. *Subject to Criticism*. Stratford, ON: Mercury, 1995.

Tyler, Carole-Anne. "Passing: Narcissism, Identity, and Difference." *Differences: A Journal of Feminist Cultural Studies* 6.2–3 (1994): 212.

Tysh, Chris. "Critical Theory, or Tooling That Thing." *Raddle Moon* 13 (1994): 44–47.

Vendler, Helen, ed. *The Harvard Book of Contemporary American Poetry*. Cambridge, MA: Belknap, 1985.

Waldman, Anne, Introduction. *Out of This World: An Anthology of the St. Mark's Poetry Project, 1966–1991*. New York: Crown, 1991. 1–6.

———. "Sexifesto." *Writing for Bernadette*. Eds. William Corbett and Michael Gizzi. Great Barrington: The Figures, 1995. n. pag.

Waldrop, Rosmarie. *The Reproduction of Profiles*. New York: New Directions, 1987.

———. "Alarms & Excursions." *The Politics of Poetic Form: Poetry and Public Policy*. Ed. Charles Bernstein. New York: Roof, 1990. 45–72.

———. Statement. *Chain* 1 (spring/summer 1994): 112–13.

———. "Differences for Four Hands." *Denver Quarterly* 31.1 (summer 1996): 123–34.

———. "Thinking of Follows." *Onward: Contemporary Poetry and Poetics*. Ed. Peter Baker. New York: Peter Lang, 1996. 73–82.

Ward, Diane. "Home Plate." *Dog City* 1 (1977): n. pag.

———. "The Narration." Symposium on Narrative. *Poetics Journal* 5 (May 1985): 94–95.

Watkins, Glenn. *Gesualdo: The Man and His Music*. 2nd edn. Preface by Igor Stravinsky. Oxford: Clarendon, 1971; 1991.

Watten, Barrett. "Russian Formalism and the Present." *Hills* 6/7 (1980): 50–73.

———. *Total Syntax*. Carbondale: Southern Illinois UP, 1985.

———. "Method and *L=A=N=G=U=A=G=E*: After Surrealism." *In the American Tree: Language,. Realism, Poetry*. Ed. Ron Silliman. Orono, ME: National Poetry Foundation, 1986. 599–612.

———. "Reinventing Community: A Symposium on/with Language Poets." *The Minnesota Review* 32 (1989): 30–39.

———. "The Bride of the Assembly Line: From Material Text to Cultural Poetics." *The Impercipient Lecture Series* 1.8 (October 1997): 1–36.

———. *Bad History*. Berkeley, CA: Atelos, 1998.

Weil, Simone. *Waiting for God*. Trans. Emma Crauford. New York: Harper & Row, 1973.

———. *Gravity and Grace*. Trans. Emma Crauford. 1952; London: Ark, 1987.

Weinberger, Eliot. "A Final Response." *Sulfur* 22 (1988): 198–202.

Weiner, Hannah. *Clairvoyant Journal*. Lenox, MA: Angel Hair, 1978.

———. *Code Poems*. Barrytown, NY: Station Hill, 1982.

———. *Spoke*. Washington, DC: Sun & Moon, 1984.

———. "Forum," *The Politics of Poetic Form: Poetry and Public Policy*. With P. Inman et al. Ed. Charles Bernstein. New York: Roof, 1990. 221–34.

———. *The Fast*. New York: United Artists, 1992.

———. *Silent Teachers Remembered Sequel*. Providence, RI: Tender Buttons, 1994.

———. Interview. Conducted by Charles Bernstein, LINEbreak program, 1995. Available at <http://wings.buffalo.edu/epc/linebreak/programs/weiner>.

———. "astral visions." *Mr. Knife, Miss Fork: Performances*. Los Angeles: Sun & Moon, forthcoming. Preview available at <http://wings.buffalo.edu/epc/authors/weiner/astral.html>.

Werner, Marta L. *Emily Dickinson's Open Folios: Scenes of Reading, Surfaces of Writing*. Ann Arbor: U of Michigan P, 1995.

West, Candace, and Don H. Zimmerman. "Small Insults: A Study of Interruptions in Cross-Sex Conversations between Unacquainted Persons." *Language, Gender and Society*. Ed. Barrie Thorne et al. Rowley, MA: Newbury House, 1983. 103–18.

Wheale, Nigel. "Uttering Poetry: Small-Press Publication." *Poets on Writing: Britain, 1970–1991*. Ed. Denise Riley. Basingstoke: Macmillan, 1992. 9–20.

Whitehead, Kate. "Broadcasting Bloomsbury." *Yearbook of English Studies* 20 (1990): 121–31.

Whitehead, Kim. *The Feminist Poetry Movement*. Jackson: UP of Mississippi, 1996.

Whitman, Walt. *Leaves of Grass*. Vol. 1 of *The Works of Walt Whitman*. 2 vols. New York: Funk and Wagnalls, 1968.

Williams, Harold. Introduction, *Journal to Stella*, by Jonathan Swift. Ed. Harold Williams. Oxford: Clarendon, 1948.

Williams, William Carlos. *In the American Grain*. New York: New Directions, 1956.

Williamson, Janice. "Citing Resistance: Vision, Space, Authority and Transgression in Canadian Women's Poetry." Diss. York U, 1987.

———. "*(f.)Lip* Sides." Letter to the Editors. *(f.)Lip* 1.1 (1987): 22.

Wills, Clair. "Contemporary Women's Poetry: Experimentalism and the Expressive Voice." *Critical Quarterly* 36.3 (1994): 34–52.

Wittgenstein, Ludwig. *Philosophical Investigations*. 3rd ed. Trans. G. E. M. Anscombe New York: Macmillan, 1958.

Wolff, Janet. *Resident Alien: Feminist Cultural Criticism*. Cambridge: Polity, 1995.

Woolf, Virginia. *The Waves*. London: Hogarth, 1931; rpt. 1990.

———. *Letters of Virginia Woolf*. Ed. Nigel Nicholson. Vol. 3. London: Chatto & Windus, 1977.

Yau, John. "Neither Us Nor Them." *American Poetry Review* 23.2 (1994): 45–54.

Young, Iris Marion. *Throwing Like a Girl and Other Essays in Feminist Philosophy and Social Theory*. Bloomington: Indiana UP, 1990.

Zizek, Slavoj. *The Sublime Object of Ideology*. London: Verso, 1989.

Zukofsky, Louis. *Prepositions: The Collected Critical Essays of Louis Zukofsky*. Berkeley: U of California P, 1967, 1981.

Selections from Joan Retallack, *AFTERRIMAGES* (Hanover, NH: UP of New England for Wesleyan UP, 1995), and the illustration from *WESTORN CIV CONT'D: AN OPEN BOOK* (Riverdale: Pyramid Atlantic, 1995–96) are used with the author's permission. She has also given permission for use of a section from "The Clouds: (This Is Not by Henrik Isbn)," *Chain* 6 (1999): 111–19, © Lyn Hejinian and Joan Retallack, and "These Are the Gay Dissolute Streets of Yoshiwara," *Dog City* 2 (1980), © Joan Retallack and Phyllis Rosenzweig.

Phyllis Rosenzweig, "Untitled," *Dog City* 2 (1980), © Phyllis Rosenzweig, is reprinted with the author's permission. "These are the Gay Dissolute Streets of Yoshiwara," *Dog City* 2 (1980), © Joan Retallack and Phyllis Rosenzweig, is reprinted with the authors' permission.

Diane Ward, "Home Plate," *Dog City* 1 (1977), © Diane Ward, reprinted with the author's permission.

The photograph from the cover of Hannah Weiner's *Clairvoyant Journal* (Lenox: Angel Hair, 1978), © Tom Ahern, is reprinted with the photographer's permission. The frontispiece to Hannah Weiner's *Silent Teachers Remembered Sequel* (Providence, RI: Tender Buttons, 1994) is used with the permission of the Estate of Hannah Weiner and the publisher. Permission has also been given by the Estate of Hannah Weiner and the Mandeville Special Collections Library, University of California, San Diego, to quote from unpublished letters in the Bernadette Mayer Papers (MSS 420) held in the Mandeville Collection.

A section of "Ratatouille" from Janice Williamson's unpublished dissertation, "Citing Resistance: Vision, Space, Authority and Transgression in Canadian Women's Poetry," is quoted with the author's permission.

Index

ABOUT THE AUTHOR

Ann Vickery is a research fellow at Macquarie University in Sydney, Australia. She has a long-standing interest in twentieth-century American poetry and its cultural contexts, as well as feminist literary theory. Since its inception, she has been a member of the editorial advisory board for *HOW2*, a journal exploring nontraditional directions in women's poetry and scholarship. She is currently working on a large project investigating constructions of sexuality and cultural identity in modern Australian women's poetry.

LIBRARY OF CONGRESS CATALOGING-IN-PUBLICATION DATA

Vickery, Ann.

Leaving lines of gender : a feminist genealogy of language writing /
Ann Vickery.

p. cm.

Includes bibliographical references and index.

ISBN 0-8195-6414-1 (alk. paper)—ISBN 0-8195-6432-x (pbk. : alk. paper)

1. American poetry—Women authors—History and criticism. 2. Feminism and literature—United States—History—20th century. 3. Women and literature—United States—History—20th century. 4. American poetry—20th century—History and criticism. 5. Experimental poetry, American—History and criticism. 6. Avant-garde (Aesthetics)—United States. 7. Language and languages in literature. 8. Authorship—Sex differences. 9. Feminism in literature. I. Title.

PS228.F45 V54 2000

811'.54099287—dc21   00-009338